Women's Experience And Education

Edited by
**Sharon Lee Rich
Ariel Phillips**

HARVARD EDUCATIONAL REVIEW
REPRINT SERIES NO. 17

Library of Congress Card Number 84-081321. ISBN 0-916690-19-9.
Printed by Capital City Press, Montpelier, VT 05602. Typography by Villanti & Sons, Williston,
VT 05495. Cover design by Cyndy Brady, Northlight Studio Press, Barre, VT 05641.

Harvard Educational Review
Longfellow Hall, 13 Appian Way
Cambridge, Massachusetts 02138

Women's Experience And Education

Preface

The articles in this volume have been brought together to allow us to explore how human experience has been and continues to be limited by conceptions of what it is to be female and male. Many readers would probably agree that, in the more than fifty years since the publication of the first edition of the *Harvard Educational Review (HER)*, those conceptions have shifted dramatically for many women, particularly following the women's movement of the late 1960s and early 1970s. In recognition of shifts over time, we believe it is important to assemble a number of original articles by and about women as they appeared in *HER* over the years. We invite you, our readers, to draw your own conclusions about patterns of change and about the limitations of current gender-related concepts.

We have several goals in publishing this edition. We wish to consolidate into a single reference articles for both education courses and women's studies courses. In addition, we would like to document one journal's treatment of the types of concerns that arose about women's lives at different times in the past four decades. Thus, we have tried to choose articles that deal specifically with women. Some of the selections describe important research and offer theoretical discussions based on recent shifts in perspective; others clearly reflect the historical perspective from which they were written.

In the process of reviewing the articles *HER* has published, we have been struck by how few articles appeared in the *Review* by or about women over the years. Not surprisingly, the majority of articles about women have been published since 1970, and these primarily focus on the lives of white, middle- to upper-class women in the United States. Therefore, this collection offers minimal information specifically about minority women, including ethnic minorities, lesbian women, and mentally and physically handicapped women. Nor did we find much concerning women from outside the United States.

Nevertheless, we still had to leave out many pieces written by and about women. Some were written by women who are well established in the social sciences and politics but whose works did not directly address women's lives. Included among these are Anna Freud, Shirley Chisholm, Marian Wright Edelman, and Eleanor Roosevelt who—in her editorial of 1938—wrote of the resentment she felt as a young woman that Harvard University did not allow girls to share in its courses. We also omitted most of the articles, essays, and book reviews that looked at women exclusively in their roles as wives and mothers. Finally, we excluded several articles due simply to space limitations.

The selections ultimately included have been separated into five sections, although there is overlap across the sections. For example, Esther Westervelt's essay, while offering information about the history of women in higher education, is also an interesting historical piece in itself.

In the first section, "Historical Perspectives," the articles, essays, and book reviews have been arranged chronologically by publishing dates in order to highlight their significance as historical documents. For example, the anger exemplified in Ann Withorn's essay captures some of the mood of feminism in the early 1970's. This section also includes historical research on women in the nineteenth and early twentieth centuries. In one article, Barbara Brenzel writes of girls assigned in the second half of the nineteenth century to the Lancaster School in Massachusetts, the first girls' reform school; through social control and benevolence, the girls were trained to fill the female role in society.

The essays in "Higher Education" reflect changing concerns about women in postsecondary education and their relationship to the surrounding society. Ordway Tead stresses the importance of college education for women, yet proposes courses that would prepare women for their *conventional* roles as wives, mothers, and members of civic groups. In contrast, Ruth Hubbard considers women's historical struggles to follow an *un*conventional path — an education in science.

"Schools and Teaching" focuses on women in primary, secondary, and higher educational institutions, as students and teachers. These articles and reviews have been organized according to the ages of the girls and women described by the authors. The subjects include women's lives as teachers, sex-role stereotyping in textbooks and classroom practices, and the importance of allowing women of all ages the opportunity to express themselves creatively.

In "Research and Theory" the authors explore the importance of incorporating women's experiences and understandings of reality into research and theory. Jane Roland Martin examines how women have been excluded from or misrepresented in educational philosophy. Carol Gilligan, in both of her articles, offers a similar argument concerning research on moral development, while Susan Squire and Sara Ruddick challenge Gilligan to take her theory on women's moral consciousness much further.

In the final section, "Ethnic Minority Voices," we offer a brief collection of writings about women from non-white cultures living in the United States. In one, Maxine Baca Zinn presents a study of eight Mexican-American families illustrating how traditional Mexican values interact with a wife's working outside of the home and with her educational level.

This retrospective volume has one other purpose. We hope it will serve as an open invitation to social researchers and educators to continue studying and writing about women's lives. We are excited about the direction of the research suggested in the pages of *HER*, including the work of Martin, Gilligan, and Gilligan's associate, Nona Lyons (*HER*, May 1983). We hope that this research continues and is expanded upon in the future.

We would like to acknowledge a number of people who contributed to this anthology. To begin with, we want to thank the original editors of the articles included here. Without their careful selection and editing, this volume would not exist. We also wish to express our appreciation to Janie Ward, Kathleen Ahern, and

Janet Hawkins, who offered many valuable suggestions and painstaking editorial assistance. Finally, we wish to recognize the special contributions of *HER*'s general manager, Margaret O'Hara, who has worked with the *Review* for the past twenty-six years. We greatly appreciate her active participation in the publication of this volume.

ARIEL PHILLIPS
SHARON L. RICH
Editors

PART I
Historical Perspectives

Some Thoughts on Education for Girls

ROBERT ULICH

Robert Ulich in this essay first published in 1941, questions the belief that women have little to offer "man-made civilization." He argues that women have the potential to contribute independent and original ideas to Western culture and that women's institutions for higher education should not simply mimic male institutions. Although Ulich's views are liberal for his times, he does focus his vision for women's education on traditional gender roles, contending that women are "citizens, wives, and mothers" who need to learn ways to overcome the boredom often found in modern family life.

In a book on the role of women in civilization which I perused some weeks ago, I found a quotation from a letter of a "lady of distinction" written to a "relative shortly after marriage." In this letter, the lady of distinction gave her young friend some rules about the proper behavior of a wife in the company of men. "I would not have you silent. Nay, when trifles are the subject, talk as much as any gentleman; but distinguish and be silent when the discourse turns upon things of importance." This letter was written in 1821, a more recent phrasing of the old *mulier taceat in ecclesia.* If one judged the influence which women exercised in earlier periods exclusively on the basis of such quotations, however, he would be wrong. Before the modern division of labor, a normal household needed a woman's initiative and circumspection much more than it does today. We also know the importance of women in the older aristocratic circles of Europe. But even in the old village and in the European courts the sphere of women was restricted to more private influences. A person like Anne Hutchinson, who divided a whole colony into factions and led a group of dissenters from Boston to Rhode Island, is a very rare exception. Not before the middle of the nineteenth century did women as a group trespass the smaller boundaries of immediate contact between them and their environment and reach over into public life. This change is characterized by their activity in education. Emma Willard, Catherine Beecher, Mary Lyon were founders of institutes for the training of girls. These pioneers showed remarkable energy in the pursuit of their plans, but they were still opposed to the participation of women in politics. It is, nevertheless, the inevitable result of their work that the next generations of women successfully asked for an increased share in public affairs.

This essay is part of an address given in an Academic Symposium of the inauguration of George N. Shuster as president of Hunter College, New York City, 11 October 1941. It originally appeared in the *Review* in the Editorial Forum section.

Harvard Educational Review   Vol. 11   No. 3   Summer 1941, 273–277

In this country, women have entered into political positions and joined boards of trustees; they are almost in the majority in classrooms and offices, and much of the public welfare work is in their hands. I still remember, however, from my own conversations as a young student with leading women in the emancipation movement, that it was not their only dream to have women working in the ranks of men; they wanted more. They were convinced that the increase in the influence of women could help to take away from our modern civilization the curse of loneliness, mechanization, and ruthless competition among individuals and nations. Each of us may judge from his own experiences to what extent these hopes have been fulfilled. He may also consider to what extent our civilization, built mainly on the standards of men, is in need of a thorough human and moral reform in which women and women's ideals would have their share. Some time ago, a friend of mine — a psychologist — tried to convince me that men were superior to women. He supported his argument by citing the undeniable fact that men rather than women had molded our civilization. I answered by asking whether he considered our western civilization of such a glorious quality that men had much reason to boast of their predominant role in its formation. The blame one could lay on women was rather that they had been too willing to accept this man-made civilization as a fate predestined by some unalterable divine decision.

So far as I can see, in spite of its enormous expansion, the work of women has been primarily imitative and adaptive and not sufficiently independent and original. As long as this situation prevails, women cannot realize fully their opportunities to correct at least some of the most striking defects in our modern civilization.

The hitherto rather adaptive attitude of women is easily explained. They had, first of all, to go into the scientific training of men and to learn the stabilized forms of reasoning and acting. Good reasoning, like good actions, follows certain inherent laws which must be learned by both men and women. It does not make any difference who is participating. Furthermore, when leaving the circle of the family, women were faced with a highly competitive civilization, a civilization perhaps still more cruel for isolated women of average quality than for isolated men. And to mention finally the most important psychological factor in this process of adaptation: the more perfectly women acquired all these manly virtues and skills, the more they convinced themselves, and hoped to convince men, that there was no God-given inferiority attached to the female sex.

But by this time, both men and women should realize that all these arguments concerning the superiority and inferiority of the sexes are obsolete and the results of false thinking. There are certainly differences in aspect, intuition, ideals, and attitudes toward life almost as marked as differences in physical structure. But these differences cannot be scored and graded like assignments of school boys or the theses of doctorate candidates. They are expressions of the mysterious richness of life which we have to accept and admire, but not to censure.

So I think I am not alone among modern men in expressing the hope that modern women will understand one important sociological fact. One cannot fight the injustice of inequality by dreading diversity, but only through enjoying diversity as a means of developing one's own individuality in its highest possible form. This insight is just as essential for a sound cooperation between men and women as it is essential for the cooperation of different individuals and social stratifications in all other democratic forms of life.

My statement on the future chances for original and enriching contributions of the feminine mind to our modern civilization must necessarily be incomplete. No one can predict what degree of reach and momentum a movement will acquire after it has found its appropriate goal and meaning. Furthermore, cultural work is not a sort of engineering for which devices and formulae can be offered. A new spirit and the initiative springing from it are the main vehicles of cultural progress. But generally I would say that the new period of woman's self-consciousness ought to begin with reforms in education just as the first period of emancipation began. The moment we concentrate on this point, several important questions emerge. In American education for girls, for example, is their future role as citizens, wives, and mothers regarded, or have they simply been dressed in boys clothes to suit the convenience of an educational system that, consciously or unconsciously, tried to equip its students to compete in a man's world? While in earlier periods, progressive men and women had to fight the short-sighted egoism of men who wanted only to enjoy women's charm and, for the rest, to confine them to house and kitchen, so at the present time progressive people may ask whether the majority of women feel themselves happier, more useful, and more dignified after having exchanged the natural skills and efficiencies of their grandmothers for the pottage of lentils they are presented by modern mechanized labor. Or, to raise another question concerning the secondary education of girls, are there fields in the arts, the teaching and cultivation of which could prevent the inner boredom which threatens the average modern household and makes wife, husband, and children dependent on the movies? Could not many useful and enjoyable activities, potentially inherent in the abilities of young women, be preserved through thoughtful training, instead of being drowned in the waves of modern standardization?

If we pass over from the secondary level to the college, was it really necessary for the majority of girls' colleges to give up so willingly the chance of elasticity and experimenting inherent in their youth and to adapt their curriculum, their course credit systems, and their judgment on the student so completely to the standards of the institutions for boys? I am far from advocating minor and easier criteria for the higher education of women. I would even advocate that they be raised at several places which seemingly tend to confuse higher education with a mixture of bookishness and comfortable country life. I am only interested in the question as to whether the colleges for men have really developed all the cultural possibilities for the perfection of the human race to such an extent that intelligent women could not contribute something of their own.

Men themselves, not always the censorious and fault-finding dilettantes, but very serious educational leaders, discuss nowadays the question of the extent to which our modern forms of higher education for boys have too one-sidedly emphasized the merely informing, job-preparing, and methodical value of studying and too little its responsibilities for a full and balanced growth of the total person. Without a fundamentally human aim, higher education is not even a good preparation for professional success; still less is it a good preparation for individual happiness and productive participation in the affairs of the community and the nation.

A Critical Look at Women's Options

MARGARET MEAD

LIFE STYLES OF EDUCATED WOMEN
by Eli Ginzberg and Associates.
New York: Columbia University Press, 1966. 224 pp.

This study of the personalities, backgrounds, and home and career experience of a group of 311 women, who were doing distinguished graduate work at Columbia University between 1945 and 1951, is presented with the clarity, economy, and sense of purpose which is characteristic of the work of Dr. Ginzberg and his associates. The research itself was undertaken in response to the finding, in an earlier study of educated persons, that the research design used was inappropriate for women. In recognition of the fact that educated women's problems were more complex, and involved more options and more complicated accommodations and compromises, a new research design was developed and used with this carefully selected group of subjects. All results are based on responses to questionnaires: 74 percent of the respondents were sufficiently caught by the questionnaire to write additional comments. The style of the book is coolly objective; the respondents are presented in their own words. Like all such "objective" reporting, selectivity plays a very important role; the present reviewer was struck with how flat most of the selected replies of this group of women were.

The bulk of the book is devoted to analysis of these 311 women, analyzed by home background, education, marital and maternal state, expressed satisfactions, and past, present, and expected work roles. The authors then use this account (of how a number of these women have been able to solve their career problems and of their successful aspirations towards careers that have utilized their higher education) as a basis for a series of exhortations to all those concerned with manpower problems. Their argument is simple: these educated women have succeeded in using their education—"half of the group had had a continuous work history, slightly over a quarter have been in and away from work throughout their adult lives, and only 11 percent never really got started on careers." Employers should take note of the large proportion who have worked successfully and should adjust their personnel practices to the needs of women employees in terms of hours, vacations, and periodic leaves. School counselors should encourage girls to undertake higher education instead of discouraging them as they so often do at present. Girls in school and college should be encouraged to attend to the possibilities that are bound to open up for the employment of more and more educated women. Women, although often discriminated against, are nevertheless more fortunate than men because they have more options, more choices.

This is an optimistic model and a constructive one. The authors present a sympathetic analysis of the position of women who must often adjust their work plans to their husbands' careers, and recognize that the exigencies of raising three children do definitely force women out of the labor market. They recognize that married women's chances of a career are definitely negatively affected by: lack of domestic help, a greater insistence on the importance of mothers' caring for their own children, and difficulties inherent in dispersed suburban living. Nevertheless, they insist women have overcome these difficulties, and what some educated women have done, more educated women can do.

The book is a sophisticated adventure in model building for a new era, and era in which, as all manpower specialists agree, the utilization of intelligent and educated women will be essential. Those specialists with the generous and constructive sympathies of Dr. Ginzberg are concerned that this utilization of women should permit women to play a role beyond that of wife and mother, commensurate with their educational level. The study tries to do, in the crisp, non-vivid idiom of contemporary problem analysis, what earlier books have done by presenting success stories about members of backward or minority groups. It utilizes the contemporary American tendency to trust statistical analyses of a large number of real cases, rather than highly individualized records of outstanding success which are likely to evoke the response, "But I'm no Einstein!" from the reader. These, the authors argue, are, it is true, superior women, but there are a lot of them, all selected from one university, in one city, in a short period of modern history. Look what they have done (more than a third have earned the doctorate) and believe that this is the future for girls and women of promise.

The strategy is openly stated and clear, to be accepted or rejected by the reader. But it does raise some rather serious problems. Is a model that is subtly based on the conditions of an earlier era, developed in order to encourage this generation to make what appear to be comparable choices, really a completely satisfactory way to produce needed and desirable social change? If the model is reasonably relevant, and sways enough readers, especially those in key educational and manpower positions to whom the book is specifically addressed, it may well strengthen a social trend in the desired direction. But if it promises too much, then disillusion may set in. This was the case in the last two decades for many educated young Negro Americans who were encouraged by the records of outstanding Negro Americans who had succeeded, sacrificed, and worked to get a college education, and then found themselves working as postmen with M.A.s.

The circumstances under which most young women conduct their lives today are not the circumstances of Dr. Ginzberg's sample. While the number of women obtaining graduate degrees has gone up, the *percentage* of women obtaining graduate degrees has actually dropped. And his sample is a group of women who were highly enough motivated to get to graduate school. Many of them were very highly motivated towards work. Only 10 percent reported any parental opposition, 30 percent had working mothers, and a fourth of the husbands made over $10,000 a year. During their graduate work, they were living in or near New York City—where husbands and wives can both work without encountering nepotism rules or blind alleys. Furthermore, these women, as a group, represented a different style of life: 28 percent were unmarried (as against only 6 percent in the general population), 18 percent of the married women had no children, 14 percent had only one child. Of those who were married, only 6 percent had married in their teens, one quarter had married after twenty-nine, and of those with children, only half had children within two years after being married. Dr. Ginzberg emphasizes the variety of solutions which these figures represent: choice of whether to work or not, choice of whether to have children or not, choice of whether to marry or not. All of this was true of the women in the sample who went to graduate school in the late forties and fifties.

But we are faced here with the same sort of dilemma that faces educators who study defects in the educational state of adolescents and then try to remedy these defects by changing nursery school education. The changes that have already occurred are likely to make the reforms obsolete before they are introduced. Most of the options which the book outlines so sympathetically are not nearly as clear for young women in the mid-1960s. The choice of single blessedness is deeply suspect today, for both young men and young women. Every social pressure pushes young women into marriage or else mutilates their development as human beings capable of pursuing their career aspirations. The possibilities of a satisfying sex life outside marriage are still largely confined to the premarital experimentations of the young without social commitments and to a few circles in large cities. The option to postpone child bearing until several years after marriage, so that a woman may finish her professional training, conflicts with present styles of young marriages and isolates the couples who elect this pattern. Domestic help is not only often unsatisfactory—as the book mildly remarks—it is often impossible to come by and will be until a whole new set of institutions are invented which make domestic help as satisfactory an occupation as being a member of a yacht club staff or an airplane hostess. The young women of today are singularly ill equipped for cooperation with other women—the other viable solution to problems of combining work and homemaking. Early dating interferes with experience in friendships between girls, and girls who never had adolescent friends escape as quickly as possible into single rooms in college and into a partnership with a man who performs the kind of services which a female relative or friend used to perform.

If the optimistic picture of how women can combine higher education and careers with homemaking is to be realized, American society will have to come to grips with some of these problems. We need a different pattern of living which makes for greater accessibility to domestic help and work opportunities, and a different pattern of late adolescent social relationships. There are also, as Ginzberg stresses, other reforms which would be easier to put into effect: tax reforms which allow realistically for deduction of homemaker services and a revision of the rules against nepotism, especially in educational fields. Teaching, and especially teaching in institutions of higher learning, is one of the fields which can be combined most successfully with homemaking and motherhood, especially if a woman can teach in the same institution in which her husband teaches and live near the campus.

Conditions in many careers today, especially educational and health work, are highly conducive to occupationally endogamous couples, who would not be available singly, but may be very available together. At the point of higher education, a certain number of steps could be taken at once: abolition of all nepotism rules, hospitality to married faculty in the same field, provision of models of successful women among those who teach both young men and women, and stress, in the education of women, upon establishing an undergraduate basis for future, if not immediate, professional work.

One statement in the book could lead to rather serious misinterpretation. Ginzberg says: "Contrary to the popular belief that educated women represent a particularly dissatisfied group, less than one out of ten (of the sample) is dissatisfied with all aspects of life. About three out of four are satisfied with their lives as a whole, and if we add the women who are satisfied with one aspect of their lives, the proportion rises to 90 percent." But the educated women about whom so much has been written lately are not the women who have succeeded in getting as far as graduate school; the word *educated*, in the more usual sense, is used for women who have had some college education before they married and took up full time homemaking, women who, on the whole, had no career aspirations beyond marriage and motherhood. There is no doubt that the early development of real career interests means also the development of a sense of herself as a person. This can protect a girl, even through the years of continuous domestic labor, by assuring her that she has interests to which she will be able to return. It is notable that of Ginzberg's sample only 16 percent were working in fields that had no connection with their undergraduate majors. A study, of twenty-six years ago, of members of the American Association of University Women showed the same dependence of later interests upon the awakening of such interests in college. A principal finding relevant to college education for women is the importance of connecting the work they do as undergraduates with the work which they may want to do later.

There is, of course, just the possibility that changed attitudes towards conception control and parenthood, consequent upon the population explosion, will spread as rapidly as the present style of large families spread after World War II. Then, for the first time, young women may really ask, on a large scale, to be treated as persons rather than potential mothers, and if they do, all but some of the most old fashioned and stubbornly conservative women's colleges may be ready to treat them as persons capable of a full life and a full career. In this case, the present economically engendered pressure to get educated women back into the labor market may have performed a prefiguratively useful service in stimulating educational institutions, at all levels, to take women's education more seriously, and arrange for both boys and girls to be taught by distinguished men and distinguished women, which is a necessary condition of such seriousness.

Three Views of Liberation

ANN WITHORN

WOMAN'S PLACE: OPTIONS AND LIMITS IN PROFESSIONAL CAREERS
by Cynthia Fuchs Epstein.
Berkeley: University of California Press, 1970. 221 pp.

THE FEMALE EUNUCH
by Germaine Greer.
New York: McGraw-Hill, 1971. 340 pp.

THE DIALECTIC OF SEX: THE CASE FOR FEMINIST REVOLUTION
by Shulamith Firestone.
New York: William Morrow, 1970; Bantam Edition, 1971.

No one is surprised any more when a woman complains about her fate. Even Martha Mitchell has had her say on the plight of womankind. Many of us have heard the statistics on women's employment, the inadequacy of women's education, unsafe birth control devices, and illegal abortions. We are aware of the hypocrisy in the laws regarding women. Moreover, we have probably heard something about the "psychology of women's oppression"; we know the female role in society is not a liberating one. We have listened to the condemnation of the "nuclear family" and realize that most advertising (and film, and art, and literature) exploits women. Kate Millet's *Sexual Politics* generated reviews in every major periodical. For whatever reasons, the press has kept the Women's Liberation Movement before the public.

We must not let the "overkill" make us numb to the totality of women's oppression as it is experienced. No matter how true, all the press stories, the statistics, and the rhetoric can never encompass the adolescent girl's terror that no boy will desire her; the despair of the woman left alone after a "one night stand"; the panic of the isolated housewife whose husband is "losing interest"; the humiliation of the prostitute or welfare mother. It is now time, however, to go beyond what we know, to overcome both the self-hatred and the newly developed self-righteousness, so that we can create viable strategies for change. We need ways to help us change ourselves individually, methods to develop strength, trust, and solidarity as a group, and tactics to help us deal with the individual men in our lives as well as with the male, white, capitalist "system" which imprisons us.

Harvard Educational Review   Vol. 41   No. 3   August 1971, 408–415

Cynthia Fuchs Epstein approaches women's problems as a detached sociologist. In *Woman's Place: Options and Limits in Professional Careers*, she dispassionately tries to answer the question, "Why have so few capable women ever fulfilled the promise of their potential and ability, and conversely, how do those few who do, manage?" (p. 16). Fulfillment here is defined by the number of us in "the prestigious occupational spheres." Perhaps this question, limited as it is, could afford significant insight into why women do not "make it" and could initiate a feminist criticism of the professions, from the inside out. But Cynthia[1] does not accomplish even this. Although she discusses the "images and ideology" which limit women and the undercutting nature of our socialization which forces us to be "sexless" in order to succeed, she sees these as nothing more than sociological "conditions," obstacles which must be overcome by each of us individually on our way to success. She sees the role of housewife, for example, as impeding the career of the professional woman, who feels that she must successfully be both worker in the office and housewife in the home. Nowhere does Cynthia consider that the role of housewife itself is destructive and that women must directly confront its effects and create new methods to deal with the tasks of running a home. Cynthia suggests only that the role of housewife can be modified: by working with the husband, in the same field with him, or by having a husband who is often away from the home, the woman can get through with housework more easily.

Cynthia does not understand that simply attaining a higher place in the hierarchy will not help women — that hierarchy is itself destructive to us. It is dominated by male values, male expectations of the limited ways a woman can behave and still be "womanly" enough for men to feel safe with and to reward. Though Cynthia never refers to her individual experience, the many suggestions she makes for how woman can "minimize the effects of their sex status" gives us a sense of the sacrifices that "successful" career women must make. "Women should not permit their own self consciousness to cause them to overreact. Women who are professional but not especially formal or aggressive, who try to be gracious as women and not deny their sex, are said to make the best impression on men and gain acceptance. . . . Problems arise only were women demand they be treated 'just like the men' causing their colleagues discomfort" (p. 195).

With this, women are right back where they started. We can "succeed" in the professions only if we impress the men in power. Thanks, but no thanks. Cynthia's

---

[1] There are lots of reasons why I call women by their first names instead of their last. First, a woman's last name is not really her own but belongs to her father or husband, indicating possession. Second, if I call Germaine Greer "Greer" or Shulamith Firestone "Firestone" it makes them sound like men (perhaps since they are writers we are supposed to try to forget their sex?) and I don't like that. Third, one of the things the Women's Movement is about is destroying the male formalities and amenities, forcing us to think of others as people, not writers or scholars or sociologists, but as whole human beings like ourselves; using first names helps to do this. Fourth, despite my disagreements with each of these women, I feel a kind of closeness with them because they too are trying to understand what is happening to us. Calling them by their first names forces me to remember that we are sisters, that I should try to understand why Germaine and Cynthia think as they do and not just try to tear them apart for the sake of my argument. Finally, I suppose I call these women by their first names because that is the way I would address them if I met them and I see no reason for treating them differently in print. A.W.

ability to read and analyze all the statistics about women's pathetic chances in the job market and still not get angry about the condition of her sisters (and herself) is a clear example of the callous, empty meaning of "male" success. Her choice of such a dry, outdated "sociological" method to deal with a problem about which she admittedly cares, warns all of us about the dangers of such "male" methods. We do not want to become men and thereby "make it" in a man's world; we want real change, both in ourselves and of that world. We must learn to reject the traditional "male" models as well as the "female" ones. What Cynthia does not understand is that *all* sex roles in this society are brutalizing, that the solution lies in changing the nature of those roles, not in assuming them or manipulating them, as in trying to remain "feminine" while playing the male role.

At first reading, it may appear that if Germaine Greer wants anything, she certainly wants change, and of the most radical sort. She demands that we stop marrying, that we start living in extended families, that we withdraw our labor (both sexual and otherwise) as a social tactic, that we stop being ashamed of our bodies and stop denying our sexuality, that we stop destroying ourselves and those around us by our demands for a nonexistent security. She argues forcefully that we have been castrated by the altruistic, security conscious "Eternally Feminine" image laid on us by our society. The title of her book, *The Female Eunuch*, describes what she thinks women have become and what we must refuse any longer to be in order to achieve our personhood. "I refuse to be a female impersonator, I am a woman not a castrate," she angrily proclaims.

Unfortunately, Germaine's understanding of the nature of women's oppression — the brutalizing roles, the socialization out of sexuality and into passivity — does not lead her to call for alternatives that are complex or radical enough to change the situation. Her anger, in fact, seems to focus on women themselves, for succumbing too easily to the destructive roles they are offered; her sympathy lies with men. Constantly she suggests that it is by our own individual hang-ups that we oppress men and force them to hate us and thereby mistreat us. She speaks strangely of the "coven of females" who help each other at a birth. Why "coven"? The "feminine way" of performing tasks is "servilely, dishonestly, inefficiently, and inconsistently" (p. 57). Germaine does not consider that most of the tasks women are given in society are dehumanizing and that it is not ignoble to perform dehumanizing tasks shoddily. But if she were able to view her sisters with more sympathy, she might see that women often show amazing strength and creativity in their limiting roles, that often we are far more imaginative and dedicated wives, secretaries, and maids than the nature of these roles would suggest, Germaine criticizes the "vain, demanding servile boor who cannot offer her husband love" so that he runs away with a "shameless hussy of nineteen" (p. 88). Other anti-woman remarks permeate the book: she likes her job as an academic even though it does mean that she has to "tolerate the antics of faculty wives, but," she continues, "they are fairly easy to ignore" (p. 127). She denigrates the romantic stories women read by exposing the "deep disgust" men feel about them. She claims that women "pervert civilized conversation about issues into petty and personal spats." But she consoles those men "who do not want *their women* (my italics) shaved and deodorized into complete tastelessness" recognizing how "powerless" they are "against women's distaste for their [own] bodies" (p. 28). She rather sympathizes with men because they must tolerate such weak, neurotic, uninteresting women.

What women must do, she argues, is make drastic changes within themselves, but nowhere does she call for basic alterations in men and the male dominated culture. Like Richard Nixon, who tells us that it is each individual's responsibility to fight pollution, Germaine argues that women must change themselves, not make revolutionary demands: "The housewife who must wait for the success of the world revolution for her liberty might be excused for losing hope. . . . She could begin, not by changing the world but by changing herself." And her role in the women self-help program is by no means a humble one, "The hope in which this book is written is that women will discover that they have a will; once that happens they will be able to tell us how and what they want." Who is "us," Germaine, and what will "you" do then?

Germaine Greer is one of those educated, sophisticated, articulate women who identify with men. She sees the reasons why other women are not like herself and deplores them. She wants women to change because "if women are to be better valued by men they must value themselves more highly" (p. 264). All men are not perfect (even though she does think they show "more grace on the battleground"); they are aggressive and cold, but women can change that: "If women liberate themselves they will perforce liberate their oppressors" (p. 8). She offers men a telling reason for supporting a woman's liberation, because they "need her joy and her strength." The liberated woman will offer men freedom because she will understand that "lovers who are free to go when they are restless always come back, lovers who are free to change remain interesting. . . . A lover who comes to your bed of his own accord is more likely to sleep with his arms around you all night than the lover who has nowhere else to sleep" (p. 242). The question remains, however, what should women do while the lover is away being restless—wait patiently by the fire?

No, Germaine would say. Why sit by the fire when you could be out enjoying the very freedom that men have, to grasp what pleasure life may bring regardless of consequences, responsibilities, or insecurities? In fact, a major theme of the book argues that women must come to recognize "insecurity as freedom." Our desire to have a safe, stable existence, especially within marriage, is the weakest, most self-destructive part of our nature. If we could but overcome our cloying, emotional dependencies, if we could learn to risk, to dare, we too could achieve "self-sufficiency" and the joys of "spontaneous association."

So in place of marriage, Germaine suggests "deliberate promiscuity" (p. 8). In place of the entrapment of what we call "love," she would have us offer "love" without "conditions." But surely we have the right to make some demands. How can we love men as most of them are today? She herself admits that women "have very little idea of how much men hate them" (p. 245). How then are we to forget this and all it means, trust men, and give up all our demands for security? Germaine says we should replace our quest for security with an application of the "pleasure principle." But what kind of pleasure can most men offer us? We can hope that most women will recognize this alternative to dependency for what it is—an escape and a trap, a return to a shallow individualism reminiscent of the "liberated" twenties. Cosmopolitan, fun, as it might be, it is no answer to the plight of women.

Granted we must learn to reject our debilitating dependency on men, but we must replace it with relationships in which sex is not the core but which do involve care, interdependence, and trust. Real security, gained by working and loving women (and those men we can trust), is strengthening, even liberating.

I am tempted to suggest that Germaine recognizes her contradictions but cannot accept what they mean. A pattern emerges from her early history that is familiar to many of us: daughter of a bitchy mother and an entrapped father, she has the additional burden of being bright and aggressive. Perhaps she cannot risk offending men; she must *not* resemble her mother. Instead she will be the woman in whom all men confide and trust because they can make love to her without feeling possessed. Her own "security" lies in being "free" while still attractive to and desired by men; to give this up would be to risk a great deal.

Many of us who have feared to become like our mothers have found a temporary security in such a position. The trouble with it is that those very men who confide in such an understanding and "free" woman are probably mistreating other, less favored, women. By giving those men a place to be safe from demands, the bountiful, sexy mama undermines any real chance for change in the condition of women. What reason is there for men who find such havens to cease their destructive behavior toward other women?

Ultimately, Germaine's call for individual self-help rests on rejection of other women besides oneself. Such a strategy makes us hate ourselves and renders us incapable of understanding why, despite all our personal changes, the world doesn't get any better. What we need is neither this nor calls to give up men entirely. We need tactics which provide us with the strength to challenge men and make the demands upon society which are essential for the liberation of ourselves and all our sisters.

Germaine herself mentions the proponents of one such alternative when she comments favorably on the "more intelligent" members of the National Organization of Women (NOW), who left that group to carry on more radical feminist work. One of these women, Shulamith Firestone, has written a book, *The Dialectic of Sex: The Case for Feminist Revolution*, which could help women like Germaine to understand that they do not have to hate men in order to confront them and make demands on them. Too, it is possible to deplore many of the bad patterns which women have developed in self-defense without hating women for their weaknesses. It is even possible to see the practical wisdom of some of the stratagems women have devised for themselves.

Shulamith offers "radical feminism" as the way for women to change themselves and society:

> It sees feminist issues not only as *women's* first priority but as central to any larger revolutionary analysis. It refuses to accept any existing leftist analysis not because it is too radical, but because *it is not radical enough*. It sees the current left analysis as outdated and superficial because this analysis does not relate the structure of the economic class to its origins in the sexual class system, the model for all class systems and thus the tapeworm that must be eliminated. (p. 37)

This overall approach allows Shulamith to analyze the situation of women without allowing her frustration to lead to easy hatred—of men or women. She too sees the nuclear family as destructive, but, unlike Germaine, she understands why women choose it. Women are either private or public property, she maintains, subject to the control and authority of one man or of many, but seldom truly free. Therefore, if a woman is married she at least acquires physical security in place of her independence: she is somewhat safer sexually and she has a chance to achieve an integrated, even loving relationship with the people in her family, something usually impossible for the unattached female. She argues that sexual "freedom," such as advocated by Germaine, does not liberate women at all, but instead only serves to provide men with an ever more compliant harem of women:

> By convincing women that the usual female games and demands were despicable, unfair, prudish, old fashioned, puritanical and self-destructive, a new reservoir of available females was created to expand the tight supply of goods for traditional sexual exploitation, disarming women of even the little protection they had so painfully acquired. . . . Those women who had decided not to marry because they were wise enough to look around and see where it led found it was marry or nothing. Men give their commitment only for a price. (pp. 142, 144)

Shulamith understands that many of the female behavior patterns which so irritate Germaine are nothing more than "desperate strategies for survival." For example, Germaine has only contempt for the romanticism and altruism in which women often indulge. Shulamith, while also viewing both as harmful to women, recognizes them as responses to the fact that society, no matter how much it promotes the role of "creative homemaker" or "glamorous playmate," considers women's lives virtually without meaning. It is much more gratifying, for example, to imagine that you are in the midst of a passionate love affair than it is to accept being used for some man's sexual pleasure. Likewise it is less destructive to think of yourself as "serving humanity" when you do volunteer work than it is to admit to being simply an easy source of cheap labor.

Shulamith recognizes that the struggle for the liberation of women will be long and hard, and she enlists the theories and techniques of traditional enemies when she thinks they will aid the cause. Most feminists, including Germaine, reject Freud entirely because his theories grew from an authoritarian, male-dominated point of view. Shulamith examines the Oedipal conflict, reinterprets it in terms of power, and finds that it has cosmic significance in the socialization of women as well as men: young boys must reject their mothers, even though they are good, in favor of their fathers, who have power, even if they are cold. Sons feel guilty about rejecting the good mother so they act out their guilt by hating women. Understandably, women are even more confused by the situation. Shulamith also accepts another traditional feminist enemy, the Man's technology. She hopes that technology, driven by ecological imperatives, will help to relieve women of the now necessary burden of bearing children. She is even willing to accept a modified idea of marriage (licensed "households" composed of groups of couples and children) as a gradual step toward eliminating the nuclear family.

Finally, Shulamith is both more angry and yet more realistic than Germaine. Because she perceives the depths of women's oppression, she does not expect change to come from individual "self-help." While women must individually work to change their socialized and romanticized notions of what they should be, such change cannot be profound unless individual men and the male culture change as well. She understands, far better than does Germaine, that men and women are locked into destructive roles and that only a drastic restructuring of our life patterns will allow any of us to survive.

But Shulamith Firestone does not have all the answers either. She, like Germaine, is limited by a strongly middle class bias: Germaine's solution to the problem of having children is to take them to Italy to grow up in a large extended family there; Shulamith assumes that everyone discusses Freud at cocktail parties. Also, she overstates her case. Everything in society simply cannot be reduced to a male-female analogy. Blacks are not merely playing the child's role in a "societal nuclear family," nor does it help much to discuss aesthetic culture as "female." Obviously, the failure of the Russian Revolution is not "directly traceable to the failure of its attempts to eliminate the family and sexual repression" (p. 212). We have to learn much more about how all people respond to differences and to power; for example, certainly *all* problems in lesbian relationships do not come from their mimicry of male-female relations. Her use of senseless, pretentious charts is distracting. Her "re-interpretation" of the Oedipal conflict is grossly over-emphasized, particularly since it is mere hypothesis, and questionable at that.

Still, Shulamith Firestone does begin a process which other feminists must continue, that of analyzing society from out of the female experience in a way which neither accuses men of constant plotting against women nor exonerates them from their misbehavior, which neither assumes all women are super-women because of their suffering nor attacks them for behaving in the only ways they are allowed to behave in this society. This is the type of approach that is positive, future-oriented, and can lead us to constructive discussions of realistic strategies toward achieving revolutionary ends. Others, like Cynthia Epstein, are not preparing for this change; they simply want to acquire what men have. We cannot win this way, first, because it is impossible for the sexist male society to grant us equality, and second, and more importantly, because any analysis of what has happened to women should teach us not to want men's roles since these roles are even uglier and more dehumanizing than our own. Women like Germaine Greer cannot help us plan for the future either. Although they might provide a scathing indictment of women's misery, they cannot accept how deeply rooted the causes of that misery are. Merely changing ourselves will not solve our problems. Men are adaptable; they will tolerate our "independence" as long as we do not threaten their power. Shulamith Firestone, however, shows us that things can change in constructive directions. We can prove the anti-feminists right: giving women their rights does result in the destruction of the family, Motherhood, the capitalist economy, and "civilization" as we know it. Good riddance.

Domestication as Reform:
A Study of the Socialization
of Wayward Girls, 1856–1905

BARBARA BRENZEL

Barbara Brenzel examines nineteenth-century juvenile reform policies by telling the story of Lancaster, a family-style progressive reform school for girls in Massachusetts. Analyzing the efforts of reformers to socialize poor girls, many of whom were immigrants, she describes the contradictory dual purposes underlying these policies—fear and benevolence. The discussion of Lancaster illustrates how particular policies and programs for potentially or already deviant girls reflected nineteenth-century thought about reform, childhood, poverty, and especially the role of women in society.

In 1857, Bradford Peirce, superintendent of the first reform school for girls in North America, reported to the Massachusetts legislature on the role of female juvenile reform:

> It is sublime work to save a woman, for in her bosom generations are embodied, and in her hands, if perverted, the fate of innumerable men is held. The whole community, gentlemen, personally interested as they are in our success because the children of the virtuous must breathe the atmosphere exhaled by the vicious, will feel a lively sympathy for you, in your generous endeavors to redeem the erring mothers of the next generation.[1]

Peirce was echoing a pervasive point of view in mid-nineteenth-century America, that in one form or another, social stability rested on women. Women would set the moral and religious tone for family life,[2] and family life itself would counterbalance the effect of unchecked economic change and the new extremes of urban wealth and poverty. Mid-century reformers had two solutions to the dilemmas created by capitalist

[1] Bradford K. Peirce, 2AR, Public Document 16, 1857, p. 26.
[2] Barbara Welter, "The Cult of True Womanhood," *American Quarterly* (1966), 151-174. In this article the author delineates the four qualities considered necessary for the ideal antebellum woman: domesticity, submission, purity, and piety. It is obvious that even in postbellum America, Lancaster's founders were very much influenced by this ideology.

Harvard Educational Review   Vol. 50   No. 2   May 1980, 196-213

modernization and its effect on the American family. One was formal schooling, which was a public and collective antidote to the disorder and chaos of the new urban environment. The other was the private family, which would offer—in a phrase recently reappropriated—a haven from the world of work and urban problems.[3]

The increasing stress on the importance of the family as a refuge crystallized expectations of women. Now they were to remain in the home, tending and educating the younger children while their spouses and older children left daily for the workplace. In addition to nurturing children, they were to create a sanctuary against the evil of the outside world. As a result of these expectations, nineteenth-century society became irreversibly dichotomized into the domestic sphere and the workplace. Obviously, poor women were frequently unable to fulfill the stereotype of true womanhood, for their lives were shaped by the need to survive rather than by social prescription. Nevertheless, this view of women—as social saviors guarding home, hearth, and family morality—continued to be the cultural norm and provided the model for social theorists and policy makers, as well as for women of all classes.

Poor girls were of particular concern to the reformers, who believed that rehabilitation of juvenile offenders was both possible and necessary. As industrialization, urbanization, and immigration surged, poor, deviant adults seemed less likely to be rehabilitated and assimilated into the new society. As optimism for rehabilitating adults waned, reformers transferred their enthusiasm for rehabilitation to children, whose innocence made them attractive candidates for reform. Children of the urban poor, potential street urchins, threatened social order; their future had to be engineered to preserve society. Reformers believed that these children could be re-formed at an early and still malleable age by giving them an acceptable type of family life. The dual motives of juvenile reform were to save the child and preserve social order. These purposes were especially clear in the case of poor girls, who were considered potentially wayward—as vagrants and prostitutes. Saving the erring mothers of the next generation became vital.

In response to this pressing concern, reformers founded in 1856 the State Industrial School for Girls in Lancaster, Massachusetts. It was not only the first reform school of any kind for girls, but the first family-style institution in North America. Lancaster fused the twin nineteenth-century emphases on schools and families. Through the combination of schooling and reform, the girls at Lancaster would be saved so they could fill the appropriate female role within the family. Thus, reform ideology blended together the confused motives of benevolence and social control.

Once the school was established, it became apparent that reformist theories had to be adjusted to reality. Adhering to their belief in the family, reformers held steadfast in their efforts to train girls for the world of domesticity. The story of Lancaster is one of the changing definition of domesticity in the treatment of wayward girls. Although the school continued to train girls to fit into the domestic sphere, the emphasis narrowed from a total domesticity of surrogate family-style living and love, to an almost exclusive vocational training for domestic service.

What follows in this article is a social portrait of the reformers, the girls, and the school itself, in which we see vividly the expectations placed on women and changing

[3] Christopher Lasch, *Haven in a Heartless World: The Family Beseiged* (New York: Basic Books, 1977).

but pervasive views of the role of domesticity. Studying Lancaster gives us access to fifty years of changing social theory about poor, wayward children, especially girls, and offers us a window on the past of the institutions we struggle to change today.

Methodology

Although historians have been interested in the lives of the poor and seemingly unimportant, they have found it exceedingly difficult to reconstruct the lives of the illiterate.[4] Until recently we assumed that many of the poor, especially poor women and children, had been lost to history. Now, material such as tax records, vital statistics, and census data as well as a more sophisticated use of computers has enabled social historians to write the history and to understand the lives of those previously forgotten. The Lancaster girls, the internal workings of the school, and reform thought are best understood by weaving quantitative and qualitative data together.

I have benefitted from the new historiography and, by using the original handwritten case records, have gained rich and carefully detailed information for every entrant, every fifth year for fifty years. By translating the data into a coding system, I marshalled certain facts about each girl: ethnicity, parental background, the family situation from which each girl entered Lancaster; her schooling, religious training, crime, complainant, behavior at the school, details of the indenture experience, and at least two "follow throughs," including place of residence and work subsequent to leaving the school. Many entries included a wealth of anecdotal materials about later events such as other employment, marriage, entrance into other institutions, or early death. I used indenture, employment, and place of residence to assess some of the school's outcomes.

Official statements made by the reformers of the day give us further information. Massachusetts state records contain many important discussions indicating attitudes toward crime, institutions, welfare, and causes of poverty and deviance. Legislative and other public documents of the Commonwealth, and early reports made by the Board of State Charities and Lancaster's trustees and superintendents contain much pertinent material. Some of the original diaries of the matrons and the budgets and personal records of the superintendent offer additional information. By concentrating on frequency distributions and cross tabulations, I have attempted to understand the interrelationships between all these variables.

The Establishment of Lancaster

Lancaster was an outgrowth of a widespread dialogue in Europe and North America that resulted in a series of institutional responses to capitalist modernization. As part of this ongoing transatlantic dialogue, state-appointed commissioners[5] went abroad to inspect institutions for juvenile reform. European reformers feared potential hordes of street urchins and, like their United States counterparts, combined a pressing need to control the urban poor with what they considered benevolent care for the deprived.

---

[4] For a comprehensive example of this work, see Michael B. Katz, *The People of Hamilton, Canada West* (Cambridge, Mass.: Harvard Univ. Press, 1975); and Peter Laslett, *The World We Have Lost* (New York: Scribner, 1965).

[5] The Fay Commission, headed by Francis Fay, a legislator, was appointed by the Massachusetts Legislature in 1854 specificially to begin plans for a state reform school for girls.

The commissioners visited many schools, the most important of which included Das Rauhe Haus, Hamburg, Germany; École Agricole, Mettray, France; and Royal Philanthropic, Surrey, England. These European schools espoused environmental theories of crime and vagrancy, and sought to counter detrimental environmental conditioning through family-style institutional life. Therefore, in all these institutions, dependent and deviant children were brought to live in home-like cottages in which they were to be treated with the firm but loving guidance of a supervising adult. The children were to live and be reformed within this surrogate family, as all were considered potentially salvageable.

The antiurban bias of most nineteenth-century social theorists was evident in juvenile reform. These schools were located in rural settings where children were considered safe from the evil influences of big-city life. The pastoral environment was believed to be purifying, a healthy retreat enabling children to redeem their lost innocence. A combination of religious training and family-style living within these rural sanctuaries was to insure that they would become reliable working adults and responsible family members.

Having studied these institutions carefully and discussed juvenile reform theories with European reformers, the Massachusetts commissioners returned to the United States convinced that family-style juvenile reform institutions were appropriate for the first American reform school for girls. Yet nineteenth-century Americans did not want to borrow blindly from the Old World. They wanted a New World version of the European reformatories and, in characteristic American fashion, placed great emphasis on education. The commissioners were determined, therefore, to draw heavily on those aspects of European juvenile reform that seemed most applicable to their mission. They embraced the family-style reform as perfect for the reformation of young girls; they envisioned that in the cottages of the heterogeneous reformatory, girls could receive the common schooling held so precious by the reformers and would acquire the habits of domesticity deemed critical for them. However, the reformers were also determined to avoid those aspects of European institutions that seemed too punitive, lacking in educational value, or inappropriate for women. They therefore rejected, for example, military routine, harsh punishment, and overemphasis on vocational training.

The commissioners returned to Massachusetts at an auspicious time. Nineteenth-century Americans were reacting to the crises of urbanization, modernization, and immigration by seeking to create institutions to mediate between older values and the consequences of modernization. Emerging cities with their large masses of poor and dislocated people, resulted in the loss of informal, familial, and community responsibility in which care for and control of the dependent and deviant traditionally occurred. Now, with towns swollen into cities, the same needy people were considered strangers; social reformers felt compelled to create new mechanisms to deal with them.

These reformers were, as a rule, driven by two motives: the hope of building a new social order, and the fear of social chaos. These motives were written into their reform innovations and characterized efforts to deal with strangers in their midst. It is important to note that Lancaster was an integral part of an institutional web[6] which had only

---

[6] For a more detailed description of this movement, see Michel Foucault, *The Birth of the Clinic* (New

partly begun to include reformatories, mental hospitals, public schools, orphanages, and various urban missions. In this light we can see Lancaster as part of an effort to care for and control the stranger—in this case, urban girls. This legacy was inherited from two sources: the egalitarian impulses which, in part, were inspired by the creation of America's democratic institutions and the common school movement.

The common school movement aptly illustrates the mixed motives of mid-century reform. Public schooling insured every child an equal education which would extend equality of opportunity to all children and teach them those habits of industry and morality considered important for responsible citizenship. By educating and socializing all children, reformers hoped to achieve social democracy and social order. Horace Mann, the father of the common school movement, articulated this dual purpose in his First Annual Report of 1837: "After the state shall have secured to all its children, that basis of knowledge and morality, which is indispensible to its own security; and after it shall have supplied them with the instruments of that individual prosperity, whose aggregates will constitute its own social prosperity; then they may be emancipated from its tutelage; each one to go whithersoever his well instructed mind shall determine."[7]

As a further effort to socialize and educate all children, the first state reform school for boys was opened in Westborough, Massachusetts, in 1847. Its purposes were to shelter those dependent and deviant boys who needed guidance beyond that offered by common schooling and to protect society from their potential evil. As Michael Katz discusses in *The Irony of Early School Reform*, a mechanism was created to educate and correctly socialize those who could not be reached by the regular process of common schooling.[8] In spite of the egalitarian rhetoric used to rationalize common schooling, however, the early reform school effort neglected girls. But the same view of children that led Horace Mann and others to promulgate common schooling for all children soon compelled reformers to offer the same reform opportunities to neglected and delinquent girls.[9] Mixed with this vision, however, was a growing concern that the family was faltering and the number of wayward girls was rising. It was, therefore, of immediate concern that girls, as future wives and mothers, be domesticated and reformed.

Given both their egalitarianism and commitment to common schooling, the reformers felt strongly that education had to be an integral part of the girls' reform program: they would learn to read and write as well as to perform household tasks and would receive rigorous religious training. Firm convictions of faith were motivational forces in the social activity of doing good for others less fortunate than oneself:

York: Pantheon, 1973); Michel Foucault, *Discipline and Punish* (New York: Pantheon, 1977): Gerald N. Grob, *The State and the Mentally Ill* (Chapel Hill: Univ. of North Carolina Press, 1965); Gerald N. Grob, *Mental Institutions in America* (New York: Free Press, 1973); David W. Lewis, *From Newgate to Dannemora* (Ithaca: Cornell Univ. Press, 1965); Barbara Gutman, *Public Health and the State* (Cambridge, Mass.: Harvard Univ. Press, 1972); David Rothman, *The Discovery of the Asylum* (Boston: Little, Brown, 1971).

[7] Lawrence A. Cremin, *The Republic and the School: Horace Mann on the Education of Free Men* (New York: Teachers College Press, 1957), p. 33.

[8] Michael B. Katz, *The Irony of Early School Reform* (Cambridge, Mass.: Harvard Univ. Press, 1968), pp. 163-211.

[9] Douglas E. Branch, *The Sentimental Years* (New York: Hill & Wang, 1965), pp. 289-318.

Intellectual development exalts the moral, and although order and direct appliances may be necessary to complete its culture, still, when you open the avenues to knowledge and supply the mind with healthy food, it ceases to long after the garbage which works such mischief with those who have nothing else to feed on. The cultivation of *self-respect*, beside the inculcation and enforcement of those great moral truths which it is the business of society to develop and to cherish, should be carefully attended to.[10]

The germ of all morality lies in self-respect; and, unless you have sufficiently stimulated and excited this, all your efforts will be as "sounding brass or a tinkling cymbal."[11]

The commissioners reported their thoughts in January, 1855 and in the same year the Massachusetts legislature established the school they wanted. The legislative resolves pulled together four critical aspects of this new social experiment. First, Lancaster was to be created and operated on state initiative. Second, this school was a manifestation of a larger enthusiasm for social reform. Third, the school was to be a great social invention, combining the best of common schooling with training in the habits of work. Fourth, its program orientation stressed meeting the unique needs of women. The Resolves expressed the theory which governed the creation of Lancaster:

The title of the Resolves under which the commissioners act is, "Resolves for the establishment of a State Reform School for Girls." *A State Reform School for Girls!* Every word is significant and suggestive. In the first place the institution established is to be a *state* school. . . . Its establishment and maintenance will certainly affect the material interest of every citizen; and its beneficial operation will as certainly it is hoped return a manifold recompense, purifying in its nature, into the bosom of society.

In the second place, it is to be a *reform* school. . . . Its aim to be the means, under the divine providence and by the divine blessing, of reconstructing . . . of rebuilding . . . or re-forming. . . .

In the next place, it is to be a reform *school*. It aims to accomplish its object in and upon its subject as *pupils*. It aims to enlighten the understanding, and to mend and re-generate the heart, by teaching the pupils what is true, and by training them to think and speak it, and by showing them what is good, and by leading them to act and do it. . . .

And, finally, it is to be a school for *girls* — for the gentler sex. . . . This circumstance is an important one, and enters into and modifies the plan of building and arrangement of rooms, with all the details relating to employment, instruction, and amusement, and, indeed, to every branch of domestic economy.[12]

The principle of in loco parentis assured the Commonwealth that the Lancaster girls were indeed to be treated as if they were under the supervision of a wise parent. The matron served as a mother; each girl was to have her own room, and no more than thirty girls were to live in the same house. In keeping with the staunch mid-century belief in the potential goodness of all children, the girls were not separated either by age or alleged crime. The older girls would set an example for their younger sisters; the younger girls would serve as gentling influences on the older girls. Corporal punishment was no longer an acceptable means of discipline; firmness and love stood in its

[10] "Commissioner's Report," Massachusetts House Document 43, 1854, p. 6.
[11] "Commissioner's Report," p. 34.
[12] "An Act," Massachusetts House Document 43, 1854, p. 51.

stead. The girls would be bound in their new home by cords of love rather than imprisoned by bars.

Both European and American reformers were caught in a struggle between the utilitarianism most clearly defined in Benthamite ideology and the romantic view of lost community idealized by nineteenth-century poets, especially Samuel Coleridge.[13] While the utilitarians rationalized the growth and expedience of policies that resulted in the creation of social institutions and laissez-faire economic policies, the romantics yearned to recover the pure and pastoral. Lancaster was to provide the perfect environment to cleanse the girls, who were considered polluted by city life. The purity of natural living would inspire the redemption and healthy growth of the potentially wayward child.

Lancaster was nestled in hilly farmland in a beautiful rural area of Massachusetts about fifty miles west of Boston. A small stone chapel was built in the center of the grounds as a symbol of the school's mission. The girls' living quarters reflected the two goals of the founders. Each girl had her own room, although the size of the rooms and the layout of the sleeping quarters made them appear cell-like. Yet, there was pleasant common living and recreational space. Girls learned domestic skills in the ironing rooms in each cottage. In spite of this homelike atmosphere, however, the square, red brick building appeared less like the neighboring homes than the New England academies of the era. In this institution the girls were to be sheltered, educated, and gently incarcerated.

The daily life at the school was based originally on a balanced three-tiered program consisting of common schooling, religious observance, and domestic training. Life at the school can best be described by looking at the "First Annual Report of the Superintendent":

> The chapel bell rings at six, at which time or before, the girls rise, and put themselves
> and their sleeping rooms in order, and prepare the breakfast; at seven this meal is
> eaten. Housework is attended to until nine, at which time the chaplain comes, to take
> the direction of the morning devotions. Labor holds as many as can be spared from
> domestic duties in the workroom until dinner; this occurs at twelve. School is held from
> half-past one until half-past four; supper at five; and sewing, knitting and reading in
> the work-room until evening; prayers at eight, after which the girls are dismissed for
> bed. During the day sufficient time for exercise is allowed in the open air.[14]

Regardless of the age at which the girls entered Lancaster, at sixteen they were to be placed as indentured domestic servants. It was presumed that the moral and domestic training received at Lancaster would ensure that they were well suited for their placements. Girls served these indentures under the jurisdiction of the state until age eighteen, considered the age of majority. During their indentures, they performed household duties within a supportive and supervisory household.

The probate court was empowered to sentence to Lancaster those girls it felt would benefit from such a rehabilitative setting. Although they could be sent for both status offenses, such as vagrancy, and more serious adult crimes, such as assault, more than

---

[13] F. R. Leavis, ed., *John Stuart Mill on Bentham and Coleridge* (New York: Harper & Row, 1950).

[14] "First Annual Report of the Superintendent and Chaplain," Massachusetts *IAR*, House Document 20, 1856, p. 35.

three-quarters of the girls had been accused of committing crimes considered morally threatening to social stability. For the full fifty years under consideration, most of the girls sent to Lancaster had been accused of stubborn, wayward, and potentially degenerate behavior; vagrancy, running away, and staying out late at night continued to be the most frequent female juvenile crimes.

Given the structure of the school, there could only be a small group of girls in residence at any one time. According to the Board of State Charities' Reports, the number of girls in the school averaged between 90 and 120. On the average, there were 69 entrants per year. It is important to note that the small group of girls who came to Lancaster had a great deal in common.

From 1856 to 1905, 75 percent of these girls were English-speaking, American-born, and very poor. Of the few who were foreign-born, almost all were Irish and therefore spoke English. Given the changes in immigration patterns around the turn of the century, it is not surprising that at that time a slightly larger proportion of the immigrant inmates were from non-English-speaking countries. Nevertheless, 85 percent of the girls still came from English-speaking countries, and the vast majority were native-born. A closer look at these girls' ethnic backgrounds indicates that most of them were the daughters of Irish Catholic parents. This is understandable, given the waves of immigration after the Irish potato famine of 1845. By the 1850s, more than half the population of Boston was foreign-born and most of these immigrants were poor Irish.[15] Therefore, it is safe to assume that their daughters were very poor indeed.

For these fifty years, Lancaster housed an almost equal number of Irish Catholic and Protestant American girls. It is considered unusual for such a large group of Catholics to be in a Protestant institution, except by force. Certainly by 1840, Catholics had issued public complaints against public schooling. In New York, for example, Catholic immigrants, through the efforts of Bishop Hughes, fought for public money to start their own schools. Catholic parents opposed the use of the King James version of the Bible, the lack of catechismal instruction in the classroom, as well as the Protestant insistence that schools be neutral. According to Carl Kaestle, many of the public school texts exacerbated this situation by containing anti-Irish slurs. In short, Catholics considered the neutral stance of the public schools to be, in effect, Protestant and, therefore, anti-Catholic.[16]

During the fifty years studied, 6 percent of the inmates were black. Although this figure is disproportionately high when compared to the number of Blacks in the state at that time, the black population was steadily growing as black families migrated from the South. They, like the Irish, were poor and dislocated, but there is no evidence that they were selected to be brought to the school in any way different from the other girls.

It is also striking that Lancaster consistently housed children whose parents spoke English. Since the majority of the girls had been born in the United States, we may also

---

[15] Oscar Handlin, *Boston's Immigrants* (New York: Atheneum, 1972); Malwyn A. Jones, *American Immigration* (Chicago: Univ. of Chicago Press, 1960); U.S. Dept. of Commerce, Bureau of the Census, *Historical Statistics of the United States: Colonial Times to 1970*, pp. 87-121.

[16] Daniel Calhoun, ed., *The Educating of Americans: A Documentary History* (Boston: Houghton Mifflin, 1969), pp. 158-171; Carl F. Kaestle, *The Evolution of an Urban School System: New York City, 1750-1850* (Cambridge, Mass.: Harvard Univ. Press, 1973), pp. 148-158.

assume that their parents had been in this country long enough to internalize the social norms, to speak the language of the probate court, and ultimately to make use of the system in order to find shelter for their daughters. Throughout these fifty years, more than half of the girls, both Catholic and Protestant, were brought to the court by members of their own families. The complainant families seemed to have had in common a sense of desperation bred by poverty, unemployment, death, or physical uprooting.[17] That most of the complainants were family members undermines two popular assumptions: that reform schools were a malevolent plot of the state to take poor girls away from their families, and that Irish Catholic parents were extremely reluctant to place their children in a Protestant state institution.

Conventional wisdom assumed that state institutions, under the aegis of *parens patriae*, were legally sanctioned to take over child rearing because the natural parents were considered incapable. They were, therefore, considered enemies to families, especially to those destitute and foreign. Dickensian images of the heartless state hauling off weeping, protesting children from their humble, helpless parents are so ingrained that we are shocked to discover the extent of parental participation in a daughter's commitment to a state home.

As we have seen, Catholic parents exhibited great hostility toward institutions which they saw as undermining their own religious and ethnic identities. Understandably, their greatest hostility was directed toward schools and other institutions which cared for their young. Yet Catholics also brought their daughters to Lancaster.[18] It seemed that, when they were desperate, Lancaster was the only concrete help available to poor parents of difficult girls.

The evidence from the Lancaster School supports historians who consider most reform institutions as mechanisms for social control. However, the story of Lancaster suggests that our present understanding of the relationship between the state and the poor does not adequately account for the complicated web of relationships created among those involved. Given the benevolent impulses and the fears of the reformers, the seemingly inadequate supervision of the girls, and the desperation of poor parents, an inextricable triangular relationship emerged in the absence of any other welfare options. In large measure, the problem was the state's inability or unwillingness to offer more reasonable and less traumatic options for aid to the poor. Instead, parents were forced to take advantage of a punitive institution.

The story of Lancaster is not one of a dream come true. The Commissioners' lofty aspirations rapidly collided with social reality. In ways unanticipated by the reformers, the school had ties to social, political, economic, and institutional circumstances that would prevent it from becoming a rehabilitative utopia. Soon after Lancaster opened, the initial optimism of the trustees began to wane and, within a year, they began to doubt the feasibility of their scheme. Although the trustees continued to defend the innocence of childhood, their ambivalence grew, as demonstrated in the following passage:

[17] By using the occupational ranking scheme devised by Michael B. Katz in *The People of Hamilton, Canada West*, pp. 343–348, I was able to assess the fathers' occupational rank. The number of fathers who were dead, had deserted, or whose occupation was "uncategorizable" showed that the girls at Lancaster were from extremely poor homes. Those mothers who worked held exceptionally low-ranked jobs.

[18] I calculated Irish or Irish-American girls as Catholics when the religion of the girls was not explicitly stated.

> When the criminal desire has developed itself into the criminal act, the question is often asked, is there any prospect for permanent reformation? The answer will, of course, be greatly modified by the circumstances of age, previous social relations, strength of character, and their future position. In reference to the youngest cases, embracing even the astonishing premature age of twelve years, a glance upon their girlish faces will afford, in part, an answer to the question.[19]

The despair and frustration of the trustees and administrators was plain. Echoing the disillusionment expressed above, just slightly over a year later, another of Lancaster's trustees began to question heterogeneous groupings. He concerned himself with separating deviants from dependents. His rationale was a chilling harbinger of the policies to come. "This would enable us to separate those of a tender age from the older girls and to conduct, with a somewhat modified discipline, a department which might be considered *preventative*, anticipating temptation, and guarding the inmates from the peril of personal contact with the young offenders whose reformation is attempted in the other homes."[20]

By 1865 Lancaster was becoming less a place of loving familial guidance and more a place of punishment and incarceration. This was due to three interrelated factors: changes in reformist ideology, changes in the clientele, and changes in the school program itself. The Howe Sanborn Report, printed in the Annual Report of the Board of State Charities for 1865, indicated with frightening clarity the direction in which reform ideology was rapidly moving. This Report was concerned with the social burden of poor and deviant children and the elderly—those considered dependent. More important than this general concern, however, are the ideas found in the discussion of the "General Causes of the Existence of Dependents, Destructives, and the Like." Drunkenness was considered to reproduce weak stock, and there was also a strong suggestion of a new hereditarianism: evil tendencies were considered to be transmitted to children by parents inebriated at the time of conception. The report warned that the children of such a coupling could threaten social order.

Unlike the discussions of mid-century social theorists which blurred the distinctions between deviance and dependence in a sentimental judgment of all those who could and should be saved, less than fifteen years later analysis focused on the various causes of deviance. The concern shifted from saving children to classifying types of depravity. Although the authors of the report claimed to be confused about who was blighted irreversibly and who was redeemable, they revealed their hereditarian bias when they attempted to explain the difference between "lack of vital force" and "inherited tendencies." Mid-nineteenth century social theories had attributed juvenile dependency and deviance to poor environment and inadequate parents. Now the blame fell increasingly on the child, to whom the bad habits of parents had been directly transmitted.

At the same time that reform ideology was evolving toward a sterner hereditarian explanation for deviance, the age and supposed character of entrants also changed. Initially, girls between ages seven and sixteen were to be admitted to Lancaster. However, from its opening in 1856, most girls were pubescent—between fourteen and

---

[19] Massachusetts 2AR, Public Document 16, 1856, p. 14.
[20] Massachusetts 2AR, House Document, 1857, p. 10.

fifteen. The age of entrants steadily increased, so that by 1875 most of the entrants were between the ages of fifteen and sixteen and by 1895, they were between sixteen and seventeen.

The contrast between the sentimental attitudes of mid-century reformers, especially toward younger girls, and the harsher attitudes later in the century are reflected in the superintendents' reports. For example, both Sarah W. (1856) and Elizabeth B. (1880) were sent to Lancaster as "stubborn" girls, on the verge of deviance, but supposedly redeemable. However, the tone of Superintendent Bradford Peirce, writing in 1856, differs radically from that of Superintendent Marcus Ames, writing in 1880.

Sarah W., brought in for uncontrollable masturbation, was described as a "pretty little girl . . . who would be a substantial comfort to anyone who would carefully train her. . . ."[21] Once it was discovered that she was suffering from erysipelas, a skin disease, rather than a need to "abuse herself," the state chose to keep her and thus be guaranteed that she would be properly trained. Bradford Peirce went on to describe her as "requiring medical attention and physical treatment."[22] It was unlikely that Sarah and girls like her would be considered incorrigible in 1856.

By 1880, however, girls were more likely to be described as Elizabeth B.: "Young as Lizzie is, her record is painfully bad. She has been off with bad men and to disreputable places on Charles Street."[23] Similarly, Winnifred C. is "unmanageable and disobedient; has been in bad company; appears hardened and utterly devoid of feeling or shame."[24] Certainly by 1890, Bradford Peirce's sensitive belief that the young "sinner" was to be pitied, loved, and redirected to a good life was replaced by the colder tone reserved for management of the unruly and depraved. The case report of Josephine C., the 1,557th entrant, reflected the officer's attitude toward newcomers to Lancaster: "[She] is said to be unchaste. Has not frequented houses of ill fame. She is not of average intelligence. Character of house not good. Father a drinking fiddler and her mother is deaf and dumb. Girl is on street. Stole a hat from a store in Holyoke. Her appearance indicates a want of teaching."[25]

This unfeeling tone colored reports for the next fifteen years. In 1905 the punitive voice of the superintendent can be heard in the description of Annie Elizabeth H.: "[She] is known to have been unchaste. Keeps low company. Out late at night. Character of home poor. Fa[ther] in H[ouse of] C[orrection] for drunkenness. Mother washes. These girls were found in a freight car with men. She has been immoral for some time."[26]

The Legislative Reports also systematically noted that the girls were harder and of a more "criminal" class, and now defined "criminality" in specifically female terms. The crimes reported at the boys' reformatory at Westborough were crimes which implied greater violence, and more damage to personal or public property. The more severe crimes for girls were those which suggested immorality, defined as wantonness and prostitution. No longer considered vulnerable to exploitation, girls now could be

[21] Bradford K. Peirce, *First Handwritten Casebook*, 1856, p. 1.
[22] Peirce, *Casebook*, p. 1.
[23] Porter N. Brown, *Handwritten Casebook*, 1880. Case 1062.
[24] Brown, Case 1070.
[25] Mrs. L. Brackett, *Handwritten Casebook*, 1890, Case 1557.
[26] Mrs. L. Brackett, *Handwritten Casebook*, 1905, Case 2751.

destructive of public morality. They were no longer seen as girls in need of protection or firmer, more loving supervision, but as threats to public safety in need of isolation and control.

The increase in the age of entrants, however, was affected by three legislated changes as well as by the emergence of new state reform institutions.[27] In 1871 the state passed a law which enabled the Board of State Charities to attend probate court and prevent younger and seemingly more innocent girls from going to Lancaster. The state could now intervene to separate the younger from older girls. This view countered the founders' conception of the family institution as a therapeutic environment. It was now important to save young girls from the potential harm resulting from exposure to older and more hardened girls. State policy now facilitated direct placement to help the young; direct placement was seen as less desirable for older girls. In 1871 other laws influenced the age composition at Lancaster. One determined that seventeen-year-olds could be sent to Lancaster. Another provided that girls of sixteen who were considered incorrigible or badly placed originally could be transferred to Lancaster from other institutions by the courts. Lancaster was rapidly becoming a dumping ground for older and tougher girls.

In 1886 the State Primary School at Monson opened.[28] The express purpose of this school was to care for young, destitute children. Younger girls who were originally to be sent to Lancaster were now to be sent to the Primary School. Although the Primary School closed in 1895, the age patterns at Lancaster remained relatively unchanged after that time.

While the original reform ideology of heterogeneous family-style life was debated until 1885, policy pressures and the working of the institutional web brought about the separation of younger from older girls long before the formal change in reform theory occurred. Segregation by age and character replaced the therapeutic vision of mid-century environmentalists and underlined an insistence on the permanence of taint. The state, through legislation, voiced its disbelief in the possibility of reclaiming innocence for everyone. It is difficult to evaluate the criminal character of these older girls, to determine whether they were, in fact, as the officers described them, harder. It is possible that they were more sexually experienced if only because they were older.

With the changes in age and supposed criminality of its clientele, Lancaster officials were forced to face pressing questions of management and control. Although, by 1877, hardened girls were being sent to Sherborn Reformatory for Women, an institution for adult female first offenders, the trustees of Lancaster felt that the increased number of

[27] The following three acts brought about de facto classification. Sects. 8 and 10, Chap. 359, Acts of 1870, allowed the Visiting Agent of the Board of State Charities to attend trials and to oversee placement once the girls received their sentences. At the same time, Chap. 365, Acts of 1871, gave the Board the power of transfer of girls to Lancaster from other institutions. It also sanctioned the commitment of seventeen-year-olds to Lancaster.

[28] Until 1872 the Primary School was really an adjunct to the Monson Almshouse. In 1872 the Primary School became independent of the Almshouse, sharing its trusteeship with the two reform schools. The increasing bureaucratization of the State Board of Charities eroded the informal mechanisms the founders felt necessary to work with these children. Bitter controversies arose over the education program and placement at Monson. In addition, hardened criminal children were placed with young destitute children. In 1886 the State Primary School at Monson was opened for the purpose of housing destitute and deprived young children; it was considered a preferable alternative to the Almshouse or reform school. The Primary School suffered the same fate at Lancaster, however. The legislature closed the school in 1895.

hardened girls created a need for the school to have its own correctional department. The policy of transferring incorrigible girls to Sherborn sufficed when transfer was not a frequent necessity. By the 1880s, however, this policy was inadequate to handle the new clientele. The mid-century belief that "cords of love are stronger than chains of iron" and that "affection and attachment are more irresistible bulwarks than stone walls . . . that iron and stone may restrain and confine the vicious, but they possess no healing properties for the morally diseased,"[29] was now undermined by the request for a more correctional measure. "Isolation or separate confinement, with or without work, as the case may require, is conceded to be one of the most effective methods of bringing to a sense of duty the insubordinate."[30]

With the new institutions for the very young and channels for shipping off the unsuitable, Lancaster assumed a new role. In 1885, the trustees stated that "the Industrial School occupied a position more important than many it has held since its establishment. It is now a middle place between the care of the Board of State Charities and a Reformatory Prison."[31] "The inmates are lodged in four separate family houses, each with its own staff of officers. This division allows a careful classification within the school, a classification depending upon the character and previous history of the girls, and not upon age or conduct within the institution. As there is no promotion from house to house, a perfect isolation is thus secured of those who might otherwise contaminate the more innocent."[32]

A system to guarantee separation of girls by age and character was now in full operation at Lancaster. This classification system formally acknowledged the acceptance of the hereditarian argument for the causes of dependence and deviance. Older girls were considered more tainted, harder, and less redeemable. Hereditarians argued that most delinquent poor children suffered the "permanence of taint." In spite of this harsh argument, some commitment to the ideas linking childhood and salvation continued. Hope for some rehabilitation, therefore, was reserved, but only for the very young. The classification system also formally sanctioned a more punitive approach to older girls whose characters were flawed. Girls would now be treated as cases, rather than as souls to be redeemed. The work at Lancaster was to manage this classified system, making sure that the girls were appropriately placed in the school. The loving family circle was a forgotten dream.

Given all the factors influencing Lancaster's program—economic shifts, changing social theory, different clientele, and internal school pressures—the school's officials kept struggling to redesign a program suitable for both the social climate and the entrants. Therefore, the appropriate roles of common schooling, domestic training, and placement were constantly debated. The success of Lancaster's program had depended upon its healthy balance of religion, common schooling, and domestic training. This internal program was to culminate in a successful indenture—one where the girls were to perform satisfactorily as decent and self-respecting domestic servants. The indenture period was the most vulnerable part of the program because it depended upon successful training at Lancaster and a welcoming climate and job market outside

[29] Massachusetts 4AR, Public Document 24, 1859, p. 6
[30] Massachusetts 22AR, to State Board of Health, Lunacy, and Charity, Public Document 20, 1877, p. 7.
[31] Massachusetts 22AR, 1877, p. 14.
[32] Massachusetts 32AR, to the State Board of Lunacy and Charity, Public Document 18, 1887, p. 14.

the school. Flaws in the indenture system frequently resulted in efforts to redesign the school's training program and educational curriculum. For example, in 1868 the program was revised to include instruction in a wider variety of housekeeping skills to improve the capacity for housework. The trustees saw in such increased versatility a greater guarantee to the girls that "[they would] readily find safe and respectable homes, liberal wages and kind friends."[33]

Although domesticity was always the prime objective of Lancaster's program, the increased stress on domestic training was now explicitly stated and justified as that aspect of Lancaster's program most relevant to the attainment of true womanhood. The details of this report read as a prescription for the happy lives of women:

> Almost every woman is destined to have a leading or subordinate part in the management of a family. Preparation for the ready and intelligent performance of household duties, the lowest as well as the highest, is therefore, of the first importance. Now, as perfect cleanliness is essential to health of body and of mind and to cheerfulness, all the arts of washing and scouring should be early learnt and practised, so as to form and fix the habit of doing them well, throughly, rapidly, and willingly.[34]

The report then goes on to list explicitly the chores most closely linked to those deemed essential for women's happiness: ". . . these arts should include not only the washing of tables and dishes, but the scouring of floors, stairs, windows and walls, and of clothes, and especially of bedclothes, and bedsteads. These duties occur every day in every family. They should, therefore, be done methodically, and the habit of method and order should be insisted upon amongst the most important attainments."[35]

Common schooling, originally seen as an essential feature of Lancaster's program, became less important as the push for domestic science increased. By 1869 education at Lancaster largely had come to mean female vocational training. The zeal of Samuel Gridley Howe and Horace Mann for common schooling was swept under the carpet with domestic training.

In spite of the newly tailored curriculum, by 1875 the indenture system was in even greater danger. The number of indentures experienced by each girl had risen, so that as many as 15 percent of those girls who where indentured had more than three placements and a few had as many as five. It seemed that many Lancaster girls were not suitable for placement and that the school would have to refine its program in order to increase the girls' employability.[36]

By 1884 the program had diverged dramatically from its original plan. The 29th Annual Report discussed the constant change of inmates due to a new policy which placed out girls as soon as they seemed ready rather than when they reached sixteen. This new policy left more openings for new girls, and since the average length of confinement was short, the whole idea of family-style care was undermined; Lancaster became less a residence and place for reformation and more a place for expedient detention.

Because many of the girls were at Lancaster for only a short while, the trustees

---

[33] Massachusetts 13AR, to the Board of State Charities, Public Document 20, 1868, p. 2.
[34] Massachusetts 13AR, 1868, p. 2.
[35] Massachusetts 13AR, 1868, p. 8.
[36] Massachusetts 19AR, to the Board of State Charities, Public Document 20, 1874, p. 8.

feared that the school would become a mere custodial institution. Therefore, they decided to speed up their training and enable the girls to earn a living within a domestic situation. If they did not comply, they were punished by being transferred to Sherborn Reformatory.

In one sense, the trustees' decision made sense; training for service all but insured the Lancaster girls employment. While employment opportunities for women expanded in the last two decades of the nineteenth century, domestic service continued to be the most available job for young women. In fact, the demand for domestic service increased as fewer women found jobs in service appealing. Many young women preferred to work in the mills and factories, away from the constant surveillance of the female employer. Moreover, many older immigrant and black women previously forced to live in as domestics preferred to live out and combine motherhood and work.[37] Given this demand, it is not surprising that the reformers chose to train Lancaster girls for domestic service. Not only was there a guaranteed market, but domestic service also continued the close and constant familial supervision of Lancaster. In many ways, the domestication of Lancaster girls continued beyond the school into domestic employment. This labor need continued well into the 1920s.

Regardless of this demand for domestics, several factors complicated the hiring of young women. One was that the marriage age had risen so that many young people remained at home longer. Given that more women had older daughters at home, it is possible that female heads of households would have been unwilling to have a non-American girl in the house. As Marcus Ames suggested, these women were no longer filled with mid-century benevolence; they were not anxious to extend their hospitality to the likes of a Lancaster girl. Rather, they wanted efficient and thorough work from their domestic employees. In addition, it seems likely that mothers might worry about the potential promiscuity between their older sons still at home and young girls; any act which led to their stay in reform school was assumed to be evidence of previous promiscuity. Given the availability of jobs for Lancaster girls in domestic service as well as the bias of employees against girls who were untrained or in need of nurturance, the new policy seemed sensible. The affectionate domestic life of mid-century Lancaster became an artifact; in its stead was an expedient vocational training program.

The trustees recognized that Lancaster had become a school solely for rapid vocational training. The school was free of its mid-century conflicts; no longer did it claim to protect and reform deprived girls. Common schooling, once considered a critically important factor in the reformation of young girls, was no longer considered essential. Lancaster was finally adopting the type of British vocational program it had previously scorned. The shift in program, however, was part of a wider educational trend in which formal industrial education sought to prepare the poor and immigrant for jobs in the new industrial world.[38] At the same time, it was assumed that learning technical skills would train the whole child, that she would learn strong moral values as well as

[37] David M. Katzman, *Seven Days A Week* (Oxford: Oxford Univ. Press, 1978).

[38] Barbara Brenzel and Walter McCann, "Education Technical," *Encyclopedia of Sociology* (Guilford, Conn.: Dushkin Press, 1974). For a more detailed and comprehensive account see Marvin Lazerson, *The Origins of the Urban Public School* (Cambridge, Mass.: Harvard Univ. Press, 1971); and Marvin Lazerson and W. Norton Grubb, eds., *American Education and Vocationalism* (New York: Teachers College Press, 1974).

skills, and therefore be prepared to participate in the broader social world. Like common schooling, Lancaster's original program was no longer appealing.

Employment and Family Life

What impact did Lancaster have on the adult lives of its inmates? In keeping with nineteenth-century expectations for women, Lancaster girls were to live domestic, industrious, and morally upright lives. Although the founders did not anticipate that the girls would rise above their station, they hoped that they would live respectably.

After leaving the supervision of the state, most Lancaster girls continued to live as the founders had hoped. Between 1856 and 1905, 75.6 percent of the girls lived with a family: parental, conjugal, in placement, or in Lancaster itself. From this group, 35 percent returned to their parents. The pattern emerging from these first follow-ups continued. Most girls remained within a family environment, usually with husbands in homes of their own. There continued to be a small number of girls living and working alone, but there was little to indicate that the majority of them were living dissolute lives.

It is dangerous to assume a cause-and-effect relationship between Lancaster's program and the subsequent lives of the girls. Lancaster may have provided no more than shelter for poor and difficult girls; it may have been little more than a way station for them. Or it may have functioned primarily as a job placement service. It is also likely that it offered slight comfort to some parents skidding from the lower class to the underclass.[39] Perhaps Lancaster prevented this fall for their daughters and returned them to society as poor but respectable women.

The inherent nature of women was presumed to be domestic. Lancaster's program was designed according to this stereotype and offered what was "natural" for the reformation of poor girls. The environmentalists blamed poverty and slum life for the unrestrained, and therefore unwomanly, behavior of the girls. Later, the hereditarians blamed vicious parents, especially mothers, for raising "unnatural" and tainted daughters. The definition of "natural" changed from a state of externally induced conditions to internal character weaknesses. Lancaster's job continued to be the domestication of girls so that they would be better able to fulfill their "natural" roles; regardless of changes in clientele or social theory, Lancaster's main objective did not change.

Conclusions

The story of Lancaster, its goals and program, tells us as much about the nineteenth-century view of women's roles in society as about the institution itself. Lancaster's primary objective was to domesticate girls who were considered potential deviants. In keeping with contemporary attitudes, it was especially important that women, as potential wives and mothers, be respectable, morally upright, and industrious.

[39] Stephan Thernstrom, *The Other Bostonians* (Cambridge, Mass.: Harvard Univ. Press, 1973), pp. 45-75; Stephan Thernstrom, *Poverty and Progress* (Cambridge, Mass.: Harvard Univ. Press, 1964), pp. 150-152. Thernstrom describes static families. The girls at Lancaster seem to come from families like the ones Thernstrom describes as "unable to rise out of the most depressed impoverished segment of the manual laboring class."

Seemingly seductive women had always been feared and shunned as dangerous, uncontrolled, and lascivious. Now, renewed pressure to secure the family increased society's expectations of women. They were expected to insure social order, especially at a time when there seemed to be precious little of it. Lancaster's program, although initially claiming a great belief in the role of common schooling as crucial to reformation, increasingly became a domestic training program. Regardless of these changes, however, most of the girls left Lancaster to lead lives of domestic respectability. Although the ideology of reformation degenerated into little more than rhetoric, the school seemed succesful because there was little evidence that Lancaster girls ended up in jail or on the streets. This program, however, perpetuated the class structure that was a major factor in the poverty of the girls' families. Few rose above their station and few skidded to the underclass or resorted to prostitution.

It is most important to remember that there were almost no options for poor parents. The story of Lancaster, therefore, is not just about a reform school, but also a drama about the devastating effects upon families of poverty and public charity. The story of Lancaster also offers an overarching view of reformers. In the fifty years covered by this study, the initial exuberance and optimism of the founders abruptly ended. In their stead came fatigue, disillusionment, pessimism, and anger. The early optimism of the founders changed partly because of changes in clientele, and partly because of economic changes and shifting trends in nineteenth-century social theories. In the end, we are left with many questions about the potential success of any social experiment over time. The trustees and state officials did not remain sensitive to Lancaster's success as a reform experiment, created from policies which attempted to accommodate the inherent ambivalence of the reformers — fear and benevolence. In an attempt to create a social institution that would protect and guide children, as well as incarcerate them for the public safety, the founders of Lancaster created an institutional experiment based on confused purposes. The school was to make restitution for the children's deprived family lives by offering them compulsory love.

Lancaster's story is a gloomy one, a tale of the decline of hopes for reform into a desire for social control. There is sufficient evidence that the institutional attempt to counter the unchecked forces of economic and technical change was not by itself sufficient. However, the story is not simply a revisionist parable of an elite imposing its will on the passive masses. It is a story of true mixed feelings and mixed results.

In 1980 historians, sociologists, and social policy analysts are questioning the beginnings of compulsory school attendance, and the growth of policies that have given the state increased jurisdiction over the lives of children, particularly those who are seen as receiving inadequate care from their families. These policies grew partly as a response to the needs of poor and potentially delinquent children in the nineteenth century and have ultimately touched the lives of all children. They are particularly relevant to policy makers currently in the process of formulating new programs for juveniles.

Today, we continue to face heartbreaking facts about the treatment of female delinquents. While the story of Lancaster is not totally unique either to the Commonwealth or to girls, parts of its history threaten to be repeated, especially in the new programs for the treatment of female juveniles. In 1973 Massachusetts took great pride in its bold and controversial policy to deinstitutionalize children. Soon after, the boys school at Westborough was closed amidst an almost celebratory event in which a cavalcade of cars and vans from the University of Massachusetts at Amherst "rescued" the last thirty-five inhabitants of the school. However, Lancaster remained partially occupied until 1976. Once again girls were neglected .[40] This suggests that, one hundred and twenty years later, fear still exists; the story of girls at Lancaster threatens to come full circle. Nevertheless, attempts are now being made to avoid some of the mistakes we have seen in Lancaster's history. It is hoped that the story of Lancaster, and similar institutions, will prove valuable so that we can learn from the glaring errors of the past.

[40] Carol Peacock, "The Massachusetts Experiment: Towards Equal Services for Girls" (Boston: Dept. of Youth Services, 1978). I have also benefited from numerous conversations with Claire Donovan, former Superintendent of State Industrial School, Lancaster.

The Most Arduous Profession

PATRICIA MEYER SPACKS

NOTABLE AMERICAN WOMEN: THE MODERN PERIOD
edited by Barbara Sicherman and Carol Hurd Green, with Ilene Kantrov and Harriette Walker.
Cambridge, Mass.: Belknap Press, Harvard University Press, 1980. 773 pp.

Polly Adler, madam. Elizabeth Arden, entrepreneur. Mary Breckinridge, nurse-midwife. Isadore Mudge, librarian, bibliographer. Ruth Nichols, aviator. Mildred Ella (Babe) Didrikson Zaharias, athlete. The women listed in this fourth volume of *Notable American Women*, like their predecessors in the previous volumes, have realized a startling range of possibilities.[1] The narratives of this female pantheon repeatedly generate a sense of genuine presence; one can only feel awe at the will, courage, ingenuity, intelligence, they evoke. "Women's history" becomes real through those who have created it; the records of individual lives, moreover, often take dramatic shape in stories of almost fictional excitement.

Notable American Women provides good reading as well as valuable reference material. Dealing only with women who died between January 1, 1951, and December 31, 1975 — the first three volumes go to the end of 1950 — the book presents a revealing perspective on the social history of a period marked by great political and social change. Many of the subjects worked in one way or another for the cause of feminism. Many more concerned themselves with government and politics, with civil rights, birth control, community affairs, conservation, consumer affairs, education — the various avenues of reform. The classified list of biographies at the end of the volume also reveals the number of women who excelled in more traditionally female activities. It records only one astronomer, but twenty-one artists; two chemists to four who made a name for themselves in cookery and six in dance; two explorers, eight leaders in fashion; one philosopher, thirteen workers for peace. The book includes many suffragists, actresses, writers, and musicians; an astounding number of physicians and medical researchers, and a good many journalists, businesswomen, and labor leaders. Even its lists, in other words, provide provocative reading: the bare bones of history.

---

[1] *Notable American Women, 1607–1950: A Biographical Dictionary*, ed. Edward T. James, assoc. ed. Janet Wilson James, and assis. ed. Paul S. Boyer (Cambridge, Mass.: Belknap Press, Harvard Univ. Press, 1971).

Harvard Educational Review   Vol. 53   No. 1   February 1983, 52–59

The individual biographies, of course, go far beyond the lists to educe reflection about the condition of American women in the twentieth century. "Being a woman," columnist Dorothy Dix wrote, "has always been the most arduous profession any human being could follow" (p. 276). These life stories suggest that efforts to combine being a woman with other kinds of professions guarantee arduous existence. What extraordinary accomplishments these people achieve! For example, "In addition to a daily column and volumes of direct correspondence, Dorothy Dix had published seven books by 1939" (p. 277). She wrote her column until she was almost eighty-eight years old. For forty-seven years — until her husband's death — she remained married to a man whose emotional instability resulted in his confinement to a mental institution. In her early thirties, she "suffered a nervous collapse" (p. 276); recovering from that, she began writing newspaper stories and sketches, then a weekly column so successful that she could soon afford to take her father to Europe for Queen Victoria's Diamond Jubilee. Dix worked as a crime reporter, championed the cause of suffrage, and reported in detail the temperance campaign of Carrie Nation. Her column of advice to readers appeared daily for more than thirty years. The record of this career, a career largely built on the capacity for sympathetic identification with other people's problems, emphasizes the traditional female virtues of concern for others, familial loyalty, devotion. But it also reveals its subject's astounding discipline, energy, and determination. By any standard, she worked remarkably hard; by any standard, she had a difficult life. So did most of the women here evoked.

Although the biographies in *Notable American Women* follow the general pattern established by such traditional reference works as the *Dictionary of American Biography*,[2] they do not sound quite like their analogues. Most of the entries begin with a summary paragraph indicating the nature of the subject's importance. Then comes an account of her parentage, a chronological narrative of her life, often a section characterizing and assessing her accomplishment in some detail, and a report of the date and cause of her death. A short bibliographical summary follows, with an explanation of sources used and a guide to further reading. Yet both because female careers assume different shapes from male ones and because different issues seem relevant in female lives, these biographies often resemble only superficially those of male counterparts. Inasmuch as they concern themselves with specific work accomplishments, their tone sounds familiar. "Building upon fundamental theories of alternating current developed by Charles P. Steinmetz, Clarke prepared charts and calculating devices from which engineers could predict the behavior of a system without the repetitive solving of complicated equations" (p. 152). A hypothetical John Clarke would fit into that sentence as plausibly as the actual Edith Clarke. On the other hand: "In 1919, Clarke received the first M.S. in electrical engineering granted to a woman by [MIT]. However, the war was over and no one would hire a woman engineer" (p. 152). Over and over, these entries report the difficulties confronted by women proposing to do what women had not previously done. The difficulties frequently sound insurmountable; over and over,

[2] *Dictionary of American Biography*, 17 vols., ed. Allen Johnson (New York: Scribners, 1964).

women surmounted them. The account of such triumphs generates dramatic excitement.

One might expect that. Less predictable, and perhaps even more interesting, is the effect of the different sorts of emphasis appropriate to female experience. In the *Dictionary of American Biography*, entries about men frequently relegate information about marriage and family to the final sentence. "[Charles Robert] Leslie married Harriet Stone of London in 1825; he died in London at the age of sixty-five" (IV, p. 185). The death occurred some thirty-four years after the marriage, but both items of information are offered with an air of tidying-up details. Even when mention of marriage finds a place earlier in the narrative, the fact assumes little importance. "On a trip home in 1845, [Robert Traill Spence Lowell] married, on Oct. 28, Mary Ann (Marianna) Duane, of Duanesberg, N.Y., by whom he had seven children" (VI, p. 470). No further reference appears to wife or children; marriage and fatherhood alike appear as more or less accidental adjuncts to the trip home.

For the women chronicled in *Notable American Women*, on the other hand, marriage and maternity, their presence or their absence, often assume central significance. Katherine Cornell, for instance, met Guthrie McClintic when she was twenty-seven. She had worked as an actress for four years, but "it was not until she met him that her desire to be a great actress crystallized" (p. 168). A year later, she married him. Subsequently, he directed many of her productions and in 1930 the couple formed a company to produce plays featuring Cornell as star, McClintic as director. She bought *The Barretts of Wimpole Street*, in which she was to play her most famous role, as a gift for her husband, but after his death, thirteen years before her own, she never acted again.

The pattern of professional collaboration runs through many marriages of these notable women. Particularly for scientists and physicians, association with a respectable male counterpart often made possible work they might otherwise not have been allowed to do. (However, biochemist Gerty Cori was told at a university that "it was un-American for a man to work with his wife" [p. 166].) Gertrude Rand, an important researcher in physiological optics, designed industrial and hospital lighting systems with her husband and taught with him at The Johns Hopkins University School of Medicine. Lillian Moller Gilbreth was studying for a doctorate in English Literature when she met her future husband, a building contractor and expert in motion study. She stopped work on the Ph.D. and became a partner in his business. Bearing twelve children in seventeen years, she edited her husband's publications while he traveled. Later, she joined him as a management consultant. After his death, however, she discovered that factory owners refused to acknowledge her competence and canceled their contracts with the firm. Nonetheless, she continued lecturing and offering courses in order to put her eleven surviving children through college.

Certainly not all of the women presented in this volume followed patterns of close professional collaboration with the men in their lives. Fannie Hurst, the popular fiction writer of the twenties, maintained a separate residence from her husband, pianist Jacques Danielson, throughout a long and happy marriage. Attacking the notion of " 'two souls with but a single thought' " as "a horrible and siamese state of freak mentality," she stated publicly her determination that marriage "should not lessen my capacity for creative work or pull me down into a sedentary state of fatmindedness" (p. 360). Some resorted to sequential love affairs rather than lasting commitments; some found their marriages facing disaster as they attempted to pursue fulfilling work. Nora Blatch Barney, for instance, with a degree in civil engineering, studied electricity and mathematics after she met Lee de Forest, in order to become his laboratory assistant. The two spent their honeymoon demonstrating radio equipment in an effort to win contracts for de Forest's company. Although her husband wanted her to stop working, Barney persisted in her involvement with the firm, criticizing (accurately) its financial practices. After the birth of their daughter, the couple divorced.

In fact, the editors' introduction notes the relative frequency of divorce and of single lives among the subjects of this volume. "Demographically, [these women] stand apart from their contemporaries: they married less often, had fewer children, and divorced more frequently" (p. xvi). A more noteworthy fact is that many actually managed marriage and motherhood in addition to their distinguished careers. Some chose not to marry, yet cultivated intimate relationships. Winifred Goldring, a paleontologist, wrote in a Wellesley class report that she had not married because she had "discovered no one more attractive than my work" (p. 283). The entry about her calls attention to her devotion to family as well as to research: until her death at the age of eighty-three, she shared a house with various sisters. In her powerful family bonds, Goldring typifies many of the single women described in the volume. Many remained in close association with their families; some formed ties with other women; many turned their emotional energies toward ways of helping others. When her younger sister complained about an embarrassing episode caused by the clumsy toilet seat she was carrying for her child, Gertrude Muller (assistant manager of a toilet seat company) designed the "toidey seat," established a new company to manufacture it, and promulgated her philosophy of childrearing in pamphlets packed with the items she sold. Never marrying, she supported her mother and helped to put several nieces and nephews through college. The facts which suggest the shape of her emotional life assume as important a position in this biographical entry as those indicating her business acumen. The typical inclusion of such facts not only reiterates the importance of interpersonal connections for women; it also unostentatiously calls attention to the new way of writing social history which *Notable American Women* exemplifies. These accounts give importance to "private" as well as "public" facts. In their emphasis on such material, they differ from the characteristic mode of earlier reference works; they suggest, without polemics, a fresh mode of locating significance.

Personal appearance has often determined the fates of women, and these biographies mention how people look. "The plainest of the sisters, Else Frenkel-Brunswik later attributed her intellectual achievements to her older sister's extraordinary beauty. . . . If her status as plainest daughter thrust her into intellectual life, her Vienna colleagues remembered her as lively and assertive but also slim, elegant, flirtatious, and an excellent dancer" (p. 251). Material for a novel lies latent in those two sentences, with their statement of the social and psychological import of beauty and their suggestion of the discrepancy between how a woman perceives herself and how she is seen by others. Seldom in the capsule histories does appearance possess this degree of importance, but frequent allusions to such attributes evoke character and define situation. Edith Clarke "was a square-faced, broad-shouldered woman of great vitality" (p. 152); her appearance suggests her forthright strength. Frieda Fromm-Reichman, four feet ten, with her braids pinned around her ears, experienced — apparently as a result of her looks —"considerable discriminatory treatment by members of the [medical school] faculty" (p. 253). Edna Gellhorn, a community leader working in the cause of reform, was "a woman of great beauty and charm" who "brought out the best in everyone" (p. 269). Elizabeth Craig, a Washington journalist, "a small woman with striking blue eyes and brown hair wrapped in a bun, . . . dressed in blue and wore flowered hats so that she would be remembered at White House, Capitol Hill, and government department press conferences" (p. 172). One may feel pity or anger over such means for remembrance, but the account of Craig's strategy also calls forth instant recognition: how often women have proceeded in such fashion!

Notable American Women, providing no explicit commentary on beauty as an element in female destiny, similarly offers without comment facts that provoke consideration of age as an issue for women. Adelaide Johnson, sculptor and feminist, married a man eleven years younger than she and falsified her age on the marriage certificate to make herself appear a year younger than her husband. At the age of eighty-eight, she reversed the process, to declare herself twelve years older than she was, attracting considerable publicity as she celebrated the birthdays from "100" to her death at "108." The story of her manipulation of chronology epitomizes the will to take command of her own life which characterizes this woman as it does many of the others described here.

Different readers will find different details to treasure in these accounts. Virginia Apgar, an expert on genetics, carried around a tiny preserved fetus in her purse and "taught medical students the anatomy of the spinal cord by having them feel her own unusually prominent coccyx" (p. 28). Selma Borchardt, an educator who believed that the development of fast foods accounted for the disintegration of the American family, explained to a union meeting that the passing of the American dining room was the root cause of juvenile delinquency. Such facts do not merely declare the eccentricity of individual women; they suggest how eccentricity may derive from and serve intellectual passion. Multiple instances of this sort generate much of the reader's pleasure in this book, whether used for reference or read as social history.

The volume's real importance, however, derives not from its compelling details but from a larger aspect of its conception: the contextuality it richly creates. Women inhabit the pages of the *Dictionary of American Biography* along with men, their appearances relatively sparse but nonetheless meaningful. To read an account of a woman's life in a context defined mainly by men, however, has an effect different from that of reading even the identical account in relation to other women's lives. The 442 separate narratives in this volume of *Notable American Women* comment on and illumine one another. Familiar lives take on new meaning when considered in relation to the various possibilities realized by twentieth-century women; unknown figures become comprehensible by comparison with their female contemporaries; unexpected similarities and contrasts emerge. The work profoundly educates its readers, and not by facts alone, although it largely eschews overt commentary.

Reading such a book, of course, reminds any reader in the 1980s of many life stories already well-known. Helen Keller, Eleanor Roosevelt, Marilyn Monroe: these women have already received considerable biographical attention. The familiar names multiply to create awareness of the startling number of twentieth-century women whose accomplishments, long attested, seem incontestable. The biographies themselves, portraying not only accomplishment but experience, call attention to costs as well as rewards to illustrate the immense difficulties of female achievement. The poignance of Keller's career has relatively little connection with her sex, although in some ways her story allegorizes the plight of women. The pathos of Eleanor Roosevelt's life and of Marilyn Monroe's, on the other hand, reveals the difficulties of overprivileged and underprivileged existence in their specifically female aspects: both women alternately evaded and attempted to meet impossible expectations. One may add to this grouping Ethel Rosenberg, the only biographee whose name precedes no listed profession or occupation (she appears in the classified bibliography under "Socialism and Radicalism"). She won fame by dying, at the age of thirty-seven, in the electric chair, convicted—almost certainly unjustly—of conspiracy to commit espionage. Her life, too, expresses a peculiarly female pathos. Her early ambitions for a career as singer or actress yielded, under her husband's influence, to political concerns; then, after her sons' births, she devoted herself almost entirely to her family, taking courses in child psychology and in music for children. Facing the accusation of espionage, she had to endure not only the threat of death, not only the loss of her children, but intense pressure from her family as well as from the government and a barrage of publicity about her alleged role as "unnatural mother and . . . domineering wife" (p. 603).

Yet these biographies by no means stress pathos. Roosevelt, Monroe, and even Rosenberg emerge as figures of genuine heroism as well as suffering, managing to triumph over social and psychological handicaps as Keller surmounted physical ones. The likeness beneath their manifest differences, the likenesses that create unexpected linkages among many of these life stories, provoke reflection about female transcendence. Relatively few of these careers follow a straight line. The women whose names we know, this volume tells us, have typically pursued convoluted and costly courses to fame.

Unfamiliar names also inhabit these pages: Elizabeth Burchenal, folk dance educator; Mother Mary Katharine Drexel, founder of the Sisters of the Blessed Sacrament for Indians and Colored People; Anne Bauchens, film editor. The editors' preface sketches the procedures which elicited such names: searches of all women's obituaries in the *New York Times* from 1951 through 1975, consultation of hundreds of individuals ("historians, practitioners in the many fields covered in this volume, and persons interested in specialized branches of women's studies" [p. x]) and hundreds of organizations—professional, labor, political, cultural, social, scientific and religious—and groups representing Afro-American, Native American, Asian-American and Hispanic-American constituencies. Further consultation with many experts decimated the 4,000 names emerging from the original search. A staggering job of research, in other words, preceded the actual writing of the entries, itself a notable accomplishment, given the scantiness of available information about many of these figures. Distinguished writers produced the biographies, often condensing a tremendous amount of information. As a result, previously "unknown" figures come to life as vividly as their better-known sisters. Women who contributed through philanthropy or community service appear along with those of more public fame; minority Americans jostle socialites.

If one finds unexpected psychological connections between diverse figures, one also encounters enormous differences. The biography of Muna Lee, an "international affairs specialist, writer, feminist," for example, immediately follows that of Gypsy Rose Lee. Both women died of lung cancer, five years apart; both manifested extraordinary vitality. (A high energy level may in fact be the single characteristic most of the women here described share.) Apart from these similarities and the obvious one of gender, it would be difficult to find common elements between the well-known stripteaser and the relatively obscure expert on Puerto Rico.

Gypsy Rose Lee's mother, characterized as frugal, brutal, ruthless, and charming, drove her daughters toward theatrical success. Deprived of all schooling, Rose led a marginal existence in vaudeville; her stripping career began at the age of fifteen. She married and divorced three times; she wrote mystery novels, essays, and autobiography; she defied the American Legion and the Un-American Activities Committee. Later she collected art and antiques, redecorated houses, cultivated the domestic arts, appeared on television. In contrast, Muna Lee's parents "nurtured their daughter's idealistic spirit and her devotion to learning" (p. 413). After college, she began writing poetry and published widely in magazines. She taught school, worked as a translator, married a Puerto Rican, had two children, moved to Puerto Rico with her husband, and served as director of international relations at the University of Puerto Rico while also running a large household. Her writing branched into many genres; she became active in the fight for women's rights. Divorcing her husband after more than a quarter century of marriage, she returned to Washington, worked for the State Department and inaugurated a new career of promoting close relations between the United States and Latin America. Continuing to write and to translate, she also cared for her mother until her death and appeared as a United States delegate at various international conferences until within two months of her own death at the age of seventy. Both biographies reveal deep parental influence on a daughter's life; both suggest the conceivable scope of female action and interest. Together they affirm a stunning spectrum of possibility.

The life stories in the volume arrange themselves at every conceivable point on such a spectrum. *Notable American Women* encourages many sorts of comparison; every pair of biographies provides provocative possibilities. Some obvious contrasts present themselves: Louella Parsons and Hedda Hopper, Judy Holiday and Marilyn Monroe, Sylvia Plath and Marianne Moore, Elizabeth Arden and Helena Rubinstein. Researchers into women's history will discover material for speculation and for further investigation; students who seek only facts about a single figure may well be lured into going farther afield. Although one might find grounds of complaint about omissions and inclusions—as one might with any biographical dictionary—there can be little question that the volume provides a valuable research tool and fills a crucial need.

The volume often leaves its readers with acute problems of interpretation. The biographer of Mahalia Jackson, Lawrence M. Levin, concludes, "[she] was one of those rare individuals whose life and career epitomized the developments shaping an entire group. Through her career one can better understand the intricate relationships between the secular and the sacred in twentieth-century Afro-American culture" (p. 373). Megan Terry quotes *The New Yorker* describing Janis Joplin's addiction to drugs as "not a personal but a cultural idiosyncrasy" (p. 386). These two performers, then, symbolize their cultures, public success and personal tragedy alike pointing to facets of cultural history. Neither the private life nor the public career of Judy Garland, on the other hand, receives comparable analysis. Although Beth Genné describes Garland as "one of the major figures of the century," and although the entry concludes that "her consistently brilliant performances helped to shape and define the film musical during a period that saw this uniquely American art form at its height" (p. 266), the shape of her life and the nature of her death do not seem to be understood as significant.

The problem of interpretation is inherent in the very enterprise of a biographical dictionary. What do these lives *mean*? The question always presents itself, and in a biographical dictionary of women, it assumes an extra dimension. To what extent is the fact of gender determinant? Should we think of these women mainly as women, or as embodiments of cultural and historical reality, or simply as individuals? The biography of architect Sophia Hayden calls attention to the danger of interpreting on the basis of gender by quoting critical response to the Woman's Building of the World's Columbian Exposition in Chicago, which Hayden designed. One critic described the building as "dainty but tasteful"; another noted its "graceful timidity or gentleness," which "at once differentiate[s] it from its colossal neighbors, and reveal[s] the sex of its author" (p. 323).

As these quotations indicate, to consider gender the most meaningful fact about a person creates risks of stereotyping, superficiality, an invidious form of separation. Granted the special shape of female careers, the substantial achievement of women often rivals that of their male counterparts. To insist on understanding a woman artist, for example, as doing one or another kind of work specifically because of her gender may trivialize her accomplishment or falsify it. If one believes that Judy Garland chose the life of an entertainer because women excel at self-display, what can one say about Fred Astaire?

Yet satisfactory alternatives to this emphasis on gender do not readily present themselves. The cultural interpretation also falsifies: Joplin's drugs belonged to her, not just to her historical era; Mahalia Jackson's personal triumph had individual, not only collective, meaning. The fact of gender *is* important: virtually all the biographies make that clear. Exactly *how* important remains hard to ascertain. *Notable American Women* is weakest in its occasional forays toward explicit answers to such questions. Its strength inheres in the ways it makes answers difficult: by providing a mass of suggestive data so complicated that it defies easy summary or analysis. "As notable women," the introduction warns, the subjects of this work "are by definition atypical" (p. xv). An important caveat—yet the volume generates a haunting sense that these lives reveal the typical as well as the extraordinary. The task of interpretation remains the task of defining "typical" and "atypical" in their full meaning for women.

The Education of Women through Domestic Service

JEANNE BOYDSTON

SERVING WOMEN: HOUSEHOLD SERVICE IN NINETEENTH-CENTURY AMERICA
by Faye E. Dudden.
Middletown, Conn.: Wesleyan University Press, 1983. 344 pp.

Until well into the twentieth century, the proportion of female wage-earners employed in domestic and personal service occupations far outstripped women's participation in any other single field of paid employment in the United States. Through most of the nineteenth century, the importance of domestic service in the shaping of female experience was even more marked: as late as 1870, the 950,000 women who undertook paid household work comprised an absolute majority of women in paid employment, and approximately one in every five wives found herself supervising the labor of at least one hired domestic worker.[1]

And yet, as Faye Dudden points out in her introduction to *Serving Women: Household Service in Nineteenth-Century America*, "historians have rarely and only belatedly considered household service a subject worthy of their note" (p. 2). The main exception to Dudden's observation is David Katzman's *Seven Days a Week: Women and Domestic Service in Industrializing America*. His book is a study of changes in the demography of the servant population rather than of the organization of the work itself. Katzman maintains that as a field of labor, domestic service remained largely impervious to change; a peculiar blend of "work, environment, and personal life," it survived into the nineteenth and twentieth centuries as "an anachronism in an industrializing and modernizing society in which workplace and home had become separate."[2]

It is against that image of stasis that Dudden brings to bear her considerable skills as historian, author, and interpreter of women's lives. She contends not only

[1] In addition to Dudden's book (pp. 77, 78), the sources for these statistics are Rosalyn Baxandall, Linda Gordon, and Susan Reverby, eds., *America's Working Women: A Documentary History—1600 to the Present* (New York: Random House, 1976), pp. 406–407; and David M. Katzman, *Seven Days a Week: Women and Domestic Service in Industrializing America* (New York: Oxford Univ. Press, 1978), Table 2–1, p. 47 and Table 2–2, p. 53.
[2] Katzman, p. 95.

Harvard Educational Review   Vol. 54   No. 2   May 1984, 220–222

that domestic service changed over the course of the nineteenth century, but that it changed in ways that paralleled transformations occuring in paid labor outside of the household. Rather than suggesting "discrete categories into which every individual case can be unerringly sorted"(p. 5), Dudden wants to pose the "models or ideal types" which are the poles of this change. She describes the process as a slow and uneven evolution from hired "help" to paid domestic "servants"— a distinction in language that is meant to convey a host of altered daily realities in the interaction of employer and employee.

The early nineteenth-century "help" or "hired girl" was often a neighbor, Dudden explains, an adolescent or young woman who entered employment on a temporary basis. Although the hired girl's own family might be less prosperous than the family that hired her, they were nearby and were usually able to offer her the option of returning home if she became dissatisfied with the conditions of her paid work. While she remained in service, both her family's proximity and the tightly-knit character of many communities provided the help with moral and physical protections against mistreatment by her master or mistress.

Other factors contributed to the relative amiability of this relationship. Family boundaries remained permeable, permitting households to absorb paid members with a minimum of internal stress and dislocation. That the help was often hired to assist with work destined for the local market demonstrated her worth in clear cash terms and further reduced potential antagonisms in the relationship. Finally, the experience of the work was shared: not only did employer and employee work side by side, but the mistress herself was likely to have worked as a hired girl.

By the mid-nineteenth century, these conditions had altered fundamentally. Often the daughter of working-class immigrants, the "servant" lacked the protections of long acquaintance with her middle- or upper-class employer, of oversight by a familiar community, of a common culture, and even of assured refuge in her parental family home. Further, she entered a work environment far more highly charged with the potential for discord than had her counterpart fifty years earlier. The growing privatization of the nuclear family made her presence a stark anomaly. Hired for "status" rather than "market" work, she performed labor that had no fixed measurement of worth. Particularly as the mistress assumed a more purely supervisory role, employer and employee came to share little common ground other than their femaleness and the fact of their wage relationship.

It is in her analysis of this developing conflict of interest between mistress and servant that Dudden provides her most fascinating insights into the history of paid household service and, indeed, of nineteenth-century white women in general. Far from sealing female consciousness in a preindustrial time warp, she argues, the servant/mistress relationship was the school in which large numbers of women (servants and mistresses alike) learned at first hand the attitudes and behaviors of workplace exploitation and resistance.

Dudden's narrative is both lively and tragic. She presents sympathetic portraits of mid-century middle-class women faced with an elaboration of household furnishings, family needs, and status responsibilities as their role of housewife became (much to their dismay) that of a vanguard practitioner of the science of management. These portraits are strikingly interlaced with chilling evidence of a growing willingness to treat domestics as a less-than-human species: to cheat on wages, to be miserly about room and board, to hold employees to arbitrary and outrageous standards of performance, and to turn them out in an instant at the first glimpse of a better bargain. Servants, of course, learned to respond in kind. They began to demand wages in advance, to resist incursions into their time off, and to master techniques for undermining mistresses' pretentions and control. Dudden includes wonderful stories of messages intentionally garbled, concessions won in the last moments before guests were due, and defiantly noisy kitchen gatherings. Most of all, what seemed to confound employers was that servants learned to base their decisions about whether to stay or leave entirely upon self-interest.

Dudden's account of the evolution of the paid domestic relationship, and of the conditions under which both mistress and servant struggled, is both fuller and more subtle than can be suggested here. For example, *Serving Women* includes an excellent analysis of the impact of new domestic technologies, and Dudden offers a provocative argument that the ultimate effect of the changes in unpaid housework was probably to drive servants out of the paid work force and into marriage.

Though there is much to praise, there is also room to challenge Dudden's rich rendering of these female-female relationships. Although she certainly has a tradition of scholarship behind her, I question Dudden's insistence that the presence of a servant in a middle-class home signalled the virtual withdrawal of the wife from household labor. The one or two women who typically made up the hired contingent of the middle-class household may have simply replaced the labor formerly provided by daughters (who, as the nineteenth century wore on, apparently were expected to do less and less housework).[3] I regret, too, that Dudden did not say more about the experiences of free black domestics — particularly since she seems to suggest that they offered an early model of what the paid domestic relation was to become for most women. Perhaps unfairly, given the already impressive range of the book, I wish Dudden had extended her analysis of the transformation of paid household labor to include some speculation on what this may mean for conventional dichotomies of "the family" and "society." If the nineteenth-century bourgeois home was as much like the industrial workplace as she implies (and I agree that it was), historians need to reassess larger assumptions about the role of the family in the industrializing process. As Dudden would have it, home was an independent training ground for, not a refuge from, these changes.

These criticisms notwithstanding, Dudden's fine critical reading of the antebellum documents enables her to write a book that is, in many ways, larger than her subject. *Serving Women* deserves to be placed, not only in the growing secondary literature specifically on domestic service and on housework, but also among those works that illuminate the larger experience of being a white woman in the nineteenth-century United States. It is a study that will prove all the more important because Dudden casts it as a narrative in two voices: that of the servant as well as of the employer. As Dudden reminds us in her conclusion, this is not a story of the triumph of sisterhood: the trajectory that freed many middle-class women

---

[3] This change is suggested in Nancy F. Cott, *The Bonds of Womanhood: "Woman's Sphere" in New England, 1780–1835* (New Haven: Yale Univ. Press, 1977), pp. 19–62 passim.

to forge a movement for equality was precisely the trajectory that bound other women into new forms of exploitation. Finally, there is no objective way to tally the account. My sympathies, however, remain with the Scandinavian woman who showed exactly how much she had learned from her mistress when she spoke her first two English words: "I quit!"

PART II
Higher Education

Women's Higher Education: Past, Present, and Future

ORDWAY TEAD

Ordway Tead, writing in 1947, challenges the limitations to the existing curriculum for women in higher education. He then elaborates on what he believes should be the similarities and distinctions between the higher education of men and women based on the "differing and social role which each sex has necessarily to play." While calling for a more equitable sharing between husbands and wives in aspects of home and community life, he nevertheless argues that women's primary sphere of influence is in the local community and that this idea should accordingly, "pervade the subject matter of all that women are taught to learn."

I

It is hard if not impossible to see our times in proper perspective. And by the same token, it is difficult to appraise the relation of modern women to the education they are offered. We are nevertheless under the compulsion of critical scrutiny of this education, because the generalization seems true that modern woman is unhappy, feels less than at home in our kind of society, and finds personal purpose, direction, and creative growth to be baffling problems. Confusion, frustration, and thwarting of personality seem the order of the day.

To be sure, men share measurably in the same responses to modern life, but probably not to the same degree. The influences which contribute to bring this condition to pass are in part world conditions of insecurity and post-war malaise, but they are seemingly even more the result of conditions in our modern life which have been growing in power for two generations and which have resulted in the gradual weakening of the home's central significance. Forces of centralization, standardization, concentration, organization, and secularization—with all that these words imply in making difficult a rich individual relation to life—these confuse us all as to ends and means. They combine to create a deep, if sometimes unconscious, restlessness and unhappiness. And in all likelihood, the impact of all this on women is greater than it is on men because it has more profoundly disturbed their familiar patterns of habit and action.

Surely it is in the light of this underlying psychic situation that we have to examine the higher education of women. I shall not pretend to do more than suggest the historical background out of which our present eastern women's colleges have

Harvard Educational Review   Vol. 27   No. 3   Summer 1947, 151–160

49

grown. For it is a familiar fact that whether we are thinking of Sophia Smith or Mary Lyon or any of the other vigorous personalities who dominated the scene in the period from 1870 to 1900, the central motive was to create for young women an opportunity for college experience in every way equal to that offered to young men. These were rightful and needful influences, and the contribution they have made to the dignifying of the role of women in American society can hardly be overestimated.

Through the early 1900s and until woman suffrage became a fact, so-called feminist forces added their weight to the educational program already under way. As we came out of the first World War, however, higher education for women had become a generally accepted reality, so much so that in the co-educational state universities, the enrollment of women students continued to mount. It is therefore not a criticism but a statement of fact to say that in all this time the resultant educational policy was one in which the pattern of education offered in the men's colleges was religiously and uncritically copied in the colleges for women. The ideas of pure scholarship, of encouraging graduate work, and of offering preliminary training for professional careers — all these had far more influence on the curriculum and on teaching methods than has sometimes been acknowledged. The assumption was tacit, if not explicit, that in all respects the role of women in society was the same as the role of men and that therefore their education had to be the same. Any claim that the role of women might in any way be distinctive was too often taken as an allegation that the role of women was in some way inferior to the role of men.

It has been difficult for us all to examine this situation with truly objective eyes. And one big reason for this in women's colleges has been the natural momentum for a continuance of established patterns of education on the part of influential women teachers who have struggled through graduate work to qualify themselves to become professors under the established standards of scholarship. Any criticism of existing practices has appeared to them to be a criticism of women's education itself. This is probably one important reason why there has been less disposition in women's colleges to take a radically fresh look at their methods than has existed in the last fifteen years in the men's colleges.

There have, nevertheless, been other influences and other programs at work in women's education. In the land-grant colleges, the offerings for women were, for better or for worse, more concretely vocational. As the first World War drew to an end, there were groups of educators who were also critical of the familiar patterns at the women's colleges. And what variously happened in the experimental efforts of Bennington, Sarah Lawrence, Stephens, and Antioch became, in effect, a specific criticism of the program of most women's colleges as it had come out of the nineteenth century.

It is, of course, true that there has been some scrutiny of curriculum in relation to objectives in the older women's colleges. But nowhere do we find as drastic an examination of the relation of means to ends as in the Columbia University college program starting in 1922, in the efforts of Colgate and Princeton Universities, or in the variegated body of proposals which Harvard, Yale, Amherst, and numerous other colleges have promulgated since World War II.

II

In the analysis of any problem, it is essential that we ask the right questions. And in this connection, I submit that the first question to ask is: What do we want women to be, to do, to know as a result of college education? And if we can achieve some clarity and agreement about the answer to this question, we would then ask: What is the kind of education that will best help us to get what we want? The answers presumably have to be in terms that yield satisfaction and have validity both for the individual woman and for the society in which she lives and to which she contributes.

I confess to sharing the view of Dr. Robert Ulich at Harvard when he says that "generally I would say that the new period of women's self-consciousness should begin with the reform of education just as the first period of emancipation began."[1] Certainly, this new period of women's self-consciousness upon which we are now embarked carries with it an insistent assurance that the woman is to be a person in her own right, a person whose integrity in making her own choices and in evolving her own destiny is complete. We may be less understanding than we should be as to the deep physical differences between men and women, although we believe that each mature person, man or woman, is characterized by a balancing of certain traits conventionally spoken of as masculine and feminine. But it is a fact that in terms of the day-to-day preoccupations of the adult in our society, there are a number of truly functional differences between men and women. At bottom, the channels, the areas, and the forms of creativity for the two sexes have certain differences. And if this be true, this difference has much to do with the kinds of work which each chooses to do and with the ways of attack of each upon all work.

Actually, between 75 and 80 percent of women-college graduates marry; and it is a safe assumption that the great majority of these marriages take place within six years after college graduation. The college woman faces the options of conforming to what Mrs. Cyrus so tellingly describes in the *Atlantic Monthly* for March, 1947, as the "home-maker-mother pattern"; or she elects to be a careerist, completely in her own right; or she strives to achieve some combination of marriage and career.[2] As Mrs. Cyrus well points out, if a young woman elects the primary role of wife and mother, her responsibility, properly conceived, presents the "need for a new philosophy and pattern of community life, not to destroy the privacy of the family, but to end the isolation of individual mothers and children."[3] Mrs. Cyrus might well have added a recognition of the need for ending the isolation of individual mothers with respect to the impact upon them of adverse community forces in the fields of health, recreation, educational opportunities, and social contacts.

Our large concern surely is with the vast majority of women who become home-makers or are able to combine homemaking with work, for the present college set-

---

[1] Robert Ulich, "Some Thoughts on Education for Girls," *Harvard Educational Review*, **11** (1941), 273–277; also see pp. 3–9 of this volume.

[2] D. D. Cyrus, "Why Mothers Fail," *Atlantic Monthly*, **179** (1947), 56–60.

[3] Cyrus, "Why Mothers Fail," p. 60.

ting is already weighted too much in favor of careerists. It is not sentimental nor is it belittling to the integrity of women to assert that both at home and at work the woman's preeminent creative talents lie in the facilitation of better human relations in every field she touches. We need, as educators, constantly to be reminded of the truth on this score. Miss Constance Warren has well voiced it, as follows:

> Women have always known instinctively how much of their success in life depends on their ability to get on with other people, with their husbands, with their children, in their social circles. This feminine instinct for human relations can now be intelligently trained and directed. Within the last fifty years the world of the inner self, which in the old days was glimpsed by a few of the more observant novelists, has been opened up and explored by trained psychologists. They have thrown much light on why and how people differ, why they act as they do, on the ways in which emotion influences thinking, on the ways in which our home surroundings, early life, cultural patterns, influence us and how we grow in body, mind, and emotions. Among other things, they have made startlingly clear the importance of the mother in shaping the development of her children and the imperative need that she be a mature person if she is to raise children to real maturity.[4]

We want also, as a part of the adult effectiveness of woman in our society, to bring it to pass out of their education that they do not become amateur dabblers or so highly personalized in their human relations as to ignore the social and economic forces at work underneath. We similarly want them to become sufficiently confident, competent, and critical in the realm of ideas so that they do not succumb to a trivial and parrot-like repetition of their husbands' opinions. A friend of mine, high in the councils of the international Y.W.C.A., recently observed that one of the difficulties with which that organization has most seriously to contend is the habit of women committee members prefacing their observations with "but my husband says . . . ." We need perennially to struggle against the kind of mental docility which this behavior illustrates.

Nothing here said implies that I consider the present higher education of men or the present conduct by them of their domestic or social obligations to be adequate and satisfactory. For women to play the role that is inherent in their integrity, it will be essential that men, far more than they now do, should take an equalitarian view towards the place of women in society, towards their place in the home, and towards their own male obligation to assume the role of father and member of a home in a more adequate way. My own personal assumption is that the choices of life, of parenthood, of vocations, and of obligations for the conduct of the home and for relations to the community have to be equally shared by husband and wife; and that the spiritual autonomy of each has to be completely respected by the other for the fulfillment of democratic fellowship.

Yet even within the frame of this credo, it has to be acknowledged that there remain differences as between the typical responsibilities and activities of the majority of men and women.

---

[4] Constance Warren, "Wife, Mother, and Citizen," *The Standard*, **33** (1947), 209–216.

III

Before the task of higher education is explicitly faced, it is necessary to offer a few realistic comments upon the special vocational problems faced by modern college women. Any one who has interviewed scores of girls just graduated from women's colleges, as I have, knows unhappily the blank look of uncertainty, the insecurity, and the humiliation with which the typical woman graduate of liberal arts colleges confronts the world of possible jobs. Typically, she has little sense of what she wants to do, of how to find out how to do it, or of how to direct herself into channels where she might be most productive. The present picture, as far as the regular women's colleges is concerned, seems to be one of shocking ineffectuality and bafflement on the part of the young graduate. This problem is real, and our present ignoring of it because of some traditional notion of a separation between the aims and methods of liberal and vocational education is far more influential than wise. This statement is not to be taken as an argument for changing women's liberal colleges into vocational training schools. The implication of this statement for the conduct of liberal colleges has to be approached in different terms.

The problem, vocationally, is always complicated by the uncertain factor of whether the woman proposes, after some professional training or experience, to have a career without marriage, within marriage, or after an interval of marriage when her children have grown. That there should be possessed by each graduate a broad type of competence that has some vocational direction, either at the end of the four years of college or at the end of a fifth year of further, more specialized training, I am prepared to advocate. And I would include here even those students who are assured economic independence after college or who are confident that the position of wife will be open to them almost immediately after they leave college. Today the confident ability of every individual, in case of emergency if not of personal intention, to enter the labor market with some definite ability to sell should be guaranteed.

As is true with men college graduates, there is wide diversity of interesting employments for which, after some apprenticeship, women can qualify to advantage. And there are still more jobs which, with some slight vocational emphasis in the third, fourth, or fifth college year, they can be equipped to enter. Finally, there are many types of positions into which they can advance if they can enter employment by the road of secretarial training, much of which can be acquired without benefit of academic credits.

But all of this assumes and requires that each student shall have, from the very start of the freshman year, informed, skilled, and continuing educational and vocational guidance, by experts who know the curriculum, who know the world of work opportunities in its shifting trends, and who can operate an employment bureau with real effectiveness. Any assumption that the woman's college has a negligible responsibility for relating its students continuously to the vocational needs of the outside world is unrealistic and fatuous.

In case this position seems alarming to some college teachers, I would point out that the very teachers who view these conclusions with alarm are usually the ones who are most zealous in viewing their own teaching responsibility as centering in the preparation of young women to take a Ph.D. and to qualify for the vocation of teaching. In other words, we cannot ignore the obvious fact that the woman's liberal college is today in some part a vocational training school, only the vocations being trained for are those which the present faculties have agreed are respectable, cultural, and liberal. But that there are other vocations beyond teaching which can today be viewed as having aspects which are cultural and liberal is clearly a conclusion for us to examine in all its varied possibilities.

IV

When we come, now, to analyze the future task of college education, we have still to be concerned with the similarities and any possible differences as between the program for men and that for women. In terms of subjects and curricular organization through the four-year period, the similarities will naturally be great. But that there also should be some differences, I am prepared to urge. My proposals as to similarities are not novel and therefore can be briefly said.

Of course, the college is concerned with the effective unfolding of the whole individual, in terms of mind, body, and spirit. Here we are confronted by two different types of newcomers. Our freshmen are typically either those who have been bored with the pace and limitations of subject matter in the secondary school, or those who have had a somewhat dynamic experience in the last two years of secondary school and find, to their consternation, that the first two years of college are not qualitatively as vigorous and exciting as the experiences from which they have come. In both cases, however, the mandate upon the college is that the first two years shall, at a more mature level, open up the world of problems — intellectual, scientific, social, economic, and aesthetic — in ways which are stimulating, provocative, and challenging. If the best teachers, capable of the most stimulating handling of their subject matter, are not available in the first two years, the student's zest is stultified and the college experience is rendered less than appealing or even adequate.

I believe it is possible to combine the rightful claim that there is a heritage of ideas, attitudes, and beliefs which should become the common possession of college students during their course, with the view that there may rightfully be some individualization of the courses taken in relation to the needs, interests, and abilities which are unique in each person. There are two extremes in curriculum building — one saying that every student should acquire substantially the same body of knowledge, and the other holding that every student should have the curriculum tailor-made to her tastes and interests. Somewhere between these two extremes is certainly an area of curriculum which can be wisely adapted to different institutional tastes.

The college has to be concerned with the whole person because everything the person does at this age contributes to or detracts from her education. In the women's liberal colleges, as in the men's, fundamental emphasis is appropriately placed upon a concern for intellectual grasp, competence, and the use of powers of reflection and upon training in orderly methods of thought, including a capacity to apply scientific methods to thinking in all problem areas — material, social, or personal. Capacity to use one's mind in making the decisions of living, in all areas and at all levels, is central. To learn where to find evidence, what evidence is necessary, how to bring it to bear upon specific problems, how to draw conclusions in an orderly and convincing way—these are the aims toward which the teaching of *every* course, every year should drive persistently. If the life of the college does not contribute to the life of rationality, it has no distinctive reason for being. And we say this with a greater positiveness today as we look out upon a world whose problems are resolvable only by a careful use of reflective processes, patiently and zealously applied to their solution. Unless the college student has both learned these methods and become indoctrinated with the desire to bring a deliberative effort to bear upon personal and social problems, the college has essentially failed.

We earnestly want, also, the fullest possible cultivation of the whole aesthetic capacity, which implies some opportunity to do creative work in one's own right. In this province, the contribution of woman's aspiration and activity throughout life can be great, if her orientation has been valid. We want, next, the capacity to read and to communicate in speech and written words, accurately, speedily, and with critical discrimination. We want understanding of and perspective concerning the background of the forces in our contemporary life which will make possible an intelligent interpretation of on-going affairs. We want some progressively sensitive and inclusive conviction about what things in life are valuable and to be cherished even, if necessary, by a courageous and sacrificial offensive. We want sufficient commitment to the sanctity of these values so that they become devotedly striven for. And we want a sufficiently strong, rugged, and wholesome physical condition undergirding this entire effort so that the student has the constitution "to stand and having done all, to stand."

These ends that we want from education are, moreover, inseparable from the content of *any* subject studied. Rightfully, these underlying aims infiltrate, are interpreted, clarified, and advanced in the handling by the wise teacher of *every* body of subject matter. And the wise college teacher knows, too, that to a large extent the handling of her subject matter is more a means of challenging youthful capacity than it is a detailed manipulation of the specialized knowledge of her field, even though, and indeed because, the subject matter in her field is one which she is thoroughly competent to interpret and to make relevant to the student.

It is in this same sense also—through the necessary interpenetration of aims in the hour by hour conduct of class work in all the subjects—that the vocational strand and orientation can best be projected and can be made most illuminating. What the vocations of the world are for women, what the vocational relevance to each particular curricular subject is, what the special vocational requirements of many important areas of work are—all this can be realized through competent instruction in every area of subject matter. And it is the role of the teacher to be sufficiently worldly-wise about her subject matter to grasp and interpret this vocational relatedness.

V

At this point, a word is important on our grasp at the college level of what the nature of learning is and what the implications of our understanding of it may be. Actually, the newer psychological wisdom on this score has had its freshest application at the lowest levels of progressive schools, to a lesser degree at the secondary level, and to a startlingly slight degree in the usual college. We must remember that we learn what we do, what we live, what we experience in some overt way. This experience is, of course, in some part mental, verbal, and conceptual; it has to be and should be. But we know now that there is little learning out of sheer memory work, out of the regurgitation of lecture notes into exam papers, out of the manipulation of abstract ideas with which the student sees no personal relation and connection. It is not enough that college education be merely "what we have remembered when we have forgotten what we learned." College teaching, for men and women alike, will achieve its necessary fruitfulness for living only when the experience of individual classes and subjects is a living reality of thoughts and feelings relevant to the student's life.

It should be noted that I have not been urging some particular courses thought to be especially designed for the functional needs of women. Courses in home economics, in homemaking, in married life, in the care of children — all of these may well have value, and should perhaps be available for women students on the verge of matrimony. But my observation is that, to a considerable extent, we do not seem to know how to give these courses effectively, in advance of the felt need by students, who are not yet confronted by matrimony and childbearing. The pedagogical doctrine, that interest and zest in subject matter is closely related to the individual's sense of need for it, is relevant here. It is probably true that the good teacher can generate a sense of need and excite interest in almost any subject. But, unhappily, there are not enough good teachers to go around. Nevertheless, the challenge remains in the established areas of natural science, social studies, and humanities; they, too, are in danger of being bodies of inert knowledge, to be memorized and forgotten, unless the teacher can bring them to bear upon the student's life in one or another facet of her interest and concern.

I am able here only to suggest that we still have some distance to go in providing, both by the methods of study and of teaching, by field work and by course offerings, for those students who are entitled to have college experience but who will never be skilled in the facile handling of abstract ideas and broad generalization. The newer women's colleges and the newer curricula have helped us to see the educational potentials in active participation in the drama, musical performance, the dance, painting, and sculpture, and creative literary effort. Our courses of study and our method of giving credit for them must, moreover, be sufficiently flexible to assure that those talented in these directions are not regarded by the college as intellectual inferiors or as academic pariahs.

VI

Thus far, I have dwelt on the type of college education for women which will bear a striking resemblance to that of men students. But, undoubtedly, the college woman needs more emphasis in her course of study upon a fairly elaborate, persuasive, and specific consideration of her local community role. As already suggested, no wife or mother conducts her home for or by herself alone. She cannot pretend social competence without knowing how to organize herself in various civic ways so as to protect her domestic interests and creatively to enrich them. Certainly college women must come to understand how to advance these vital interests, not only at the local level, but, hopefully, to a greater and greater degree at state, national, and international levels. It is one of the unresolved problems of college education, both for men and women students, that so many of them are personally drawn away from the smaller communities from which they have come, and that the talents of civic and cultural leadership which should be poured into the smaller communities of our country are siphoned off into the big cities and their suburbs. A partial step toward preventing this is to be sure that the entire instruction orients the student to her possible leverage in her local setting and spells out her obligation to focus her creativity wherever she may be.

Possibly, for a certain few students, it has been justifiable to conduct the college course as a high intellectual effort, dissociated from the world at large. But for the great majority of young women, the college experience, if it be wholly without relation to community ties, community setting, and community relationships, will be artificial and empty; and such an experience conduces to a sterile and irresponsible conception of the intellectual life as a whole. Here again, whether the instruction be in the natural sciences, the social studies, or the humanities, the ways in which their contributions can make for cultural enrichment, both for the individuals and for the community from which they come and to which they go, should be a pervading undercurrent of all instructional effort. Otherwise, culture becomes pedantry, and the life of the mind and of the creative human spirit, as cultural forces, is absurdly and falsely divided between the so-called educated persons and the rest of society. Either culture is seen as a democratic composite of the heritage, background, and active forces in our society, accessible to and meaningful for all people, or it becomes some trivial thing, segregated in the hands of a smug, ineffectual, and spiritually barren few. And unless the college interprets the culture in this democratic way, it might as well close up shop for all the good it has for our society. Its real function is to help its students to carry a truly modern culture into the stream of life wherever they find themselves.

The difference, then, between higher education for men and higher education for women has to do with the slanting and with the emphasis of subject matter rather than with the subject matter itself. For when all is said and done, college women do have more time to bring their contribution to bear upon the community in a greater variety of ways than do those men who are presently tied to a business desk. This fact is at once a social privilege, obligation, and opportunity. And it dictates something of the emphasis which has, therefore, to pervade the subject matter of all that women are taught and learn.

As women face out upon society, it is not untrue to say that, on the whole, their influence can potentially be more meliorative, more constructive, more independent of economic influences, less hampered by a prudential point of view, more aesthetically concerned, than can the influence of most men in the same social position. Given the necessary sense of commitment which we still do not sufficiently arouse, there should be far more women than now who are active in local politics and members of local school boards; articulate through leagues of women voters, business and professional women's clubs, church groups, little theatres, local art schools, and forums. It is thus, with their feet in a solid and informed way planted firmly in the local community, that hundreds of college women can, if they are so minded, relate themselves to the ongoing process of maintaining and improving social well-being. For the fact is crystal-clear that everything which relates to the psychological and social success of the home requires that each college woman shall assume her share and take her part in local civic affairs, to the infinite toning up of the quality of health, recreation, art, education, and worship of her community. And from their outlook, influence, and concern for the local scene, many of them will be instructed by the logic of events to take their place also in affairs of the state and the nation.

The important point is that we shall be agreed upon the approach, the principle, and the mandate as to these few, yet highly important, differentials between the higher education of women and that of men.

VII

If we are to have separate women's colleges — and presumably we shall for the foreseeable future — the challenge today is to do a more vitalized job in the light of an imperious need. We agree that we want women happier and better adjusted, just because our day is one of turmoil and distress. Of course, we want all this, too, no less for men; and in that area, you may be assured that the men's colleges are today deeply concerned. It is no longer a question of equality of status in higher education or of a just-the-same-as policy. It is a question of examining with complete candor the functional differentials and of acting accordingly.

It is because woman's role today is as sensitized and as crucial as it is that we want her to be sensitively, superbly, and serenely fitted for it. We want her to go out from college, confident, directed, focused, committed to a high enterprise. Indeed, only thus will she be able to undertake that necessary assignment of helping a brutish man's world along toward being a common world of men and women, which women inarticulately long for and know that they do not see about them. If by virtue of their education, with consequent discernment of the total spiritual needs of our day, women can supplement and improve upon the limitations of vision and purpose of this man's world, the education of women will then be justified and will have high meaning for them and for society.

Surely the education of the women of the future will be different in important ways from the education of the male, which is tortured by his preoccupation during and after college with what William James termed the "bitch-goddess success," with all the limitations and constrictions of the human spirit which that motive has imposed upon men in recent generations. In opposition to this, there are ends and purposes which the women's college should struggle valiantly to find and to help each woman student to realize. I plead for recognition of these vital differences in the quality and substance of women's higher education because I am pleading also for that true equality of personality as between modern men and women, in which the clear mind and sensitive, upreaching spirit of women can help them to register their fullest contribution to the great gain of men as well.

Who is there today who will dare to say that the steps by which we do ascend are precisely the same for men and women, when we realize the differing and supplementary social role which each sex has necessarily to play in the comic-tragedy of our time?

Has Higher Education Been Wasted on Women?

HELEN PHELPS BAILEY

A Century of Higher Education for American Women
by Mabel Newcomer.
New York: Harper & Brothers, 1959. 266 pp.

This eminently readable book concerns everyone interested in the education of women in the United States. Young women already in, or soon to enter, college; parents, fiancés, husbands; alumnae, professional educators, college trustees: all will find pertinent facts and issues discussed with the objective authority of a trained scholar and with a woman's sympathetic concern.

Miss Newcomer speaks from the experience of forty years as a teacher of economics at Vassar College and eighteen years as chairman of the Department of Economics there. Let no one be misled, however, by the information that her present study was undertaken at the request of the Committee on Publications for the Vassar College Centenary Celebration.

This is no mere chart of the vagaries of a single female college. The pattern it weaves of Vassar's contribution, along with the contributions of the other earlier women's colleges, to the development of education for women does honor to the pioneers. But the book goes beyond this. Its scope is the whole field of formal higher education for women in this country. Its substance is an analysis of the problems, aims, and values at issue.

The author takes as her point of departure that time "two hundred and one years after Harvard College opened" when Oberlin — undaunted by the prevailing conviction that women belonged to an intellectually inferior order of creatures — admitted four young women to the course of study regularly pursued by male candidates for the A.B. degree. She attempts to assess the changes and predict some of the developments implicit in the fact that, over the past one hundred and twenty years, the enrollment of women in American colleges has risen to well over one million. Now that women have established their right to education at any level and in any field they choose, carrying off more than their proportionate share of academic honors in the process, where are we? And, what next?

Harvard Educational Review   Vol. 30   No. 2   Spring 1960, 169–172

It is the glory of the early women's colleges that they gave women their opportunity for higher education at a time when established institutions were reluctant to admit them. In 1870, more than two-thirds of the number of women enrolled in the collegiate departments of institutions offering the A.B. degree were in women's colleges. Vassar, alone, had over 200 of these or one-third of the number enrolled in some 40 private coeduational colleges and more than the combined total enrolled in eight state universities. Now, however, that women may pursue at least a four-year course leading to the bachelor's degree in any one of more than nine hundred institutions, the original function of the women's colleges no longer seems important.

Miss Newcomer finds her evidence for this view in the decline, since 1930, in the number of established private, independent, four-year liberal arts colleges for women. The one area of exception is the growth of Roman Catholic institutions during the past twenty years; and even here, the author notes a perceptible trend toward coeducation. Her statistics show that, excluding the Catholic women's colleges, the private four-year colleges today account for only three out of every hundred college women, as compared to nearly three out of every ten in 1880. We are reminded that, with the single exception of Claremont Men's College, which is a coordinate institution, all the new liberal arts colleges, both public and private, which have opened in the course of the past twenty-five years, have been coeducational.

The conclusion is inescapable that one of the most conspicuous developments in higher education for American women, apart from absolute numbers, has been the shift from segregation to coeducation or, at least, to coordinate education of the kind offered by university-affiliated colleges like Barnard and Radcliffe. The principal explanation offered by the institutions for this shift has been an economic one related to periods of declining enrollment. But the students, themselves, have helped to bring it about by an increasing insistence on attending a college near home (for reasons of economy or marriage, or both) and by the simple fact (also related to the earlier age of marriage) of their preference for coeducation.

The women's colleges have done more than open the way to higher education for women. They have also contributed significantly to the ranks of women scholars and artists as well as business and professional women. Women's colleges as a whole have produced more than twice the number of women scholars than might be expected from their proportion of enrollments. The eight largest women's liberal arts colleges that were in operation throughout the period from 1900–1950 (Bryn Mawr, Mount Holyoke, Barnard, Vassar, Radcliffe, Wellesley, Goucher, and Smith) accounted for only 2 percent of enrollment but produced over 17 percent of the scholars (cf. p. 195 and Table 15, p. 196). Comparison of these statistics with data tabulated for a group composed of Swarthmore, Carleton, and Oberlin — all three liberal arts colleges and coeducational — demonstrates that it is the liberal arts college *per se* — not specifically women's colleges — that produce scholars in large numbers (cf. p. 200).

Yet despite their hard-won and proven right to equal education, women have not kept pace with men in college enrollments. Although the numbers of women enrolled in institutions of higher learning has multiplied nearly one hundred times since 1870, and the proportion of women of college age attending college has also increased significantly (cf. Table 2, p. 46), the percentage of women among total college students has decreased over the past forty years, until today the men outnumber the women in college by nearly two to one. Moreover, women prove less likely than men to continue through the entire course.

Whereas 40 percent of the recipients of master's degrees in 1930 were women, only one out of three of the M.A. degrees conferred in 1956 went to a woman. But it is most of all in obtaining doctor's degrees that the women are lagging behind. Here, too, while the absolute number has increased conspicuously, particularly in the field of education, the proportion to the total recipients of the Ph.D. has dwindled from one in six in 1920 to one in ten in 1956 (cf. pp. 47–48).

These sobering facts lead Miss Newcomer to conclude: "Now that women are free to go to college, they are not so eager after all! And now that the majority of college men appear to prefer college women for wives there are only about half enough to go around" (p. 50).

The fault, it would seem, lies in a lack of motivation on the part of the women themselves. Even the accepted belief that a college education may improve a girl's social position and not only make her a social asset to her future husband, but even improve her chances of marriage, is apparently not enough to outweigh the pressure to choose marriage rather than college, if the choice is offered. Moreover, too often the parents, facing higher college costs, are not convinced of the economic value of higher education for their daughters, especially since the financial return usually is smaller and comes later than for their sons. Finally, with the increasing tendency of women to defer professional and vocational pursuits until middle age, the high school senior with marriage in view too often fails to see any immediate use to her of a college education.

Are we to believe that the higher education of women is wasted? Or is it a waste not to educate a greater number of our ablest young women? Who, if not they, will educate their children, now that 93 percent of all women marry, and half are married by the time they are twenty? And in this age of time-and-labor-saving devices, what will the homemaker do with those forty-five years of life remaining after her youngest child starts to school? These are some of the questions Miss Newcomer poses.

Today, she reminds us, all indications point to the probability of a woman's working outside the home for a fairly considerable period of her life. In our time, only one woman in ten will never enter the labor market, and today's women workers are expected to average from twenty to twenty-five years in paid occupations. The majority of college women are now in professions that normally require higher education, including all those traditionally regarded as "men's" professions. The highest percentages, as one would expect, are still to be found in the fields of social work, teaching, library work, and nursing (cf. Table 12, p. 179). To the dean of a teacher's college who protested that taxpayers' money was wasted on women students who would "just get married," Miss Newcomer points out that "something like half of the women teaching today are married women" (p. 236).

What can our institutions of higher education do to prepare women to deal with the complex demands of their multi-faceted lives? If, as Miss Newcomer believes, the usual case that is made for the women's colleges no longer has validity, what, if any, is their role? "They," she declares, "more than coeducational institutions, are in a position to dramatize the changing needs in the higher education of women today and to lead in providing for them" (p. 255).

They might begin, she suggests, by taking a fresh look at their offerings. "If women are to be persuaded to go to college in the same proportions as men, and to obtain at least the first degree before they become absorbed in family responsibilities, they must be convinced that such education is important both for family life and for a profession, and they must be assisted by more flexibility in college schedules and requirements" (p. 249).

More subject matter and fewer techniques in professional training; more advice and guidance toward choice of a profession; reduction of course offerings; greater flexibility in the granting of credit to "transfer" students and "guest" seniors; more use of early admissions and admission with advanced standing; more liberal provision for differential living costs; arrangements for payment of college fees on the installment plan; greater diversification of the student body on the basis of fathers' occupations and through the acceptance of older women who seek to complete their college education with professional goals in view; and increased opportunities for women scholars on the faculties of men's colleges and coeducational institutions, on university faculties, and in research. These are some of the ways that Miss Newcomer suggests for helping potential women college graduates to get the education they will need and must be encouraged to seek.

It would help, too, "if instead of attempting to excel in everything, the colleges would make up their minds to specialize a little . . . [and] if they would decide whether intellectual curiosity or well-roundedness was their chief concern either in selecting students in the first place, or turning them out in the end" (pp. 70–71).

Many of these proposals are not new. Some of them relating to "deferred education" would seem to lend themselves to the argument for the development of appropriate colleges of adult education leading to the degree. It must be of comfort to the author of this provocative book, and to those who share her concern, to know that a number of the measures she recommends are already in effect in certain of the women's colleges.

The Higher Education of Women: A Carnegie Study

ESTHER MANNING WESTERVELT

OPPORTUNITIES FOR WOMEN IN HIGHER EDUCATION:
THEIR CURRENT PARTICIPATION, PROSPECTS FOR THE FUTURE, AND
RECOMMENDATIONS FOR ACTION.
A Report and Recommendations by the
Carnegie Commission on Higher Education.
New York: McGraw-Hill, 1973. 269 pp.

Women's movements in the United States are yet another illustration of the symbiotic relationship between institutionalized higher education and organized opposition to the *status quo*. Superficially this association may appear paradoxical. But education is always part of a communal system of socialization, and higher education reflects and expresses established social and cultural values, including, in times of rapid social evolution, some whose foundations are cracking. This holds true whether, as in the United States, higher education is instituted by public leaders in response to social and cultural exigencies, or is, like the medieval universities, the creation of communities of scholars. Among those inevitably attracted to higher education are many of society's most inquiring minds. Higher education encourages troubling questions about societal conditions and perhaps provides a bastion from which to organize an assault upon those conditions. Academia's potential for internal disruption and for attacks upon eternal societal targets constitutes a perpetual and sometimes punishing dilemma for academic administration: events of the 1960s have been echoed over hundreds of centuries and in dozens of societies.

The *Report on Opportunities for Women in Higher Education* prepared by the Carnegie Commission on Higher Education is an effort to recommend solutions for one such societal dilemma arising from demands by women for fairer representation as students and as academic employees in our colleges and universities. The Commission makes this objective explicit early in the *Report* when it states: "Generally we should seek the maximum gains for women but at the minimum costs to academic institutions and to society" (p. 8). This effort alone, considering the prestige of the source, would make the *Report* an historic document; other characteristics

Harvard Educational Review   Vol. 44   No. 2   May 1974, 295–313

also make it historically significant. A prefatory glance at the history of the interplay between American movements and women's rights and institutions of higher education may put the *Report* in more lucid perspective.

The Social Utility of Women's Education

Women, not all of whom were feminists by any definition of the term, have long demanded increased access to American colleges and universities. Although the faculties of some medieval universities (as in Italy) had women members and some convents in the Middle Ages were well-known centers of learning, by the time higher education was institutionalized in America with the founding of Harvard, it was both acceptable and expected that colleges would exclude women. The exclusion did not have to be made explicit, for the *raison d'etre* of our earliest colleges was education for the professions and public leadership, in order that, in the words of a Harvard Commencement speaker three hundred years ago, the "ruling class [would not] be subjected to mechanics, cobblers and tailors; . . . [nor to] plebiscites, appeals to base passions, and revolutionary rumblings. . . ." (Rudolph, 1965, p. 7). In the colonial view, women had neither the intellectual nor the physical stamina for these responsibilities, and in any case their duties as family members were so arduous and varied that neither the society nor the economy could have spared them for other roles.

From the founding of Harvard as "the orthodox instrument of the community and its faith" (Hofstadter & Metzger, 1955, p. 81) to the opening of the newest community college as a vehicle for general, occupational, and service-related learning, American higher education owes its existence and its forms to ideals more utilitarian than utopian. For example, the University of Virginia opened as a *de facto* graduate professional institution not because scholars sought such a resource but because Thomas Jefferson believed "every branch of science, deemed useful at this day, should be taught in the highest degree" in "professional schools" intended primarily for "those . . . destined for learned professions (from law to rural economy), as a means of livelihood" (Jefferson, 1714, in Padover, 1956, p. 239). The extraordinary proliferation and heterogeneity of American institutions of higher education derives far less from conflicting notions cherished by self-constituted communities of scholars regarding form, process, and content for the educational enterprise than from the determination of differing power structures to conserve and enhance the social utilities defined by their religious, social, political, and/or economic values.

Inevitably, the most efficacious arguments for opening higher education to women were utilitarian rather then idealistic, although themes of individual liberty and human equality were not absent from the discourse. Newcomer (1959) states that "the principal argument *for* higher education of women was a matter of human rights . . . [although] the social good was also strongly emphasized" (p. 32). From this historical distance, however, arguments grounded in social utility appear to have exerted by far the greater leverage. On the eve of the American Revolution the academy was the most usual source of terminal higher education for the priviledged; there were only nine colleges in the colonies. Some academies were coeducational, such as the Moravian Seminary in Bethlehem, Pennsylvania, where women were first admitted in 1749, but there were few comparable institutions solely for young ladies. To what extent the rationale for women's education in these academies reflected Christian conceptions of the rights and dignity of human beings, regardless of sex and of accepted restrictions on sex roles, and to what extent it reflected ideas like those advanced by Benjamin Rush in support of academies for women, I cannot say. Rush argued that in a young country where families were isolated, a women needed a broad education to be a useful and "agreeable companion to a sensible man" and a mother competent to raise sons to participate in democratic government (Savin & Abrahams, 1957, p. 64).

Both Emma Willard and Catherine Beecher, who founded female seminaries in Troy in 1821 and in Hartford in 1824, stressed the importance of educating woman for her role as teacher, a role she could fulfill at home as well as in the primary schools. Beecher founded three other teacher-training "colleges" and was a voluble exponent of raising the level of women's education to the level of woman's status. But that status was a function of the moral and social significance of woman's domestic roles, including teaching. "The family state . . . is the aptest earthly illustration of the heavenly kingdom, and in it woman is its chief minister" (Beecher & Stowe, 1869 in Cross, 1965, p. 83). Mary Lyon's Mount Holyoke Seminary, founded in 1832, also emphasized the preparation of women for teaching; it was so successful that, according to Newcomer (1959), more than 70 percent of alumnae from the first forty years taught. Neither Beecher nor Lyon regarded anything less than a college-level education comparable to that available to men as adequate preparation for women's roles as teachers and moral leaders in the home, and they strove for this in their curricula. Beecher considered Georgia Female College, opened in 1839, and Mary Sharp College in Alabama, opened in 1850, "merely high schools" (Rudolph, 1965, p. 312).

In 1837 Oberlin, which had accepted women in its preparatory department since 1834, admitted women to candidacy for the baccalaureate degree (and/or for a diploma from the "Ladies Course"). Mundane considerations, not unknown today, may have hastened Oberlin's decision to open the way for coeducation at the collegiate level; 1837 was the single year in which Oberlin was too poor to publish a catalogue (Wirkler, 1948, p. 5).

Women's usefulness as teachers in the steadily growing numbers of elementary schools and later in the more recently established public high schools provided a strong stimulus for the establishment of full-fledged women's colleges and for the inauguration of coeducation in a number of private and public colleges and universities. Traditionally, primary teachers in the dame schools had been women. Moreover, it was advantageous to train women as teachers because women accepted salaries at less than half the level demanded by men. In any case, in an expanding economy oriented far more to production than to service, teaching the young was not a career to attract many able men. It was one of the few employment opportunities open to able women; thus women, as Newcomer (1959) points out, tended to appear superior to men in that field. Male educators possibly tended to concur with Francis Wayland, president of Brown, who wrote in 1854 that "women have a much greater natural adaptation to the work of instruction than men" (Newcomer, 1959, p. 15).

Other forces helped open new places for women later in the nineteenth century. Among these were a shortage of students during the Civil War, and increasing emphasis on the moral, religious, character-building, cultural, disciplinary, and personal improvement aspects of a college education, all acceptable as pursuits for the daughters of upwardly mobile middle-class parents. Rather sketchy reports from the United States commissioner of education indicate that by 1870 approximately 11,000 women comprised 20 percent of the students in higher education. Only about 3,000 of these were students in departments offering the baccalaureate degree, however; of these, the majority (about 2,200) were in women's colleges, although about forty coeducational institutions existed (Newcomer, 1959).

Influence of Feminism on Women's Higher Education

Forces of resistance to higher education for women also persisted. Professional courses or schools did not yet welcome women and professional education was the prototype of higher education in America. Feminism had emerged, however, and among its other activities was broadening the rationale for women's education through both rhetoric and example. According to Newcomer (1959), the 1870 census reported 525 women physicians, 67 women clergy, and 5 women lawyers. While sequence does not imply causality, particularly in history, it is worth noting that organized feminism did not begin to gain momentum in America until after higher education began to admit women. The record shows that educated women made a disproportionate contribution to the cause of feminism in the nineteenth century, and this is still the case today. This is evidence of the effect of educational advantages on inquiring minds, but it is definitely not evidence that nineteenth century colleges and universities condoned, much less encouraged, feminist ideas. Some advocates of women's education, including Almira Phelps, sister of Emma Willard, opposed women's suffrage and other tenets of feminism addressed to an extension of women's roles beyond the traditional ones. Lucy Stone was invited to write an essay for commencement at Oberlin, but was not to read it; she declined upon learning this limitation. Elizabeth Cady Stanton's daughters attended Vassar in the 1870s but she was never invited to give an address there. As late as 1917, Mabel Newcomer, then a young instructor, was reproved by the head of her hall at Vassar for chaperoning some students to a suffrage rally on the eve of New York's approval of the suffrage amendment. Institutional pressures doubtless limited student involvement in feminist causes. College-educated women as a group were not strong supporters of feminist causes, including suffrage. Most women's colleges did not support that movement; in a straw vote at Mount Holyoke in 1895 and one at Wellesley in 1912, majorities of the students voted against suffrage (Newcomer, 1959). Not until M. Carey Thomas became president of Bryn Mawr in 1894 did feminism have an outspoken advocate at a top level in higher education.

The feminist minority pressed on undaunted in higher education and elsewhere. They worked to increase women's participation in graduate and professional study and to widen their employment opportunities in professional fields outside teaching. They urged higher standards for women's college education. In an effort to raise standards, the Association of Collegiate Alumnae (parent association of the American Association of University Women) restricted its membership to graduates of colleges it specifically approved, although in no other respect could the association have been described as militant (O'Neill, 1969). Standards were not an exclusively feminist concern, however; the male founders of Wellesley, Vassar, and Bryn Mawr all declared their institutions must offer women an education comparable to that in first-class colleges for men.

Both the validity and the content of women's higher education were still issues. On these, the feminist postition was crucial. The thesis that higher education was ruinous to women's health, especially their reproductive capacities, attracted popular attention. In *Sex in Education*, published in 1873, Edward H. Clarke, a professor at Harvard Medical School, fanned fears of physical degeneracy and depopulation that Thomas and other women educators were still busy refuting with hard data in the first decade of the twentieth century. Psychologists urged a special curriculum for women; for example, G. Stanley Hall, dean of American psychology (who had said, "I envy my Catholic friends their Maryolatry"), proposed a "pre-maternal curriculum" to be organized around the "Sabbath" of the menstrual period (Fraser, 1972, p. 234). To these and other proponents of what Charlotte Perkins Gilman called "matriolatry" (Fraser, 1972, p. 234), M. Carey Thomas responded,

> it is not we, but the man who believes such things about us, who is himself pathological, blinded by neurotic mists of sex, unable to see that women form one-half of the kindly race of normal, healthy human creatures. . . . (Cross, 1965, p.160)

Catherine Beecher's glorification of women's teaching and maternal roles was lost on Thomas, who noted early in life that "of all things taking care of children does seem the most utterly unintellectual" (Cross, 1965, p. 33).

Thomas was higher education's leading feminist from the turn of the century until her retirement in 1922, a date that coincided roughly with an eclipse of feminism. Her position was based on principles of both social utility and individual liberty. She argued women should have the right to choose whether or not to marry, and if they married, to limit their families, become self-supporting, and employ others for "household drudgery"; "all women, like practically all men, must look forward after leaving college to some form of public service . . . paid . . . or unpaid" (Thomas, 1908, in Cross, 1965, p. 166). She felt women and men should have equal access to graduate study and teaching, including specially endowed research fellowships and chairs and that there should be open competition between the sexes for all chairs. She advanced the now familiar proposition that "women scholars can assist women students, as men can not . . ." and proclaimed that

> we [the college women of this generation] can do no more useful work than . . . make it possible for the few women of creative and constructive genius born in any generation to join the few men of genius in their generation in the service of their common race. (Thomas, 1908, in Cross, 1965, p. 169)

There matters rested for quite some time. College women did tend to enter public service although more were probably unpaid than paid. An increasing proportion became at least partially self-supporting and women found their way into every field of graduate and professional education, although in many fields their numbers were infinitesmal. By 1939 women comprised 28 percent of all academic faculties (Bernard, 1964, cited in the *Report*). But neither the passage of the Suffrage Amendment nor the growing numbers of college-educated women resulted in any significant movement of women into positions of political or economic power. Feminist concerns faded from view under the successive impacts of the Depression, war, a post-war retreat to domestic privacy, and persistent national and international tensions. During the middle decades of this century proportions of young people entering college grew with great rapidity but women students as a proportion of the whole actually declined, although girls remained more apt than boys to complete high school. Women's representation in the professions also declined.

New Utilities and New Demands

Then Sputnik flashed across the heavens and America mounted a talent hunt. Groups pondering education's role in meeting manpower needs advocated tapping the pool of female talent (National Manpower Council, 1957, 1960). Some skeptics countered with arguments that college women were already over-educated for the jobs they held; that women preferred marriage to employment; that they failed to pursue graduate education; and that university employment policies would be a bar to their useful employment on graduate faculties (Berelson, 1960; Havighurst, 1960).

Simultaneously, women themselves reopened the long-quiescent discussion of women's opportunities in higher education from a new and, at first glance, rather unlikely vantage point, that of the middle-class, middle-aged, married woman who found that motherhood (touted in the 1950s with a vigor Catherine Beecher could not have surpassed) was an activity that ended in the prime of life. Women began seeking entry or reentry into higher education and higher education began to consider the continuing education needs of women. The American Council on Education appointed a Commission on the Education of Women that identified continuing education as a top priority. The first such continuing education programs opened in 1960 and 1961, several with the assistance of Carnegie Corporation. In 1962 the American Council on Education held a national invitational conference on the topic, funded by the Carnegie Corporation (Dennis, 1963). President Kennedy appointed a Commission on the Status of Women; the chapter on education in its 1963 report, *American Women*, emphasized adult education for women and counseling for life-planning for women of all ages. Most women leaders of the continuing education movement were not feminists, however; they emphasized women's "dual roles" at home and at work and the inevitability of "intermittency" in most women's lives. Their activities did draw attention to women's participation in higher education and statistics revealing the relative decline in that participation aroused some concern.

Then Betty Friedan, an educated, frustrated housewife, opened the way for the rebirth of feminism with the publication of *The Feminine Mystique* (1963). Most of the new feminism's early converts came not from among Friedan's peers but from college and university campuses, particularly from the ranks of graduate students and younger faculty. As women who had been active in the civil rights struggles of the 1960s, these new feminists had learned that their male peers, however radical their thought in other respects, held traditional views of women's roles. As fledgling members of the academic community, they promptly turned their attention to the position of women in higher education. Together with newly-organized groups like the National Organization of Women and the Women's Equity Action League, they lobbied for legislation to ensure equal opportunity for women in colleges and universities and joined in filing suits against recalcitrant institutions. Throughout the late 1960s and early 1970s commissions and committees on the status of women emerged on many campuses and in virtually all professional and academic associations; these groups conducted studies of sex discrimination on campuses and in larger sectors of higher education and issued detailed reports, a number of which attracted national attention.

In its section on affirmative action, the Carnegie Commission's *Report on Opportunities for Women in Higher Education* traces the steps which led from the prohibition of sex discrimination in employment under Title VII of the Civil Rights Act of 1964, through the filing of a complaint of industry-wide sex discrimination against the entire academic community by the Women's Equity Action League under the Executive Order banning discrimination by employers having federal contracts, to Revised Order No. 4 of December, 1971, and the Office for Civil Rights guidelines of October, 1972, for implementing affirmative action for women and minorities in all educational institutions with federal contracts of over $10,000. Other legislative advances included the provisions of the Public Health Service Act of 1971 and the Education Amendments of 1972 intended to eliminate sex discrimination in higher education. Sex discrimination suits have threatened and delayed federal contracts at several major universities with considerable discomfiture to both institutions and the federal government. Some affirmative action plans are still being revised to meet federal standards.

Historical Implications of the Carnegie Commission's Report on Women

Women's quest for equal opportunity in higher education has moved rapidly ahead in the past few years, at least on paper, although it has not yet attained the goals set by M. Carey Thomas. Radicals, moderates, and conservatives among academic women of all ages have coalesced around the ends sought, although they remain divided on the means. The Carnegie Commission describes this breadth of support in the opening pages of its report. But the Commission's more significant acknowledgment is implicit in its decision to undertake the study that led to the report. During the six years of the Commission's work it has examined and weighed every salient issue in higher education. Publication of the *Report on Opportunities for Women in Higher Education* places women's access to study and status it held when President Thomas of Bryn Mawr was taking President Eliot of Harvard to task on the subject.

By focusing its discourse on questions of opportunity, the Commission implicitly attests that questions of the relative appropriateness of various curricula for women, and of the validity of equal opportunity for the two sexes which were so hotly argued in the nineteenth and early twentieth centuries, are no longer debatable, except possibly the question of academic employment for women. Perhaps even more indicative of the dawning of a new era is the relative lack of emphasis on the social utility of higher education for women, an issue that was still stimulating some controversy in the late 1950s and early 1960s. The major ideological underpinning for the Commission's stance toward women (a stance not fully in accord with its protective posture toward institutions) appears to be the individual's freedom to choose. That this theme should have outlasted its once sturdy companions is an encouraging portent.

Social utilities are not absent from the Commission's considerations but, as we might expect, in view of the nature of the larger undertaking of which this study is only one part, emphasis is on institutional utilities. The Commission points out that changes in colleges and universities cannot be accomplished without costs to the institutions and to society: cost in money, to white and minority males seeking academic employment, in efforts to change recruitment and other policies, in extension of centralized control within and without institutions to enforce revised policies, and possible costs in frustrations for women. Throughout the *Report* the Commission's attempts to suggest ways to minimize these costs reflect its protective attitude toward the essential characteristics of higher education as presently constituted, an attitude that pervades the Commission's work. In the summary of its final report (*Priorities for Action*, 1973) it states: "We believe that higher education will continue to recover from the effects of the several crises that have recently affected it" (p. 92). Concerning fuller absorption of women and minorities, however, the same report is less sanguine: "a rapid closing of the . . . gaps is difficult . . . it may take until the year 2000, or even beyond, before the levels of normal expectations for the inclusion of women and members of minority groups in the American professoriate are generally reached." But they add, "There are many unknowns, including how much frustration may develop . . . and how much pressure may be exerted . . . there will be some largely unanticipated new developments . . . American higher education and American society are in an unusual state of flux" (pp. 79–80).

The Commission's cautious optimism about higher education and its tendency to hedge its bets when it comes to minorities and women are both apparent in the report on women, but at the same time their concern for women as individuals is equally apparent. For example, the first and second of the major themes set forth in the introductory section concern, respectively, the cost to society of the loss of women's intellectual talents and women's past and present disadvantages as individuals in higher education; the nineteenth theme notes the need to give women more freedom of choice; and the twentieth, the necessity for continuing review and "revolution" in academic policies and procedures to reflect "revolutionary changes" in the lives of women and their families (pp. 1,8, and 9).

The Commission's staff deserves high commendation for pulling together an extraordinarily useful collection of data from reliable sources, as well as for developing data from their further analysis. The appendices in which most of these are found constitute a small reference work in themselves. These data document the Commission's examination in successive sections: the uses to which women put college education; women's patterns of entry into higher education; their modes of participation as undergraduate, graduate, and professional students; the status of women in the faculty and administration of higher education; affirmative action remedies; and needed campus facilities.

Women's Uses of Higher Education

The Commission examines what it terms "the impact of a college education on women as adults" (p. 16) in a section entitled "The Many Roles of College-Educated Women." As the title and the terminology suggest, the emphasis tends to be on women's patterns of exercising options rather than on the social utility of the outcomes. The summary statement about the "social benefits of higher education for women" suggests these include "elements that cannot be quantified by conventional methods of measuring the social return to investment in education" (p. 16), that is, economic input as measured by labor force participation and income. The section reviews evidence that college-educated women are more likely to participate in the labor force, to place a higher value on spending time with their children, to be more concerned about child-rearing practices, to report happy marriages, to share the intellectual interests of their spouses, and to engage in constructive volunteer community activity than are women with less education, and that their non-labor force activities resemble those of college-educated men, except the women have slightly higher rates of volunteer activity. The Commission cautions us, however, against the conclusion that a college education is universally beneficial and reminds us of their earlier recommendations intended to discourage the enrollment of "reluctant attenders" of either sex (Carnegie Commission, 1970).

Despite the emphasis on the manifold effects of higher education on women's life styles, two-thirds of this section are devoted to examination of labor force participation. These present familiar data on increases in participation since World War II, particularly among married women, and on the tendency of women with graduate degrees, especially doctorates, to persist in the labor force. Data on the actually rather slight increases in women's participation in certain so-called male professions since 1960, on relatively small increases in female enrollment in professional schools during recent years, and on career aspirations of women students showing a sharp decline in interest in homemaking as a career are adduced as evidence that women will increasingly tend to aspire to traditionally masculine professions, although the Commission expresses uncertainty about the permanence of some changes in women's attitudes towards their roles. The aspirations of women in selective institutions do appear to be rising sharply (the Commission cites 1972 data from Stanford), but data from the American Council on Education national studies of freshmen indicate that college women are, for the most part, simply shifting their career goals from elementary and secondary teaching to another "feminine" field — nursing and the allied health professions (excluding medicine and dentistry) (American Council on Education, 1967–1973). As the Commission notes, black women are somewhat more apt than white women to seek traditionally masculine careers. The Commission believes the trends it cites pose a question about whether college and university policies facilitate or inhibit women's potential exercise of these new options. In view of the fact that there have been some women in traditionally male professions for considerably more than a hundred years and of the efforts of leaders of women's movements to encourage women to enter such fields, it seems possible that the Commission poses the question with tongue in cheek.

A table developed by the Commission's staff suggests that, contrary to common belief, the participation of American women in traditionally male professions is not strikingly less than that in certain Western European countries, although it is markedly less than in certain Eastern European countries, particularly the U.S.S.R. It seems to me, however, that the data are too scattered to support any one conclusion. The Commission's point that professions like medicine and dentistry are more accessible to Western European women than to American women because of the shorter period of training required in those countries, and to Eastern European women because of the lower prestige of these professions in those countries, seems valid, however.

The Commission's almost total lack of attention to the economic sources of motivation for women's labor force participation is puzzling. No one is likely to disagree with the statement, "We believe that highly educated women are frequently motivated to work, not just for the income they will receive, but because they find their work intrinsically interesting and rewarding" (p. 25). However, it is important to recognize that many professional women make an important contribution to their families' incomes, and, in addition, their income gives their husbands more flexibility in the exercise of career options. Economic considerations can be potent motivators.

Considerations and Recommendations Regarding Students

The section on women's patterns of entry into higher education reviews the possible effects of all major factors frequently indentified by other sources as probable influences on sex differences in entry rates: age of first marriage and of first childbearing; changes in the birth rate; socio-economic status; cultural and sub-cultural stereotypes of sex differences; attitudes of high school guidance counselors towards women's educational and career aspirations, including the effect of social class differentials on these attitudes; biases in tests of vocational interests and aptitudes; sex differences in curricular choices in secondary school; sex differences in grades and in scores on standardized tests of aptitude and achievement; and institutional variations in admissions policies affecting women. The Commission notes that trends in sex differences in attainment of bachelor's and first professional degrees during the twentieth century show a rise for women until 1940, then a sharp decline during the next decade, followed by a gradual rise to the 1940 level by 1970. These tend to parallel changes in age of first marriage and in the birth rate.

Since Title IX of the Education Amendments of 1972 expressly prohibits sex discrimination in admission of students to public colleges and universities (except those that have been consistently single-sex), there is no need for a Commission recommendation on this point. The discussion points out, however, that private institutions should recognize "certain undesirable social and educational consequences of high male-female ratios" (p. 56) and not justify such a ratio by the dubious belief that male alumni contribute more heavily to their colleges than do female alumnae. The Commission recommends changes in those pre-elementary, elementary, and secondary school policies and programs that depress women's career aspirations and suggests these changes should have "first priority in the nation's commitment to equal educational opportunity for women" (p. 56). Specifically, they state that there should be no discrimination on the basis of sex in the use of grades or test scores as admissions criteria (the Commission observes that evidence that women receive higher grades than men in college in relation to prior grades and test scores could argue for *lower* cut-off scores for women); that elimination of sex bias from vocational interest tests, together with appropriate research, be encouraged (The Strong Vocational Interest Inventory has now been revised to eliminate sex bias); and that policies pertaining to the admission of adults to full or part-time study be liberalized.

In contrast to the scope of these recommendations and the supporting discussion, the Commission's treatment of the possible effect of sex differences in financial aid on entry rates seems cursory and somewhat equivocal. A 1973 report from the American Council on Education is cited to indicate that "there is no clear-cut evidence of discrimination against women in the provision of scholarships and grants" (p.57). This report, however, covers only students already in college, and data are given in percentages by sex, although women are a minority of the toal group; it thus tells nothing about effects of financial aid on entry rates by sex. In introducing the subject of financial aid, the Commission makes a glancing reference to data cited earlier in the section showing that in the two lowest socio-economic quartiles, men are more apt than women to enter colleges and that increase in entry rates from these quartiles between 1957 and 1967 has been markedly greater for men than for women. These statistics were cited elsewhere in the *Report* as evidence that the highest proportion of high–ability students not entering college is found among women in the lowest socio-economic quartiles. There is no mention of women's almost total lack of access to G.I. benefits or athletic scholarships. The Commission notes the tendency of women students to express concern about financing their education more frequently than do men, and attributes this to their greater dependence on parental support (also remarking the higher income levels of parents of women students) and to the fact that "opportunities for part-time employment frequently seem . . . more favorable for men than for women in college communities" (p.58).

The omission of any explicit recommendation regarding financial aid for women is troubling. The Commission does refer to earlier recommendations, first for a National Student Loan Program, with a variable repayment period and rates of payment determined by income level (combined for husband and wife), and second, for full funding of the Basic Opportunity Grants. The first, the Commission believes, would encourage borrowing by women who anticipated early marriage and child-bearing and the second would encourage both young men and young women from low–income families to enter colleges of their choice. There is no direct mention of the financial needs of part-time students, many of whom are mature women; it is true that full funding of the Basic Opportunity Grants would offer some aid for part-time study, but this point is not made.

On the subject of women as undergraduates, both discussion and recommendations underscore the need to diversify women's curricular choices and career aspirations. According to the Commission, the continuing tendency of women undergraduates to cluster in programs leading to such so-called feminine careers as education, nursing, allied health occupations, and social work, where there now is or is apt soon to be an over-supply of workers, is costly to women and to the economy. Their emphasis is nevertheless on freedom of choice: "We are not suggesting that women should be encouraged to enter traditionally male fields solely for job market reasons. . . . Women should have the opportunity to develop their mental capacities and utilize their abilities in whatever field of study is of greatest interest to them" (p. 70). The first three of its five recommendations regarding undergraduate education for women, however, are, first, that colleges and universities should not only strengthen career counseling in general but also take special steps to strengthen it for women (not overlooking the need to train counselors to discard outmoded sex stereotypes); second, that colleges and universities develop policies intended to eliminate administrative and faculty antagonism to admitting women to traditionally male fields; and third, that women be encouraged to make up mathematical deficiencies (by what means, the Commission does not say) when these are an obstacle to a desired career option. Perhaps the most surprising recommendation is for increased opportunity for women to participate in competitive sports; a footnote to the discussion (p. 75) cites Riesman's belief that sports encourage "antagonistic cooperation" (1969, pp. 81–82).

The fifth recommendation concerns women's studies. In both discussion and recommendation, the Commission makes clear its view that women's studies have transitional value and that when they have brought about "the discarding of outmoded and stereotyped ideas about the relative roles of the two sexes in many disciplines" (p. 78) the necessity for them should disappear. The recommendation explicitly opposes the organization of women's studies under separate departments; the discussion notes that this approach may delay the incorporation of relevant material into the curricula of the various disciplines and also may give women's studies second-class status. Not all proponents of women's studies will agree with the Commission's recommendation, although most recognize the possible merit of the rationale.

In the text of this section the Commssion makes a strong case for women's colleges. In the introductory summary of major themes, their continuation is also endorsed but no formal recommendation is made regarding them. Supporters of women's colleges would have been encouraged by a recommendation that women's colleges weigh any proposed change to coeducation with great caution in view both of the unique educational advantages such institutions appear to offer young women and of the superior achievements of their graduates. A recommendation that women's colleges prepare for the possibility of legal obstacles to their continuance by gathering further evidence of their unique educational service to women would also have been warranted. When one recalls the preeminent contribution women's colleges have made to women's higher education throughout most of its history, their failure is bewildering and rather depressing.

The seven recommendations pertaining to women in graduate and professional schools propose little more than is presently required under federal legislation and regulations—Titles VII and VIII of the Public Health Service Act of 1971, Title IX of the Education Amendments of 1972, and the affirmative action guidelines of the Office of Civil Rights. Some recommended policies and practices, such as those for the maintenance of full records regarding recruitment, applications, and admissions, the elimination of marital status as a bar to admissions, expansion of time limits on degree candidacy when family circumstances require part-time study, and eligibility of part-time students for fellowships are obvious safeguards against anti-discrimination suits. There is no recommendation for active recruitment of women to fellowships, although, as the Commission reports, a study by the Association of American Colleges suggested a need for this. There is a recommendation that college and university administrations adopt measures to encourage positive attitudes of faculty members toward women. The Commission does not specify what such measures might be. The recommendation that a woman desiring to enter graduate education after some years away from higher education "under no circumstances . . . be denied admission because her undergraduate education occurred some years earlier" (p. 107), also asks that such a student be given an opportunity "to make up for her inability to meet any special requirements." This recommendation does not directly address the related matter of age ceilings on admissions, a policy that also has been an obstacle to graduate study by women. Lacking, too, is any recommendation concerning transfer of credit from one graduate institution to another, although advocates for women in higher education, as well as the Newman Commission and the Commission on Non-Traditional Study, have repeatedly pointed out that restrictions on transfer of graduate credit, as well as restrictions on acceptance of undergraduate credits, have frequently been a deterrent to women in pursuit of graduate degrees.

The Commission, has, however, provided us with a thorough review of data on women in graduate and professional schools. While many of these facts are now familiar to those involved in the issues, the Commission's review meets a need for a concise compilation addressed to a wider audience. Data include sex differences in fields and levels of degree candidacy, in drop-out rates, in measures of ability, and in age. They observe that discrimination is "difficult to document" (p. 92) but appear to adduce evidence of dicrimination through active discouragement in both recruitment and admissions policies, as well as through the absence of policies designed to facilitate graduate and professional study for women whose family responsibilities place limits upon the time and mobility they have to pursue degree candidacy. The Commission apparently believes that women's lower rate of participation in graduate study, particularly at the doctoral level, is not solely a function of women's lower aspirations but also of the depression of aspirations by current policies and practices.

In a brief final section entitled "Needed Campus Facilities," the Commission considers continuing education and child care facilities. Although they state that "Women are major beneficiaries of (the) movement to provide more varied opportunities for higher education" (p. 153), data available from the 1970 Current Population Reports of the Bureau of the Census indicate that women then were still a minority of candidates for degrees, certificates, and diplomas in adult education programs. The Commission recommends more opportunity for external degrees and other non-traditional programs of high quality; continued opportunities for adults to study full or part-time; and separate centers for continuing education of women on campuses where circumstances suggest the necessity. The Commission's expectation, however, is that such centers are probably transitional resources, since "in the future the concept of continuing educational opportunities for mature women is likely to be . . . thoroughly accepted" (p.158). Again, there are no suggested solutions to problems of transfer of credit among traditional institutions, and there is no mention of acceleration for adults in such institutions, despite a reference to it in the section on undergraduate women. The Commission recommends that institutions respond to requests for child-care services by establishing committees, but favors separate sponsorship of such services, on grounds consistent with earlier recommendations in other reports that institutions avoid assuming functions not central to their main purposes. These several recommendations, except for the omissions noted, seem consonant with recommendations of many women's groups on campuses and leaders in the area of continuing education for women.

*Considerations and Recommendations Regarding Women
as Faculty Members and Administrators*

The sections on women as faculty members and academic administrators, and on affirmative action, are, in my opinion, the most significant in the *Report*. They exemplify the Commission's habitually meticulous approach to documentation and its scrupulous effort to chart a course that will, in its words quoted earlier, achieve "maximum gains for women . . . at . . . minimum costs to academic institutions . . . ." Interest is high, too, since academic employment of women and affirmative action remedies have been primary targets of women activists in academia; we have already remarked that a majority of the activist leaders hold or hope to hold academic posts.

Elizabeth Scott, chairman of the Department of Statistics at the University of California at Berkeley, undertook a study of the existence and the extent of discrimination and produced some of the best data yet available on this topic for the Commission. Her multilinear regression analysis of faculty salary differences by sex based on the 1969 Carnegie Commission Survey of Faculty and Student Opinion supplements data from other sources on sex differences in representation and in rank in general, and for different types of institutions and certain disciplines. Her findings confirm and extend those of Astin and Bayer (1972) indicating that a sex differential in salary remains after controlling for all the predictor variables, and further that these residual salary differences are larger in some types of institutions and in some selected fields than in others. They are greatest in leading research universities and least in comprehensive universities and colleges. Among disciplines, they are greatest in the biological and physical disciplines at the leading research universities but also exist in the humanities. Other findings are also of interest: examples include findings that sex discrimination in faculty salaries prevail for all races, while apparent discrimination associated with race is small and not statistically significant; that salary increases with increasing years in academic employment occur about 1.7 times as rapidly for men as for women; and that men's salaries vary directly with quality of the employing institution, while this factor has relatively little effect on women's salaries. Commenting on this evidence of "a pervasive pattern of lower compensation for women . . . not explained by the predictor variables," the Commission says, "it is possible that a close examination of the files of these women would reveal some justification for the relatively low compensation, but the probability of so many unusual cases is very small" (p. 119).

The Commission concludes that this discrimination, which is largely a function of slower promotion rates for women and of appointing women to positions outside the tenure line, results not from deliberate policies at top administrative levels but from recruitment, selection, and promotion practices within departments tending to favor men. This conclusion has also been drawn, as the Commission acknowledges, by most commissions and committees on the status of academic women. The Commission also enters some *caveats*. First, marriage may interfere with a woman's mobility and thus her pursuit of advancement although they admit that married women are becoming more mobile. Second, as "secondary earners" women have less need to strive for salary increases, a dubious and unjust contention, especially when one considers how many men are paid according to need. Finally, they suggest women may avoid achieving status superior to their husbands'. The last point is supported by reference to research on women's achievement motivation that has been questioned on both methodological and theoretical grounds and to ideas derived from relatively unstructured observations.

These *caveats* could be construed as questions regarding the validity of women's competitive pursuit of academic recognition with men. A more troubling question of validity is also raised; it appears in the "Major Themes" and a number of times thereafter. In the themes it reads, "Unfortunately, the years of high intellectual fertility in some fields and high child-bearing fertility overlap in the same period of life" (p. 2). While the language of the report in raising this ghost of ancient objections to women's intellectual pursuits is cautious, and suggests the cost to women will be greater in the sciences than elsewhere, the reiteration of the point may lend encouragement to a persistent belief among some academicians that motherhood and academic achievement cannot normally coexist. We must remember that data indicating that the early decades of life are the periods of highest productivity in certain "hard sciences" are derived from studies whose subjects were predominantly male. Fairly recent research (Dennis, 1966) found the highest rate of output for scholars and scientists from a variety of fields was reached in the forties and suffered little detriment thereafter until after age sixty; the fields included history, philosophy, biology, botany, chemistry, and geology. A recent study of sociologists (Clemente, 1973) found that neither the age of attaining the Ph.D., the years between degrees received, nor sex were reliable predictors of later productivity. The only reliable predictors were age at first publication and publication before the Ph.D. The size and quality of the employing institution were not taken into account in the analysis, however.

Assumptions regarding the chronology of intellectual productivity are also distorted by earlier failures to recognize the limitations of intelligence tests as measures of adult intelligence. Debate on this issue is still unresolved, however, and evidence remains inconclusive, except for findings that exercise of mental capacities is associated with their maintenance and enhancement. One recent longitudinal study (Riegel & Riegel, 1972) found a sharp drop in intellectual performance in the five years immediately preceding death, and no average decline in intellectual performance for subjects when test scores of subjects in this five–year period (regardless of age) were eliminated. Perhaps a more critical bar to premature conclusions about associations between chronological age and women's intellectual fertility is the lack of adequate data on possible sex differences in chronological patterns of intellectual productivity among men and women engaged in intellectual pursuits, whatever their marital and parental status.

While it cannot be said that the Commission's five recommendations regarding affirmative action meet the standards set by the most activist academic women nor, consequently, that they will effect rapid amelioration of women's disadvantages in academic employment, it can be said they are well within the limits of institutional feasibility. They recommend the establishment of goals and timetables based on careful research and implemented through active recruitment, availabilty of part-time appointments (in the tenure line where appropriate but no guarantee of later full-time appointment), maternity leave (with no mention of paternity leave), abolition of anti-nepotism rules, and establishment of internal grievance procedures — in other words, measures required by affirmative action guidelines. Opening more administrative posts to women through both appointment and training is also advised.

The Commission makes lengthy recommendations concerning needed limitations on federal power to enforce affirmative action. It urges federal regard for "the sensitive characteristics of academic employment" (p. 150); delay in cancellation of contracts "unless a pattern of discrimination has persisted for a considerable period of time and the institution has failed to take steps to correct it" (p. 150) and elimination of delays in federal procedures pertaining to the "development or implementation of adequate affirmative action plans" (pp. 150–151). The Commission's definition of a pattern of discrimination, in the same recommendation, seems to allow considerable flexibility in deciding what constitutes a "reasonable period of time" for developing and achieving affirmative action goals and what constitutes "lack of evidence" of adequate affirmative action effort or "evidence of antagonistic administrative or faculty attitudes" (p. 151). Some may accuse the Commission of equivocating, but both the scope and the particularity of the recommendations are necessarily limited by such immutable realities as marked differences among institutions in size, resources, and staffing patterns, and by the sharp variation among fields in availability of women recruits. Scott's projections show that, even if women were 50 percent of new hires, they would still comprise a minority of faculties in all types of institutions by 1990. Since such a percentage is unrealistically high for most institutions, in terms both of the pool of available talent and of equal treatment for other groups, progress will inevitably be slow as the Commission warns. It is unlikely that any conservative tendencies reflected in the recommendations will further retard it.

In Perspective

As a whole, the *Report* is a remarkably accurate description of the status quo for women in higher education today. It is also surprisingly, if not entirely, free of prejudice against women as students and as employees. Prejudice may be reflected in certain assumptions regarding the interaction among marriage, motherhood, and academic pursuits, as well as in those regarding the economic utilities of employment for married women. The Commission's assumptions about the vulnerability of the "balance" within institutions to rapid alterations of policies and procedures are undoubtedly a more potent influence on its position toward women than are any latent prejudices. In advocating restraint in coping with ineluctable pressures for change in women's status in higher education, the Commission is hewing to a line laid down in earlier reports on other issues.

Since a cautious approach has to be more palatable to most institutions than revolutionary proposals would be, the *Report* may serve as a greater stimulus to change than now seems likely. In any case, as the Commission repeatedly emphasizes, change is already under way and is the product of a great many forces. The capacity of a single publication, no matter how prestigious its source, to facilitate or impede that process is narrowly limited by the very nature of social change.

The *Report* does nevertheless represent a milestone in the history of women in higher education: the point at which a group clearly identified with the establishment accepted the authenticity of women's demands for equality. It is also the point at which such a body could consider issues of individual liberty and social utility but stops short of raising major questions of validity and of the necessity for curricular conformity to traditional assumptions about sex differences. Historians of women's higher education a century hence, if there are any, will surely study the *Report* with lively interest. Perhaps one of them, versed in history's footnotes, will be reminded of the Algerian president's recent speech of welcome to the Algerian Women's Union Congress in which he said, "Women's emancipaion must not be made at the expense of morals and tradition"[1] *(New York Times*, April 2, 1974).

The question is, of course, "Whose morals? Which tradition?"

References

American Council on Education. *National norms for entering college freshman*. Washington, D.C.: American Council on Education, 1967–1973.

Astin, H.S., & Bayer, A.E. Sex discrimination in academe.*Educational Record*, Spring, 1972.

Beecher, C.E., & Stowe, H.B. *The American woman's home*. New York: J. B. Ford, 1869. Chaps. 1 and 22 abridged in B. M. Cross (Ed.), *The educated woman in America*. New York: Teachers College Press, 1965.

Berelson, B. *Graduate education in the United States*. New York: McGraw Hill, 1960.

Carnegie Commission on Higher Education. *Less Time, more options: Education beyond high school*. New York: McGraw-Hill, 1970.

Carnegie Commission on Higher Education. *Priorities for action*. New York: McGraw-Hill, 1973.

Clemente, F. Early career determinants of research productivity. *American Journal of Sociology*, 1973, **79** (2), 409–419.

Dennis, L. E., (Ed.) *Education and a woman's life*. Washington, D.C.: American Council on Education, 1963.

Dennis, W. Creative productivity between the ages of twenty and eighty years. *Journals of Gerontology*, 1966, **21** (1).

Fraser, D. B. The feminine mystique, 1890–1910. *Union Seminary Quarterly Review*, 1972, **27** (4), 225 – 239.

Friedan, B. *The feminine mystique*. New York: W. W. Norton Co., 1963.

Havighurst, R. J. *American higher education in the 1960's*. Columbus: Ohio State University Press, 1960.

Hofstadter, R., & Metzger, W. P. *The development of academic freedom in the United States*. New York: Columbia University Press, 1955.

Jefferson, T. Letter to Peter Carr, September 7, 1714. In S. K. Padover (Ed.), *A Jefferson profile as revealed in his letters*. New York: John Day, 1956. pp. 247–243.

National Manpower Council. *Education and manpower*. New York: Columbia University Press, 1960.

National Manpower Council. *Womanpower*. New York: Columbia University Press, 1957.

Newcomer, M. *A century of higher education for American women*. New York: Harper, 1959.

O'Neill, W. L. *Everyone was brave: The rise and fall of feminism in America*. Chicago: Quadrangle, 1969.

Riegel, K. F., & Riegel, R. M. Development, drop, and death. *Developmental Psychology*, 1972, **6** (2), 306–319.

Riesman, D., with N. Glaser and R. Denney. *The lonely crowd*. New Haven: Yale University Press, 1969 (abridged edition).

Rudolph. F. *The American college and univeristy: A history.* New York: Random House, Vintage Books, 1965.

Savin, M. B., & Abrahams, H. J. The young ladies academy of Philadelphia. *History of Education Journal*, 1957, **8** (2), 58–67.

Thomas, M. Present tendencies in women's college and university education. *Educational Review*, 1908, **25**. Abridged in B. M. Cross (Ed.), *The educated woman in America*. New York: Teachers College Press, 1965.

Wirkler, J. E., Ed. *Oberlin College, catalogue of graduates, 1948*. Oberlin, Ohio: Oberlin College, 1948.

Paths and Pitfalls: Illuminating Women's Educational History

PATRICIA A. PALMIERI

COLLEGIATE WOMEN: DOMESTICITY AND CAREER IN TURN-OF-THE-CENTURY AMERICA
by Roberta Frankfort.
New York: New York University Press, 1977. 121 pp.

The fitness of women for higher education was a controversial topic in the nineteenth century; at issue today is the fitness of education for women. Has it promoted women's equality or perpetuated their second-class status? Which type of institution — single-sex or coeducational — serves women better? A chorus of disaffection from graduates of the Seven Sisters has recently rekindled the debate. In novels, essays, and popular histories, these writers decry the ideology of separate educational institutions for women.[1] In contrast, social analysts cite empirical evidence to praise women's colleges for producing a disproportionate share of achievers.[2]

Historians of higher education have contributed surprisingly little to the debate. In part, this failure is attributable to the parochialism of a discipline which until recently consisted largely of booster histories of elite institutions and biographies of their "great presidents."[3] Another reason for the relative silence among historians has been their tendency to assume that the life of the mind in the United States has been the exclusive preserve of the white male. Not all education historians have

---

[1] See, for example, Nora Ephron, "Reunion," in *Crazy Salad* (New York: Knopf, 1975); Diana Trilling, *We Must March, My Darlings* (New York: Harcourt Brace Jovanovich, 1977); Rona Jaffe, *Class Reunion* (New York: Delacorte, 1979); Liva Baker, *I'm Radcliffe! Fly Me!* (New York: Macmillan, 1976); Elaine Kendall, *Peculiar Institutions* (New York: Putnam, 1976).

[2] Mabel Newcomer, *A Century of Higher Education for American Women* (New York: Harper, 1959); M. Elizabeth Tidball and Vera Kistiakowsky, "Baccalaureate Origins of American Scientists and Scholars," *Science*, **193** (1976), 646–652; M. Elizabeth Tidball, "Perspective on Academic Woman and Affirmative Action," *Educational Record*, **54**, No. 2 (1973), 130–135.

[3] James McLachlan, "The American College in the Nineteenth Century: Toward a Reappraisal," *Teachers College Record*, **80** (1978), 287–306.

Harvard Educational Review   Vol. 49   No. 4   November 1979, 534–541

been so blinded, of course, but even ecumenical historians such as Richard Hofstadter, Laurence Veysey, and Frederick Rudolf have not plumbed the collegiate experience of American women.[4]

Two developments in historical scholarship augur a change. First, revisionism is sweeping the field of higher education as a new generation of scholars pursues novel topics, sources, and interpretations. Second, women's history has emerged as a legitimate field of inquiry, and since so little is known about women's higher education, almost any work casts some light on heretofore uncharted territory. As a result, many studies, including Roberta Frankfort's *Collegiate Women*, have been hailed as beacons. But beacons can lure as well as guide, distort as well as illuminate. As monographs proliferate, however, it becomes easier to distinguish those that lead the way from those that mark pitfalls. Such is the pace of research that now, only two years after its publication, *Collegiate Women* can be identified as one of the latter.

Frankfort's central thesis is that higher education for women in the nineteenth-century United States developed against the backdrop of the cult of domesticity. This ideology assigned to women, on the basis of their biological role as mothers, the social role of moral guardians of the home: for a woman to work outside the home was to violate her prescribed destiny. Before women's colleges were established, women bent on careers had to improvise their own solutions — solutions exemplified by the author in brief studies of Elizabeth Palmer Peabody and Margaret Fuller. According to Frankfort, colleges provided the next generation of women with frameworks for reconciling domesticity and career. She uses Wellesley and Bryn Mawr to illustrate the range of institutional responses by comparing the leadership styles and educational ideals of Presidents Alice Freeman (Wellesley, 1881–1887) and M. Carey Thomas (Bryn Mawr, 1894–1922). In Frankfort's judgment, Freeman did not openly defy domesticity; rather, in seeking to balance a traditional feminine style with her presidential role, she created at Wellesley an intimate, "homelike" atmosphere, and called for her "girls" to concern themselves with the "home, and with educational and charitable enterprises" (p. 43). Frankfort interprets Alice Freeman's marriage and retirement from the presidency not only as a sign of Freeman's ambivalence, but as the triumph at Wellesley of domesticity over career.

On the other hand, Frankfort sees Bryn Mawr, under the staunch leadership of M. Carey Thomas, as dedicated to producing not wives and mothers, teachers and charity workers, but scholars. Thomas, militantly antidomestic in style and philosophy, created a tense, competitive atmosphere at Bryn Mawr: students wore caps and gowns to class as symbols of their scholarliness. While in public, Thomas described the Bryn Mawr woman as one who would work and marry, inside Bryn Mawr she inculcated the norm of "intellectual renunciation" (p. 34), praising the "sexless scholar who would compete with men and shun domesticity" (p. 42). Thomas herself "of course" never married.

[4] Richard Hofstadter and Walter Metzger, *The Development of Academic Freedom in the United States* (New York: Columbia Univ. Press, 1955); Lawrence Veysey, *The Emergency of the American University* (Chicago: Univ. of Chicago Press, 1965); Frederick Rudolph, *The American College and University: A History* (New York: Knopf, 1962).

Frankfort then attempts to confirm her reading of the two colleges by using occupational and marriage statistics: in the "Years of Definition" (1885–1908), Bryn Mawr produced more working women than Wellesley; more Bryn Mawr graduates remained unmarried. Thus, the author tells us, only Bryn Mawr genuinely broke the canons of domesticity for its graduates. However, this lasted only for a short time. By 1918, the two colleges had converged; graduates of both, if they sought careers at all, typically entered domestically oriented "women's" professions such as home economics. Frankfort chooses Ellen H. Swallow Richards to exemplify this type of woman and traces the growing popularity of her conservative outlook in a discussion of the Association of Collegiate Alumnae.[5] Thus, as Frankfort would have it, the women's colleges ultimately lost their revolutionary potential, succeeding only in reinforcing, by making respectable, women's traditional domestic roles.

Even if one accepts this thesis, the book has serious shortcomings. First, the title is inaccurate. This is not a book about collegiate women, but about the responses to domesticity of four women, of whom only three attended college. There are other problems. Frankfort bases her entire argument about the changing milieu at Wellesley from 1885 to 1918 on Alice Freeman, who served only two of those years. She never examines the careers of the four women presidents whose administrations spanned the remainder of the period under study. If college presidents do dictate career ideals and leave their imprint on alumnae — a proposition that remains doubtful — surely the author is obliged to present the ideologies of all the presidents covered in her chosen time span. Frankfort undertakes a comparison of Alice Freeman and M. Carey Thomas with only slight reference to the fact that their presidencies were not contemporaneous. Moreover, the portraits of Freeman and Thomas are so misdrawn as to be falsely dichotomous.

Alice Freeman is presented as if she sought to enshrine college women as enlightened housewives. But as president of Wellesley College, Freeman wanted to produce teachers, not educated mothers. She envisioned an educational "empire," controlled and operated by women, no less broad and powerful than the Queen of England's.[6] She successfully founded such an empire, channeling many Wellesley graduates into the fifteen feeder schools she established and placing many others as teachers and deans in colleges and coeducational universities. Frankfort's claim that Freeman counseled Wellesley undergraduates toward domesticity and not "sex solidarity" is false. Freeman, no less than Thomas, fervently believed that women should band together in order to increase their power and influence.

For Frankfort, Freeman's marriage to George Herbert Palmer confirms her and Wellesley's domestic impulses. Although she did retire from the Wellesley presidency, she hardly "submerged" her identity in that of her husband, but continued

---

[5] The Association of Collegiate Alumnae, now known as the American Association of University Women, was founded in 1882 by women college graduates to lessen their social isolation and promote the status of women within higher education and the professions. See Marion Talbot and Lois Kimball Mathews Rosenberry, *The History of the American Association of University Women, 1881–1931* (Boston: Houghton Mifflin, 1931).

[6] Alice Freeman, "Dear Graduates of Mt. Holyoke Seminary," in *Semi-Centennial Celebration of Mount Holyoke Seminary, 1837–1887*, ed. Sarah Locke Stow (South Hadley, Mass.: Mount Holyoke Seminary, 1888), pp. 137–138.

actively to promote women's higher education, achieving national renown. In fact, it was Palmer's identity that was submerged—he was widely known as the husband of Alice Freeman. Wellesley's reactions to Freeman's marriage are instructive: many considered it a betrayal of the college's creed of dedication to public service; others felt it a "revolutionary"; attempt to combine career and marriage; few within the Wellesley community equated it with a retreat to domesticity.

In Frankfort's view, M. Carey Thomas had few of the conflicts that beset Alice Freeman and had no difficulty reconciling her dual roles as woman and college president. However, although Frankfort mentions that Thomas had women companions, she fails to explore in any depth the part that these serial "marriages" played in Thomas's personal life and public career. These relationships reduced the conflict between Thomas's twin roles, facilitating her presidency, but at times they generated tensions within the college community and within Thomas herself. For example, Thomas suffered a severe depression when Mary Garnett, who had lived with her in the deanery at Bryn Mawr, died in 1915. Her ensuing retreat from presidential responsibilities loosened her hold on the college.[7] Frankfort tells us only that Thomas's power declined after a 1916 battle with the faculty. Frankfort's characterization of Thomas as a single-minded career woman whose conflicts were solely in the domain of college policy is simply not true. Similarly, her presentation of Wellesley women as "hybrids" and "neurasthenes," while Bryn Mawr women are depicted as conflict-free, blatantly misrepresents both student bodies.

Frankfort's use of the career and marriage statistics of alumnae also fails to substantiate her thesis that there were distinct differences between the two colleges. Her quantitative evidence—that prior to 1908, 90 percent of Bryn Mawr graduates had careers, against only 35 percent for Wellesley—is based on a 20 percent sample of various registers compiled from time to time by the colleges' respective alumnae offices. This procedure not only results in some very small sample sizes for Bryn Mawr, but raises doubts about the comparability of the data. It is unlikely that compilers at the two institutions utilized equivalent definitions and adopted identical editorial policies, since the Wellesley registers differ markedly over time. The 1942 Wellesley register, which appears to have been Frankfort's principal source, provides far less complete alumnae work histories than do earlier registers. This may account for Frankfort's finding that Wellesley, which considered the preparation of teachers one of its highest missions, had only 21 percent of its graduates enter teaching between 1889 and 1898, while data compiled in 1900 indicate that proportion to be 43 percent.[8]

Even if the data were comparable, problems would remain. First, it is not legitimate to judge by the same criteria the educational outcomes of institutions founded a decade apart, with different purposes, and which presumably attracted students with different goals. Bryn Mawr was modeled after Johns Hopkins, a research university, while Wellesley was patterned after the New England liberal arts

[7] Edith Finch, *Carey Thomas of Bryn Mawr* (New York: Harper, 1947). See also Marjorie Housepian Dobkin, "M. Carey Thomas: Childhood and Adolescent Influences on the Growth of a Feminist Consciousness," paper presented at the Third Berkshire Conference on the History of Women, 1976.

[8] Computed from "Statistics in June 1900 of Classes '79–'99," comp. Mary Carswell in Louise McCoy North, *Historical Address* (Boston: Frank Wood, 1900). Wellesley College Archives.

college. Second, the difficulty of reconstructing students' social history, which reinforces historians' predilection for presidents, has led David Allmendinger, Jr. to call students the "inarticulate" group in education history.[9] Thus, Frankfort's attention to students is laudable, but insufficient. Merely to sample data from alumnae registers will not help us elucidate the impact of college on students' lives. To do that we must probe more deeply into students' class and family backgrounds and reconstruct their life histories before, during, and after college. This will entail a good deal of tedious but ultimately rewarding research.[10]

Beyond all the factual errors and omissions, this book is disappointing because it treats its fresh subject in such conventional ways. Frankfort borrows wholesale shopworn frameworks from several disciplines. From educational history, she resurrects the traditional focus upon the college president, disregarding students, parents, faculty, and trustees. Clearly a pluralistic model that captures the dynamic interplay among these factions—a dynamic that, over time, varies across institutions and within them—is necessary for a full portrait of the culture of a women's college.[11]

From women's history, Frankfort adopts the concept of the "cult of domesticity," first articulated a decade ago by historian Barbara Welter.[12] In this formulation, women are viewed as victims of an ideology holding them hostage in the home, segregating them from the working world, and depriving them of autonomy. Frankfort cites, but does not incorporate, more recent works which stress the salutory psychological and social aspects of a separate women's culture.[13] Here, unique "bonds of womanhood" are seen as creating a gender-based solidarity which became the starting point for a number of radical and reform activities, of which the movement for higher education was one.

By subscribing only to the old definition of domesticity, narrowly defined as involving marriage, Frankfort misses the potency of a domesticity that promoted female bonding and made homosocial subcultures intrinsic to the women's colleges of the late nineteenth century. Wellesley, a total female community, had an emotional, almost revolutionary fervor, a flavor not captured by Frankfort's description

---

[9] David Allmendinger, Jr., *Paupers and Scholars: The Transformation of Student Life in 19th Century New England* (New York: St. Martin's Press, 1975), p. 1.

[10] The best reconstructions to date are: David Allmendinger, Jr., "Mount Holyoke Students Encounter the Need for Life-Planning, 1837–1850," *History of Education Quarterly*, **19** (1979), 27–47; and Sarah H. Gordon, "Smith College Students: The First Ten Classes, 1879–1888," *History of Education Quarterly*, **15** (1975), 147–167.

[11] My own work on Wellesley College has led me to this conclusion. For example, students at Wellesley often cite stellar faculty like Katherine Coman, Vida Scudder, Emily Greene Balch, and Mary Calkins as having influenced their careers. Patricia A. Palmieri, "In Adamless Eden: A Portrait of Academic Women at Wellesley College, 1875–1920," Diss. Harvard Univ. 1981.

[12] Barbara Welter, "The Cult of True Womanhood," *American Quarterly*, **18** (1966), 151–174.

[13] Carroll Smith-Rosenberg, "The Female World of Love and Ritual: Relations between Women in Nineteenth Century America," *Signs*, **1** (1975), 1–29. Since the publication of Frankfort's book, several studies have developed further the concept of a separate woman's culture: Nancy Cott, *The Bonds of Womanhood* (New Haven: Yale Univ. Press, 1977); Nancy Sahli, "Smashing: Women's Relationships Before the Fall," *Chrysalis*, **8** (Summer 1979), 17–29; Lee Chambers-Schiller, "A Review of *Miss Marks and Miss Wooley* by Anna Mary Wells," *Frontiers*, **4**, No. 1 (1979), 73–75; Patricia A. Palmieri, "A Social Portrait of Academic Women at Wellesley College, 1890-1910," Unpub. Qualifying Paper, Harvard Univ., 1978.

of "subdued familial grace" (p. 64). Rather, students identified strongly with their mentors and peers, committing their lives to service and scholarship. It seems likely that Bryn Mawr shared at least some elements of this flavor, yet because domesticity is narrowly defined as involving marriage, Frankfort must label Bryn Mawr graduates as "sexless" Amazons, and the college itself as a "militant monument" to celibacy (p. 55).

Frankfort's near-equation of domesticity with "cleaning house," as in the *Feminine Mystique* (p. 23), is untrue to Welter's rich vision of nineteenth-century domesticity. She fails to distinguish between the religiously rooted, prescriptive ideology of the mid-nineteenth century, and the secular, capitalist version described by Friedan.[14] Not only does Frankfort blur the changing socioeconomic context of domesticity in American life, but she also omits any discussion of other social forces. This results, for example, in the failure to acknowledge the economic shifts which had made the culture of domesticity an anachronism by the late nineteenth century. Much of the work that middle-class women had formerly done shifted to factories, where it fell to immigrant and working-class women. In the face of an idle, "parasitic" womanhood, reformers like Thorstein Veblen and others developed a critique of the ideology of domesticity.[15] The opening of the women's colleges can be traced to this growing movement, which demanded that women's roles be independent of consumption and domesticity.

Without an adequate discussion of the complex cultural context within which the women's colleges operated—a discussion which should include analyses of industrialization, urbanization, demographic patterns, marriage rates, and class ideology—we cannot possibly begin to unravel the roots of women's higher education. Nor can we know for sure how and to what degree the wider culture impinged on the colleges or the role of colleges in advancing radical cultural shifts in the United States.

Another framework appropriated by Frankfort from women's history is the metaphor of decline. Long the standard interpretation of the feminist movement following the passage of the suffrage amendment, the metaphor was first applied to college women by Jill Conway in 1968.[16] To Conway, the élan of the first generation waned over time. Moreover, this generation hinged their career choices on romantic notions that the feminine temperament was uniquely fit to cure social injustice. In thus elevating the "eternal feminine," they left themselves vulnerable to Freudian dicta of the twenties that the truly feminine woman disavowed careerism. Women careerists were thus labeled "deviant," and the pioneers ceased to function as role

---

[14] Betty Friedan, *The Feminine Mystique* (New York: Norton, 1963).

[15] Thorstein Veblen, *The Theory of the Leisure Class* (Boston: Houghton Mifflin, 1973). Women's college founders like Henry Durant (Wellesley) and Matthew Vassar conceived of higher education as a reform movement that would abolish "idle" womanhood.

[16] Jill Conway, "The First Generation of American Women Graduates," Diss. Harvard Univ. 1968. See also Jill Conway, "Women Reformers and American Culture, 1870–1930," *Journal of Social History*, 5 (1971–72), 164–177. For the theory applied to professional women in academe, see Jessie Bernard, *Academic Women* (New York: New American Library, 1964). Two general works that discuss the decline of feminism are: Eleanor Flexner, *Century of Struggle: The Woman's Rights Movement in the United States* (Cambridge: Harvard Univ. Press, 1959); William O'Neill, *Everyone Was Brave: A History of Feminism in America* (Chicago: Quadrangle, 1969).

models to young women. Frankfort closely follows this line of analysis: Bryn Mawr and, to a lesser extent, Wellesley epitomize for her this first generation (1889–1908). By the second decade (1908–1918), she asserts, attending college was no longer special, and the women's colleges had lapsed into a reaffirmation of domesticity, channeling women into such fields as domestic science and home economics.

Despite the apparent applicability of the metaphor of decline to women's colleges, it does not take into account campus activism by both faculty and students throughout the Progressive era. Indeed, women's colleges were labeled "hotbeds of radicalism" in the 1920s for their support of suffrage, consumer leagues, trade unions, pacifism, anarchism, and socialism.[17] Similarly, the contention that a second generation of college women failed to remain committed to a full range of career goals is not borne out by recent studies of professional women. Margaret Rossiter traced the flow of women into the scientific professions from 1920 to 1938, concluding that women, even married women, continued to pursue careers, although their entry and advancement varied with the growth rate of their chosen profession; in crowded fields they encountered the most discrimination.[18] Frank Stricker also suggests that women from 1920 to 1960 maintained career objectives, although these changed over time; often women sought to combine marriage and career only to retreat home after finding that the sheer lack of institutional and societal support made the dual roles impossible.[19]

The decline metaphor tends to overemphasize the pioneers who struggled to gain access in the 1860s and 1870s. While Frankfort rightly directs needed attention to "pre-collegiate" women, precursors to the much studied first generation, we may question the appropriateness of her decision to focus on Peabody and Fuller. Emma Willard, Zilpha Grant, and Mary Lyon, all of whom founded seminaries, seem more direct forerunners of collegiate women. The biographies of Peabody and Fuller do remind us, however, that some women in the pre-Civil War era educated themselves. Sally Kohlstedt discusses three generations of amateur women scientists (1830–1880) who operated on the periphery of the formal disciplines, paving the way for their "public and professional" sisters who graduated from the women's colleges.[20] Likewise, Sally Schwager traces the roots of Radcliffe College to the rising expectations of the women between 1840 and 1880 who exploited summer schools, literary societies, family libraries, and ladies' clubs to gain "self-culture" and education.[21] When the full range of women's educational activities before

[17] Calvin Coolidge, "Enemies of the Republic: Are the Reds Stalking Our College Women?," *The Delineator*, June 1921, p. 67. For a discussion of campus activism at Vassar College, 1890–1920, see Lynn Gordon, "Women with Missions: Varieties of College Life in the Progressive Era." Diss. Univ. of Chicago, 1980. Student and faculty activism at Wellesley is briefly explored by Grace Hawk, "A Motto in Transit," in *Wellesley College: A Century of Women*, ed. Jean Glasscock (Wellesley, Mass.: Wellesley College, 1975). See also Palmieri, "In Adamless Eden."

[18] Margaret Rossiter, "Sexual Segregation in the Sciences: Some Data and a Model," *Signs*, **4** (1978), 146–152.

[19] Frank Stricker, "Cookbooks and Law Books: The Hidden History of Career Women in Twentieth-Century America," *Journal of Social History*, **10** (1976), 1–19.

[20] Sally Kohlstedt, "In from the Periphery: American Women in Science, 1830–1880," *Signs*, **4** (1978), 81–97.

[21] Sally Schwager, "Harvard Women: A History of the Founding of Radcliffe College." Diss. Harvard Univ., 1982.

formal access to colleges becomes better known, our conception of the first generation of college women as unique may have to be revised. Meanwhile, we can begin
to appreciate that each generation of women is in some sense pioneering, as previous gains are internalized and new agenda are set.[22] Only the gross outlines of
this generational cycle are known — from women's rights to higher education, to careers, to career and marriage — but these are enough to suggest that continuity co-
exists with decline; both are appropriate metaphors for women's contribution to
culture in the United States.

Unfortunately, Frankfort perpetuates the tradition of blaming the victim. She
erroneously chastises women for entering fields like child psychology, domestic science, and social service that did not command high salaries or status. Her analysis
is replete with presumptions about which careers are "legitimate" and "professional." In denigrating the accomplishments of women such as Ellen H. Swallow
Richards (portrayed in this volume as someone who did little more than dignify
housework), Frankfort can only treat them as failures who "clung to domesticity
under the guise of sanitary science and domestic hygiene" (p. 74). She terms their
desire to merge scientific investigation with humanitarian ethics "a conservative
outlook" (p. 98), yet their extraordinary achievements in social reform and social
service administration mark the Progressive era. Frankfort's wholesale dismissal of
women involved in social reform precludes an understanding of the dynamics of
what amounts to an interlocking directorate of elite women, trained in Eastern colleges, who put their intellectual stamp on colleges and public-policy programs
throughout the United States. It also prevents us from considering how these
women shaped the professions. Studies of Hull House, the college settlement
movement, and women in academe reveal that women held ideals about careers
that were distinct from men's. Since most of these women lived and worked in totally female communities, they produced special subcultures, the characteristics of
which are only now beginning to be understood.[23] And yet this distinctiveness
must also be assessed against the backdrop of discrimination, which, by denying
women access to key positions in professional organizations and research universities, robbed them of the experience crucial to success in modern careers.[24]

Unaddressed in Frankfort's study, as in most of the literature, is the degree of
difference between collegiate women and collegiate men. Frankfort assumes that
the educational ideals of a New England college such as Wellesley, which lauded

[22] Barbara Sicherman has suggested that successive generations of women each rebelled against limitations on women's behavior, albeit with different styles and goals. Barbara Sicherman, "American
History: Review Essay," *Signs*, **1** (1975), 461–487.
[23] John Rousmaniere, "Cultural Hybrid in the Slums: The College Woman and the Settlement
House," *American Quarterly*, **22**, No. 1 (1970), 45–66; Jill Conway, "The First Generation of American
Women Graduates"; Melissa Heild, "The Ladies of Chicago: Women, Social Reform and Social Work,
1920–1935." Diss. Univ. of Texas at Austin; Palmieri, "Social Portrait of Academic Women."
[24] For discussions of the rise of professionalism, see Burton Bledstein, *The Culture of Professionalism*
(New York: Norton, 1976); Thomas Haskell, *The Emergence of Professional Social Science* (Urbana: Univ.
of Illinois Press, 1977); Bruce Kuklick, *The Rise of American Philosophy* (New Haven: Yale Univ. Press,
1977). All of these works make scant effort, however, to investigate or incorporate women's experiences.
Two books which do treat women's emerging professionalism are: Roy Lubove, *The Professional Altruist:
The Emergence of Social Work as a Career, 1880–1930* (New York: Atheneum, 1977); Mary Roth Walsh,
Doctors Wanted: No Women Need Apply (New Haven: Yale Univ. Press, 1977).

service to society, emphasized character, and called for self-abnegation, are somehow peculiarly feminine and conservative. But the men's colleges in New England upheld strikingly similar ideals. The "symmetrical woman" had her counterpart in the "symmetrical man": both were to be the reformers of the Progressive era.[25] We know too little about the actual distinctions between student culture on men's and on women's campuses. No detailed study of curriculum exists for either; comparisons of academic men and women are also lacking. We ought to be circumspect in our claims about uniqueness or presumptions of similarity until such comparisons are completed.

Although *Collegiate Women* disappoints and frustrates, its many deficiencies serve indirectly to indicate the pathway women's educational history ought now to follow. Needed urgently is information from sources heretofore uninvestigated — women's diaries, reminiscences, notebooks, letters — as well as data from more traditional materials, such as curricula, trustees' reports, departmental reports, and faculty and presidential papers.

In the 1940s, historian Mary Beard described women as a "force in history," emphasizing their contribution to culture.[26] Beard tended to gloss over the oppression of women, but historians today are revising her framework to allow for a dialectic between women's success and victimization. Such an approach would serve historians of women's higher education well. After years of omitting women from the educational history of the United States, more than a cursory study of prescriptive norms of a few notable women is required. We need to examine closely the experiences of women of various periods, ethnic groups, classes, and ages. In all our investigations we should remember that successes and failures are both important; winners and losers, women and men, deserve our attention. Our exploration of the history of women in higher education need not be sentimentalized. A full portrait of collegiate women will reveal real people, sometimes submitting, sometimes subverting, often substantially contravening what was expected of them. A better understanding of women's experience would permit, even force, a far-reaching revision of the broader fields of higher education and intellectual life in the United States.

---

[25] George E. Peterson, *The New England College in the Age of the University* (Amherst: Amherst College Press, 1964) links the "symmetrical man" of the New England men's colleges with Progressivism. Wellesley's educational ideals (1875–1900) called for the development of the "symmetrical woman."

[26] Mary Beard, *Woman as Force in History* (New York: Macmillan, 1956). For an excellent reevaluation of Beard's contribution to women's history, see Ann J. Lane, *Mary Ritter Beard: A Sourcebook* (New York: Schocken Books, 1977), esp. pt. 1. See also "Roundtable: The Legacy of Mary Ritter Beard," Fourth Berkshire Conference on the History of Women, 1978.

Scientific Women

RUTH HUBBARD

Women Scientists in America: Struggles and Strategies to 1940
by Margaret W. Rossiter.
Baltimore: Johns Hopkins University Press, 1982. 439 pp.

Science is both a social activity and the kind of knowledge about nature that this activity produces. The people who "do" science and so produce that knowledge are called scientists. Because of the time and place in which modern Western science — and that is what people nowadays mean by science — developed, scientists predominantly have been men. As this kind of knowledge and its applications have expanded into a dominant world view over the past two or three centuries, men have become so identified with all phases of it — the activity, product, application, and world outlook — that science as both product and activity has come to be thought of as essentially masculine. This book documents the steady, careful, and politically astute efforts that women have expended between approximately 1820 and 1940 to be able to join the scientific world, and the different barriers that have in turn been erected to make their entry difficult.

Even among present-day feminists there has been a tendency in some quarters to postulate a quasi "natural" antipathy between women and science. Men, one argument goes, because of their early psychosocial experience of being nurtured by women, learn to objectify and manipulate people and the environment, whereas women learn to be comfortable with relationships that involve nurturance and mutuality. It is, of course, true that since for historical reasons science has been produced largely by men, it has built into it marks of its male parentage, such as objectivization and instrumentality. But I see no reason to believe that men and women divide into nonoverlapping categories with respect to instrumentality and domination of nature any more than we do regarding other social characteristics. The exclusion of women from science is too dramatic and quixotic to be explained on the basis of differences in intellectual or temperamental preferences between women and men as groups.

In this book, Margaret Rossiter shows the apparent arbitrariness with which certain fields of science allowed women in, whereas others were much more adamant about excluding them. One must look to the history and the growth of professionalization of various areas of science rather than to individual or group psychology to find explanations for why women were more able to gain footholds in

Harvard Educational Review   Vol. 54   No. 4   November 1984

some fields than in others. Women were far more successful in botany than in zoology, in astronomy than in physics, in biochemistry than in physiology or anatomy, in statistics than in mathematics, and in anthropology than in geology or paleontology. Reasons why women were able to be better represented in nutrition (with its links to home economics) than in chemistry, or in psychology more than in biology, are easier to deduce from the congruence of those subjects with the ideology of "woman's nature"—her supposedly inherent preference for domesticity and human relationships. But the other pairs mentioned lack that kind of easy social logic and must be explained, as Rossiter has done, on the basis of what else was happening at the time these fields of inquiry came into prominence or became professionalized; what political and economic forces small groups of well-placed women could muster; or where they could find politically effective male allies who were not biased against women, were feminists, or merely preferred to surround themselves with women for sexist reasons.[1]

Until I read this book, I had always been much more interested in women *and* science—that is, the relationships women have had to the content and practice of science—than in women *in* science. Rossiter has changed my mind. Her book is so full of fascinating tables of data, fleshed out with biographical stories and historical analyses and interpretations, that I have spent hours poring over details of where women scientists came from, where they went, and how they managed to accomplish what they did. The nearly 100 pages of footnotes and bibliography are themselves a gold mine!

Rossiter has culled her facts from membership lists of professional societies, government indexes, autobiographies, biographies, obituaries, and listings in consecutive editions of *American Men of Science* (a title to which the feminist and psychologist Christine Ladd-Franklin had objected as early as 1920 but which was not changed until 1971). With these she has woven together a story that is fascinating in its detail, while at the same time she offers a broad perspective on the work and life experiences of the women who tried initially just to become educated and eventually to be scientists.

She shows that women's early hope that if they became educated they then would be accepted as the equals of men was not fulfilled. To be permitted an education, women had to accept the compromise that their education would be structured to make them better wives and mothers, not educated people ready to earn their livings the same as men. Later, when educated women did begin to encroach on men's professions, men erected new barriers, such as the requirements for advanced degrees to which women did not yet have access. Once women, too, were earning Ph.D.s, then, as Rossiter explains, "universities were showing themselves to be liberal educators, [but] they were also proving themselves to be highly discriminatory employers" (p. 314). It was well-nigh impossible for women, even with doctorates, to get the kinds of jobs that equally- or less-qualified men were getting. Women were limited either to low-paying, dead-end jobs assisting men in univer-

[1] As far as the juxtaposition of biochemistry with anatomy and physiology is concerned, it is interesting that especially in Germany (which later became the source of much of American biochemistry) biochemistry, which came into prominence after World War I, was also much more accessible to Jews than were the older, more established, disciplines of anatomy and physiology.

sity, government, or industrial laboratories, or to stereotypically feminine subjects, such as home economics or, later, child psychology. The only institutions that made some room for them were the women's colleges. But even these colleges sought the prestige that men brought. Furthermore, they tended to impose serious limitations on the amount of research their science professors could do, whether they were women or men. The difference for women was that they had many fewer opportunities than men to move on to professorships in prestigious universities which not merely permitted but encouraged their faculty to combine research and teaching. In fact, numerous male scientists who later became well known began their academic careers at a woman's college and moved to such places as Harvard or Columbia or the University of Chicago when they felt the need for more research stimulation and support. In time, when women qualified to apply for membership in scientific societies, there, too, new barriers were erected in the name of "raising standards," such as the two-tiered "associate" and "full" memberships.

During the most active period of feminist politics, between about 1890 and the early 1920s, women collected funds to open up opportunities in coeducational institutions such as Johns Hopkins, the "women's table" at the Zoological Station at Naples, Italy, or at the Marine Biological Laboratory in Woods Hole, Massachusetts.[2] They also began preparing reports to document discrimination in employment. However, since the women depended solely on the good will of individual men, nothing much changed. Rossiter points out that patterns of sex-segregated employment were so thoroughly established in academia, government, and industry that by the 1920s, when larger numbers of women scientists with doctorates became available, neither the documentation of discrimination nor the weak kinds of political pressure the women could muster produced jobs and recognition, except in rare individual cases.

I completely agree with Rossiter's assessment that the resulting tokenism worked to the disadvantage of women in general. By celebrating and occasionally hiring an "exceptional" woman (the "Madame Curie syndrome"), men could profess fairness while continuing to pass over the women who were no better, *but also no worse*, than the men who were being hired. Women's brave accommodation to this cruel reality, and their resignation to having to achieve more for fewer rewards, makes sad reading. And it is infuriating to meet evidence of the often explicit and unashamed discrimination against them, such as Nobel physicist Robert Millikan's advice in 1936 to the president of Duke University not to appoint the highly qualified physicist Hertha Sponer, a refugee from Germany, because chances of build-

---

[2] The Zoological Station at Naples, Italy, one of the first and most important international, biological research centers, accepted donations for research tables which were reserved for scientists from the donor institutions. In the 1890s, Harvard, Johns Hopkins, the Smithsonian, and a number of other U.S. organizations supported "tables" at Naples, but as a matter of course these were available only to men (which, in the spirit of the times, meant *white* men). Rossiter tells how the physiologist Ida Hyde, after receiving her doctorate at Heidelberg, "was invited to continue her researches at one of the German tables at the Naples station" (p. 48). Stimulated by that experience, she initiated a committee which founded a "Naples Table Association for Promoting Laboratory Research by Women" and so opened access to the Naples station to a succession of women biologists from the United States. In 1901 the Association expanded its activities and began to support a "woman's table" also at the recently opened Marine Biological Laboratory in Woods Hole, Massachusetts.

ing an outstanding physics department were better if he "picked one or two of the most outstanding younger men, rather than if [he] filled one of [the] openings with a woman" (p. 192).

Another topic that interests me very much is the role of the women's colleges as both producers and employers of women scientists. As a Radcliffe A.B. and Ph.D., I am sorely aware of the bad bargain Radcliffe struck when it chose to contract for Harvard's faculty rather than build its own. This meant that, as time passed, Radcliffe could not offer employment to the increasing number of well-qualified Ph.D. women scientists, or, indeed, scholars in all fields. It also meant that, out of self-interest, Radcliffe continued to exhort its students to feel privileged to be able to study under Harvard's "great men," apparently oblivious of the fact that it was thereby withholding from them the realistic expectation that they themselves might some day be equally "great" women. Indeed, the only example of "great" women that Radcliffe could provide were its administrators (although during part of my tenure as a student even the president of Radcliffe was a man) and the faculty wives who "helped" their husbands, often as unpaid and unacknowledged collaborators ("research assistants" or "associates"), but more often as hostesses at student teas. Small wonder that many fewer women listed in the 1938 edition of *American Men of Science* earned their A.B. or Ph.D. degrees at Radcliffe than at the other "seven sister" colleges and at many coeducational schools (pp. 146–147).

Rossiter's book, the first of two projected volumes, ends in 1940, the year before I entered Radcliffe with the intention of later going to medical school. I should therefore like to end this review with a brief description of my early college science education. As an entering freshman in the fall of 1941, I enrolled in introductory chemistry. The teacher Harvard sent us was a young man recently out of Dartmouth who always wore green blazers and dripped disdain for Radcliffe science students. The following summer, under a wartime accelerated program, I took the full-year introductory biology course (botany and zoology) and the first half of a two-term introductory physics course at the Harvard Summer School. Zoology was taught by one of the elder statesmen in the Harvard biology department (whose research, incidentally, dealt with hormonal changes during pregnancy and birth). The rumor in class was that he had had to be pressured into teaching in the Summer School because the mixed company would force him to clean up the humor in his lectures.

In summer school physcis, I found myself one of two women in a class of about 300 students. Not until the end of the course did I wake up to the facts that the other woman did not go to Radcliffe, that I was the only Radcliffe student wanting to take the second semester of introductory physics that fall, and that the course therefore would not be offered at Radcliffe. Indeed, I would have to wait two terms before it would be given at Radcliffe. When I presented my problem to the professor and to the chairman of the physics department, they agreed that the only reasonable thing for me to do was to take the second semester at Harvard with the rest of the class. But rules were rules: both the Harvard and Radcliffe administrations flatly refused. (Because of wartime pressures, the rule in question was rescinded within the year, but too late to do me any good.) The physics department was sufficiently annoyed by this absurd decision that they offered to teach the course at Radcliffe if I could recruit three students to take the second semester of introductory physics before they had taken the first. So, once I had located the victims, the Harvard physics department sent us two young men, one to lecture and the other to teach labs, and we embarked on what was undoubtedly the worst physics course ever taught at Harvard or Radcliffe. The young men were barely older than we students and had not taught before; the other women were not prepared for the course; we all thought the situation ridiculous; and little teaching or learning occurred. The only gain was that I became close friends with one of the young men and his wife.

Margaret Rossiter's book cannot help but stir such memories in someone of my generation, as well as speculations and questions in everyone about the past and future of women's educational and professional experience in science. I look forward eagerly to the next volume.

PART III
Schools And Teaching

Sex Role Stereotyping in the Public Schools

TERRY N. SAARIO

CAROL NAGY JACKLIN

CAROL KEHR TITTLE

The authors investigate sex role stereotyping in three major areas: elementary school basal readers, educational achievement tests, and differential curricular requirements for males and females. The section on basal readers documents the extent and kind of sex role stereotyping in the kindergarten to third grade textbooks of four major publishers. The section on educational testing raises the issue of sex bias in item content and language usage and shows the presence of sex role stereotyping in test batteries from major test publishing companies. The curriculum section discusses the presence and ramifications of different curriculum patterns for males and females.

> If the children and youth of a nation are afforded
> opportunity to develop their capacities to the fullest,
> if they are given the knowledge to understand the
> world and the wisdom to change it, then the prospects
> for the future are bright. In contrast, a society
> which neglects its children, however well it may
> function in other respects, risks eventual
> disorganization and demise.
>
> (Bronfenbrenner, 1970, p. 3)

The concern of one generation in a society for the next has been variously described and labeled by historians, psychologists, sociologists, and anthropologists. Such concern is a constant in all societies, and is frequently called socialization. Socialization is the process of preparing children to assume adult statuses and roles. The family, the school, the church, peer groups, economic institutions, political institutions, and the media would be identified by most thoughtful people as the principal socializing institutions in our society. Of these institutions only the school has the socialization of youth as a principal function. Schools, whether formal or informal, whether inner city or rural, function as transmitters of certain societal norms and mores from one generation to the next.

Harvard Educational Review   Vol. 43   No. 3   August 1973, 386–416

It is our argument that schools not only socialize children in a general way but also exert a powerful and limiting influence on the development of sex roles. Instead of encouraging diversity within broad limits of conduct, they define specific attitudes, modes of acting, and opportunities which are appropriate for boys and girls. This serves to limit the choices open to each sex and contributes to a sense of inadequacy when individuals do not live up to the stringently defined norm or average. We acknowledge that a child's gender awareness and self-identification is critical to her or his development. However, it is reasonable to question the utility of inculcating within our children "fixed patterns of behaviors defined along traditional sex-role lines" (Emmerich, 1972, p. 7). Traditional sex role categories are simply conventions which hold significance in the social order of the day.

Educational reformers and critics in the last decade have heightened our awareness of the symbolism and hidden messages inherent in the structure of the school. They have shown us how schools function as sorting and classifying mechanisms and how schools foster and amplify such questionable personality traits as passivity, conformity, and dependency. Schools usually function in these ways *sub rosa*. Obviously, most students learn much more than reading, writing, and arithmetic. The content of the school or classroom may include curriculum materials, testing materials, and programmatically prescribed curricular patterns—which are the focus of this article—as well as teacher behavior, counseling practices, peer group influences, and many other instructional factors. All these factors convey multiple messages to children.

It is in these many ways that schools and their content carry hidden messages to the young about sex role mythologies in our society. The very structure of the school portrays males and females in somewhat idealized, rigid, and non-overlapping roles. As many developmental psychologists have noted, role models do contribute to the definition of the limits or boundaries of a child's self-expectations (Mischel, 1970). These limits may be set very early in life (Mead, 1971; Kagan, 1969; Levy, 1972). And yet, as Betty Levy (1972, p. 5) and others have noted, "as children grow older their awareness of 'appropriate' sex role behavior increases and becomes more restricted and stereotyped." Looft (1971), for example, asked a sample of six to eight-year-old children what they wanted to be when they grew up. He found a striking contrast between the variability of the boys' responses and the unanimity of the girls'. Seventy-five per cent of all the girls' responses in this age group were in two categories—teacher and nurse. The two most popular categories for boys—football player and fireman—were selected by less than ten per cent of the boys. In all, eighteen potential occupational categories were elicited from the males in the sample, eight from the girls. Differential socialization could account for these results.

There is increasing reason to believe that agents outside the home are important as differential socializers. Developmental theory, for example, points to the influence of the environment, including the family, in the rate and mode of children's development. Evidence of differential treatment of the sexes has not been well documented before the age of six (see Maccoby, 1972, for a review); but the research literature in this area is not ample. Perhaps acts of parents subtler than the looks, smiles, touches, and amount-talked-to counted by developmental psychologists are the important variables. Subtle expectations or punishments and sanctions against inappropriate sex-stereotyped behaviors may be the real differential socializers that parents are consciously or unconsciously using.

Although home influences certainly contribute to the sex role modeling which is prevalent in our society, we feel other influences such as schooling are important determinants to be considered. Research to date into the nature and origins of sex role stereotyping in schools has been limited and scattered at best. In undertaking the present studies, we sought to focus our research on some concrete aspects of schooling where stereotyping was blatantly fostered, and where changes in policy could be effected in relatively short order. Certainly hidden curriculum aspects of classroom interactions contribute to the images children have of themselves; and yet this area is so vague and undefined that mere documentation of the effects would not serve to change educational policy. The hidden curriculum exerts influence despite policy. Sex role stereotyping pervades every aspect of education and gradually it must be documented and rooted out of each area. For the moment, however, we have chosen to investigate its presence in elementary basal readers, to describe the sex bias in educational achievment tests, and to discuss some of the curricular requirements which are differentially imposed on male and female students throughout primary and secondary education.

We focus on elementary readers because a child's first contact with school is likely to leave a lasting impact. Since learning to read is the principal task of the early years at school, the content of the books with which children spend so much time merits investigation. Similarly, the study of sex bias in the content of achievement tests is important because the child so frequently encounters them during the school years. Finally, differential curriculum requirements for girls and boys automatically limit the choices each can make while they are in school and in later life.

We outline the research and findings in each of these three areas, and conclude with some recommendations for policy and research which begin to point the way to a less restricted system of education.

Sex Role Stereotyping in Early Readers

Much of the content of the school day in the first few grades is focused upon learning to read and write. Whether the child is taught in an open classroom or a traditional one, at some point the child encounters reading textbooks. These readers sustain an image of authority merely by being textbooks (California Advisory Commission, 1971; Child, Potter, and Levine, 1946). Unlike the substance of the textbooks a student encounters in later grades, the substance of early readers is not usually assumed to be central to the teaching and learning activity. The child is being taught to read, not to remember the intricacies of the story of Jack and Jill falling down the hill. Hence, we usually assume the content of the stories in the early readers is innocuous. But is it really? Do children learn something beyond how to read when they encounter these basal readers?

One of the first studies which examined this question of stereotyping in reading textbooks was the Child, Potter, and Levine (1946) content analysis of portions of third grade readers. They assumed, as have many researchers since, that principles of reinforcement and avoidance learning are operative as a child reads. "It is assumed that in reading a story a child goes through symbolically, or rehearses to himself, the episode that is described. The same principles, then, are expected to govern the effect of the reading on him as would govern the effect of actually going through such an incident in real life" (p. 3). Given these assumptions, they examined the role third grade readers would play in determining what motives children develop, how they learn to satisfy these motives, and what expectations they develop about the consequences of trying to satisfy these motives in various ways.

Their unit of analysis was the major theme of the reader. A theme was defined as a recurrent pattern of events, including the situation confronting a persons, the behaviors with which the person responded, and the consequences of that behavior to that person. They found striking differentiation of roles by sex in their sample of readers. Female characters more often showed affiliation, nurturance, and harm-avoidance, and were the ones nurtured. Males more often provided information, showed activity, aggression, achievement, construction, and behavior directed at gaining recognition. The general absence of females in these readers was as prominent as any differences in behavior: seventy-three per cent of all central characters were male, only twenty-seven per cent female.

Zimet (1970) studied primers spanning the period from 1600 to 1966 to determine whether boys and girls had always been portrayed as engaging in the undifferentiated activities found in modern readers. She found that diffusion or ambiguity of sex role models had increased over the period studied. However, "diffusion" was not clearly defined or quantified. A N.O.W. task force, Women on Words and Images (1972), reviewed 134 readers from fourteen publishers. Each story was categorized in terms of its hero or heroine by sex (male or female), age (adult or child), and whether it was a biography or fantasy story.

In 1972, Blom, Waite, Zimet, and Edge examined the activities portrayed in the first grade readers in twelve frequently used textbook series. They classified the activities according to: a) age of the child to which the activity would appeal (six, older, or younger); b) sex of the child to which the activity would appeal (as determined by agreement of the researchers); and c) the outcome of the activity in terms of success or failure. They found that masculine activities in these stories ended in failure more often than did feminine activities. (A caveat should be inserted here. These stories seem to have contained some ambiguity about the relationship between sex roles and activities, since forty-six per cent of all activities were performed by both boys and girls while only twenty-six per cent were performed by boys alone and only twenty-eight per cent by girls alone.)

When U'Ren (1971) studied textbooks recommended by the California State Board of Education she found seventy-five per cent of the main characters in these stories were male with less than twenty per cent of story space devoted to females. Many stories with male main characters presented no females at all, but female centered stories usually included males. Stories about girls were usually shorter than stories about boys. In another recent study, Graebner (1972) tried to determine whether the role of women has changed in elementary texts over the last decade. Five hundred and fifty-four stories were analyzed using texts from Scott, Foresman, 1962-63 and 1971, and Ginn, 1961 and 1969. She concluded that almost no change in the portrayal of the role of women has occurred and that texts "have not kept pace with a changing society" (p. 52).

In an analysis of a series of social studies books and readers produced by ten publishing houses, De Crow (1972) found no women portrayed as working outside the home except as a teacher or nurse. Those who were teachers and nurses were all labeled "Miss," perhaps implying that no married women work. Men were more often depicted as making decisions, including household decisions. Boys showed initiative, were creative, and did things while girls were fearful, dependent, and watched other people doing things. Friendships between boys, and between girls and boys, were frequently displayed, but friendships between girls were quite rare.

Potter (1972) has described the effect of books as symbolic models much as Child, Potter, and Levine did in justifying their content analysis. She argues that sequences of behavior which are punished or rewarded in stories should be vicariously rewarding and punishing to the reader. This effect is expected to vary with the ease the child has in identifying with a specific character, a phenomenon which may be partially dependent on such variables as age and sex.

These studies strongly suggest pervasive sex role stereotyping in early readers. But all are generally limited in that they seldom provide reliability data on categories used in content analysis, and they provide only descriptive statistics. While most of the studies agree that textbooks do portray stereotypic sex role models for children, few specify the types of stereotyping that occur.

Carol Jacklin and her associates (1972) undertook the present study to provide some information on the magnitude, direction, and type of stereotyping present in early basal readers.[1] If stereotyping does exist in these readers, they also wanted to find out whether it changed from one grade level to the next, from kindergarten to third grade, and whether publishers differ very much in the amount or kind of sex role stereotyping which occurs in their texts. Answers to these questions would be a basis for estimating the role early readers play in constricting and reinforcing

[1] The Jacklin research was sponsored by the Ford Foundation.

the behavior patterns and psychological characteristics a child associates with particular sex roles.

Four elementary reading textbook series were chosen for analysis. Those published by Ginn, Harper and Row (the California state approved series), and Scott, Foresman were chosen because of their widespread use. The Bank Street series was included because of its reputation for innovation. A complete list of specific texts analyzed can be obtained from the authors.

A systematic sample of every third story in the selected books was examined.[2] The total number of stories analyzed, by publisher, were: Bank Street, sixty-one; Ginn, sixty-nine; Harper & Row, sixty-three; and Scott, Foresman, seventy-seven.

Publisher, grade level, book and story title were recorded. Each character in each story, classified by age and sex, was coded on five additional categories: a) occurrence as main character; b) occurrence in specific environments; c) occurrence as exhibiting specific behaviors; d) occurrence as bearers of specific consequences; e) occurrence as recipients of specific behaviors and consequences. Stories were analyzed person by person, i.e., the environments, behaviors, and consequences related to a given character were scored for the entire story before the next character was begun. The actual taxonomy of attributes and categories employed in the procedure is presented below, with selected examples.

1. Main and secondary characters
2. Type of environment:
    Home
    Outdoors
    Place of business
    School
3. Behavior exhibited:
    Nurturant (helping, praising, serving)
    Aggressive (hitting, kicking, verbal put-downs)
    Self-care (dressing, washing)
    Routine-repetitive (eating, going to school)
    Constructive-productive (building, writing story, planning party)
    Physically exertive (sports, lifting heavy objects)
    Social-recreational (visiting someone, card games)
    Fantasy activity (doll play, cowboys and Indians)
    Directive (initiating, directing, demonstrating)
    Avoidance (stop trying, run away, shut eyes)
    Statement about self—positive, negative, neutral ("I have blue eyes," "I'm too stupid.")
    Problem-solving (producing idea, unusual combinations)

[1] The Jacklin research was sponsored by the Ford Foundation.
[2] Individual stories were analyzed as titled and listed in the table of contents of each book. To limit the number of stories examined, every third story listed was analyzed. Poems were omitted, as were animal or fantasy stories without people. Stories with historical settings were included. In cases where a single plot was continuous throughout an entire book, the procedure of analyzing every third unit listed in the table of contents was maintained.

Statements of information ("I know . . ."; non-evaluative observations about other people)

Expression of emotion (crying, laughing)

Conformity (express concern for rules, social norms, others' expectations, do as told)

General verbal (trivial motor behavior such as dropping something, looking for something, listening)

4. Types of consequences:

Positive consequences—

From others—directed toward subject (praise, recognition, support, signs of affection)

From self—self-praise, satisfaction

From situation—reaching goal, unintended positive results

Chance

Author's statement, text

Negative consequences—

From others—directed toward subject (criticism, correction, rejection of ideas)

From self

From situation—inability to reach goal, unintended negative results

Chance

Author's statement, text

*Neutral consequences—*not clearly positive or negative

In addition to the above, the agent and recipient of all consequences was noted. Changes in environment were recorded as they occurred. Data from individual stories at each grade level were collected separately for each publisher.

All scoring was performed by trained graduate students. Four potential sources of error in scoring existed: a) classification of the person-type; b) classification of the behavior; c) classification of the consequences; and d) classification of the environment. In order to assess inter-rater scoring reliability, eight stories were selected and each of the scorers was asked to score each of the stories, according to the taxonomy presented above. The total number of behaviors, consequences, and environments was recorded for each person-type in each of the eight stories. Pearson product moment correlation coefficients were computed among scorers on the total number of counts in each of these categories. Correlation coefficients for behaviors and consequences ranged from .953 to 1.00 with seventy-five per cent of the correlations greater than .98. There was perfect agreement between scorers for the environment categories.

Results

Combining data across all publishers and grade levels (first through third), fewer female than male characters appeared in these stories. A breakdown of the total number of characters by person-type in the sampled stories is presented in Table 1.

Because female characters occurred less frequently than males, comparisons of total frequencies within each category would reflect this difference. To avoid such

TABLE 1

Total Number of Characters in the Sampled Stories Displayed by Person-Type

	Child	*Adult*	TOTAL
Female	241	124	365
Male	324	256	580
	565	380	945

a misrepresentation, proportional comparisons were made within each category (i.e., behaviors, environments, and consequences), and chi-square tests of significance for differences in proportions were computed. Thus, taking into account the smaller total number of adult female characters, female adults are still significantly under-represented as main characters (see Table 2).

TABLE 2

Number of Main Characters by Age and Sex

	Female	*Male*
Adults		
Number main characters	7	33
Total number in stories	124	256
Chi square = 3.95; df = 1, p .05		
Children		
Number main characters	61	110
Total number in stories	241	324
Chi square = 3.49; df = 1, p. 05		

The behaviors, environments, and consequences associated with each person-type are presented in Tables 3, 4, and 5. Although only significant findings are discussed in the text, the results for all categories of behaviors, environments, and consequences are presented. In this way, each reader can examine the results from her or his own point of view.

The data are organized according to the frequency of each category by person-type, and the percentage of each category of the total counts for that attribute for each person-type. Two chi-square statistics were computed for each category. The first compared child female vs. child male proportions for each category. The second comparison was adult female vs. adult male proportions for each category.

As shown in Table 3, boys were portrayed as demonstrating significantly higher amounts of aggression, physical exertion, and problem-solving. Girls were significantly more often displayed as characters enveloped in fantasy, carrying out directive behaviors, and making (positive and negative) self-statements.

Adult males were shown in significantly higher proportions of constructive-productive behavior, physically exertive behavior, and problem-solving behavior. Adult females were shown in significantly higher proportions of conformity behavior and verbal behavior other than statements about themselves.

TABLE 3

Types of Behaviors Performed by Children (C) and Adults (A) of each Sex (M/F) Given in Frequencies and in Percentages of Total Behaviors by each Age and Sex

Behaviors	Frequencies and Percentages			
	CF n = 241	CM n = 324	AF n = 124	AM n = 256
Nurturant	101 6.3%	169 6.1%	109 14.3%	156 11.3%
Aggressive	19 1.2%***	90 3.3%	14 1.8%	26 1.9%
Routine-Repetitive	131 8.2%	261 9.5%	94 12.3%	153 11.1%
Constructive-Productive	21 1.3%	56 2.0%	2 0.3%***	60 4.4%
Physically Exertive	60 3.7%***	195 7.1%	5 0.7%***	68 4.9%
Fantasy	39 2.4%***	30 1.1%	5 0.7%	14 1.0%
Directive	221 13.8%	282 10.2%	156 20.5%	212 15.4%
Statements about self — positive	53*** 3.3%	46 1.7%	11 1.4%	12 0.9%
Statements about self — negative	8 0.5%*	2 0.1%	2 0.3%	5 0.4%
Statements about self — neutral	50 3.1%	64 2.3%	15 2.0%	23 1.7%
Problem solving	39 2.4%***	118 4.3%	12 1.6%***	65 4.7%
Statements of Information	203 12.7%	372 13.5%	99 13.0%	73 12.5%
Expression of Emotion	94 5.9%	153 5.6%	36 4.7%	85 6.2%
Conformity	121 7.5%	170 6.2%	21 2.8%*	17 1.2%
Watching	61 3.8%	111 4.0%	15 2.0%	37 2.7%
Other Verbal	224 14.0%	389 14.1%	131 17.2%*	186 13.5%
Totals: Frequency Percentage	1,604 90.1%	2,763 91.1%	763 95.6%	1,830 93.8%

* = p < .05
** = p < .01
*** = p < .001

NOTE: The percentages do not add to 100% because of the three omitted behaviors. Self-care, avoidance, social-recreational activities, expression of emotion, and the miscellaneous categories mentioned in the taxonomy were omitted due to their infrequent occurrence.

In examining the data of Table 4, we find no significant sex differences in the

TABLE 4

Types of Environments in Which Children (C) and Adults (A) of Each Sex (M/F), are Shown Given in Frequencies and in Percentages of Total Environments Shown by Each Age and Sex

Environment	Frequencies and Percentages			
	CF n = 241	CM n = 324	AF n = 124	AM n = 256
Home	97 34.2%	111 29.0%	83*** 54.6%	59 23.6%
Outdoors	157 55.2%	234 61.1%	47*** 30.9%	144 57.6%
Business	15 5.3%	16 4.2%	8*** 5.3%	40 16.0%
School	15 5.3%	22 5.7%	14*** 9.2%	7 2.8%
Totals: Frequency Percentage	284 100%	383 100%	152 100%	250 100%

* = p < .05
** = p < .01
*** = p < .001

environment categories in which children appear. However, there are significant sex differences for *every* environment category for adults. Adult males were found significantly more frequently outdoors or in business. Women were portrayed significantly more frequently in the home and in the school.

Table 5 presents the consequences experienced by each person-type. Young females were significantly more often shown as the recipients of positive consequences coming from a situation, and young males were significantly more often the recipients of positive consequences from their own action. Adult males were more frequently shown as the recipients of positive consequences coming from others and were shown as experiencing significantly more self-delivered negative consequences. In contrast, women more frequently experienced neutral consequences of acts.

In examining differences across grades, the total number of female characters declined sharply from the primers through the third grade readers. An analysis of the stories revealed two factors which contributed to this decline: a decrease of child females and an increase of adult males. One also finds an increase (with each grade level) in the number of significant sex differences between males and females for both child and adult behaviors, consequences, and environments. The stereotypic portrayal of male and female roles (both child and adult) increased with grade level.

TABLE 5

Types of Consequences for Children (C) and Adults (A) of Each Sex (M/F) Given in
Frequencies and in Percentages of Total Consequences for Each Age and Sex

Consequences	Frequency and Percentages			
	CF n = 241	CM n = 324	AF n = 124	AM n = 256
Positive-other	115 16%	230 17.1%	27 8.3%*	94 14.1%
Positive-self	17 2.4%*	57 4.2%	6 1.8%	14 2.1%
Positive-situation	336 46.6%***	488 36.3%	173 53.1%	328 49.3%
Positive-author	4 0.6%	14 1.0%	1 0.3%	7 1.1%
Neutral	87 12%	197 14.6%	57 12.5%	70 10.5%
Negative-other	73 10.1%	153 11.4%	30 9.2%	39 5.9%
Negative-self	4 0.6%	16 1.2%	0 0.0%*	12 1.8%
Negative-situation	84 11.7%	180 13.4%	32 9.8%	95 14.3%
Totals: Frequency Percentage	721 98.7%	1,346 98.3%	326 98.5%	666 99.1%

* = p < .05
** = p < .01
*** = p < .001

There were also significant differences in the way the sexes were portrayed in each publisher's series. Not one of the series was egalitarian in its presentation of the sexes, that is, not one presented either adult males or females or male and female children as more *alike* than different in behavior characteristics, personality traits, and expected behaviors. Harper & Row, among the texts examined, presented the fewest number of total sex differences among children and adults. Scott, Foresman and Bank Street had the greatest differentiation in the presentation of adult characters. Conversely, Ginn portrayed children more stereotypically in their series. The pattern of each publisher is similar to the general pattern across grades. In each case, incidence of child females in the stories declines from grades K through three and incidence of adult males in the stories increases from grades K through three. Also, number of adult females stays uniformly low, and number of child males stays uniformly high.

It may be argued that the authors and publishers of these books are simply mirroring the real world and that they should not be expected to provide a false picture of equality. But reality belies such an assertion. Children encounter women far more frequently than the average reading textbook would suggest. Even more to the point, children encounter women in many occupational roles and activities. As the 1973 *Economic Report of the President* noted, "One of the most important changes in the American economy in this century has been the increase in the proportion of women who work outside the home" (p. 89). Women constitute approximately thirty-eight per cent of the labor force and are distributed across a wide variety of occupational statuses. What is presented in the texts reviewed is an *idealized* view of society with the breadth and diversity of human endeavors eliminated.

Thus, it appears that these texts do not mirror the reality experienced by large groups of children: urban children, ghetto children, children with working mothers, children of divorced parents. Since we cannot depict for children what their lives will be, especially as we witness the rapid changes our society and culture are undergoing, the critical question becomes: What are we doing to children's aspirations when a sterile and unrealistic world is portrayed in the books that they read?

Although it is true that women today have fewer roles and opportunities than men and engage in more limited behaviors in more restricted settings, what are the consequences of portraying this state of affairs in elementary texts? Since textbooks reach a child at an early and impressionable age, children may attempt to perpetuate the stereotypes which the textbooks portray. The pervasiveness of sex role stereotyping in basal readers has been documented in this article. Future research efforts should explore in greater depth the relationship between such literary stereotypes and the development of sex roles.

In passing, it should be noted that many other stereotypes exist in these texts. The real world is more varied than the one depicted in elementary readers. Boys and girls, and men and women, are fat and skinny, short and tall. Boys and men are sometimes gentle, sometimes dreamers. Artists, doctors, lawyers, and college professors are sometimes mothers as well. Rather than limiting possibilities, elementary texts should seek to maximize individual development and self-esteem by displaying a wide range of models and activities. If the average is the only model presented to a child and therefore assumed to be the child's goal, most children—and most adults—would probably be unable to match the model.

Sex Bias in Educational Testing

Soon after children enter school they encounter a barrage of testing which is likely to continue throughout their school careers. Educators use tests for diagnosis and prescription in classrooms and for assessment and normative placement purposes as they sort, select, and classify students. Test data and comparative performance information are recorded on permanent cards which are transferred to each school a child attends. The child's placement on a variety of instruments is then noted by counselors as they advise the child about her or his future potential. Teachers also view the scores and often sort students into learning groups accordingly.

The wide usage of test data has been documented by a number of sources (Holmen & Docter, 1972; College Entrance Examination Board, 1970; Educational Testing Service, 1968). Holmen and Docter noted, for example, that approximately two hundred million achievement test forms and answer sheets are used annually in the United States alone. Moreover, there is evidence that students, teachers, and parents believe in the accuracy of intelligence test results (Brim *et al.*, 1969; Kirkland, 1971) and in the results of standardized achievement tests, and act upon them (Goslin, 1967). Tests are most widely used to assess educational achievement in the schools; Holmen and Docter point out that sixty-five per cent of all educational tests are achievement tests, while five per cent are used for counseling and guidance, and thirty per cent are used for selection and placement purposes. No one until now has systematically reviewed educational achievement tests to determine whether these tests contribute to the stereotyping of male and female roles. Are tests structured so as to reinforce existing stereotypic notions of male and female academic performance? Are the items selected to favor individuals who have encountered specific academic subjects (i.e., mathematics, science, home economics)? And do the items connote preference for males or females in their content or in the pronouns which dominate the content?

Carol Tittle and her associates (1973) noted this absence in the field and undertook a study[3] to examine two aspects of potential sex discrimination in achievement tests: sex bias in language usage (see Gunderson, 1972) and sex role stereotyping in item content. The goal of their study was to examine aspects of test content for potential sex bias; their study did not deal with bias in the uses of test results.

Several writers have recently noted the general male orientation of the English language, and what appears to be sex-typed usage of language. Strainchamps (1971) and Key (1971) have discussed the stereotyped characterization of English as masculine. Key outlined some of the preliminary work in language research which reported differing male and female usage of language, and several studies have examined classroom transcripts of four female and four male social studies teachers (Barron, 1971; Barron & Marlin, 1972; and Barron, Loflin, & Biddle, 1972). These latter studies begin to suggest the type of linguistic analysis which may be required to understand more fully the relationship between attributes of language, language usage, and the continuation of prejudice against women. Thus, bias in testing could arise in selecting item content (i.e., items drawn from chemistry or home economics), bias could be mainly a function of language use (i.e., word choice such

[3] This research was sponsored by the Ford Foundation. In addition to discussing the research described here in more detail, Tittle *et al.* review literature on test bias and the use of vocational and occupational tests, and present an extensive annotated bibliography on women and testing.

as generic pronouns) and not subject to change by the test publisher, or bias could result from a combination of selection and usage. A large ratio of male to female references, for example, could result primarily from the use of generic nouns and pronouns, and would be less susceptible to change than if bias had resulted from content selection.

While a series of studies which have examined stereotyping in children's books and textbooks are available (Key, 1971; Frasher & Walker, 1972; and Grambs, 1972; as well as Jacklin's study described in the previous section), not one study has systematically reviewed the educational measurement literature and analyzed educational and occupational achievement tests for sex role stereotyping. Tittle's study included an exploratory survey of several aspects of educational testing, with a view toward identifying stereotypic presentations of women. It provides an important sequel to Jacklin's work.

The data examined in this study consist of test batteries from each of the major test publishing companies.[4] The procedures and recording forms for data collection were developed and pretested by two graduate students specializing in educational measurement.[5] The recorders first tabulated language usage defined as the ratio of male nouns and pronouns to female nouns and pronouns. A ratio close to 1.00 would indicate an equal use of male and female nouns and pronouns. A ratio above 1.00 would indicate that males were referred to more frequently than females, and in this sense would be indicative of biased content.

Two sets of analyses were performed to determine whether bias resulted from content selection or from the nature of the English language. The first analysis was designed to examine each subtest in each test battery. Generic nouns and pronouns were tallied. Ratios of male to female nouns and pronouns were then compared to determine whether language usage or content was sexually biased. One set which is based on all nouns and pronouns, including generic ones, is labeled *All*. A second set, labeled *Regular,* excludes the generic nouns and pronouns and counts only those nouns and pronouns which refer specifically to males and females. If the ratio of males to females is greater than 1.00 for the *Regular* ratios as well as for the *All* ratios, then it can be concluded that the bias is largely a function of content selection and is therefore readily subject to change. Additionally, there are nouns which are not sex-designated in and of themselves, but are designated by a pronoun following them. Here, the test publisher can provide a balance in designating the sex as female in such contexts as "the doctor" or "the lawyer."

In the second analysis, recorders were asked to identify stereotypic content and list such instances on the same form used to record nouns and pronouns. General

[4] The tests analyzed include the California Achievement Tests, Iowa Test of Basic Skills, the Iowa Test of Educational Development, Metropolitan Achievement Tests, Sequential Tests of Educational Progress, SRA Achievement Series, Stanford Early School Achievement Test, and the Stanford Achievement Test.

[5] The graduate students were Karen McCarthy and Jane Stekler of the City University of New York.

guidelines were given the recorders to suggest types of sex role stereotypes which might occur in test content. Do females appear in other than traditional jobs such as teachers and nurses? Are girls shown as active and independent? The question was whether educational achievement tests contain the same sex role stereotyping of women that is present in other educational materials. Stereotyped activities for women were identified: Mary helped her mother set the table. Women mentioned in a stereotyped profession were also listed: the teacher . . . Mrs. Jones; the secretary . . . Miss Ward. Items or descriptions which assign women to a secondary or helpless status were included as stereotypic: Bob was elected class president and Susan was elected secretary.

Two other categories listed as identifying stereotypic content were those which limited female occupational pursuits and references to activities which were distinctly male or female. It should be noted that the purpose of this aspect of the study was to produce examples of sex stereotypes and was not considered a formal content analysis.

Results

Table 6 shows the ratio of male noun and pronoun referents to female noun and pronoun referents for the educational achievement test batteries analyzed. These total battery data were obtained by summing the male-female references for all the tests in the battery and computing the ratios for the total counts.

There are few differences between the conclusions which would be drawn by using the ratios based on *All* nouns and pronouns and those based only on *Regular* nouns and pronouns. As can be seen in the table, deleting the generic pronouns reduces only a few of the ratios. Thus, any bias which exists is primarily a function of the content of educational achievement tests rather than the nature of the language, and should be amenable to change by test developers and publishers.

Each test battery, with one exception, showed a higher frequency of male nouns and pronouns. In Table 6 the distribution of *All* noun and pronoun ratios indicates that in all but eight of the twenty-seven batteries analyzed, the ratios of male to female are greater than 2.00. In one case, the ratio is as high as 14.00. There is a tendency for the test batteries developed for the early grade levels, kindergarten through grade three or four, to have lower ratios than the test batteries for the higher grades. This is largely because the tests at the early grades have fewer extended reading passages. Another reason for the low ratio may be the home orientation of primary education. Examples and discussion may revolve more around the home and mother. These findings are analogous to those in the previously discussed Jacklin *et al.* report; the pattern of stereotypic portrayal of males and females heightens and intensifies as grade level is raised.

Our analysis of language usage suggests that educational achievement tests reflect the general bias in school instructional materials, referring much more frequently to males and their world, seldom balancing references and drawing on content equally for the two sexes. Nevertheless, since this bias results from the use of regular rather than generic nouns and pronouns, it is susceptible to change.

Sex role stereotypes evident in item content were also recorded for each test analyzed. Women were portrayed almost exclusively as homemakers or in the pur-

TABLE 6

Ratios of Male Noun and Pronoun (nM) Referents to Female Noun and Pronoun (nF) Referents — Educational Achievement Test Batteries

| Test | Total No. of Test Items
Items | Nouns and Pronouns | | | |
		All nM/nF = Ratio		Regular nM/nF = Ratio	
Test A					
Grade level 4 – 6	343	190/47	4.04	190/47	4.04
Grade level 6 – 9	337	84/46	1.83	84/46	1.83
Grade level 9 – 12	349	93/36	2.58	93/36	2.58
Test B					
Grade level 3 – 8	1,232	1221/368	3.31	1211/368	3.29
Test C					
Grade level 9 – 12	330	262/195	1.34	219/195	1.12
Test D					
Grade level 1.5 – 2.4	174	51/59	.86	48/54	.89
Grade level 2.5 – 3.4	257	137/86	1.59	137/86	1.59
Grade level 3.5 – 4.9	300	124/42	2.95	121/42	2.88
Grade level 5.0 – 6.9	534	181/44	4.11	178/44	4.05
Grade level 7.0 – 9.5	524	198/51	3.88	195/51	3.82
Test E					
Grade level 3 – 5	420	366/103	3.55	322/98	3.29
Grade level 6 – 9	420	443/150	2.95	408/149	2.74
Grade level 9 – 12	470	468/134	3.49	360/120	3.00
Grade level 13 – 14	320	448/32	14.00	390/32	12.19
Test F					
Grade level 1 – 2	320	179/88	2.03	179/88	2.03
Grade level 2 – 4	276	333/241	1.38	330/234	1.41
Grade level 4 – 9	1,070	1513/231	6.55	1462/229	6.38
Test G					
Grade level K – 1	126	217/93	2.33	217/93	2.33
Grade level 1	259	192/168	1.14	190/168	1.13
Grade level 1.5 – 2: Form 1	251	134/53	2.52	123/51	2.41
Grade level 1.5 – 2: Form 2	251	119/78	1.53	115/78	1.47
Grade level 2 – 3: Form 1	409	209/89	2.34	192/87	2.20
Grade level 2 – 3: Form 2	409	143/87	1.64	143/87	1.64
Grade level 4 – 5	540	221/83	2.66	198/71	2.78
Grade level 5 – 6	544	171/58	2.95	166/58	2.96
Grade level 7 – 9	532	181/46	3.93	157/46	3.41
Grade level 9 – 12	478	245/40	6.13	242/39	6.21

suit of hobbies (e.g., "Mrs. Jones, the President of the Garden Club . . .").[6] Young girls carry out "female chores" (e.g., Father helps Betty and Tom build a play-house; when it's completed, "Betty sets out dishes on the table, while Tom carries in the chairs . . .").[7]

In numerous activity-centered items, boys were shown playing, climbing, camp-ing, hiking, taking on roles of responsibility and leadership. Girls help with the cooking, buy ribbon and vegetables, and, when participating in any active pursuit, take the back seat to the stronger, more qualified boys (e.g., Buddy says to Clara, "Oh, I guess it's all right for us boys to help girls. I've done some good turns for girls myself, because I'm a Scout.")[8]

In addition, some items implied that the majority of professions are closed to women. A reading comprehension passage about the characteristics and qualifica-tions required for the Presidency began with the statement: "In the United States, voters do not directly choose the man they wish to be President." It repeatedly says "he must be," "he must have . . ."[9] Most short biographies were written about men. Practically all teachers were listed as female, while professors, doctors, and presi-dents of companies were listed as male. If a team was mentioned, it usually had all male members. Thus an examination of the content of these tests for sex role stereotypes suggests that achievement tests do not differ from other instructional materials in education: their content contains numerous sex role stereotypes.

Tittle's analysis of educational achievement tests demonstrates both substantial bias in the number of male and female noun and pronoun references, and frequent stereotypic portrayals in the content. These aspects of testing could easily be altered to present a more equitable and less prejudiced view of women, for example, by showing women in a variety of occupations and activities. Test publishers can easily address these criticisms by initiating a review procedure very early in the test de-velopment process. Specifications to item writers can encourage a less stereotypic presentation. Examples can be drawn from history, literature, science, and other areas where women have made contributions. Test editors can review the content before specific items are tried out. Review procedures to ensure balanced presenta-tion of males and females can be instituted when a test is assembled.[10]

One last point should be stressed. Tests have been used extensively in school settings with little thought given to the socializing aspects of their content. The last decade has heightened awareness of potential cultural bias in the content of

[6] *California Achievement Tests*—Language Usage, Level 5, Form A, 1970, item no. 43, p. 43.
[7] SRA Achievement Series—Reading 1-2, Form D, 1963, p. 17.
[8] SRA Achievement Series—Grammatical Usage, Multilevel Edition, Form D, 1963, p. 45.
[9] *SRA Achievement Series*—Reading, Multilevel Edition, Form D, 1963, p. 76. See also *Sequential Tests of Educational Progress*, Series II Reading Form 1A, 1969, p. 18.
[10] Women on Words and Images (1972) describe a form for evaluating sexism in readers. A similar form could be developed for test content, considering the illustrations, main characters and char-acteristics of children and adults. The categories developed by Jacklin *et al.* could also be valuable in a review procedure.

testing. Perhaps now is the time to stress that testing instruments not only *assess* but also convey and *teach* much about the latent aspects of our culture—our prejudices, our mores, and our way of life.

Curricular Requirements

The small amount of evidence available on school curriculum suggests it too may promote sex role stereotyping and sex discrimination. Acceptable avenues for the expression of a variety of interests are prescribed differently for males and females. Girls are told at an early age that boys are mechanically and scientifically inclined while girls excel at reading and language. To some extent this is reinforced by a division of males and females into seventh grade shop and home economics. Later vocational education tracks usually vary by sex; boys acquire a series of shop and mechanical skills while girls prepare for a life as a wife and mother, sometimes with secretarial skills on the side in case there is need to supplement a husband's income. Physical education classes for the most part are segregated by sex and as such often establish different physical expectations for individual performance by sex. All males are expected to be athletic superstars, while girls are not expected to aspire to anything beyond a good intramural fray. These expectations are often vigorously reinforced with substantially different financial allocations to boys' and girls' physical education programs.

Sex bias in vocational and physical education curricula is relatively easy to document and shall be the focus of this discussion. The deliberate segregation of the sexes according to preconceived notions of appropriate curricular activities is open to question in terms of the limitations it imposes on both sexes. Whose decision has led to sex-segregated classes? How pervasive is such segregation? Are such decisions made by students and their families or tacitly made *a priori*?

Education is not specifically mentioned in the United States Constitution, and hence its control constitutionally becomes the prerogative of each state. All fifty states have explicit constitutional provisions and numerous statutes and regulations which establish specific state responsibilities for the education of their citizenry. The National Education Association is one of the few existing sources of information about states' curricular and graduation requirements (Thompson, 1972). Most state requirements address only a limited number of academic subjects and a few non-academic ones like physical education, health, and practical arts. According to the NEA Educational Research Service (1972), no states patently discriminate by sex in the specification of their curricular requirements although variations by state do occur in those curricular items specified as mandatory and those considered to be the option of local school boards and administrators. Decisions about curricula and sexual composition of classes largely become the prerogative of local authorities.

Perhaps the most extreme form of discrimination in the exercise of local options occurs in metropolitan areas where a high concentration of students allows specialized high schools to appear. By design or default they usually become unisexual institutions and often male institutions. Given that public funds support these public schools, simple equity would require that male and female students have equal access to the programs offered. Females frequently are not admitted, and, when they are, often face more stringent entrance requirements, i.e., higher academic performance is demanded (Bryan, 1972; New York N. O.W., 1972). For example, of those courses listed in *Public High Schools, New York City* (New York City Board of Education, 1970), seventy-seven are designated as technical courses restricted to males and thirty-six are designated for females. Discrimination does not stop at the door to the classroom; as the New York City Board of Education (1972) notes, the system of vocational education in New York City discriminates against girls in three significant ways. First, more class slots are open to boys than to girls. Second, a "greater variety of more useful courses" are offered to boys than to girls, and, finally, even within a vocational program, such as fashion or dentistry, courses are labeled as being appropriate for one sex or the other. Such sex distinctions in vocational courses limit potential occupational roles for both males and females.

In the case of the vast majority of secondary schools in the United States local educational options are translated into some variation on the comprehensive high school theme James Conant advocated (1959). These options often result in a curriculum which is discriminatory in terms of specified vocational tracks and physical education courses. Frequently such discrimination occurs with the implicit consent of school boards. Data available from the USOE's Bureau of Adult, Vocational and Technical Education (1972) substantially reflect this skewed sorting of students into "sex-appropriate" vocational tracks. Ninety-five per cent of all students registered in vocational agriculture courses are male. These figures represent the beginning of a new trend, for in 1970 no females were enrolled in agriculture. The field of health has also recently experienced a shift of minimal magnitude. In 1965, males constituted 4.9 per cent of those registered in health courses, as compared to 12.3 per cent of the health student population in 1971. Male and female distributions in other categories for which the Bureau aggregates data conform to the same stereotypic pattern: ninety-three per cent of all students registered in consumer and homemaking courses are female; eighty-five per cent of those enrolled in home economics courses which lead to gainful employment are female; ninety-two per cent of those registered in technical courses—metallurgy, engineering, oceanography, police science—are male; seventy-five per cent in office occupations are female; and eighty-nine per cent of all registered in trade and industrial courses are male.

These issues take on particular urgency when it is realized that recently there has been renewed interest in questions of career education and choice. The year 1971 saw the largest investment ever in vocational education by federal, state, and local governments, a combined increase of twenty-two per cent over 1970 ($1,952,-000,000 by state and local governments and $396,000,000 by the federal government). In addition, career education has become a banner program of the current

Secretary of Health, Education, and Welfare. Renewed interest in vocational and career education is thus reflected in financial and political support, and yet the distribution of the sexes into fields over the last decade has continued to follow traditional sex role patterns.

Perhaps such simple injustices could be accepted if labor market statistics revealed a different reality. In 1971, however, according to the Women's Bureau of the United States Department of Labor (1972), one-third of the thirty-two million women who were in the labor force were clerical workers. These figures included 3.6 million stenographers, typists, and secretaries. Seventeen per cent of the thirty-two million were service workers, fifteen per cent were professional or technical workers, of whom 1.9 million were teachers, and thirteen per cent were operatives, chiefly in factories. Women who were employed full-time in 1970 earned as a median income $5,323, or 59.4 per cent of the $8,966 median income earned by fully employed men. Surely no one would argue that women deliberately prefer such narrow, low paying, and low status sectors of the labor market. In fact, once given the opportunity, a noticeable insurgence of women is found in those fields which traditionally had been masculine domains. Soon these fields aggressively recruit female participation (Hedges, 1970; Zellner, 1972; Levitin, Quinn, and Staines, 1973).

As Crowley, Levitin, and Quinn (1973) point out:

The 'average woman' is a statistical creation, a fiction. She has been used to defend the status quo of the labor market, on the assumption that knowing the sex of an employee reliably predicts his or her job attitudes. This assumption is false. Knowing that a worker is female allows us to predict that she will hold a job in a 'woman's field,' and that she will be substantially underpaid for a person of her qualifications. But knowing that a worker is female does not help us much to predict what she wants from her job. (p. 96)

While half of all women employed in 1969 were concentrated in 21 of the 250 distinct occupations listed by the Census Bureau (Hedges, 1970), an increasing proportion of these women assumed responsibility for some portion of their own or their household's income during their lifetime (Levitin, Quinn, and Staines, 1973). Thus to argue that women prefer low incomes and less secure positions in the labor market is fallacious. Unfortunately, the onus of such occupational distributions must lie at the feet of industries seeking unskilled cheap labor, and on the shoulders of schools which counsel and prepare women for limited future occupational roles.

Allocation of money to support sports and physical education programs represents another very clear instance in which resources are allocated differentially on the basis of sex. The tendency to support a major sports program for boys but not for girls starts early, often at the initiative of the local community. While there have been a few recent outstanding exceptions, communities typically organize Little League baseball and football teams, leaving young girls to their dolls. Eight-year-old girls quickly learn that only males "are proficient enough to form leagues, play regulation length games with paid umpires, uniforms, full schedules, and championship playoffs" (Dunning, 1972, pp. 28-29). Such activities are usually neither sponsored nor organized by the elementary school, but do set the precedent for sex-segregated physical education after the fourth or fifth grade. Little rationale other than tradition exists for such segregation when students are being taught the same sport and are of approximately the same height, strength, weight, and skill level. Of course, young males are encouraged by their family, the media, and their peers to spend many hours a week on athletic activities outside of school, and by the time they are ten or eleven their athletic skills have been finely honed.

Real discrimination in the allocation of time, financial resources, and physical facilities is most evident in junior and senior high school. The largest swimming pool, the best playing fields, the finest tennis courts are usually reserved for male sporting events. Most schools offer male students a sports program composed of varsity competition in football, basketball, baseball, track, swimming, and other sports. These activities are considered to be an essential element in the comprehensive educational package offered by the school. Coaches are hired, uniforms purchased, and facilities built. Such expenditures are considered to be legitimate line-items in a school's budget. Seldom does a school's budget reflect comparable line-item expenditures for a girls' athletic program. Girls Athletic Associations (GAA) are usually voluntary, "out-of-school" programs. At a high school in California, for example, "the GAA must sell hot dogs at football games, bake cupcakes and other such things to support their limited program which . . . includes field hockey, basketball, volleyball, tennis and softball. In other words, there is no pre-existing program at the high school for female athletes or those girls who wish to become athletes. If the GAA cannot sell enough hot dogs and popcorn, there will be no field hockey team. If enough cupcakes aren't sold or bottles collected, basketball may have to go. The boys' programs do not face similar problems" (Dunning, p. 26).

Even the salary supplements that coaches receive highlight the school's discrimination in physical education. According to the N.E.A. (1972), in 1971-72 the extracurricular salary supplements for head coaches ranged from a low of $1,226 to a high of $5,500. Intramural sports coaches received supplements which ranged from $554 to $1,920 and the cheerleader advisor received from a low of $347 to a high of $2,240. These salary supplements were not reported by sex but it is highly likely that the head coach is a male and the cheerleader advisor and possibly some of the intramural coaches are females. Schools do communicate in many ways that boys' athletic programs are of greater significance to the school's educational programs than are those for girls; the best physical facilities are reserved for male use, financial support of girls' programs is minimal, and an elaborate system of athletic options for girls and boys of varying abilities is nonexistent.

It is not our intent in this article to substitute one curricular prescription for another, nor do we suggest that any arbitrary concept of equal curricular opportunity is either desirable or feasible. We do assert that girls and boys should be treated by the school as individuals each with her or his own individual curricular interests and needs. Schools should make available to girls as well as boys a full range of options in physical education and interscholastic athletics. Shorthand and typing skills are at least as useful to boys as woodworking. The school curriculum has clearly functioned to reinforce rigid, educationally discriminatory, and sexually stereotypic attitudes in both students and school staff. Schools seeking to free the next generation of youth from the dysfunctional constraints of the past will have to change curricular requirements and redress inequities in the options open to boys and girls. But in order to accomplish these structural reforms schools must face the serious problem of changing the attitudes of administrators, counselors, and teachers.

Conclusions

Until quite recently, no one had challenged the long-standing tendency of school boards, state boards of education, and other authoritative educational bodies to mandate curricular requirements and other educational practices which differ by sex. Now a substantial number of local groups have begun to do just that. Organizations have begun to analyze the textbooks being used in districts around the country, to challenge physical educational policies, to press for class action suits on vocational educational issues, and to review employment advancement practices.[11]

Many of these activities have been spurred by recent federal legislation, specifically, Title IX of the Education Amendments Act of 1972, Executive Order #11246, Title VII of the Civil Rights Act of 1964, and the Equal Pay Act, all of which prohibit discrimination on the basis of sex in federally assisted programs. Unfortunately, to date no substantial federal effort has been launched to notify states and local school systems of the content of this legislation. Guidelines for enforcement of Title IX are in the process of being designed by H.E.W.'s Office of Civil Rights. Once these guidelines are adopted, legal action against school districts in violation of the intent of the legislation becomes an imminent possibility. Until such guidelines are issued, complaints are processed under the aegis of Executive Order #11246 and Title VII of the Civil Rights Act of 1964, both of which prohibit discrimination in employment on the basis of sex, and the Equal Pay Act, which prohibits discrimination in salaries on the basis of sex. Once issued, the guidelines

[11] Best known among these groups are Women on Words and Images in New Jersey; the Emma Willard Task Force in Minneapolis; Know, Inc., in Pennsylvania; and numerous local chapters of the National Organization for Women. An excellent source for information regarding these groups and the grounds upon which they intend to test these issues is the Resource Center on Sex Roles in Education which has been established under the auspices of the National Foundation for the Improvement of Education, in Washington, D.C. The Resource Center was established to offer technical assistance to state departments of education and local school districts as they begin to understand and adjust to recent federal landmark legislation which bears on the issue of sex discrimination in public education.

will indicate the extent to which federal leverage will be applied to reduce sex discrimination in public educational agencies. Evidence regarding H.E.W.'s record to date, however, does not support an optimistic outlook (Knox & Kelly, 1972).

There are, of course, many actions which local school districts, school boards, state educational agencies, and textbook and test publishers can take which need not wait for the prod of federal legislation (see Lyon & Saario, 1973). Much of the structure and content of the American school system has evolved rather haphazardly over time and without grand design; there is very little that ought to be sacrosanct about the system. Local administrators and educational policy makers need to identify and eradicate all those elements of sex discrimination in their schools which prohibit and constrain the options of every adult and student in the system. Textbook and test publishers need to marshal their products in the same way. The issue ultimately becomes a matter of conscience and simple justice.

This article has presented a few examples of the way in which existing elements of the school contribute to sex role stereotyping and discriminate against both male and female students. Textbooks and other curricular materials, testing and counseling procedures, and mandated curriculum and sports requirements sort and classify students in alignment with society's reified notions regarding appropriate sex role behaviors.

We have not addressed a series of far knottier questions. To what extent are children already socialized by the time that they reach the school so that changing school policy will make little or no difference in shaping attitudes? Even if it is assumed that schools have an impact on children's attitudes, how can aspects of the schooling process which contribute most strongly to sex role stereotyping be isolated? And once relevant schooling factors have been identified, what is the best way to study their impact upon children? Questions about the ways in which teachers react to, reward, and reinforce the behaviors of male and female students have not been addressed in this article. Some researchers argue that girls more than boys tend to imitate and respond positively to teacher reinforcements (see Smith, 1972, for a review). If that is the case, then girls are responding to strong pressures to be compliant, passive, tractable, and dependent. The same researchers suggest that an opposite trend may be operating for boys. Getting less approval from teachers and needing less from their peers, boys may become more self-motivated and more confident. There is a school of thought which argues the converse, i.e., that schools reinforce femininity in boys (Sexton, 1969). Obviously, more empirical research on the impact of teachers' behaviors upon sex role development is needed.

Little longitudinal research has been conducted in the field of sex role development, and its absence has contributed to confusion regarding the relative impact of hormones and socialization upon the development of sex role differences. At Stanford University, Maccoby and Jacklin recently initiated an eight-year study of two cohorts of children from birth to the age of first school attendance to examine the interaction of hormones and parental socialization practices. This study and similar or related research, such as John Money's at Johns Hopkins, should illuminate to some extent the "nature-nurture" argument as it is related to the development of sex differences. Parallel and longitudinal studies which simultaneously test the multiplicity of theories in the field of sex role development could clarify the significance of some of these models and could move the field toward greater theoretical sophistication (see Emmerich, 1972).

A new concept has been introduced into the common parlance of the field of sex role development by Sandra Bem (1972). Many individuals, according to Bem, do not fall at the extremes in the distribution of such sex-related characteristics as aggression, dependence, and sociability. Rather, most people evidence behaviors which are truly androgynous, i.e., neither representative of maleness nor femaleness. Bem is now attempting to develop instruments which could establish the degree to which such traits are present in an individual's behavior. Studies like Bem's have begun to question the stereotypic perception of male and female behavior which is implicit in many research designs. Too frequently variations between the sexes have been reported and magnified while the variation which exists within each sex category has been overlooked or masked.

Once research has documented the impact of all school factors upon sex role development (i.e., guidance counselors, peer group influences, the media used in school settings, the intervention of the home, in addition to those variables already discussed), then the task becomes one of developing and testing new behavioral models for school settings. As yet, little is known about how effective androgynous materials and behaviors will be upon future generations of students. Most studies simply scratch the surface. Present understanding of the socialization and maturation processes which lead toward mature sex role identities is rather limited.

The examples of sex discrimination addressed in this article are merely symptomatic of a far greater and more pervasive phenomenon in our society. All social institutions promote stereotypic conceptions of male and female roles; all societies contain their own peculiar sex role mythologies. Some permit far greater latitude in the definition of boundaries between male and female roles than others. The definition of these boundaries, as Ruth Benedict (1961) so eloquently argued, is nothing more than a cultural artifact. Some societies rigidly adhere to a bimodel distribution of behavioral traits, aptitudes, and emotional expression; others acknowledge the necessity of having a community of adults whose characteristics overlap considerably on a number of dimensions.

We argue for such diversity, and for more flexible and more tolerant definitions of sex roles, because the livelihood and health of the American nation depend upon the talents of all its members, because the absence of restrictive stereotypes enhances the liberty and human potential of all persons, and because simple fairness and equity demand it.

References

Barron, N. M. Sex-typed language: The production of grammatical cases. *Acta Sociologica*, 14, No. 1 & 2 (1971), 24-42.

Barron, N. M., Loflin, M. D., & Biddle, B. J. *Sex role and the production of case frames.* Columbia, Mo.: University of Missouri, 1972.

Barron, N. M., & Marlin, M. J. Sex of the speaker and the grammatical case and gender of referenced persons. Technical Report C153. Columbia, Mo.: Center for Research in Social Behavior, University of Missouri, 1972.

Bem, S. L. The measurement of psychological androgyny. Unpublished paper, Stanford University, 1972.

Benedict, R. *Patterns of culture.* New York: Houghton-Mifflin, 1961.

Blom, G. E., Waite, R. R., Zimet, S. G., & Edge, S. What the story world is like. In Zimet (Ed.), *What children read in school.* New York: Grune & Stratton, 1972, 1-18.

Boserup, E. *Women's role in economic development.* New York: St. Martin's Press, 1970.

Brim, O. G., Jr., Glass, D. C., Neulinger, J., & Firestone, I. J. *American beliefs and attitudes about intelligence.* New York: Russell Sage Foundation, 1969.

Bronfenbrenner, U. *Two worlds of childhood.* New York: Russell Sage Foundation, 1970.

Bryan, G. Discrimination on the basis of sex in occupational education in the Boston public schools. Paper prepared for the Boston Commission to Improve the Status of Women, Eastern Massachusetts Chapter of N.O.W., 1972.

California Advisory Commission on the Status of Women. *California women.* Sacramento, Calif.: Author, 1971.

Child, I. L., Potter, E. H., & Levine, E. L. Children's textbooks and personality development: An explanation in the social psychology of education. *Psychological Monographs,* 60, No. 3 (1946), 1-54.

Civil Liberties in New York, Vol. XX, No. 8, May 1973.

College Entrance Examination Board. *Report of the commission on tests: I. Righting the balance.* New York: 1970.

Collins, R. A conflict theory of sexual stratification. In H. P. Dreitzel (Ed.), *Family, marriage and the struggle of the sexes: Recent sociology.* No. 4. New York: Macmillan, 1972.

Conant, J. B. *The American high school today.* New York: Macmillan, 1959.

Crowley, J. E., Levitin, T. E., & Quinn, R. P. Seven deadly half-truths about women. *Psychology Today,* 6 (March 1973), 94-96.

De Crow, K. Look, Jane, look! See Dick run and jump! Admire him! In S. Anderson (Ed.), *Sex differences and discrimination in education.* Worthington, Ohio: Charles A. Jones, 1972.

Dunning, R. Discrimination: Women in sports. Unpublished manuscript, F35 No. Campus Way, Davis, California, 1972.

Economic report of the President. Washington, D.C.: U. S. Government Printing Office, 1973.

Educational Testing Service, Evaluation and Advisory Service. *State testing programs: A survey of functions, tests, materials and services.* Princeton, N. J.: Author, 1968.

Emmerich, W. Continuity and change in sex role development. Paper presented at a Symposium in Sex Role Learning in Childhood and Adolescence, American Association for the Advancement of Science, Washington, D.C., December, 1972.

Emmerich. W. Socialization and sex-role development. In P. B. Baltes & K. W. Schaie (Eds.), *Life-span developmental psychology: Personality and socialization.* New York: Academic Press, 1973.

Frasher, R., & Walker, A. Sex roles in early reading textbooks. *The Reading Teacher,* 25 (May 1972), 741-9.

Goslin, D. A. *Teachers and testing.* New York: Russell Sage Foundation, 1967.

Graebner, D. B. A decade of sexism in readers. *The Reading Teacher,* 26 (October 1972).

Grambs, J. D. Sex-stereotypes in instructional materials, literature, and language: A survey of research. *Women Studies Abstracts,* 1 (Fall 1972), 1-4, 91-94.

Gunderson, D. V. Sex roles in reading and literature. Paper presented at the meeting of the American Educational Research Association, Chicago, April, 1972.

Hedges, J. N. Women at work: Women workers and manpower demands in the 1970's. *Monthly Labor Review,* 93 (June 1970), 19-29.

Holmen, M. G., & Docter, R. F. *Educational and psychological testing: A study of industry and its practices.* New York: Russell Sage Foundation, 1972.

Jacklin, C., Heuners, M., Mischell, H. N., & Jacobs, C. As the twig is bent: Sex role stereotyping in early readers. Unpublished manuscript, Department of Psychology, Stanford University, 1972.

Kagan, J. The three faces of continuity in human development. In D. A. Goslin (Ed.), *Handbook of socialization theory and research.* Chicago: Rand McNally, 1969.

Key, M. R. The role of male and female in children's books—dispelling all doubt. *Wilson Library Bulletin,* 46 (October 1971), 167-76.

Kirkland, M. C. The effects of tests on students and schools. *Review of Educational Research,* 41 (October 1971), 303-350.

Knox, H., & Kelly, F. A look at women in education: Issues and answers for HEW. Report of the Commissioner's Task Force on the Impact of Office of Education Programs on Women. Unpublished report, Washington, D.C., November, 1972.

Levitin, T. E., Quinn, R. P., & Staines, G. L. A woman is fifty-eight per cent of a man. *Psychology Today,* 6 (March 1973), 89–91.

Levy, B. Sexism, sex role, and the school in the sex role stereotyping of girls: A feminist review of the literature. Unpublished manuscript, Columbia University, 1972.

Looft, W. R. Sex differences in the expression of vocational aspirations by elementary school children. *Developmental Psychology,* 5 (November 1971), 366.

Lyon, C., & Saario, T. Women in public education: Sexual discrimination in promotions. *Phi Delta Kappan,* 54 (October 1973), 120–123.

Maccoby, E. Differential socialization of boys and girls. Paper presented at the meeting of the American Psychological Association, Honolulu, September, 1972. In E. E. Maccoby and C. N. Jacklin, *Psychology of sex differences.* Palo Alto, Calif.: Stanford University Press, 1974.

Malcolm, A. H. Most common verb in schools, study finds, is . . . is. *New York Times,* September 4, 1971, p. 22.

Mead, M. Early childhood experience and later education in complex cultures. In M. L. Wax, S. Diamond, & F. O. Gearing (Ed.), *Anthropological perspectives on education.* New York: Basic Books, 1971.

Mischel, W. Sex-typing and socialization. In P. H. Mussen (Ed.), *Carmichael's manual of child psychology.* Vol. 2. New York: John Wiley & Sons, 1970.

Money, J., & Ehrhardt, A. A. *Man and women, boy and girl.* Baltimore: Johns Hopkins University Press, 1972.

National Education Association Educational Research Service. *State graduation requirements.* Washington, D.C.: Author, May, 1972.

National Education Association. *Salary schedule supplements for extra duties,* 1971-72. Research Memo, Washington, D.C.: April, 1972.

New York Chapter, N.O.W., Education Committee. *Report on sex bias in the public schools.* New York: Author, 1972.

New York City Board of Education. *Public high schools, New York City 1970-71.* New York: Bureau of Educational and Vocational Guidance, 1970.

New York State Commission on the Quality, Cost and Financing of Elementary and Secondary Education Report. Vol. 2. New York: Viking Press, 1972.

Potter, B. A. The shaping of woman. Unpublished manuscript, Stanford Univeristy, 1972.

Sexton, P. *The feminized male*. New York: Random House, 1969.

Smith, M. He only does it to annoy. . . . In S. Anderson (Ed.), *Sex differences and discrimination in education*. Worthington, Ohio: Charles A. Jones, 1972.

Strainchamps, E. Our sexist language. In V. Gornick & B. K. Moran (Ed.), *Women in sexist society: Studies in power and powerlessness*. New York: Basic Books, 1971.

Thompson, M. Sex discrimination in the schools. Unpublished manuscript, 3400 Dent Place, N.W., Washington, D.C., 1972.

Tittle, C. K., McCarthy, K., & Steckler, J. F. Women and educational testing: A selective review of the research literature and testing practices. Unpublished manuscript, Office of Teacher Education, City University of New York, 1973.

U. S. Department of HEW, Office of Education, Bureau of Adult, Vocational, and Technical Education. *Trends in vocational education*. Washington, D.C.: General Services Administration, 1972.

U'Ren, M. B. The image of woman in textbooks. In V. Gornick & B. K. Moran (Ed.), *Woman in sexist society: Studies in power and powerlessness*. New York: Basic Books, 1971.

Women on Words and Images. *Dick and Jane as victims: Sex stereotyping in children's readers*. Princeton, N.J.: Central New Jersey N.O.W., 1972.

Women's Bureau, Employment Standards Administration, United States Department of Labor. *Highlights of Women's Employment and Education*. Women's Bureau WB72-191, Washington, D.C.: U. S. Government Printing Office, March 1972.

Zellner, H. Discrimination against women, occupational segregation, and the relative wage. *American Economic Review*, 62 (May 1972), 157-160.

Zimet, S. G. Little boy lost. *Teachers College Record*, 72 (September 1970), 31-40.

Women's Images in Indian Education

ARUN P. MUKHERJEE

SEXISM IN INDIAN EDUCATION: THE LIES WE TELL OUR CHILDREN
by Narendra Nath Kalia.
New Delhi: Vikas Publishing House, 1979. 193 pp.

When India became independent in 1947, Indian women had much cause for optimism. They had taken an active part in the *satyagraha* ("struggle for truth"), the term used by Gandhi for India's civil disobedience movement against British colonial rule, as well as in the revolutionary underground. Equality between the sexes was a declared goal of the freedom movement. In 1965 the Education Commission of India further promised them an education curriculum free of sex-role biases so that India's youth would not be forced to conform to sex-role stereotypes.

There seemed no reason why such a curriculum could not be implemented. School textbook production in India is heavily subsidized by the state. Moreover, India's educational officialdom enjoys an almost dictatorial hold on the syllabus, content, and number of textbooks to be used at various grade levels in every Indian school. Yet the promise remains unfulfilled. In this study, rather appropriately subtitled *The Lies We Tell Our Children*, Narendra Nath Kalia painstakingly documents the dominance of sexism in Indian school curricula. He analyzes more than forty-two English and Hindi literature textbooks, annually prescribed for more than 1.5 million students in the North Indian regions of Haryana, Punjab, Rajasthan, Uttar Pradesh, and Delhi. His sample includes texts prepared or approved by various state bureaucracies, including two national agencies, the prestigious National Council of Education Research and Training (NCERT) and the Central Board of Secondary Education.

Kalia found that authors and editors of Indian textbooks, as if catering to a male readership alone, use nouns and pronouns that exclude females in generalizations about human society. Not only are male characters in the majority in fiction, but 75 percent of the dominant figures in plots are similarly male. Forty-seven biographies of men are used, but only seven of women. More than 100 female characters appear as victims and in many lessons men routinely abuse and violently beat women. Both inside and outside the home, men are portrayed as the dominant decisionmakers; women's authority to make decisions is generally restricted to domestic matters. Finally, of the 465 occupations held by characters in the plots, women are completely excluded from 344. Women are mostly relegated to low-

Harvard Educational Review   Vol. 51   No. 1   February 1981, 218–220

status, low-income positions such as housewife, servant, or prostitute.

In lesson after lesson, the belittlement of females continues. When a princess dares to propose marriage to an exiled prince, he hacks off her ears and nose to discourage such overtures made by a female. A father, trying to arrange his highly talented daughter's marriage, presents her to the prospective in-laws as a beautiful but stupid person. A husband practices witchcraft to obstruct his wife's occupational aspirations. An urban housewife languishes over the greater benefits of being male: men do not have to curl their hair; they are not slaves to fashion; and they have more pockets than they will ever need. Even those female characters who distinguish themselves as political activists, scientists, or poets are usually highlighted as homemakers and breast-feeders. Their domestic roles are seldom as neatly ignored as are those of their male counterparts. The pattern holds for subjects of fiction as well as of biography. As the author wryly observes, men make history, while women do the dishes.

The Indian textbooks also tend to rely heavily upon English classics, perhaps more out of a colonial deference to the West's supposed superiority than because the editors want to expose students to good writing. Most textbook adaptations of classics are rewritten in grotesquely synopsized form. *Othello*, for example, comes across simply as the story of an enraged man who kills his wife.

Kalia's most important contribution is in showing us the reality of a patriarchal education system beneath the veneer of egalitarian pretensions. The irony is that traditionally the Indian woman was not the silly sister or protected property. Neither was she the mythological embodiment of evil in the style of Eve. In the Indian myths of creation, she is the *prakriti* ("female personification of matter") of Sankhyan philosophy who complements the male spirit as a necessary prelude to creativity. Androgyny and female worship are as ancient in India as its gods.

In the United States, feminists now have begun to direct attention toward forgotten female achievers. These are mostly women who challenged the sexist myths of their society. In India, the women were the myths: *Bhuvaneshwari*, ruler of the world and devourer of evil; *Graam-Maataa*, protectress of villages; *Aditi*, the personification of freedom; *Saraswati*, patroness of learning and fine arts; *Vak,* omniscient counterpart of the Creator; *Shakti*, eternal, life-sustaining energy; and the female half in the *Ardhanaarishwar*, the androgynous Siva. But women were more than just the myth. They were Rigvedic poets; female warriors of the aboriginal Dasas; Rudamba, the thirteenth-century Kakteya queen; the reigning monarchs Tara Bai, Ahalya Bai Holkar, and Rani Durga Vati; female historians, judges, and accountants of the Vijay Nagar empire; and the political activists in British India. On and on goes the line.

Given such materials, Indian textbook writers did not have to rely on esoteric sagas of jargon-spouting mem-sahibs. Nor did they have to resort to digging for fictional female role models to appease rabid feminists. They had all they needed, ripe for retelling, in India's distant and not-so-distant past. Yet, as Kalia shows, the Indian textbooks continue to draw upon the worst of Indian tradition and bastardize the best of it. In most lessons, the males retain their absolute dominance. Fathers bemoan the birth of a daughter, while praising sons. A married woman is expected to obey her husband unquestioningly while he lives and to follow him to the pyre when he dies. Even today, the Indian textbooks idealize *sutti*[1] and *jauhar.*[2]

To remedy the above, Kalia ends his study with a plea for balance in literary selections, for language that does not discriminate, for a critical evaluation of the patriarchal assumptions out of which such sexist writing grows, for recognition of the full equality between sexes, and for an end to subliminal messages which imply that what is masculine is somewhat better than what is feminine. On this last point, however, I must pause to debate with Kalia. For while he says (sincerely, I believe) that we should trash the scales that bear more weight on the masculine side, he unwittingly uses those very scales. In discussing the images of male and female characters in fiction, Kalia content-analyzes those that characterize males as more suited to marketplace success than nonmarketplace roles. The opposite he finds to be true of female characters. Consequently, he argues, the females in these books are not whole human beings—they are cutouts. To undo the imbalance, he recommends more portrayals of women as assertive, innovative, bold achievers.

Here, I believe, he is on slippery ground because his advocacy relies on those qualities of aggression that are typically associated with men—pushiness, pride, adventurousness, heroism—and are typically valued as instruments of marketplace success. As a feminist, I can find no fault with Kalia's preferences. But from a liberal educational standpoint, I think we need to review our definitions of success and failure. I would have liked to see Kalia invent a new scale, one which is totally nonoppressive and therefore truly radical.

Kalia does not investigate why India's official educators have preferred to highlight nonegalitarian themes over those conducive to sex-role equality in Indian and non-Indian literary materials. I understand that, under a UNICEF project, Kamlesh Nishchal in New Delhi is studying sex-role bias in the perception of Indian school teachers. Krishna Kumar at the Ontario Institute for Studies in Education and a team of researchers at the Srimati Nathibai Damodar Thackersey Women's University in Bombay are reported to be examining the current sex-role biases in Indian classroom instruction. Until the publicaton of these studies, however, Kalia's monograph remains the first comprehensive and empirically sound analysis of a major problem in curricular development in Third World education.

[1] An ancient Hindu practice whereby a widow immolated herself on her husband's funeral pyre. The practice was banned by the British.

[2] A practice prevalent among Rajput women whereby residents of a beseiged fort, to avoid being captured by their victors, committed mass suicide by burning themselves on a communal pyre.

"I Took my Childhood into my Hands": Some Voices from High School

KATHLEEN MURPHEY
BARBARA GATES
ADRIA REICH

DAUGHTERS IN HIGH SCHOOL: AN ANTHOLOGY OF THEIR WORK
edited by Frieda Singer.
Plainfield, Vt.: Daughters, Inc., 1974. 244 pp.

Daughters in High School is a collection of poems and short stories by young women in high schools throughout the United States. The editor, Frieda Singer, states that the anthology is intended "to represent the many concerns of American women in high school and to present as many sections in the nation as possible" (p. viii). She explains that unlike other anthologies this one "is concerned *both* with creative excellence *and* the responses of a selected segment of the population on a given theme — mainly the realities of growing up female in American society today" (p. vii). Singer is struck by the urgency, honesty, and depth of these writings, in which young women confront growing up, identity, self-pride, death, and social justice.

As high school teachers, we value this work of high school students because poems and stories by young writers inspire other young people to think and write about their own lives. And we commend the publishing company, Daughters, Inc., a new feminist press, in their first attempt at such an anthology. As women, we are particularly interested in this attempt to bring together the voices of young women. In our relationships with students — male and female — we have tried to encourage them to expand their images of themselves and of their futures beyond traditional social roles. It is our experience that this is often difficult for them to accomplish. The curriculum, the social climate, and the behavior expected of students in school settings all serve to reinforce traditional sex roles. Young men's futures are taken more seriously than young women's; young men in high school often are encouraged to achieve not only in academic studies but also in vocational and athletic programs as well. As girls become young women, social pressures and societal expectations subdue their voices, and possibly subvert them. They become ever more quiet and passive in the classroom and are labeled "normal" for this inexpressive behavior. This adjustment to social norms obscures the fact that young women are serious, thinking, growing people.

Harvard Educational Review   Vol. 45   No. 3   August 1975, 394–399

We gave *Daughters in High School* to several of our young women students at The Group School, an alternative high school in Cambridge, Massachusetts, for adolescents from largely white workingclass backgrounds.[1] The students were enthusiastic about the book, responding in particular to the poems and stories that were written in a direct and simple style, and that dealt with life experiences and problems. The poem "Childhood" by Lynn Stein elicited strong, though differing, responses about the process of growing up:

> I wanted to hold it —
> hug it tightly
> but they were around and
> i was afraid
> so i picked it up
> and ran with it hidden
> . . . .
> underneath my shirt
> i brushed the dust off
> took my childhood into my
> hands, and wept. (p. 4)

Although all the young women liked this poem, some expressed relief that childhood was over. One wanted "to be a kid again." Others felt there were both advantages and disadvantages of being a child. As one said, "You can't do nothin'. But it's good because you don't worry and stuff. I like being sixteen." All these young women, sixteen and seventeen years old, were sure childhood was over for them, a response which might vary among young people of different social class, race, sex, or ethnic background.

Related to the theme of growing up is teenage culture. Carol Parker's "Freeze-Dried Dharma," a stream-of-consciousness play of words, loosely links together names and lyrics of pop songs, singers' names, and current slang (p. 129). It excited our students as they read it through with recognition. One girl's comment, "I got to get a copy of that poem," indicates their pride and nostalgia for what is truly theirs, something between childhood and "being grown up."

Our young readers also reacted to poems and stories dealing with the theme of intuition, particularly in relation to an impending death. One such story, "You Don't Have to be Told to Know" by Debbie Kameros, tells of a young woman's premonition that something is wrong with her grandfather and ends with her aunt's calling to ask "When is the funeral?" (p. 9). Another favorite, "Tinky" by Roslyn James, has an even stronger emphasis on intuition and a more unexpected twist at the end (p. 58). A young girl is upset that her cat is to be put to sleep; she has a strange encounter with the ghost of the cat, and later finds out that the ghost has saved her life.

These stories intrigued our students partly because the plots were "weird" and "freaky" and "surprised you at the end." But their interest in these stories goes beyond a fascination with the strange. These stories connect to their own experiences:

[1] We would like to give particular thanks to Annie Bithoney, Coleen Long, and Robbin Luzaitis, and also to Stacey Croucher, Lyz Etter, Janet Ferreira, and Marie Lange, for their comments and judgments.

the death of a grandparent, the loss of a loved pet, the loyalty of an animal they have cared for. The attraction of these young women to the supernatural may reflect their fears of the future and what life will bring them. Perhaps at this point in their lives they put more trust in intuition or fate than in their own ability to control their futures.

Forebodings about the future also carried over into the two themes of death and war. In "Please God, Don't Let Mommy Die" (p. 18), Kathy Fonwit describes a young girl's renewed appreciation of good health during the terrifying time surrounding her mother's mastectomy. Poems about the tragedy of war — poems that question whether winning a war but losing lives is really winning — also moved our students. "A Small Battle" by Sharon Kramer counts up all those affected when "[W]e suffered only light casualties" (p. 127). The last two lines reiterate the theme:

> We won the battle.
> Or did we? (p. 127)

War was only one of the social and ethical issues that interested all the young women. They also liked the writings that depicted personal racial encounters. In the form of a series of letters that she calls "Flexagon" (p. 144), Jennifer Rice describes the growing friendship of a black and a white girl. The poem "Hybrid" by Reiko Obata also affected our students by its directness of feeling:

> Mama's white
> her lover, Black
> (They probably forgot in the dark)
> I'm neither
> and hate them both. (p. 158)

Like all young people, these young women seek strong positive models to grow through. They were especially enthusiastic about writings which showed women proud to be themselves. Ellen Gray's "For the Daughter I May Someday Have" impressed them all. The first line, "Walk tall, daughter," captures the tone.

> Liberation is a thing of the soul
> And bears no relation to laws passed
> Or battles won.
> We will have succeeded only if
> From our bittersweeet choices,
> You are born with what we fought
>   to attain.
> Daughter, I give you pride. (p. 179)

"Song 16" by Anne Fullerton lists ways in which its author is not going to conform. For example,

> I want to wear jeans today
> I don't have to play games that way.
> I want to be looked to for my
>   brain not my breasts. (p. 229)

In "Dear J," also by Anne Fullerton, the writer speaks to another woman caught in social roles and struggling to be herself.

> The struggling woman lawyer
> is you, my sister.
> The secretary sex kitten
> is also you, my sister. (p. 220)

Our students picked up on the strong, proud tone of the poem. As one student explained, "Her sister's a chick and she's trying to tell her."

The theme of self-pride surfaced again in our students' discussion of "I Sit Alone" by Laurie B. Lommen (p. 228), a poem about a girl who is "waiting" for someone who may never come. "She's a sucker!" they agreed. However, they liked the story, "Sand is a Useless Necessity," by Julia Ann Ward, even though, after a summer friendship with a boy, the heroine is left alone and ends up "waiting" too. Here the waiting is different, because the heroine learns self-respect. Thinking of the past as over, she cuts her hair and is ready to go on. Our students respect the heroine who respects herself and grows through suffering. They are uncomfortable with a young woman who suffers for suffering's sake.

"I Am a Bitch" by Reiko Obata expresses a young woman's angry self-realization:

> I didn't just all of a sudden
> become bitchy
> I used to be quiet
> People even called me shy
> Maybe because I've held it all in
> for too many years. (p. 180)

One student saw herself in the poem. Another commented, "I like it, but I don't think I'm a bitch." After the laughter subsided, she continued, "Well, maybe everyone is once in a while."

Our students also liked poems like "Housewife" by Shoshana Volkas, that indirectly criticize the social roles into which men and women are forced.

> The house is clean
> but
> your mind rots,
> something's in there
> aching to come out. . . . (p. 198)

But the few writings, like "Sisters" by Reiko Obata, that speak more explicitly of Women's Liberation were unpopular with our students.

> Sisters,
> We've got to come together.
> Our men are putting us down
> Without our even noticing.
> We've got to get off the feminine trick. (p. 181)

Their reactions tell us of a tension between their own struggle with self-definition and their discomfort with the Women's Liberation Movement. Their understanding of the Women's Movement is vague, and Movement rhetoric seems disconnected from their own lives. In their search for positive male and female models, these young women are angered to hear men condemned simply for being men. Writings which call for flexible, expanded social roles for women and men alike speak to them more directly.

The young women did not respond to some writings at all. They did not dislike them; they simply did not remember them. Although they responded to writings about social identity, they did not seem to be moved by the many stories and poems which explored questions of inner, psychological identity—poems like "i am" by Jessica Teich, which begins,

> i am a figment of my own imagination
> a reflection of my shadow.... (p. 39)

Marie Piche confronts these issues also in "Inertia."

> There are no answers; only questions.
> ....
> There is no reality; only a universe of illusions. (p. 124)

In contrast, our students were intrigued with poems and stories which dealt with conflicts between friends, struggles against sickness, death, war, race, and sex prejudice. These concerns grow directly out of their lives as young working-class women.

Concern with inward problems may be more characteristically middle class, and the preponderance of writing exploring inward rather than outward conflicts may reflect a middle-class bias in the selections of this anthology. This could be an unintended consequence of the selection process. The editor notes that material was solicited "only through a brief notice in selected newspapers and periodicals throughout the nation," and that "many faculty members were kind enough to encourage their students to submit material" (p. 3). From our experiences as teachers in urban and suburban schools, with young men and women from varying social-class backgrounds, we would expect more academically motivated, verbal young women from middle-class backgrounds to respond in greater numbers to random solicitation. If this is true, then *Daughters in High School* is not representative of all young women in the United States. Indeed, it is difficult to tell whether the selections in the book represent a cross section of age, social class, and racial backgrounds. Many anthologies include valuable background information on the authors, but in this collection such information is missing. The editor simply gives us each author's name and home city.

When we asked our students if anything was missing from the anthology, they were specific. "There's nothin' about violence, about what goes on in the city and in the streets. You know, excitement." "There's nothin' about cops and politicians." "There's nothing about being rich or poor." "They don't write about problems." "Problems" to these young women are not strictly intellectual and abstract, they are practical, everyday, getting-through-life problems. Their comments again reinforce our analysis of the middle-class bias in the anthology.

Editors of the next high school women's anthology might hopefully avoid this kind of unintentional bias by publishing writings of specific groups of young women. In particular, the often unheard voices of young women from poor and working-class backgrounds and authors whose native language is not English need to be heard.

Since many young women are not likely to respond to random solicitation, obtaining writings from a broader range of young women might be accomplished by going directly to where students work together with their teachers. This also would make possible a description of the teaching-learning process. When published writings are seen as the end result of a work process, readers and potential authors can better understand and identify with the process of writing.[2] Moreover, simply being in classrooms would help editors to recognize the issues which concern students. Themes students mentioned cut across the six areas into which Frieda Singer divided this anthology. Organization which flows from the concerns of the material, rather than from the concerns of editors, would be more useful to the reader and would show greater respect for the voices of authors.[3]

After reading this anthology, one of our students "went right home and tried to write to see if I could do stuff like that." And she has. No doubt these writings will inspire many young people to do the same. We hope that teachers will use this anthology in their classrooms. It speaks to the concerns of young people in provocative ways, and through classroom use, it would reach young people who otherwise might not have access to it. Moreover, *Daughters in High School* gives adults an appreciation for how much we have yet to learn from young women who are just beginning to find and have pride in their own voices. We recommend *Daughters in High School* to everyone, especially to students, teachers, and educators.

[2] Some authors have successfully carried out such a writing-as-process presentation. See Kenneth Koch and the students of P.S. 61 in New York City, *Wishes, Lies and Dreams: Teaching Children to Write Poetry* (New York: Vintage Books/Chelsea House, 1970); and Kenneth Koch, *Rose, Where Did You Get That Red?: Teaching Great Poetry to Children* (New York: Vintage Books, 1973).

[3] As an example of organization that follows more directly from the concerns of students, see Stephen M. Joseph, ed., *The Me Nobody Knows: Children's Voices from the Ghetto* (New York: Discus Books, 1969).

Overcoming Silences:
Teaching Writing for Women

ALIX KATES SHULMAN

SILENCES
by Tillie Olsen.
New York: Delacorte Press/Seymour Lawrence, 1978. 306 pp.

The reading list I distribute to students in my writing workshops for women usually has two parts. One lists stories, novels, and memoirs by women which turn
the daily lives of ordinary women into works of art; the other includes works that
analyze directly the complex problems facing women writers in a male-dominated
society. Only two writers have consistently appeared in both parts. One is Virginia
Woolf, whose novels are among the triumphs of English literature and whose 1928
essay, *A Room of One's Own*, constitutes the first complex feminist study of the problems of women writers and is still stunningly accurate fifty years after it was written.[1] The other is Tillie Olsen, whose short stories have inspired a generation of
women writers and whose 1962 essay "Silences" considers aspects of the problems
inhibiting, interrupting, and silencing women (and men) writers that Woolf either
neglected or only briefly explored.

Since her short story collection *Tell Me a Riddle* was published in 1961, Tillie Olsen has occupied a special place in the consciousness of American women writers.[2]
The title story, "Tell Me a Riddle," won the O. Henry Award as best American story
of 1961 and brought Olsen immediate literary acclaim. "I Stand Here Ironing," the
1957 story of a mother and daughter wounded by poverty, is an artistic masterpiece
which, Olsen tells us, was the first story she considered publishable. Born in 1913,
Olsen came of age and began to publish fiction during the Depression but was effectively "silenced" for twenty years by the necessity of raising and supporting four
children, despite her constant efforts to continue writing. After she began publishing again in her mid-forties, she suffered further silences. As she tells us in *Silences*,
"In the twenty years I bore and reared my children, usually had to work on a paid

[1] Virginia Woolf. *A Room of One's Own* (New York: Harcourt, Brace & World, 1929).
[2] Tillie Olsen. *Tell Me a Riddle* (Philadelphia: Lippincott, 1961; New York: Dell, 1976).

Harvard Educational Review Vol. 49 No. 4 November 1979, 527–533

job as well, the simplest circumstances for creation did not exist" (p. 19). Although the publication of *Tell Me a Riddle* gained Olsen an immediate literary following, she did not publish any more fiction until 1974, when her early novel *Yonnondio: From the Thirties*, begun forty years earlier, was finally issued.[3] In between, instead of publishing fiction, Olsen gave us a number of essays including "Silences: Why Writers Don't Write" (1962) in which she catalogues many of the insidious, unjust, and overwhelming circumstances that too often interfere with a writer's "sustained creation"—from poverty, marginality, and illiteracy ("two-thirds of the illiterate in the world today are women," she tells us in *Silences*, p. 184) to the less obvious literary brotherhood, damnation of women, demands of motherhood ("almost no mothers—as almost no part-time, part-self persons—have created enduring literature . . . so far," p. 19).

Writing on the acknowledged plight of the mother-writer, Olsen explains:

> More than any other human relationship, overwhelmingly more, motherhood means being instantly interruptable, responsive, responsible. Children need one *now* . . . the very fact that these are real needs, that one feels them as one's own (love, not duty); *that there is no one else responsible for these needs*, give them primacy. It is distraction, not meditation, that becomes habitual; interruption, not continuity; spasmodic, not constant toil. . . . Work interrupted, deferred, relinquished, makes blockage—at best, lesser accomplishment. Unused capacities atrophy, cease to be. (pp. 18–19)

Like her stories, the essay "Silences" quickly became a classic of feminist literature. Tillie Olsen, because of her own artistic mastery and her sympathy for the plight of other artists, became a model to aspiring women writers. Facing many handicaps, she published little, yet everything she wrote was recognized as important and inspiring. Her life and work thus demonstrated for the unrecognized or would-be artist that the huge effort required to overcome the countless difficulties confronting writers in a sexist, racist, class-stratified society was worthwhile.

Olsen's work, like Virginia Woolf's, has long seemed to me essential for my students to explore. But while Woolf's work was from the start available in print, Olsen's essay and occasionally her stories were so hard to find that I often had to circulate Xerox copies or place my own treasured copies on library reserve. No wonder the publication of Olsen's new book *Silences* seems an occasion for rejoicing. Not only does *Silences* contain the celebrated essay of the same title, but it includes as well many important pieces of evidence revealing the woman writer's plight, like those I used to carry around in a stuffed briefcase from class to class to share with my students: condescending reviews of women's works, outcries against them by women writers, counts of the paltry number of women authors listed in college catalogues and popular anthologies. I wanted to share this evidence with my students because I felt that my own power to overcome the impediments awaiting many of us who write had come partly through my acknowledging and defying them and by studying the ways other women writers have dealt with similar problems. Like Olsen's, my evidence collected over the years illustrated the insults, subtle or blunt, to women writers and the denigrations, veiled or artless, of women's

[3] Tillie Olsen. *Yonnondio: From the Thirties* (New York: Delacorte, 1974).

experiences that steadily appear in print to erode women's confidence. What woman writer has not felt discouraged reading the dismissals of women's writing as minor, domestic, intuitive, precious, or delicate? "As delicate as a surgeon's scalpel," retorted Katherine Anne Porter to that charge leveled against Katherine Mansfield, Olsen pointedly tells us (p. 41). What should a woman writer make of assessments of style as feminine or masculine, as in that invidious compliment, "she writes like a man" or of dismissive phrases like lady novelist, female poet, poetess, spinster, old maid, or of injunctions like poet John Berryman's, "Them lady poets must not marry, pal" (p. 31n), or the opposite advice given Ellen Glasgow, "Stop writing and go back to the South and have some babies" (p. 199)? It is difficult to avoid Olsen's conclusion that, with "critical judgment predominantly a male domain, the most damaging, and still prevalent, critical attitude remains [as Virginia Woolf noted] 'that women's experience, and literature written by women are, by definition, minor.' Indeed, for a sizable percentage of male writers, critics, academics, writer-women are eliminated from consideration, consciousness, altogether" (p. 232).

But *Silences* is not simply a collection of valuable essays and fragments conveniently housed in one volume. The book is a distillation of a lifetime's observations by one very perceptive, learned, and generous artist who has set out to "expand the too sparse evidence on the relationship between circumstances and creation" (p. 262) and show that "where the gifted among women (*and men*) have remained mute, or have never attained full capacity, it is because of circumstances, inner or outer, which oppose the needs of creation" (p. 17). More than a collection, the book is an eloquent argument presented in a fluid, unorthodox form. It is a case carefully documented and substantiated by testimony from writers spanning time, gender, race, and class, which grows increasingly powerful as the evidence accumulates from topic to topic. It begins with Olsen's 1962 essay, here called "Silences in Literature," and follows with a second essay, "One Out of Twelve: Writers Who Are Women in This Century," which explores in depth the continuing limitations on contemporary women writers and asks:

> Why are so many more women silenced than men? Why, when women do write (one out of four or five works published) is so little of their writing known, taught, accorded recognition? What is the nature of the critical judgments made throughout that (along with the factors different in women's lives) steadily reduces the ratio from one out of three in anthologies of student work, to one out of seventeen in course offerings? (p. 25)

In a later section of the book, eight pages of woman-counting statistics show the low ratio of acknowledged women writers to men even today, in literature courses, critical surveys, reference works, anthologies, textbooks, literary prizes and awards, all published fiction, and so forth.

Following these is an exemplary, detailed case study of the silences suffered by one important and original but now little known nineteenth-century writer, Rebecca Harding Davis. Tracing Davis's progress as a writer, Olsen shows how her creative powers were diminished by the demands of father, husband, and children; how her best efforts at writing were thwarted by circumstances and the need to earn money; how her originality was never acknowledged; and how, finally, her work fell into undeserved obscurity in her lifetime and near oblivion after her death.

In the sections called "Silences — II" and "The Writer-Women — II" are testimony culled from the correspondence, notebooks, and published works of many variously silenced writers, deepening our understanding of the causes and subtle varieties of silences described in the opening essays. A sampling (without Olsen's insightful clustering and discussion):

> You're brought up with the . . . curious idea of feminine availability in all spiritual ways and in giving service to anyone who demands it. And I suppose that's why it has taken me twenty years to write this novel; it's been interrupted by just anyone who could jimmy his way into my life. (Katherine Anne Porter, p. 261)

> A writer needs time to write a certain number of hours every day. This is particularly true with prose fiction and absolutely necessary with the novel. . . . It is humanly impossible for a woman who is a wife and mother to work on a regular teaching job and write. (Margaret Walker, author of *Jubilee*, thirty years in the writing, p. 209)

> I should have liked a closer and thicker knowledge of life. I should have liked to deal with real things sometimes. (Virginia Woolf, p. 244)

> At Iowa . . . a classmate told me he believed that to be a woman poet was "a contradiction in terms." (poet Jane Cooper, p. 197)

Silences is neither literary criticism nor literary history nor even a history of silences. It is, rather, the personal response of a writer to situations impeding writers. Still, it does include many illuminating items of literary history. For example, there are provocative lists of writers who did not begin writing until their later years and of women writers who never married. There are revealing facts, such as a report of Margaret Atwood's telling 1973 survey, "Sexual Bias in Reviewing," which concludes that the works of women writers, but not of men, are often assessed on the basis of the author's sex. There is a report of research showing that in the century from 1850 to 1950 few black writers published more than two novels; but after 1960, when circumstances had in some ways improved for blacks, "any single year has seen more than nine novels by black writers that are their second, third, or fourth books" (p. 146). Here also are cutting insults and outbursts against women writers by such powerful literary misogynists as Samuel Johnson, who stated, "A woman's preaching is like a dog's walking on his hind legs. It is not done well, but you are surprised to find it done at all" (p. 229), and Norman Mailer, who observed, "I doubt if there will be a really exciting woman writer until the first whore becomes a call girl and tells her tale. . . . A good novelist can do without everything but the remnant of his balls" (p. 238). And all these excerpts collected by Olsen over a span of fifty years are here transformed through her probing intelligence, pain, and wisdom into a powerful argument. It gives us not only new understanding, but also a foundation for our own observations and personal responses to impediments. *Silences* is a book women writers need to read, especially those women who, without understanding why, may feel discouraged as they are beginning to write.

Since traditional writing workshops focus chiefly on the students' own works and perhaps a few exemplary texts, it is not unreasonable to ask why one would want to burden beginning writers with the seemingly discouraging information in *Silences*. Reflection on my experiences both in writing and teaching writing to women has convinced me that to remain ignorant of the forces opposing you is to remain forever vulnerable to them.

When I first began to teach, shortly after my first novel had been published, I lacked all experience as either a teacher or a student of writing, save for a single freshman writing course I had taken some twenty years earlier. But I welcomed the opportunity because there was much in my own experience of beginning to write at the age of thirty-five that I felt I could pass on to others. How I had found the words, the style, the materials to use in my writing was mysterious to me, but the inhibitions that had kept me silent for so many years, as well as the encouraging ideas, the inspiring books, the stimulating questions, and the varied circumstances that had enabled me to begin finally to write I now felt I understood and was eager to share with other women. I was equally aware of that peculiar combination of circumstances and luck that had finally freed me to write, including the luck to have started writing at a time when the age-old denigration of women's experience was being challenged and examined in the light of feminist ideas. I hoped that by revealing these circumstances to other women writers, I could inspire in them the same confidence I had found through feminism, and that they too might overcome some of the obstacles to writing.

Several things combined to end my own long "foreground silence," as Olsen calls the silence of late starters. First, I stumbled on the short stories of Grace Paley (*The Little Disturbances of Man*) and Tillie Olsen (*Tell Me a Riddle*) which showed how ordinary daily concerns of contemporary women could be transformed into art.[4] The stories portrayed common struggles of women with children, without money, in the city playground or kitchen, experiences not unlike my own, which, until I read Paley and Olsen, I had unconsciously accepted as unsuitable subjects for artistic treatment. Next, a writer of some reputation moved in with our family for a few weeks, long enough to let me discover that, contrary to popular mystique, writers are fallible, ordinary folk. Fortified against the notion that it was pretentious of me to write despite the stories inside me burning to be told, I decided to secretly try. At about that time, my youngest child began nursery school, leaving me with two and a half free hours each weekday for the first time in six years. I jealously guarded those hours, neither washing a dish nor answering the phone, forcing myself to concentrate on writing.

Less than a year after beginning my regimen, I chanced to join a group of ardent young theorists of the radical feminist movement, then in its infancy, who together were developing a new understanding of the pervasive societal forces restricting women. In those discussions, where new ideas were constantly being tested, I learned to explore long-suppressed feelings and to risk confronting my own experience with what Olsen calls "the writer's deepest questions: what is happening here? what does this mean? (p. 61) . . . is this true? is this true in my own experience and life-knowledge?" (p. 253). In that stimulating atmosphere I was able to believe

---

[4] Grace Paley. *The Little Disturbances of Man* (New York: Doubleday, 1959).

in the validity of my own perceptions and the importance of my own experience.

I had managed, then, at the right time, to come upon inspiring examples in the works of women writers, a means of demystifying fictional creation, uninterrupted time of my own, self-discipline, confidence that what I had to say might be interesting or even important to others, and a community in which I was taken seriously. It was my hope to share these with my students. At New York University's School of Continuing Education, my students range in age, experience, and occupation. As they have chosen to take my classes, and seldom for credit, they are in some sense already committed to writing. I shall try to outline here what I believe to be the most important services women's writing workshops can offer such students —services reinforced by Olsen's *Silences*.

First of all, I encourage respect for and familiarity with a large and varied literature by women. A writing workshop is not a literature course, but ignorance of this literature by women has caused a great injury to women's confidence in the value of their own experiences, literary or otherwise, an injury that Olsen calls "the great crippler" (p. 252). Though certainly a rich women's literature exists, little of it is studied or honored, so that, as Elaine Showalter argues in *A Literature of Their Own* "each generation of women writers has found itself, in a sense, without a history."[5] The few women writers who are included in the traditional literary canon are usually viewed as exceptions—hardly useful, as we know we are not exceptions. Although it is true that women writers have usually managed to find some of their female literary predecessors, a female literary tradition is not a resource most women grow up with or come by easily. Its absence produces the suspicion that what one knows intimately enough to write about is not acceptable material for fiction. My reading list contains many fine and varied books by women and I urge students to concentrate their reading on women's works if possible because, as Olsen says, "predecessors, ancestors, a body of literature, an acceptance of the right to write" (p. 23) constitute great advantages to the writer.

Second, a workshop should provide a group of sympathetic readers and co-writers who take women's creations seriously. Ideally, a writing workshop is a laboratory for risk-taking and exploration, a place where students can present their written creations without fear of the backbiting, ridicule, dismissal, or disregard that, as *Silences* demonstrates, too often await women's writing outside. Many students come to my classes as refugees from other writing workshops in which the very subjects and insights they chose to write about were attacked or questioned as false, insignificant, or uninteresting by fellow students and teachers who share our society's prejudices. Unless one is aware of the general cultural tendency to devalue women's experiences, criticism—particularly criticism of content, but also approach—is often felt as an attack on the self. In all-female writing classes where these prejudices are noted, many women find they are able for the first time to take for granted the acceptability of the experiences and truths they choose to explore and can get on to the main concerns of a writing workshop: form, style, technique, meaning, feeling—in other words, the effects of the written word. They are able

---

[5] Elaine Showalter. *A Literature of Their Own: British Women Novelists from Brontë to Lessing* (Princeton, N.J.: Princeton Univ. Press, 1977), p. 11.

to ignore being women writers and to examine their own and each other's work simply as writers. As Adrienne Rich observes in an essay on "Taking Women Students Seriously":

> If there is any misleading concept, it is that of "coeducation": that because women and men are sitting in the same classrooms, hearing the same lectures, reading the same books, performing the same laboratory experiments, they are receiving an equal education. They are not, first because the content of education itself validates men even as it invalidates women. Its very message is that men have been the shapers and thinkers of the world, and that this is only natural.[6]

Third, women benefit from access to a large literary community. Working in isolation from other women writers, women have had to accept by default the literary community of the dominant culture with its exclusion of all but a few token women writers from serious consideration and its frequently trivializing judgments of women's art and experiences. With the resurgence of feminism, an international literary community of women has formed, in which women's creative achievement is assumed and desired. There now exists an exciting array of women's cultural and critical journals, newspapers, presses, salons, schools, meeting places, workshops, readings forums, and discussion groups where women's art flourishes and in which students may often participate. Writing in a vacuum is discouraging. One task of teachers of writing is to help women students escape the traditional isolation of women writers and connect with this community and network. My students are encouraged to continue meeting in workshop groups independent of the institution through which they initially came together.

Fourth, I try to demystify creative writing as the exclusive province of the "great"— those mysteriously talented, biologically privileged, usually white, usually male, successful few. If identifying the biases and questioning the judgments of the dominant cultural establishments do not demystify writing sufficiently to free students to attempt to write what they "know to be true," if reading moving, masterly works by the less privileged and little known does not do it, if even the example before them of a small, female, part-time teacher and mother of two who did not begin writing until the age of thirty-five yet still manages to get her books read will not do the trick, then perhaps hearing the testimony of the many fine writers invoked in *Silences*, including the incomparable Tillie Olsen herself, will accomplish it. As Olsen in her wisdom and generosity says, "There is so much unwritten that needs to be written. . . . The greatness of literature is not only in the great writers, the good writers; it is also in that which [in Virginia Woolf's phrase] explains much and tells much" (p. 45).

Finally, a room of one's own, uninterrupted time, and self-discipline are crucial. Although these necessities will continue to be chancy for most women until sexism and every other inequity are only memories, determination, for whatever part it plays in enabling the writer to take full advantage of the resources available, should be carefully nourished in the workshop. There is still power to be gained from the suggestions, understanding, and encouragement of others in the same situation.

---

[6] Adrienne Rich. *On Lies, Secrets, and Silence: Selected Prose 1966–1978* (New York: Norton, 1979). p. 241.

There is hope in one of the lessons of *Silences*: others have done it; maybe I can too.

Every feminist artist and educator already understands these needs: the need to know our predecessors, the need to support each other's efforts, the need to free ourselves from the restrictions imposed on us by cultural and educational traditions, the need to find and speak the truth of our own experience. Many of the facts in *Silences* are by now well known to feminists. Yet the book remains moving and important, for one has only to take one step outside the feminist community to find widespread ignorance and denial of these truths and to be confronted by the very conditions Olsen documents and decries. Indeed, recently a new pernicious obstruction has been erected before the woman writer — too new, even, to have been considered in *Silences* — which insists that the woman's story has now been written, woman's experience rendered, the market saturated, the subject a cliché, and that there is no longer any need for more "women's books." As if there were but one woman's story, or as if woman's awareness of her otherness were a fad or a publishing trend instead of a condition of her history, or as if it would ever be suggested that there were now enough "men's books"! Until such suggestions are impossible, writers and students will need to acknowledge the facts presented in *Silences*, be comforted and encouraged by the company the book provides, and then proceed with their writing.

To me, reading *Silences* is rather like sitting in a circle with a group of trusted fellow writers for mutual encouragement and support, so much of the experience described is recognizable. Our circle spans generations. As I was first inspired to write fiction after reading about ordinary women in the stories of Grace Paley and Tillie Olsen, so here in *Silences* is Tillie Olsen herself, in her essay on Rebecca Harding Davis, testifying that Davis's obscure novel, *Life in the Iron Mills* (together with a few other books) revealed to her that "literature can be made out of the lives of despised people" and said to her, "you, too, must write" (p. 117).[7] In the same way, a century earlier Davis, according to Olsen, was inspired to write when she discovered in three stories about an ordinary American town by her contemporary, Hawthorne, that "the commonplace folk, and things which I saw every day had mystery and charm . . . belonged to the magic world [of books]" (p. 52). Recognizing the importance of such revelatory literary experiences, Olsen first taught Davis's *Life in the Iron Mills* at Amherst in 1961, using Xerox copies of the April 1861 *Atlantic Monthly* where it first appeared, just as I, a decade later, taught Olsen's essay "Silences" from Xerox copies placed on library reserve.

Here we all are, then, the writers invoked in *Silences* and those of us who read them, comprising a writers' workshop. We are sitting in a circle, sharing our experiences and ideas, reading and discussing each other's work, searching for a common truth, growing stronger and more confident and more determined through our mutual support and inspiration. Let us continue to expand the circle.

---

[7] Rebecca Harding Davis. *Life in the Iron Mills, or the Korl Woman* (Old Westbury, N.Y.: Feminist Press, 1972). Excerpts from this work are appended to *Silences*, pp. 265–283.

A Historical Look at Women Teachers

JACQUELINE JONES

WOMAN'S "TRUE" PROFESSION: VOICES FROM THE HISTORY OF TEACHING
by Nancy Hoffman.
Old Westbury, N.Y.: Feminist Press, 1981. 327 pp.

Nineteenth-century schoolteacher. The words conjure up two equally popular, yet contradictory images: one of a sweet young woman, patient, kind, biding her time until marriage, surrounded by appreciative and adoring pupils; the other of an older woman (perhaps the first one forty years later, having been disappointed in love and life), tight-lipped and humorless, alternately drilling sullen pupils in meaningless rote exercises and tormenting them with the ferule. Real nineteenth-century female teachers, of course, fell somewhere between these two extremes, and their experiences were much richer, their personalities much more complex, than these images would suggest. In editing this volume of primary documents, Nancy Hoffman attempts "to reproduce the experience of teaching in the past from the *perspective of the teacher*, and at the same time, to highlight critical themes which define teaching and characterize it as women's work" (p. xv). The result is a valuable collective portrait of nineteenth-century women who took their work seriously and did daily battle against restless youngsters and mean-spirited bureaucrats.

The documents themselves offer a wealth of detail that conveys the human drama implicit in the everyday classroom experience. Certainly neither annual school board reports nor policymakers' pronouncements offer such a compelling perspective on nineteenth- and early twentieth-century public education. Here is rural Vermont's Lucia B. Downing, planning her ensemble for her first day of teaching in 1882, desperate to make herself look older than her fourteen years: "[A] difficulty was my hair. . . .But, after many experiments, I achieved a way of folding it up, under and under, tying it close to my head, and I thought it resembled a real pug" (p. 31). Here, too, are the northern teachers of the former slaves, beleaguered by the Klu Klux Klan, fleas, and rattlesnakes, yet devoted to the enlightenment of the downtrodden. We watch as Marian Dogherty, an instructor in Boston's Hancock School for Girls, guides her immigrant pupils through a harrowing yet hilarious examination conducted for the benefit of the male principal, a "stickler for the proprieties" (p. 265).

The book spans the period 1830 to 1920, focusing on northeastern educational reformers and innovations, and chronicling the feminization of the teaching force

Harvard Educational Review   Vol. 53   No. 3   August 1983, 335–338

and the rise of urban school bureaucracies. Hoffman provides detailed introductions to the major sections and presents individual documents under three headings: "Seminary for Social Power: The Classroom Becomes Woman's Sphere"; "A Noble Work Done Earnestly: Yankee Schoolmarms in the Civil War South"; and "Teaching in the Big City: Women Staff the Education Factories." The voices we hear are those of genteel young ladies as well as rough-and-ready pioneers in the wild West, the strife-torn South, and the immigrant ghetto.

Despite the century-long time span and the variety of physical settings revealed in the volume, certain themes weave in and out, binding the teachers together and signifying their universal concerns. Several recount in loving detail their first day at the head of a class: "I can no more forget that class than a man forgets his first love or a warrior his first battle" (p. 259), writes one. Others provide blow-by-blow descriptions of their disciplinary techniques, including examples of spectacular successes. For example, the young Emma Willard managed to rein in her first class, but only after spending an afternoon "in alternate whippings and exhortations, the former always increasing in intensity, until at last, finding the difference between capricious anger and steadfast determination, they submitted" (p. 21). Still other accounts describe the end of the school year with the triumphant public exhibition and a renewed commitment to the work, unless, as in some cases, an exceptionally attractive bachelor enters the picture and seduces the teacher away from her children. On the other hand, if this creature never appears, the teacher might have few choices but to spend a lifetime of noble self-sacrifice in the classroom.

This period in women's history is fraught with irony. On the one hand, as a profession for women, teaching was considered a "sacred office" (p. 4), cloaked in sentimental rhetoric. Certainly Catherine Beecher did more than anyone else to glorify the role of the mother-away-from-home when she proclaimed that the future well-being of the nation rested on the teacher's sturdy shoulders. Hoffman has chosen Beecher's address, "Remedy for Wrongs to Women," which reads like an early Victorian melodrama as she warns of the chaos that will engulf American society if women neglect their "sphere" at home and in the school. On the other hand, the teacher received only a pittance for financial compensation. Local school boards rejoiced over the fact that they could pay females less than a living wage, and only half what their male counterparts earned for the same job. According to conventional wisdom, the vast majority of women teachers were unmarried and had no dependents to support and so they "needed" less pay. Here then was a labor of love with a vengeance.

Many of the poems, essays, letters, diary excerpts, short stories, and reminiscences in *Women's "True" Profession* convey the exhiliaration experienced by women who sought to use their physical and intellectual resources to their full limits; these women "revelled in [their] independence" (p. 79); they "loved [their] work so thoroughly that its very difficulties but lent it zest" (p. 83). But "shadows" (p. 15) remained—the realization that this was, in society's view, "only women's work," and it often yielded the teacher little but emotional exhaustion and the contempt of her better-paid male superiors. Indeed, as urban schools systematized, standardized, and bureaucratized their procedures, the teacher herself was reduced to the status of a child, burdened with paperwork and terrorized by associate superintendents like the Honourable Timothy O'Shea—"Gum Shoe Tim"—immortalized in Myra Kelly's essay.

Perhaps the greatest irony of all was that, despite the rigorous professionalization of teaching on the one hand and, on the other, paeans to women's innate sweetness, the instruction of young children seemed to require a very specific kind of temperament not found in all women. "It's a God-given something and you never get away from that, never" (p. 241), observed Mary Agnes Dwyer when Nancy Hoffman interviewed her in 1977. Dwyer knew this from long experience, having taught her first class in 1906. All of the women in this volume had that "God-given something" and knew what to do with it. This makes their writings particularly fascinating, but also a bit self-righteous at times.

Issues of class loom large throughout the book. In the early nineteenth century, school-teachers favorably compared their lot to that of their sisters in the New England textile mills, slaving away at the machines all day. But by the end of the century, teachers—most of whom remained relegated to the primary grades—chafed under the contemptuous glance of upper-middle-class female reformers.

Efforts to unionize teachers came from within their own ranks, as women in the early 1900s sought to achieve power and dignity for their profession, beleaguered as it was, by corrupt urban political machines and mindless administrators. Margaret Haley's address to the 1904 General Session of the National Education Association, "Why Teachers Should Organize," signaled a new era in labor history. As business agent of the Chicago Teachers Federation, Haley ushered her group into the mainstream of American trade unionism. Although Beecher would not have approved of Haley's combative spirit, she would have admired the sense of pride that this Chicago teacher and other union organizers derived from their work as professionals and as women.

Certainly local school districts rarely made a financial commitment to education commensurate with their rhapsodies about its social significance. Various documents suggest that, as a means of impressing teachers with their lowly status, the meager pay was matched by the demoralizing, and at times primitive, physical conditions of the schoolroom—a "murderous hole of darkness" set among "distinctly offensive" and "foul" corridors, according to one New York observer (p. 226). Americans as a whole placed education low on their list of fiscal priorities.

Through their own words, these teachers reveal themselves to be a tough-minded, spirited lot, all with a similar message about morality and goodness to impart to their students. They overcame relatives' objections to their vocation with a combination of stubbornness and defiance. Anzia Yezierska, for example, gives a moving account of the ensuing estrangement between a young "Americanized" Russian Jewish teacher and her Orthodox parents in her short story, "Children of Loneliness." For the heroine of the story, assimilation had its price: "The terrible loneliness of their abandoned old age, their sorrowful eyes, the wrung-out weariness on their faces, the whole bleak picture of her ruined, desolate home burned into her flesh" (p. 284). Moreover, spinsters, in their "single blessedness" (p. 74), withstood the scorn heaped upon them from people of both sexes and all ages. And many crusading northern teachers measured the justness of their own cause by the degree of hatred they inspired in native southern whites.

Indeed, regardless of their race, class, age, or ethnic background, all of the women in *Women's "True" Profession* seem to be self-consciously literate, imbued with a sense of mission and a love for their work. Missing from this collection, however, are the women who taught even though they were unsuited for the job. The harm they inflicted on their students—their attempt to perfect the fine art of humiliation—is only alluded to in third-person accounts. Teachers could also be agents of all that was petty and prejudiced in American society. In her exposé of the New York public school system in 1903, Adele Marie Shaw tells of teachers who murdered their pupils' instinctive love of learning, of women who engaged in pedagogical and disciplinary rigidity akin to rigor mortis, and had not the common decency—or common sense—to address an immigrant child politely.

Moreover, through her choice of selections, Hoffman neglects to illuminate competing visions about what should or could be taught in the classroom. Her emphasis on public schools includes little material to suggest that Roman Catholics and non-English speaking immigrants waged fierce battles over these questions in the nineteenth century. The best example of this omission deals with the freed people's schools established during the Civil War and Reconstruction eras. Throughout the South, blacks hired their own teachers in an effort to assert independence from whites and control their lives and those of their children. Afro-American culture, with its tradition of mutual assistance, stood in stark contrast to the individualistic, materialistic ethos implicit in the Yankee teachers' world view. Archives of the American Missionary Association include letters written by southern black teachers who struggled to serve their own people during this turbulent period. Their perspective on the political implications of schooling would have provided a nice corrective to the white and middle-class biases of this book.

Nevertheless, *Women's "True" Profession* contains many useful and revealing documents relating to the history of women and education. Significantly, Hoffman ends on a rather pessimistic note, suggesting that "while more women than ever before are in the work force, fewer, and less accomplished women are choosing to work at teaching—or so statistics would indicate (pp. 302–303). Not too long ago, a very bright, sensitive student at an elite women's college was overheard discussing her career plans. She said that she really wanted to teach American history to public high school students because it was important for them to learn about the role blacks and women had played in this country's past. She had a fiery sense of idealism, but felt troubled by the fact that teaching was traditional "women's work." As her peers entered business and the "male" professions, she worried that she would feel stigmatized in following a more conventional, "womanly" path. American society has so effectively devalued "woman's 'true' profession" that young women today who are capable of choosing a more prestigious career than teaching automatically shun it. In her candor, this student spoke eloquently to the tragic legacy left by the feminization of teaching in the nineteenth century.

PART IV
Research
And
Theory

Feminist Criticism of the Social Sciences

MARCIA WESTKOTT

The tensions and contradictions that permeate women's lives create simultaneously the potential for both alienation and liberation. These antithetical conditions form the outline of the debate within the social sciences concerning the interpretation of women's experiences. Marcia Westkott discusses the feminist criticism of the content, method, and purpose of knowledge about women as defined by the social sciences, and she offers a dialectical alternative to conventional analyses.

One of the struggles and, indeed, one of the sources of intellectual excitement in women's studies is the critical dialogue that feminist scholars create within the various traditional disciplines. These dialogues are not debates between outsiders and insiders; they are, rather, critical confrontations among those who have been educated and trained within particular disciplines. The feminist debate arises because some of these insiders, who are women, are also outsiders.[1] When women realize that we are simultaneously immersed in and estranged from both our own particular discipline and the Western intellectual tradition generally, a personal tension develops that informs the critical dialogue. This tension, rooted in the contradiction of women's belonging and not belonging, provides the basis for knowing deeply and personally that which we criticize. A personally experienced, culturally based contradiction means that in some fundamental way we as critics also oppose ourselves, or at least that part of us that continues to sustain the very basis of our own estrangement. Hence, the personal struggle of being both insider and outsider is not only a source of knowledge and insight, but also a source of self-criticism.

As the debate becomes institutionalized within the academic sphere through women's studies programs and journals, it begins to develop its own critical traditions, which, in the social sciences, have been directed to issues of content and method. More

An earlier version of this paper was presented at the National Women's Studies Association First National Conference, 1 June 1979. I am grateful to Lee Chambers-Schiller for reading the original draft and discussing these ideas with me.

[1] See Vivian Gornick, "Women as Outsiders," in *Woman in Sexist Society: Studies in Power and Powerlessness*, ed. Vivian Gornick and Barbara K. Moran (New York: New American Library, 1971), pp. 126-144.

Harvard Educational Review   Vol. 49   No. 4   November 1979, 422–430

specifically, the criticism has focused upon the invisibility or distortion of women as objects of knowledge, and upon conventional modes of establishing social knowledge. These issues of content and method are hardly fleeting matters, for they strike at the very foundation of the contemporary practice of social science. At the same time, the criticism also implies alternatives to contents and methods judged to be inappropriate. Criticism is not practiced in a vacuum; it is always criticism of something by someone. By clarifying what a social science is not or should not be, we can begin to realize what it can and should be. My intention is to adumbrate the alternatives that are implied by the criticism for the purpose of suggesting more appropriate (from a feminist perspective) approaches to social knowledge. My focus is upon themes and ideas rather than upon a paraphrasing of particular criticisms. I shall discuss first the criticism of and implied alternatives to *content*, then *method*, and finally *purpose* of social knowledge of women.

Among the major arguments that feminist criticism directs at social science is that it concentrates on the distortion and misinterpretation of women's experience. Women have not only been largely ignored in traditional approaches to knowledge[2]; where women have been considered at all we have been measured in masculine terms.[3] The concept of the human being as a universal category is only the man writ large. "Woman" is considered an abstract deviation of this essential humanity[4]; she is a partial man, or a negative image of man, or the convenient object of man's needs.[5] In any case, a woman is defined exclusively in terms of her relationship to men, which becomes the source from which female stereotypes emerge and are sustained.[6]

Moving beyond these stereotypes requires renaming the characteristics of women, not in terms of deviations from or negations of a masculine norm, but as patterns of human responses to particular situations.[7] In this view, masculinity and femininity are simply different human possibilities that have emerged historically. This understanding has led feminist scholars to rethink the concept of the person to include traditionally female characteristics.

[2] The invisibility of women in all disciplines is an early and recurrent theme of feminist criticism. See Nona Glazer, "General Perspectives," in *Woman in a Man-Made World: A Socioeconomic Handbook*, ed. Nona Glazer and Helen Youngelson Waehrer, 2nd ed. (Chicago: Rand McNally College Publishing, 1977), pp. 1–4; Sally Slocum, "Woman the Gatherer: Male Bias in Anthropology," in *Toward an Anthropology of Women*, ed. Rayna Reiter (New York: Monthly Review Press, 1975), pp. 36–50; Delores Barrancano Schmidt and Earl Robert Schmidt, "The Invisible Woman: The Historian as Professional Magician," in *Liberating Women's History: Theoretical and Critical Essays*, ed. Bernice A. Carroll (Urbana: Univ. of Illinois Press, 1976), pp. 42–54.

[3] Naomi Weisstein, "Psychology Constructs the Female," in *Woman in Sexist Society*, pp. 207–224; Susan Carol Rogers, "Woman's Place: A Critical Review of Anthropological Theory," *Comparative Studies in Society and History*, 20 (1978), 123–162.

[4] Carol C. Gould, "The Woman Question: Philosophy of Liberation and the Liberation of Philosophy," in *Women and Philosophy: Toward a Theory of Liberation*, ed. Carol C. Gould and Marx W. Wartofsky (New York: Putnam, 1976), pp. 5–44.

[5] Caroline Whitbeck, "Theories of Sex Difference," in *Women and Philosophy*, pp. 54–80.

[6] Dorothy Dinnerstein, *The Mermaid and the Minotaur: Sexual Arrangements and Human Malaise* (New York: Harper & Row, 1976) among others, has argued that female stereotypes are male creations based upon role-defined male-female relations. See also Juanita H. Williams, "Woman: Myth and Stereotype." *International Journal of Women's Studies*, 1 (1978), 221–247; Linda Gordon, Persis Hunt, Elizabeth Pleck, Rochelle Goldberg Ruthchild, and Marcia Scott, "Historical Phallacies: Sexism in American Historical Writing," in *Liberating Women's History*, pp. 55–74; Michele Wallace, *Black Macho and the Myth of the Superwoman* (New York: Dial, 1979).

[7] Jean Baker Miller, *Toward a New Psychology of Women* (Boston: Beacon Press, 1977).

Another strand of feminist criticism of content concerns the assumption that the human being and "his" social environment are mutually compatible. According to this assumption, the personality is formed by and therefore reflects its social contexts. The male character structure and patriarchal culture mutually reflect and support one another through social, political, and economic institutions. For this approach to person and society to remain consistent, women and other deviants must either become invisible or their estrangement from, or failure in, such a society must be explained in terms of their "natural" inferiority. In calling attention to women's invisibility in social science and in rejecting the notion of women's natural inferiority, feminists have challenged the assumption that self and society are mutually reflective and supportive.[8] Instead, they have stressed the idea that girls and women have grown up and have lived in social contexts that are opposed to their needs as human beings. These social contexts, they argue, are patriarchal: through the organization of social relations, women are controlled by men and are culturally devalued. Feminist scholarship has attended to both the material base of that control[9] and to the cultural and psychological aspects of female devaluation. Recent work has focused on how family organization influences that devaluation at psychological—often unconscious—levels.[10] Whether a woman manages to struggle against this subjugation or succumbs to it, or more likely both, in a patriarchical culture, she is still an outsider, an other, a marginal person, a deviant. In short, she is alienated.

By stressing female alienation in a male world, feminist scholars have shredded the happy functionalist assumption of a mutually supportive relationship between personality and culture. Moreover, they have suggested a theoretical approach to social knowledge that defines the socially constituted world "out there" as alien and opposing. Women's alienation from the man-made world suggests an alternative approach to social knowledge that is critical rather than functionalist, emphasizing the discontinuities rather than the continuities, the oppositions and the contradictions rather than the coincidence between persons and social contexts.[11]

Most feminist criticism of social science methods is derived from the criticism of content. According to this criticism, the patriarchal bias is reflected in the ways in which questions about women are posed: the absence of concepts that tap women's experience,[12] the viewing of women as an unchanging essence independent of time and place,[13] and the narrowness of the concept of the human being reflected in limited ways of understanding human behavior.[14] Although these criticisms address

[8] See Greer Litton Fox, "Nice Girl: Social Control of Women through a Value Construct," *Signs*, 2 (1977), 805-817.

[9] See Heidi Hartmann, "Capitalism, Patriarchy, and Job Segregation," *Signs*, 1 (1976), 137-169.

[10] See Dinnerstein, *The Mermaid and the Minotaur*, and Nancy Chodorow, *The Reproduction of Mothering* (Berkeley: Univ. of California Press, 1978).

[11] An excellent example of scholarship that illuminates such contradictions is Nancy F. Cott, "Passionlessness: An Interpretation of Victorian Sexual Ideology, 1790-1850," *Signs*, 4 (1978), 219-236.

[12] Joan I. Roberts, "The Ramifications of the Study of Women," in *Beyond Intellectual Sexism*, ed. Joan I. Roberts (New York: David McKay, 1976), p. 8; Arlene Kaplan Daniels, "Feminist Perspectives in Sociological Research," in *Another Voice: Feminist Perspectives on Social Life and Social Science*, ed. Marcia Millman and Rosabeth Moss Kanter (New York: Doubleday, 1975), pp. 340-370.

[13] Sheila Ryan Johansson, " 'Herstory' as History: A New Field or Another Fad?" in *Liberating Women's History*, pp. 402-403.

[14] Arlie Russell Hochschild, "The Sociology of Feeling and Emotion: Selected Possibilities," in *Another Voice*, p. 283.

methodological issues, they do not directly challenge the epistemological basis of mainstream social science. The epistemological criticism remains implied or sketchy, although exceptions exist, such as the work of Canadian sociologist, Dorothy Smith.[15]

Like the Marxist tradition within which she works, Smith's criticism directly challenges the norm of objectivity that assumes that the subject and object of research can be separated from one another through a methodological screen. The subject-object dichotomy in social science refers to the distinction between the person conducting the research and the person about whom knowledge is being developed. The ideal of objectivity was advocated by nineteenth century positivists, including Emile Durkheim, who argued that the object of social knowledge should be regarded as any other physical phenomenon and that the subject who conducts research must always be on guard not to let feelings "infect" research.[16] More recent versions of this ideal of objectivity have emphasized the importance of the universal application of social science methods as the best guarantee against the bias of subjectivity.

Marxists, especially those affiliated with the Institute for Social Research at Frankfurt,[17] criticized this ideology of objectivity and challenged the positivist idea of generalizing science and the notion that truth can be expressed in causal relations independent of time and place. They charged that positivist methods shatter and abstract concrete social relations into ahistorical relationships among things. Smith underscores this Marxist critique with a concern for women as agents of knowledge. She argues that the methodological norm of objectivity is itself socially and historically constituted, rooted in an ideology that attempts to mystify the social relations of the knower and the known through procedures that appear anonymous and impersonal. This aura of objectivity can be maintained so long as the object of knowledge, the "known," can be an "other," an alien object that does not reflect back on the knower. Considering women only as *objects* of social knowledge fails to challenge this disassociation. Moreover, it is consistent with the wider cultural objectification of women, in which our basic humanness is denied, but our externally determined characteristics can be categorized and related to one another like other phenomena. It is only where women are also brought in as the *subjects* of knowledge that the separation between subject and object breaks down. Smith comments: "So long as *men* and the pronouns *he, his,* etc. appeared as general and impersonal terms, there was no visible problem. Once women are inserted into sociological sentences as their subjects, however, the appearance of impersonality goes. The knower turns out not to be 'abstract knower' after all, but a member of a definite social category occupying definite positions within the society."[18]

The specificity of the knower is revealed when women become subjects of knowledge, because women are not identified with the abstract human being but with

[15] Dorothy Smith, "Women's Perspective as a Radical Critique of Sociology," *Sociological Inquiry,* 44 (1974), 7-13; "Some Implications of a Sociology for Women," in *Woman in a Man-Made World,* pp. 15-22.

[16] Emile Durkheim, *The Roles of the Sociological Method* (New York: Free Press, 1964), pp. 32-44.

[17] See Jurgen Habermas, *Knowledge and Human Interests,* trans. Jeremy Shapiro (Boston: Beacon Press, 1971); Theodor W. Adorno et al., *The Positivist Dispute in German Sociology,* trans. Glyn Adey and David Frisby (New York: Harper & Row, 1976); Herbert Marcuse, *Reason and Revolution* (New York: Oxford Univ. Press, 1941).

[18] Smith, "Some Implications of a Sociology for Women," pp. 16-17.

particular deviations or negations of this abstracted universal. Women studying women reveals the complex way in which women as objects of knowledge reflect back upon women as subjects of knowledge. Knowledge of the other and knowledge of the self are mutually informing, because self and other share a common condition of being women.

This emphasis upon the idea that subject and object are humanly linked converges with the interpretive tradition in the social sciences. Like the Marxist tradition, the interpretive tradition dissents from the mainstream positivist emphasis upon objectivity.[19] It emphasizes instead the idea that social knowledge is always interpreted within historical contexts, and that truths are, therefore, historical rather than abstract, and contingent rather than categorical. The interpretive approach also assumes that these historical truths are grasped not by attempting to eliminate subjectivity but through the intersubjectivity of meaning of subject and object. This intersubjectivity does not mean the identity of subject and object, but rather their dialectical relationship. Thus the questions that the investigator asks of the object of knowledge grow out of her own concerns and experiences. The answers that she may discover emerge not only from the ways that the objects of knowledge confirm and expand these experiences, but also from the ways that they oppose or remain silent about them. Hence, the intersubjectivity of meaning takes the form of dialogue from which knowledge is an unpredictable emergent rather than a controlled outcome.

This feminist critique of conventional social science methods intersects with the Marxist and interpretive criticisms at the points where their methodologies reflect women's experience. The idea of grounding inquiry in concrete experience rather than in abstract categories is reflected in women's historical identification with the concrete, everyday life of people and their survival needs. The idea of knowledge as an unpredictable discovery rather than a controlled outcome is reflected in women's historical exclusions from institutions, where planned rational control is the mode of operation, and in women's historical identification with domestic spheres which have been less rationally controlled or predictable. And finally, the idea of knowledge emerging from a self-other dialectic is reflected both in the historical exclusion of women from educational institutions where knowledge has been transmitted through books and lectures and in women's participation in societies and friendships where social knowledge has emerged from dialogue, a practice recently exemplified by women's consciousness-raising and support groups.

These historical experiences of women reflect the particular social relations implied by Marxist and interpretive methodologies. Threading itself throughout the social contexts of women creating and gaining knowledge is an affirmation of the idea of the human being as fully and freely creating herself and the world in which she lives, a process which includes negotiating that creation through dialogue with others. It is this sense of humanism that feminist social science affirms in these other critical traditions that have preceded it.

The third criticism that feminist scholars direct against traditional social science actually prefigures the other two. Containing implications for both content and method,

---

[19] The relationship between Marxist and interpretive approaches is drawn in Janet Wolff, "Hermeneutics and the Critique of Ideology," *Sociological Review*, 23, NS (1975), 811-828.

it is concerned with the purpose of the social knowledge of women. It certainly takes no more than a modicum of perception to realize that women have become the latest academic fad. As objects of knowledge, women have become marketable commodities measured by increasing profits for publishers and expanding enrollments in women's studies courses. While women are riding the crest of the wave which we ourselves have helped to create, it may be a rather sobering, albeit necessary, task to reflect on the ephemeral nature of the academic market in which we are now valued.

In this respect we have much to learn from the academic social-science exploitation of the poor, expecially the blacks, in the sixties. In the name of academic liberal concern and compensation the black ghetto was measured, analyzed, processed, dissected— —in short, reduced to manipulable data that advanced the career interests of the investigators but did little to improve the plight of the investigated.[20] The fact that research on the black ghetto is now passé, although black ghettos continue to exist, and research on women is now *au courant*, should give us pause. Once women have had "their day," once the academic market has grown tired of this particular "area," once the journals are glutted with information about women, minority as well as white women, how then shall we justify the importance of studying women? Shall knowledge of women also recede in the shadow of benign neglect?

The issue here concerns the exploitation of women as objects of knowledge. So long as we endorse the idea that the purpose of the study of women is justified solely in terms of our past exclusion as objects of knowledge, we inadvertently contribute to this exploitation as well as to its faddish nature. Women are an attractive subject to exploit so long as we hold that the purpose of social knowledge is simply getting more information. In social science's unrestrained pursuit of information, any new object of study that can generate mounds of data is of interest so long as it is a prolific source.[21] When the data are no longer new, the object of study loses its primacy.

Along with this flimsy market valuation of content is the problem of simply recording the present or past conditions of women. The methodological approach which recognizes as valid only the factual recording of what is allows no justification for attending to alternatives to present conditions. The effect of this approach is to justify the present. Ironically, in the practice of conventional social science,[22] this methodological conservatism is frequently accompanied by an ideology of social change. Hence, it is not at all unusual to see social scientists, who openly advocate social change, practicing a social science that on the epistemological level denies the possibility of that change.[23] Women's devaluation and the consequences of this devaluation are reinforced by a social science which records these conditions while systematically ignoring alternative possibilities. A depressing pall hangs over this litany of past and present

---

[20] Alvin W. Gouldner, "The Sociologist as Partisan: Sociology and the Welfare State," in *The Relevance of Sociology*, ed. Jack D. Douglas (New York: Appleton-Century-Crofts, 1970), pp. 112-148; Frances Fox Piven and Richard A. Cloward, *Regulating the Poor: The Functions of Public Welfare* (New York: Random House, 1971).

[21] Eric Voegelin, *The New Science of Politics: An Introduction* (Chicago: Univ. of Chicago Press, 1952), p. 8.

[22] The following critique of the conservatism of the practice of positivist social science has been influenced by the work of those associated with the Institute for Social Research at Frankfurt. See fn. 18.

[23] Marcia Westkott, "Conservative Method," *Philosophy of the Social Sciences*, 7 (1977), 67-76.

subjugation of women, precisely because its methodological principles allow for no future that is not an extension of present facts.

This approach to knowledge, impoverished by a flat and rigid literalness, reinforces the exploitation of women as data-generating objects of research. The method mirrors the idea of the person as a passive recorder of social reality. It is assumed that neither the process of recording data, nor the object about whom the data are recorded, has any imaginative capacity to transcend the present. Both the recorder and the recorded, the researcher and the researched, must necessarily resign themselves to the apparently self-perpetuating facts, facts which one can amass but cannot change. Social science, conceived in this way and applied to women, is an extension of the more-equals-better principle: the more information about women the better. If past examples are reliable clues, the only result can be an academic discipline in which initial excitement soon slips into the drudgery and cynicism of the accumulation of information for its own sake.

Opposed to this social science *about* women is an alternative social science *for* women.[24] A social science for women does not exclude information about women, but informs the knowledge it seeks with an intention for the future rather than a resignation to the present. The intention is not an historical inevitability but a vision, an imaginative alternative that stands in opposition to the present conditions of the cultural domination of women and is indeed rooted in these conditions. This dialogue with a future suggests a social science that is not simply a doleful catalogue of the facts of patriarchy, but an opposition to the very facts that it discovers.

The tension between describing and transforming which is first perceived in the knower, the subject of knowledge herself, implies a concomitant tension in the object of knowledge. From this perspective, women as objects of knowledge are viewed not as passive recipients nor as active, confirming reflections of society. Instead, the tension which informs the method suggests a concept of women in society which also expresses a negation: women opposing the very conditions to which they conform.

This tension requires at the very least a reconsideration of the assumption in social science research that there is a basic continuity between consciousness and activity. Conventional social science research continues to assume a fit between consciousness and activity,[25] despite the recognition of the possibility of a discontinuity between consciousness and activity. The assumption reflects the condition of being a male in patriarchal society, a condition of freedom, which admittedly varies greatly by race and class, to implement consciousness through activity. Because this freedom has been historically denied to women, the assumption of a convenient parallel between consciousness and activity does not hold. The idea of women simultaneously conforming to and opposing the conditions which deny their freedom suggests a breach between consciousness and activity that does not exist, at least not in the same way for the men who have had the power to implement consciousness through activity and to create the concepts that reflect that power.

[24] In the constitution developed at its founding conference in 1977, the National Women's Studies Association affirmed the importance of this distinction. "Constitution of the NWSA," *Women's Studies Newsletter*, 5, Nos. 1 and 2 (1977), 6.

[25] See esp. Talcott Parsons, *Toward a General Theory of Action* (New York: Harper & Row, 1951).

Such a dissociation between conforming behavior and consciousness emphasizes the crucial importance of women's consciousness in patriarchal society in at least two respects. In the first place, consciousness can be viewed as it is split off from activity,[26] freed from conforming behavior, imagining and fantasizing oneself in a world freed from oppression. In short, consciousness can be viewed as women's sphere of freedom, a sphere that exists simultaneously with unfree, conforming behavior. This is a split that women poets and novelists have long recognized. Witness Doris Lessing's account of a woman lunching with her husband and his colleague: "Having handed them coffee and chocolate wafers, she set an attentive smile on her face, like a sentinel, behind which she could cultivate her own thoughts."[27] The thoughts that are hidden behind the appropriately silent, feminine smile tell us who this woman is and who she could be. Historians have been discovering these thoughts in women's journals, memoirs, and letters. This is the area of women's creative imagination that mainstream social science, with its methodological insistence on recording behavior, has not tapped. To ignore women's consciousness is to miss the most important area of women's creative expressions of self in a society which denies that freedom in behavior.

Secondly, the idea of women's dissociation of consciousness from behavior suggests not only a freeing of consciousness, but also a tension between consciousness and behavior. Considering behavior alone is insufficient to understanding women in patriarchy, nor is it adequate to link women's behavior only to the dominant, male-created ideology. As Nancy Cott has shown, the meaning which women ascribe to their own behavior is reducible to neither the behavior itself nor to the dominant ideology.[28] It is derived from women's consciousness, which is influenced by the ideas and values of men, but is nevertheless uniquely situated, reflective of women's concrete position within the patriarchal power structure. Finally, this emphasis on consciousness suggests that women's unique interpretation of their own conforming behavior affects that behavior in ways that are intelligible only through reference to women's consciousness itself.

The opposition to patriarchal domination within both subject and object, knower and known, is a profound expression of a longing for freedom from that domination. For those of us who are seeking knowledge of women, this idea of freedom can be expressed as a future intention which indicates to us which facts in the present are necessary to know. These facts, including those concerning the ways in which we may unreflectively participate in our own victimization, may not be convenient or comfortable for us. But facts, even difficult ones, become important sources of self and social knowledge as a means of creating a future free of domination. Without this sense of what knowledge is important for our liberation, we are in the situation of gathering any and all information we can about ourselves so long as it sells, and thus we exploit ourselves as objects of knowledge. The difference between a social science about women and a social science for women, between the possibilities of self-exploitation and those of liberation, is our imaginative capacity to inform our understandings of

---

[26] This argument has been made with regard to class consciousness by some Marxists. See esp. Georg Lukacs. *History and Class Consciousness: Studies in Marxist Dialectics* (Cambridge, Mass.: MIT Press, 1971), pp. 83-109.

[27] Doris Lessing. *The Summer Before the Dark* (New York: Knopf, 1973), p. 14.

[28] Nancy F. Cott. "Passionlessness," pp. 219-236.

the world with a commitment to overcoming the subordination and devaluation of women.

The feminist criticisms of social science content, method, and purpose are not tightly integrated into an academic discipline. They are, rather, strands that are just beginning to emerge. What all three share is a dialectical approach to social knowledge. To emphasize the dialectics of self and other, person and society, consciousness and activity, past and future, knowledge and practice, is to approach social knowledge as open, contingent, and humanly compelling, as opposed to that which is closed, categorical, and human-controlling.

This is the exciting challenge and hope that feminist criticism brings to social science. As a result, women's actions are being reinterpreted and profoundly illuminated from the perspective of women's consciousness.[29] Social institutions such as motherhood are being re-examined for their patriarchal assumptions and are being countered with a vision of decent and humane parenting.[30] A psychology of women emphasizes its intention to be *for* women by not only explaining the conditions that affect the psychology of women and men, but also by exploring the bases from which those conditions can be transformed.[31] Self-knowledge and social knowledge are being creatively mediated in women's studies programs, through collaborative scholarly work, and in professional dialogue.[32]

The practice of these alternatives is not without its practical risks, especially for those who employ them within academic contexts where the model of mainstream social science is the unexamined standard. The dialogue concerning the criticism and its alternative practices has been limited primarily to women's networks, caucuses, and organizations. Yet it offers intellectual excitement and vitality to the practice of social science as a whole. To attend to the feminist criticism is to open the social sciences to both the feminist challenge and its hope.

[29] See esp. Caroll Smith Rosenberg, "The Female World of Love and Ritual," *Signs*, 1 (1975), 1-29; and Nancy F. Cott, *The Bonds of Womanhood* (New Haven: Yale Univ. Press, 1977).

[30] Adrienne Rich, *Of Woman Born: Motherhood as Experience and Institution* (New York: Norton, 1976).

[31] Miller, *Toward a New Psychology of Women*.

[32] See Deena Metzger and Barbara Meyerhoff, "Dear Diary (or Listening to the Silent Laughter of Mozart while the Beds are Unmade and the Remains of Breakfast Congeal on the Table)," *Chrysalis*, 7 (1979), 39-49.

Excluding Women from
the Educational Realm

JANE ROLAND MARTIN

Women have been traditionally underrepresented in the scholarship of the academic disciplines. Jane Roland Martin, continuing a line of thought she initiated in an earlier article (HER, August 1981), examines the exclusion of women from philosophy of education both as subjects who have written about education and as objects of educational study and thought. She traces this exclusion from a misunderstanding of the writings of Plato, Rousseau, and Pestalozzi on the education of women, and builds a comprehensive critique of the concepts of education, liberal education, and teaching which are accepted by analytic philosophers of education. Martin proposes a possible reconstruction of the field of philosophy of education to include women and describes the benefits of such a needed undertaking.

In recent years a literature has developed which documents the ways in which intellectual disciplines such as history and psychology, literature and the fine arts, sociology and biology are biased according to sex. The feminist criticism contained in this literature reveals that the disciplines fall short of the ideal of epistemological equality, that is, equality of representation and treatment of women in academic knowledge itself—for example, in scientific theories, historical narratives, and literary interpretations. The disciplines exclude women from their subject matter; they distort the female according to the male image of her; and they deny the feminine by forcing women into a masculine mold. While certain aspects of philosophy have been subjected to feminist scrutiny,[1] the status of women in the subject matter of philosophy of education has not yet been studied. This is unfortunate, for philosophy of education has more than theoretical significance; in dealing with prescriptive questions of education which touch all our lives, it has great practical signifi-

This essay was written while I was a fellow at the Mary Ingraham Bunting Institute, Radcliffe College. I wish to thank Naomi Chazan, Anne Costain, Ann Diller, Carol Gilligan, Diane Margolis, Michael Martin, Beatrice Nelson, and Janet Farrell Smith for helpful comments on the original draft.

[1] See Kathryn Pyne Parsons, "Moral Revolution," in *The Prism of Sex*, ed. Julia A. Sherman and Evelyn Torton Beck (Madison: Univ. of Wisconsin Press, 1979), pp. 189–227; and Lawrence Blum, "Kant's and Hegel's Moral Rationalism: A Feminist Perspective," *Canadian Journal of Philosophy*, **12** (1982), 287–302.

Harvard Educational Review   Vol. 52   No. 2   May 1982, 133–142

cance. Furthermore, as a consequence of state teacher certification requirements and the fact that public school teaching is primarily a woman's occupation, a large proportion of philosophy of education students are women. It is important to understand, therefore, that, although throughout history women have reared and taught the young and have themselves been educated, they are excluded both as the subjects and objects of educational thought from the standard texts and anthologies: as subjects, their philosophical works on education are ignored; as objects, works by men about their education and also their role as educators of the young are largely neglected. Moreover, the very definition of education and the educational realm adopted implicitly by the standard texts, and made explicit by contemporary analytic philosophers of education, excludes women.

Invisible Women

In an earlier issue of this journal I argued that the common interpretation of Rousseau's educational thought cannot explain what he has to say about the education of Sophie, the prototype of woman.[2] Rather than admit to the inadequacy of the accepted interpretation, the standard texts either ignore Rousseau's account of the education of Sophie or treat it as an aberration in his thought.

Rousseau's account of the education of girls and women is no aberration; on the contrary, it is integral to his philosophy of education. Nor is Plato's account of the education of women in Book V of the *Republic* an aberration; yet a number of the standard texts and anthologies omit all references to Book V. Others neither anthologize nor comment on those sections containing Plato's proposal that both males and females can be rulers of the Just State and that all those who are suited to rule should, regardless of sex, be given the same education.[3] Moreover, the texts which mention Plato's views on the education of women do so in passing or with significant distortion.[4]

A study done by Christine Pierce has shown that translators and commentators have consistently misinterpreted Book V of Plato's *Republic*; they have been unable

---

[2] Jane Roland Martin, "Sophie and Emile: A Case Study of Sex Bias in the History of Educational Thought," *Harvard Educational Review*, **51** (1981), 357–372.

[3] See Robert Ulich, ed., *Three Thousand Years of Educational Wisdom* (Cambridge, Mass.: Harvard Univ. Press, 1948) and his *History of Educational Thought* (New York: American Book, 1945); Robert S. Brumbaugh and Nathaniel M. Lawrence, *Philosophers on Education: Six Essays on the Foundations of Western Thought* (Boston: Houghton Mifflin, 1963); Paul Nash, Andreas M. Kazemias, and Henry J. Perkinson, ed., *The Educated Man: Studies in the History of Educational Thought* (New York: Wiley, 1965); Kingsley Price, *Education and Philosophical Thought*, 2nd ed. (Boston: Allyn & Bacon, 1967); Paul Nash, comp., *Models of Man: Explorations in the Western Educational Tradition* (New York: Wiley, 1968); and Steven M. Cahn, comp., *The Philosophical Foundations of Education* (New York: Harper & Row, 1970).

[4] For example, although Brumbaugh and Lawrence call Plato "the great educational revolutionist of his time" in part because of his "insistence on the equality of women" (*Philosophers on Education*, p. 38), they say not another word about that insistence. Robert S. Rusk, who presents Plato's position on the education of women in some detail in his anthology, is apparently so distressed by it that he says what any reader of the *Republic* knows to be false, namely, "Plato can only secure the unity of the state *at the cost of sacrificing all differences*" (*The Doctrines of the Great Educators*, rev. 3rd ed. [New York: St. Martin's, 1965], pp. 28–29, emphasis added). Nash comments that Plato's model of the educated person applies "only to those rare men *and rarer women* who are capable of understanding the underlying harmony of the universe," (*Models of Man*, p. 9, emphasis added) without acknowledging that Plato himself never makes a comparative judgment of the ability of males and females in his Just State to grasp The Good.

to comprehend that such a great philosopher sanctioned the equality of the sexes.[5] Few writers of the standard texts in the history of educational philosophy seem able to grasp this either. Other scholars, for example John Dewey and Thomas Henry Huxley, have also treated women's education seriously.[6] Nonetheless, only one standard text lists girls and women in its index.[7] The others do not perceive sex or gender to be an educational category, even though many of the philosophers whose thought constitutes their subject matter did.

The standard texts have also ignored what philosophers of education have said about the educative role of women as mothers. In his classic pedagogical work, *Leonard and Gertrude*, Johann Heinrich Pestalozzi presents Gertrude neither — to use his biographer's words —"as the sweetheart of some man nor, in the first place, as the wife of her husband but as the mother of her child."[8] As such, Pestalozzi presents her as the model of the good educator. When the nobleman Arner and his aide visit Cotton Meyer in Gertrude's village, Meyer describes Gertrude as one who understands how to establish schools which stand in close connection with the life of the home, instead of in contradiction to it.[9] They visit Gertrude and closely observe her teaching methods. Arner's aide is so impressed by Gertrude that he resolves to become the village schoolmaster. When he finally opens a school, it is based on principles of education extracted from Gertrude's practice.

Pestalozzi is not discussed in as many of the standard texts as are Plato and Rousseau. Insofar as the texts do include his thought, however, they scarcely acknowledge that he thinks Gertrude's character and activities "set the example for a new order."[10] Pestalozzi's insight that mothers are educators of their children and that we can learn from their methods has been largely ignored in educational philosophy.

Just as the exclusion of women as objects of educational thought by historians of educational philosophy is easily seen from a glance at the indexes of the standard texts, their exclusion as subjects is evident from a glance at the tables of contents in which the works of women philosophers of education have been overlooked. The one exception is Maria Montessori, whose work is discussed at length by Robert Rusk.[11] However, she is neither mentioned nor anthologized in the other texts I have surveyed, including Robert Ulich's massive anthology, *Three Thousand Years of Educational Wisdom*.

Montessori's claim to inclusion in the standard texts and anthologies is apparent, for her philosophical works on the education of children are widely known. She is not, however, the only woman in history to have developed a systematic theory of education. Many women have been particularly concerned with the educa-

---

[5] Pierce, "Equality: *Republic* V," *The Monist*, **57** (1973), 1–11.

[6] See, for example, John Dewey, "Is Coeducation Injurious to Girls?," *Ladies' Home Journal*, **28** (1911), pp. 60–61; Thomas Henry Huxley, "Emancipation — Black and White," *Lay Sermons, Addresses, and Reviews* (New York: Appleton, 1870; rpt. in Nash, pp. 285–288).

[7] Nash, *Models of Man*.

[8] Kate Silber, *Pestalozzi* (New York: Schocken Books, 1965), p. 42.

[9] John Heinrich Pestalozzi, *Leonard and Gertrude*, trans. Eva Channing (Boston: Heath, 1885), ch. 22.

[10] Silber, p. 42.

[11] Rusk, ch. 12.

tion of their own sex. For example, in *A Vindication of the Rights of Woman*, Mary Wollstonecraft challenged Rousseau's theory of the education of girls and developed her own theory.[12] Wollstonecraft, in turn, was influenced by the writings on education and society of Catherine Macaulay, in particular her *Letters on Education*.[13] In numerous books and articles, Catharine Beecher set forth a philosophy of education of girls and women which presents interesting contrasts to Wollstonecraft's;[14] and the utopian novel *Herland*, written by Charlotte Perkins Gilman, rests on a well-developed educational philosophy for women.[15]

While Montessori's work was certainly familiar to the authors and editors of the standard texts and anthologies, it is doubtful that Macaulay, Wollstonecraft, Beecher, and Gilman were even known to these men, let alone that they were perceived as educational philosophers. It is possible to cite them here because feminist research in the last decade has uncovered the lives and works of many women who have thought systematically about education. The works of these women must be studied and their significance determined before one can be sure that they should be included in the standard texts and anthologies. This analytic and evaluative endeavor remains to be done.

It should not be supposed, however, that all the men whose educational thought has been preserved for us by the standard texts are of the stature of Plato and Rousseau or that all the works represented in the anthologies are as important as the *Republic* and *Emile*. On the contrary, a reader of these books will find writings of considerable educational significance by otherwise unknown thinkers, and writings of questionable educational value by some of the great figures of Western philosophy. Thus, while criteria do have to be satisfied before Macaulay, Wollstonecraft, Beecher, Gilman, and others are given a place in the history of educational thought, they cannot in fairness be excluded simply for being regarded as less profound thinkers than Plato.

The question remains whether the women cited here can be excluded because their overriding interest is the education of their own sex. In view of the fate of Sophie, Gertrude, and Plato's female guardians as objects of educational thought, one can only assume that, had the works of these women been known to exist, they also would have been ignored by the standard texts and anthologies of the field. From the standpoint of the history of educational thought, women thinkers are in double jeopardy: they are penalized for their interest in the education of their own sex because that topic falls outside the field; and, as the case of Montessori makes clear, those who have written about education in general are penalized simply for being women.

[12] *A Vindication of the Rights of Woman* (New York: Norton, 1967); see also Mary Wollstonecraft Godwin, *Thoughts on the Education of Daughters* (Clifton, N.J.: Kelley Publishers, 1972).

[13] *Letters on Education*, ed. Gina Luria (New York: Garland, 1974). For discussions of Macaulay's life and works, see Florence S. Boos, "Catherine Macaulay's *Letters on Education* (1790): An Early Feminist Polemic," *University of Michigan Papers in Women's Studies*, 2 (1976), 64–78; Florence Boos and William Boos, "Catherine Macaulay: Historian and Political Reformer," *International Journal of Women's Studies*, 3 (1980), 49–65.

[14] For a list of Beecher's published works, see Kathryn Kish Sklar, *Catharine Beecher: A Study in American Domesticity* (New York: Norton, 1973).

[15] *Herland* (New York: Pantheon Books, 1979).

Defining the Educational Realm

Lorenne Clark has shown that, from the standpoint of political theory, women, children, and the family dwell in the "ontological basement," outside and underneath the political structure.[16] This apolitical status is due not to historical accident or necessity but to arbitrary definition. The reproductive processes of society—processes in which Clark includes creation and birth and the rearing of children to "more or less independence"—are by fiat excluded from the political domain, which is defined in relation to the public world of productive processes. Since the subject matter of political theory is politics, and since reproductive processes have been traditionally assigned to women and have taken place within the family, it follows that women and the family are excluded from the very subject matter of the discipline.

The analogy between political theory and educational philosophy is striking. Despite the fact that the reproductive processes of society, broadly understood, are largely devoted to childrearing and include the transmission of skills, beliefs, feelings, emotions, values, and even world views, they are not considered to belong to the educational realm. Thus, education, like politics, is defined in relation to the productive processes of society, and the status of women and the family are "a-educational" as well as apolitical. It is not surprising, then, that Pestalozzi's insight about Gertrude is overlooked by historians of educational philosophy; for in performing her maternal role, Gertrude participates in reproductive processes which are by definition excluded from the educational domain. If Gertrude is outside the educational realm, so is Sophie, for the training Rousseau intends for her aims at fitting her to be a good wife and mother, that is, to carry on the reproductive processes of society.[17] Yet, the exclusion of these processes from education does not in itself entail the exclusion of training *for* them; people could be prepared to carry on reproductive processes through bona fide educational activities even if the processes themselves are outside of education. However, since educational philosophy defines its subject matter only in terms of productive processes, even this preparation is excluded.

We can see the boundaries of the educational realm in the distinction commonly made between liberal and vocational education. Vocational education is clearly intended to prepare people to carry on the productive processes of society.[18] Liberal education, on the other hand, is not seen as preparation for carrying on its reproductive processes. Even though disagreements abound over which intellectual disciplines are proper to liberal education and the way they are to be organized, no one conceives of liberal education as education in childrearing and family life. The distinction between liberal and vocational education corresponds not to a distinc-

---

[16] "The Rights of Women: The Theory and Practice of the Ideology of Male Supremacy," in *Contemporary Issues in Political Philosophy*, ed. William R. Shea and John King-Farlow (New York: Science History Publications, 1976), pp. 49–65.

[17] See Susan Moller Okin, *Women in Western Political Thought* (Princeton: Princeton Univ. Press, 1979), ch. 6; Lynda Lange, "Rousseau: Women and the General Will," in *The Sexism of Social and Political Theory*, ed. Lorenne M. G. Clark and Lynda Lange (Toronto: Univ. of Toronto Press, 1979), pp. 41–52; and Martin, "Sophie and Emile."

[18] See Marvin Lazerson and W. Norton Grubb, ed., *American Education and Vocationalism* (New York: Teachers College Press, 1974).

tion between the two kinds of societal processes but to one between head and hand *within* productive processes. Liberal education is thus preparation for carrying on processes involving the production and consumption of ideas, while vocational education is preparation for processes involving manual labor.

Historians of educational philosophy have no more interest in Sophie than they do in Gertrude, for Rousseau places Sophie in the home and tailors her education to the role he assigns her there. Indeed, educational philosophy has no ready vocabulary to describe the kind of education Rousseau designs for Sophie. It is not a liberal education, for she will learn coquetry and modesty and skill in lacemaking, not science, history, literature, or rational thinking.[19] Like vocational education, her training has narrow and clearly specified ends. Yet vocational education programs prepare their graduates to enter the job market, whereas Sophie's education is designed to keep her out of that arena.[20]

Philosophy of education has no ready classification for the training Rousseau would provide women because it falls outside the educational domain. However, there is a classification for the training Plato would provide the women guardians of his Just State. For Plato, ruling is a matter of knowing the Good, which involves using one's reason to grasp the most abstract, theoretical knowledge possible. Thus, the education he prescribes for the guardian class is a type of liberal education — one which greatly influences educational thought and practice even today. How, then, are we to explain that historians of educational philosophy ignore Plato's theory of the education of women? In a field which excludes the reproductive processes of society from its subject matter and identifies women with these processes, Plato's theory is an anomaly. Plato places women in the public world and prescribes for them an education for the productive processes of society. Although their education falls squarely within the educational realm as defined by the field and can be readily classified, the fact that *women* are to receive this education is lost to view. The position of women in the history of educational philosophy is not an enviable one. Excluded from its subject matter insofar as they are commonly tied by theory to the reproductive processes of society, women are denied recognition even when a particular theory such as Plato's detaches their lives and their education from childrearing and the family.

The Analytic Paradigm: Peters's Concept of Education

Contemporary philosophical analysis has made explicit the boundaries of the educational realm assumed by the standard texts in the history of educational philoso-

[19] Rousseau, ch. 5. For the account of liberal education which dominates the thinking of philosophers of education today see Paul H. Hirst, "Liberal Education and the Nature of Knowledge," in *Philosophical Analysis and Education*, ed. Reginald D. Archambault (London: Routledge & Kegan Paul, 1965), pp. 113–138; rpt. in Paul H. Hirst, *Knowledge and the Curriculum* (London: Routledge & Kegan Paul, 1974). Page references will be to this volume.

[20] I recognize that I have omitted from this discussion all reference to home economics education. Briefly, home economics education has historically been classified as vocational education (see Lazerson and Grubb). However, in the form which is relevant to the present discussion, namely, the preparation of women for their place in the home, it lacks the distinguishing mark of other vocational studies in that it is not intended as training for jobs in the marketplace. Furthermore, contemporary philosophy of education has seldom, if ever, recognized its existence.

phy. In *Ethics and Education*, R. S. Peters writes that education is something "we consciously contrive for ourselves or for others" and that "it implies that something worthwhile is being or has been intentionally transmitted in a morally acceptable manner."[21] Peters distinguishes between two senses of the word "education." As an activity, education must fulfill three conditions — intentionality, voluntariness, and comprehension — for it involves the *intentional* transmission of something worthwhile, an element of *voluntariness* on the part of the learner, and some *comprehension* by the learner both of what is being learned and of the standards the learner is expected to attain.[22] As an achievement, education involves also the acquisition of knowledge, understanding, and cognitive perspectives.[23]

The analytic literature in philosophy of education is filled with discussions of Peters's concept of education, and at various points in his career he has elaborated upon and defended it.[24] Over the years he has come to acknowledge that there are two concepts of education: one encompassing "any process of childrearing, bringing up, instructing, etc.," and the other encompassing only those processes directed toward the development of an educated person.[25] Peters considers only the second, narrower concept to have philosophical significance. He has analyzed this concept in one work after another and has traced its implications in his book, *The Logic of Education*. This narrow concept is the basis not only for his own philosophical investigations of education but also for those of his many collaborators, students, and readers.

Peters is no insignificant figure in the philosophy of education. Indeed, his concept of education, which excludes the reproductive processes of society, defines the domain of the now-dominant school of philosophy of education — analytic philosophy of education.[26] Peters has given analytic philosophy of education a research paradigm which defines the types of problems, approaches, and solutions for the field only in terms of the productive processes of society. Thus from its standpoint, when Gertrude teaches her children, she is frequently not engaged in the activity of education. While a good deal of what she does fulfills Peters's condition of intentionality, and although she always acts in a morally acceptable manner, there are many occasions on which the children fail to meet the condition of voluntariness.

At times, however, the children are voluntary learners, as when the neighbor children implore Gertrude to teach them spinning:

[21] *Ethics and Education* (Glenview, Ill.: Scott, Foresman, 1967), pp. 2, 3.

[22] Peters, p. 17.

[23] Peters, p. 27.

[24] See Peters, "What is an Educational Process?," in *The Concept of Education*, ed. R. S. Peters (London: Routledge & Kegan Paul, 1967); Paul H. Hirst and R. S. Peters, *The Logic of Education* (London: Routledge & Kegan Paul, 1970); R. S. Peters, "Education and the Educated Man," in *A Critique of Current Educational Aims*, ed. R. F. Dearden, Paul H. Hirst, and R. S. Peters (London: Routledge & Kegan Paul, 1972); R. S. Peters, J. Woods, and W. H. Dray, "Aims of Education — A Conceptual Inquiry," in *The Philosophy of Education*, ed. R. S. Peters (London: Oxford Univ. Press, 1973).

[25] See, for example, Peters, "Education and the Educated Man," p. 8.

[26] In this section and the ones to follow I will only be discussing paradigms of analytic philosophy of education. There are other schools within philosophy of education, but this one dominates the field today as the recent N.S.S.E. Yearbook, *Philosophy and Education*, testifies (ed. Jonas Soltis [Chicago: The National Society for the Study of Education, 1981]).

"Can you spin?" she asked.

"No," they answered.

"Then you must learn, my dears. My children wouldn't sell their knowledge of it at any price, and are happy enough on Saturday, when they each get their few kreutzers. The year is long, my dears, and if we earn something every week, at the end of the year there is a lot of money, without our knowing how we came by it."

"Oh, please teach us!" implored the children, nestling close to the good woman.

"Willingly," Gertrude replied, "come every day if you like, and you will soon learn."[27]

However, with her own children, Gertrude constantly instills manners and proper conduct without their permission:

"What business was it of yours to tell the Bailiff day before yesterday, that you knew Arner would come soon? Suppose your father had not wished him to know that he knew it, and your chattering had brought him into trouble."

"I should be very sorry, mother. But neither of you said a word about its being a secret."

"Very well, I will tell your father when he comes home, whenever we are talking together, we must take care to add after each sentence: 'Lizzie may tell that to the neighbors, and talk about it at the well; but this she must not mention outside the house.' So then you will know precisely what you may chatter about."

"O mother, forgive me! That was not what I meant."

Gertrude talked similarly with all the other children about their faults, even saying to little Peggy: "You mustn't be so impatient for your soup, or I shall make you wait longer another time, and give it to one of the others."[28]

There are numerous questions about the transmission of values by the family which philosophy of education could answer: What does "transmit" mean in this context? Which values ought to be transmitted by the family? Should the values transmitted by the family be reinforced by schools or should they be challenged? Do schools have the right to challenge them? Yet as its subject matter is presently defined, philosophy of education cannot ask them, for they are questions about the reproductive processes of society which are inappropriate to raise, let alone to answer.

From the standpoint of contemporary analytic philosophy of education, Gertrude's educational activities and those of mothers in general are irrelevant. Indeed, any account of mothering is considered outside the field. For example, Sara Ruddick's recent innovative account of maternal thought, which gives insights into a kind of thinking associated with the reproductive processes of society, has no more place in the field than Pestalozzi's insights about Gertrude in her capacity as mother.[29]

The kind of maternal thought Ruddick describes and Gertrude embodies is the kind Sophie must exhibit if she is to perform well the traditional female role Rous-

---

[27] Pestalozzi, pp. 87–88.

[28] Pestalozzi, p. 44.

[29] "Maternal Thinking," *Feminist Studies,* **6** (1980), 342–367.

seau assigned her. As Ruddick makes clear, however, "maternal" is a social, not a biological category: although maternal thought arises out of childrearing practices, men as well as women express it in various ways of working and caring for others.[30] Thus it is something Sophie must learn, not something she is born with. Notice, however, when Sophie learns maternal skills from her mother and in raising her own children, this learning will also fall outside the educational realm. It will lack Peters's voluntariness and intentionality and will be part of the childrearing processes he would have philosophers of education ignore. In sum, the definition of education used by analytic philosophers today excludes the teaching, the training, and the socialization of children for which women throughout history have had prime responsibility.[31]

The Analytic Paradigm: Hirst's Concept of Liberal Education

Yet Sophie's learning would not be admitted to the educational realm even if it were designed in such a way that it met Peters's criteria of an educational process. It would still include unacceptable goals and content. According to Peters, the goal of education is the development of the educated person, who does not simply possess knowledge, but has some understanding of principles for organizing facts and of the "reason why" of things. The educated person's knowledge is not inert, but characterizes the person's way of looking at things and involves "the kind of commitment that comes from getting on the inside of a form of thought and awareness." This involves caring about the standards of evidence implicit in science or the canons of proof inherent in mathematics and possessing cognitive perspective.[32] At the center of Peters's account of education and the educated person is the notion of initiation into worthwhile activities, the impersonal cognitive content and procedures of which are "enshrined in *public traditions*."[33] Mathematics, science, history, literature, philosophy: these are the activities into which Peters's educated person is initiated. That person is one who has had, and has profited from, a liberal education of the sort outlined by Peters's colleague Paul Hirst in his essay, "Liberal Education and the Nature of Knowledge":

> First, sufficient immersion in the concepts, logic and criteria of the discipline for a person to come to know the distinctive way in which it "works" by pursuing these in particular cases; and then sufficient generalization of these over the whole range of the discipline so that his experience begins to be widely structured in this distinctive manner. It is this coming to look at things in a certain way that is being aimed at, not the ability to work out in minute particulars all the details that can be in fact discerned. It is the ability to recognise empirical assertions or aesthetic judgments for what they are, and to know the kind of considerations on which their validity will depend, that matters.[34]

---

[30] Ruddick, p. 346.

[31] I do not mean to suggest that these activities have been in the past or are now carried on exclusively by women. On the contrary, both men and women have engaged in them and do now. Our culture assigns women responsibility for them, however.

[32] Peters, *Ethics and Education*, p. 8ff.

[33] Peters, *Education as Initiation* (London: Evans Brothers, 1964), p. 35, emphasis added.

[34] Hirst, "Liberal Education," p. 47.

If Peters's educated person is not in fact Hirst's liberally educated person, he or she is certainly the identical twin.

Hirst's analysis of liberal education has for some time been the accepted one in the field of philosohy of education.[35] In his view, liberal education consists of an initiation into what he takes to be the seven forms of knowledge.[36] Although in his later writings he carefully denies that these forms are themselves intellectual disciplines, it is safe to conclude that his liberally educated people will acquire the conceptual schemes and cognitive perspectives they are supposed to have through a study of mathematics, physical sciences, history, the human sciences, religion, literature and fine arts, and philosophy. These disciplines will not necessarily be studied separately; an interdisciplinary curriculum is compatible with Hirst's analysis. But it is nonetheless their subject matter, their conceptual apparatus, their standards of proof and adequate evidence that must be acquired if the ideal liberal education is to be realized.

In one way or another, then, the intellectual disciplines constitute the content of Peters's curriculum for the educated person. Since the things Rousseau would have Sophie learn — modesty, attentiveness, reserve, sewing, embroidery, lacemaking, keeping house, serving as hostess, bringing up children — are not part of these disciplines and are not enshrined in public traditions, they fall outside the curriculum of the educated person. But this is to say that they fall outside of education itself for, as we have seen, education, in Peters's analysis, is necessarily directed to the development of the educated person. Just as Rousseau's curriculum for Sophie is excluded from the educational realm, curricula in Beecher's domestic economy, Ruddick's maternal thinking, and Nancy Chodorow's mothering capacities would also be excluded.[37] Given the analyses of the concepts of education, the educated person, and liberal education, which are accepted in general outline by the field of philosophy of education, no curriculum preparing people for the reproductive processes can belong to a realm which is reserved for the ways of thinking, acting, and feeling involved in *public* traditions. Since girls and women are the ones who traditionally have carried on the reproductive processes of society, it is *their* activities of teaching and learning and *their* curriculum which are excluded from the educational realm. Sophie and Gertrude are as irrelevant to analytic philosophers of education as they are to the writers of texts in the history of educational philosophy.

The Analytic Paradigm: The Rationality Theory of Teaching

I have said that Gertrude teaches her children even though analytic philosophers of education would say she is not educating them. Yet according to Peters, only a fraction of what Gertrude does could be called "teaching." This is because the

[35] For an extended critique of Hirst's analysis in this respect, see Jane Roland Martin, "Needed: A New Paradigm for Liberal Education," in *Philosophy and Education*, pp. 37–59.

[36] In "Liberal Education," p. 46, Hirst listed the seven as: mathematics, physical sciences, human sciences, history, religion, literature and fine arts, and philosophy.

[37] See Ruddick; Chodorow, *The Reproduction of Mothering* (Berkeley: Univ. of California Press, 1978); and Catharine M. Beecher, *Suggestions Respecting Improvements in Education* (Hartford, Conn.: Packard & Butler, 1829).

concept of teaching is so closely linked to the concept of education that, in ruling out so many of Gertrude's activities as instances of education, Peters's analysis also rules them out as instances of teaching.

But quite apart from Peters's criteria, Gertrude fails to qualify as a teacher according to the accepted analysis of the concept of teaching. Perhaps the best brief statement of this analysis—what I have elsewhere called the rationality theory of teaching[38]—is found in a little known essay by Israel Scheffler. Beliefs, Scheffler says,

> can be acquired through mere unthinking contact, propaganda, indoctrination, or brainwashing. Teaching, by contrast, engages the mind, no matter what the subject matter. The teacher is prepared to *explain*, that is, to acknowledge the student's right to ask for reasons and his concomitant right to exercise his judgment on the merits of the case. Teaching is, in this standard sense, an initiation into open rational discussion.[39]

In this passage Scheffler harks back to the original account of teaching he gave in his earlier book *The Language of Education* where he states that to teach "is at some points at least to submit oneself to the understanding and independent judgment of the pupil, to his demand for reasons, to his sense of what constitutes an adequate explanation." And he adds:

> Teaching involves further that, if we try to get the student to believe that such and such is the case, we try also to get him to believe it for reasons that, within the limits of his capacity to grasp, are *our* reasons. Teaching, in this way, requires us to reveal our reasons to the student and, by so doing, to submit them to his evaluation and criticism.[40]

Scheffler is not the only contemporary philosopher of education who has emphasized connections between teaching and rationality. Numerous colleagues and critics in the field have elaborated upon and modified his analysis of teaching, and others have arrived independently at conclusions similar to his.[41] The relevant point for the present inquiry is that, according to this analysis of the concept of teaching, the learner's rationality must be acknowledged in two ways: the manner in which the teacher proceeds and the type of learning to be achieved. Thus, the rationality theory holds that to be teaching one must expose one's reasons to the learner so that the learner can evaluate them, and also that one's aim must be that the learner also have reasons, and attain a level of learning involving understanding.

On some occasions Gertrude does approximate the conception of teaching which the rationality theory embodies. When she tries to get her children to learn that virtue must be its own reward, she cautions them to give away their bread quietly so that no one may see them and reveals to them her reason that "people

---

[38] Martin, *Explaining, Understanding, and Teaching* (New York: McGraw-Hill, 1970), ch. 5.
[39] "Concepts of Education: Reflections on the Current Scene," in Israel Scheffler, *Reason and Teaching* (Indianapolis: Bobbs-Merrill, 1973), p. 62.
[40] *The Language of Education* (Springfield, Ill.: Thomas, 1960), p. 57.
[41] See, for example, Thomas F. Green, "A Topology of the Teaching Concept," *Studies in Philosophy and Education*, **3** (1964–65), 284–319; and his "Teaching, Acting, and Behaving," *Harvard Educational Review*, **34** (1964), 507–524.

needn't think you want to show off your generosity."[42] When one son asks her to give him a mouthful of bread for himself since he is giving his portion away, she refuses to do so. He asks for her reason and receives the reply: "So that you needn't imagine we are only to think of the poor after our own hunger is satisfied."[43] Yet one is left wondering what Gertrude would say and do if her children ever questioned the values she instills in them. One suspects that she would quickly resort to appeals to authority, a move of which the rationality theory would not approve.

Consider now the occasion on which Gertrude attempts to transmit her values to some neglected children by washing them, combing their hair, dressing them with care, and scrubbing their house. She neither gives reasons for the values of cleanliness and order in which she so firmly believes nor tries to *acknowledge the rationality* of the children in other ways.[44] And on another occasion when Gertrude invites these children to pray with her own children, and then accompanies them to their house with a "cheery parting, bidding them to come again soon,"[45] the intention is that they acquire good habits, but the mode of acquisition is quite divorced from the giving of explanations and the evaluation of reasons. Gertrude expects that through her kindness, good example, and the efficacy of unconscious imitation, these derelict children will adopt her values. She does not seem to care whether they understand the habits and values they are adopting or have proper backing for the associated beliefs they are acquiring.

It must be made clear, however, that the rationality theory does not function as an account of *good* teaching. It is not meant to be prescriptive; rather its function is to tell us what *constitutes* or *counts as* teaching. If Gertrude's actions do not meet its twofold requirement of rationality in the manner in which the teacher proceeds and in the type of learning to be achieved, adherents of the theory will not judge her teaching to be deficient; they will judge her not to be teaching at all. They will do so, moreover, no matter how reasonable or appropriate her actions may be. That Gertrude's actions are appropriate, given the value she places on cleanliness and godliness, the age of the neighbor children, and their condition, will be evident to readers who know young children. However, the rationality theory is not concerned that teaching be a rational activity in the ordinary sense that the actions constituting it be suited to the ends envisioned. Its sole concern is that the learner's reason be taken into account. Thus there are many contexts in which an activity meeting the requirements of the rationality theory of teaching will not be rational from the standpoint of the demands of the particular context.

In the process of bringing new infants to the point of independence, parents often do things which fit the rationality theory's criteria of teaching. Yet most of the teaching and learning which takes place in relation to the reproductive processes of society do not fit these criteria.[46] Values are transmitted, sex roles are internal-

---

[42] Pestalozzi, p. 55.
[43] Pestalozzi, p. 54.
[44] Pestalozzi, p. 87.
[45] Pestalozzi, pp. 88–89.
[46] Philosophy of education is not alone in placing Gertrude and the mothers she represents in the "ontological basement." In ch. 2 of *Worlds Apart* (New York: Basic Books, 1978), Sara Lawrence Lightfoot discusses mothers and teachers but never acknowledges that mothers *qua* mothers teach.

ized, character traits are developed, skills are acquired, and moral schemes and world views are set in place. Yet, if the teacher's reasons are not revealed or the learner's rationality is not acknowledged, the rationality theory denies the labels of "teacher" and "learner" to the parties involved.

The analysis of teaching which occupies a central position in philosophy of education today embodies a Socratic conception of both teaching and learning. The give and take of Socrates and his friends philosophizing in the marketplace, the Oxford tutor and his tutee, the graduate seminar: these are the intuitively clear cases of teaching and learning on which the analytic paradigm is based. Gertrude teaching her children a song to sing to their father when he returns home or the neighbors to count as they are spinning and sewing, Marmee helping Jo to curb her temper, Mrs. Garth making little Lotty learn her place — the activities and processes of childrearing which have traditionally belonged to women as mothers are at best considered to be peripheral cases of teaching and learning and are more likely not to qualify under these headings at all.[47]

A Servant of Patriarchal Policy

In defining education and the questions that can be asked about it, the analyses of contemporary philosophy of education make women and their activities and experiences invisible. The question naturally arises whether this matters. As long as women can enter the educational realm in practice — as they can and do today — what difference does it make that educational philosophy does not acknowledge gender as a bona fide educational category? As long as Plato and Rousseau discussed the education of girls and women in major works and Pestalozzi recognized the ability of mothers to teach, what difference does it make that the texts in the history of educational philosophy ignore their accounts and that the paradigms of analytic philosophy of education do not apply to Sophie, Gertrude, or women in general?

It matters for many reasons. When the experience of women is neither reflected nor interpreted in the texts and anthologies of the history of educational philosophy, women are given no opportunity to understand and evaluate the range of ideals — from Plato's guardians to Sophie and Gertrude — which the great thinkers of the past have held for them. When Wollstonecraft and Montessori are ignored in these texts, students of both sexes are denied contact with the great female minds of the past; indeed, they are denied the knowledge that women have ever thought seriously and systematically about education. What is more important is that, when the works of women are excluded from texts and anthologies, the message that women are not capable of significant philosophical reflection is transmitted.

By placing women outside the educational realm or else making them invisible within it, the contemporary paradigms of philosophy of education also contribute to the devaluation of women. Peters's conviction that only the narrow sense of education is worthy of philosophical inquiry keeps us from perceiving the teaching which takes place in childrearing as a serious, significant undertaking; it makes women's traditional activities appear trivial and banal. Similarly, in defining teach-

---

[47] These examples of mother-teachers are taken from Louisa May Alcott, *Little Women* (Boston: Little, Brown, 1936); and George Elliot, *Middlemarch* (Boston: Houghton Mifflin, 1956).

ing in terms of a very narrow conception of rationality—the giving and under-standing of reasons—the rationality theory of teaching makes the educational ac-tivities of mothers, and, by implication, mothers themselves, appear nonrational, if not downright irrational.

In a report on recent contributions to philosophy of education, Scheffler pro-tested that philosophy is not a handmaiden of policy. "Its function is not to facilitate policy," he said, "but rather to enlighten it by pressing its traditional questions of value, virtue, veracity, and validity."[48] Yet by its very definition of its subject matter, philosophy of education facilitates patriarchal policy; for in making females invis-ible, philosophy of education helps maintain the inequality of the sexes. It rein-forces the impression that girls and women are not important human beings and that the activities they have traditionally performed in carrying on the reproduc-tive processes of society are not worthwhile. Furthermore, philosophy's traditional questions of value, virtue, veracity, and validity cannot be asked about the educa-tion of females because females are unseen in the educational realm. Thus the en-lightenment that philosophy is capable of giving is denied to policies which directly affect girls and women.

I do not know if philosophy can ever be as divorced from policy as Scheffler would have it. But as long as there is no epistemological equality for women in phi-losophy of education, that discipline will serve patriarchal policy, albeit uninten-tionally. For when the activities and experiences of females are excluded from the educational realm, those of males provide our norms. Thus, the qualities Socrates displays in his philosophical conversations with his male companions in the mar-ketplace are built into our very definition of teaching even as the ones Gertrude displays in her interactions with her children are overlooked. Similarly, the tradi-tional male activities of science and mathematics, history and philosophy are built into the curriculum of the educated person even as activities traditionally assigned to females are ignored.

Do not misunderstand: I am not suggesting that the curriculum Rousseau pre-scribed for Sophie should become the norm or that cooking and sewing should be placed on a par with science and history. An education for coquetry and guile is not good for either sex; and, while there is nothing wrong with both sexes learning how to cook and sew, I am not advocating that these skills be incorporated into the liberal curriculum. Nor am I endorsing Pestalozzi's claim that Gertrude's par-ticular mode of teaching should be a model for all to emulate. My point is, rather, that when the activities and experiences traditionally associated with women are excluded from the educational realm and when that realm is defined in terms of male activities and experiences, then these become the educational norms for all human beings.

It has been shown that psychological theories of development have difficulty in-corporating findings about females because they are derived from male data.[49] It should now be clear that the paradigms of analytic philosophy of education are also

[48] "Philosophy of Education: Some Recent Contributions," *Harvard Educational Review*, **50** (1980), 402–406.

[49] See Carol Gilligan, "In a Different Voice: Women's Conceptions of Self and Morality," *Harvard Educational Review*, **47** (1977), 481–517; "Woman's Place in Man's Life Cycle," *Harvard Educational Review*, **49** (1979), 431–446; also in this anthology on pp. 187–223, 224–239.

based on male data. The examples which generate the rationality theory of teaching, Peters's concept of education and the educated person, and Hirst's theory of liberal education all derive from male experience. The response of the psychologists to the difficulty presented them by female data is to impose on their female subjects a masculine mold. The response of philosophers of education to female data is similar: Gertrude's teaching is at best defective; education for carrying on the reproductive processes of society is at best illiberal. Thus, the male norms which are implicit in the concepts and theories of philosophy of education today devalue women, and thereby serve patriarchal policy. But this is only part of the story. A corollary of this devaluation of women is that men are denied an education for carrying out the reproductive processes of society. In this way, the traditional sexual division of labor is supported.

Reconstituting the Educational Realm

The exclusion of women from the educational realm harms not only women; the field of philosophy of education itself is adversely affected. As the example of Rousseau's *Emile* illustrates, interpretations of works by major educational thinkers in which the education of both males and females is discussed will be deficient when they are based solely on material concerned with males. My discussion of the rationality theory of teaching — a theory which is quite implausible as an account of the teaching of young children — makes clear that analyses of concepts are likely to be inadequate when the cases which inform them and against which they are tested are derived solely from male experience. Furthermore, when gender is not seen to be a relevant educational category, important questions are begged.

When the educational realm embodies only male norms, it is inevitable that any women participating in it will be forced into a masculine mold. The question of whether such a mold is desirable for females needs to be asked, but it cannot be asked so long as philosophers of education assume that gender is a difference which makes no difference.[50] The question of whether the mold is desirable for males also needs to be asked; yet when our educational concepts and ideals are defined in male terms, we do not think to inquire into their validity for males themselves.

Perhaps the most important concern is that, when the educational realm makes women invisible, philosophy of education cannot provide an adequate answer to the question of what constitutes an educated person. Elsewhere I have argued at some length that Hirst's account of liberal education is seriously deficient — it presupposes a divorce of mind from body, thought from action, and reason from feeling and emotion — and that, since Peters's educated person is for all intents and purposes Hirst's liberally educated person, Peters's conception should be rejected.[51] Simply put, it is far too narrow to serve as an ideal which guides the educational enterprise and to which value is attached: it provides at best an ideal of an educated *mind*, not of an educated *person*, although, to the extent that its concerns are strictly cognitive, even in this sense it leaves much to be desired.

[50] Jane Roland Martin, "Sex Equality and Education," in *"Femininity," "Masculinity," and "Androgyny": A Modern Philosophical Discussion*, ed. Mary Vetterling-Braggin (Totowa, N.J.: Littlefield, Adams, 1982).
[51] Martin, "Needed: A Paradigm for Liberal Education"; "The Ideal of the Educated Person," *Educational Theory*, **31** (1981), 97–109.

An adequate ideal of the educated person must join thought to action, and reason to feeling and emotion. As I pointed out in an earlier section, however, liberal education is designed to prepare people to carry on the productive processes of society, in particular those involving the production and consumption of ideas. Thus Peters's educated person is intended to inhabit a world in which feelings and emotions such as caring, compassion, empathy, and nurturance have no legitimate role to play. To incorporate these into a conception of the educated person would be to introduce traits which were not merely irrelevant to the desired end, but very likely incompatible with it.

Peters's conception of the educated person is untenable, yet the remedy for its narrow intellectualism is unavailable to philosophers of education as long as the criteria for what falls within the educational realm mirrors the distinction between the productive and the reproductive processes of society. An adequate conception of the educated person must join together what Peters and Hirst have torn asunder: mind and body; thought and action; and reason, feeling, and emotion. To do this the educational realm must be reconstituted to include the reproductive processes of society.

It is important to understand that the exclusion of both women and the reproductive processes of society from the educational realm by philosophy of education is a consequence of the structure of the discipline and not simply due to an oversight which is easily corrected. Thus, philosophical inquiry into the nature of those processes or into the education of women cannot simply be grafted onto philosophy of education as presently constituted. On the contrary, the very subject matter of the field must be redefined.

Such a redefinition ought to be welcomed by practitioners in the field, for there is every reason to believe that it will ultimately enrich the discipline. As the experiences and activities which have traditionally belonged to women come to be included in the educational realm, a host of challenging and important issues and problems will arise. When philosophy of education investigates questions about childrearing and the transmission of values, when it develops accounts of gender education to inform its theories of liberal education, when it explores the forms of thinking, feeling, and acting associated with childrearing, marriage, and the family, when the concept of coeducation and concepts such as mothering and nurturance become subjects for philosophical analysis, philosophy of education will be invigorated.

New questions can be asked when the educational realm is reconstituted, and old questions can be given more adequate answers. When Gertrude, Sophie, and Plato's female guardians are taken seriously by historians of educational thought and when Rousseau's philosophy of education is counterbalanced by those of Wollstonecraft, Beecher, and Gilman, the theories of the great historical figures will be better understood. When analyses of the concept of teaching take childrearing activities to be central, insight into that prime educational process will be increased. When the activities of family living and childrearing fall within the range of worthwhile activities, theories of curriculum will be more complete.

It is of course impossible to know now the precise contours of a reconstituted educational realm, let alone to foresee the exact ways in which the inclusion of women and the reproductive processes of society will enrich the discipline of philosophy of education. Yet the need for a redefinition of its subject matter is imperative if philosophy of education is to cease serving patriarchal policy. The promise of enrichment is real.

Success Anxiety in Women: A Constructivist Interpretation of its Source and its Significance

GEORGIA SASSEN

Georgia Sassen examines the popular notion that women are afraid to succeed. In analyzing women's anxiety in the face of competitive success, Sassen argues that recent research reveals that it is the climate of competition which arouses the anxiety, not success itself. Drawing upon a constructivist-developmental concept of anxiety, she points out that the "success anxiety" attributed to women might well be a reflection of their essentially female way of constructing reality, as elaborated in recent feminist theory. Sassen concludes by questioning the idea of removing women's success anxiety by training them to compete; she calls instead for a restructuring of institutions so that competition is not the only avenue to success.

In 1964, Matina Horner sought to explain difficulties experienced by psychologists in understanding women's achievement motivation (Alper, 1971, 1974) with the hypothesis that there was a "motive to avoid success" found predominantly in women. Scoring undergraduates' responses to Thematic Apperception Tests,[1] she found that 65 percent of the women showed anxiety over success, compared to 8 percent of the men. This led her to believe that women had a fear of success (FOS) which would explain behavior that achievement motivation researchers had failed to explain with a theory of fear of failure. She concluded that FOS, or success anxiety, "exists because for most women the anticipation of success in competitive achievement activity, especially against men, produces anticipation of certain negative consequences, e.g., threat of social rejection and loss of femininity" (Horner, 1968, p. 125).

---

[1] The Thematic Apperception Test is a projective test in which a series of ambiguous pictures or verbal "cue" sentences are presented to the subject with instructions that she or he tell a story based on the scene or complete a story beginning with the cue. Subjects are usually told there are no right or wrong answers and are given a time limit in which to respond. The test is based on the theory that ambiguous cues will be perceived in the light of the subject's motives, needs, fears, conflicts, and attitudes, and that these will be expressed in the story she or he writes or tells. Achievement-motivation theorists have used the story completion test with standard cues designed to elicit stories that will give information on the subject's need to achieve, avoid failure, or—in some cases—fail.

Harvard Educational Review   Vol. 50   No. 1   February 1980, 13–24

Horner's data were widely accepted as proof that women feared or were anxious over the expectation of success. Her idea was popularized in the late sixties by articles in *Time, Newsweek*, the *New York Times Magazine, Ms.*, and even the *National Enquirer*. Fear of success also became a common independent variable in experiments reported at professional meetings and in journals (Karabenick, 1976, 1977; Esposito, 1977; Makosky, 1976; Sorrentino, 1973; Major & Sherman, Note 1; Midgely & Abrams, 1974). Many undergraduate theses (see Shaver, 1976) and graduate dissertations took up the topic, often using the concept unquestioningly.[2] Fear of success was accepted as a variable that could be quantified, and a large body of scholarly literature developed on the subject even in the midst of debate as to what it was, in what form it existed, and how it should be measured. Scholarly pursuit of the issue has raised critical questions, but these have not reached the popular press. Thus, many people continue to believe there is something wrong with women called "fear of success."

Because of this popular and enduring interpretation of Horner's original work, it is important to consider an alternative view of the data on FOS. This view does not conclude that there is something amiss with women, but takes into account some of the recent work on differences in women's conceptions of self and morality, as well as recent research in constructivist-developmental theory. But before we move on to this critique, we must look closely at Horner's methodology and her interpretation of her results.

Horner's Original Research

In addition to standard Thematic Apperception Test cues, Horner presented the cue, "At the end of first term finals, Anne finds herself at the top of her medical school class" (Anne's name was changed to John for male respondents). She considered success anxiety to be present if the subjects' responses contained "negative imagery which reflected concern about the success." Horner writes:

> Any of the following types of imagery was scored as Fear of Success:
> a. negative consequences because of the success;
> b. anticipation of negative consequences because of the success;
> c. negative affect because of the success;
> d. instrumental activity away from present or future success, including leaving the field for more traditional female work such as nursing, school teaching, or social work;
> e. any direct expression of conflict about success.
> Also scored was evidence of
> f. denial of the situation described by the cue;
> g. bizarre, inappropriate, unrealistic or non-adaptive responses to the situation described by the cue.
>
> (1968, p. 105)

In the first test session, each of Horner's subjects worked alone at anagram tasks. In the second session, additional anagrams were assigned. This time subjects worked in one of three experimental conditions: a noncompetitive condition working alone; a

---

[2] Psychological Abstracts lists twelve such dissertations as of June 1979.

mixed-sex competitive condition; and a competitive condition in which they worked in randomly chosen same-sex groups. The results showed that women high in fear of success scored lower when they competed with others than when they were tested alone, while those low in success anxiety performed equally well in the competitive and noncompetitive conditions. From this performance decrement, Horner concluded that women not only had a higher level of success anxiety than men, but that success anxiety interfered with their performance under competitive conditions.

In 1973, Horner, Tresemer, Berens, and Watson (Note 2) retained Horner's basic design but refined the scoring criteria. They took as an additional indicator of fear of success "interpersonal engagement," which was scored when two or more persons were involved with each other in a response. A story mentioning any involvement with another person was said to indicate fear of success, while a story involving only the cue character was considered to be an indicator of less fear of success or of its absence. This scoring criterion appears to correlate fear of success with the subjects' concern for relationships, a point we will return to.

The problem with Horner's methodology arises in her documentation of the *cause* of the anxiety her female subjects felt. While her documentation that FOS existed was thorough, her documentation of its cause consists only of examples of subjects' responses to the cue about Anne in medical school. Because she found specific references to femininity, men, marriage, and wifehood in the women's stories, she concluded that the loss of femininity is a specific fear. Because she found some stories in which specific negative consequences befell Anne, she concluded that it is fear of these sorts of consequences that constitute the success anxiety.

But her scoring criteria show us that more than these specifics were considered to show fear of success, and I question whether they have the same implications as the specific references to loss of femininity. And nowhere does Horner give a quantitative breakdown of the frequency of these more complex manifestations of success anxiety.

The complex manifestations I am referring to are:

—fear of becoming isolated, lonely, or unhappy as a result of success (without specific reference to unattractiveness to men or longing for marriage)

—any direct or indirect expression of conflict about success, such as doubting one's . . . normality or feeling guilty and in despair about the success (Horner, 1972, p. 159)

—negative imagery which reflected *concern* about the success

—any direct or indirect expression of *conflict* about success [emphasis added]. (Horner, 1968, p. 105)

These images do not necessarily indicate that the subjects are acting out of a motive related to their sex-role socialization. Rather, they could indicate a heightened perception of the "other side" of competitive success, that is, the great emotional costs at which success achieved through competition is often gained—an understanding which, while confused, indicates some underlying sense that something is rotten in the state in which success is defined as having better grades than everyone else.

Success: Competitive or Noncompetitive

What is the significance of this interpretation of Horner's subjects' responses? I suggest that Horner's findings, interpreted as the discovery of a motive to avoid success, actually reveal anxiety regarding competitive success. Research by Zuckerman and Alison (1976) is particularly relevant to this alternative interpretation. Using a twenty-seven item, agree-disagree instrument, they found significantly more fear-of-success responses in women than in men. However, examination of the questions employed reveals that they were testing for fear of a specific kind of success: success in competition. For example, subjects who disagreed with the following were scored as fearing success: "The rewards of a successful competition are greater than those received from cooperation," and "I am happy only when I am doing better than others." Subjects who agreed with the following were also scored as fearing success: "I think success has been emphasized too much in our culture" (pp. 422–424). Subjects who agreed with the idea of "winning no matter what" (p. 423) were scored low in fear of success; if they felt that "it is more important to play the game than to win it," they were scored as high in fear of success (p. 424).

In contrast to the work of Zuckerman and Alison, research using another objective measure of fear of success revealed no significant sex differences (Pappo, Note 3). Pappo developed an eighty-three item questionnaire which searches out self-doubt, preoccupation with competition, preoccupation with evaluation, self-sabotage, and repudiation of competence, all of which score as indicators of fear of success. Unlike Zuckerman and Alison, however, Pappo was not testing for fear of competitive success in particular, and in fact, she found preoccupation with competition an indicator of fear of success.

Thus, sex differences did not appear when objective tests looked for immobilizing or self-sabotaging behavior against any kind of success; sex differences showed up only when experiments tested for fear of competitive success.[3] For the purposes of this paper, this is the most important finding to come out of the research stimulated by Horner's original work. Against a background of studies which contradict each other on the question of sex differences in fear of success, the difference between fear of competitive success and fear of any success stands out.[4]

----

[3] Since Horner's original work, many studies have reexamined the question of sex differences in the presence of FOS. Zuckerman and Wheeler (1975)-collected the results of fifteen studies, the majority of which showed no significant sex differences using instruments identical or similar to Horner's. Brown, Jennings, and Vanik (1974) found marginally more FOS in college men than in college women while Weinreich-Haste (1978) and Griffore (1977) found no significant differences when they tested undergraduates and graduate students respectively.

The question of racial differences in FOS led to conclusions that black college women had significantly lower FOS than white college women (Mednick & Puryear, 1976; Weston & Mednick, 1970; Bright, 1970; Horner & Fleming, Note 4). Darity, using a refined test for FOS, found no significant sex differences between black male and black female college students.

Among the other questions that arose was whether subjects were responding to the idea of "deviant" success implied by a cue in which a woman succeeds in a "man's field" (Olsen & Willemsen, 1974; Monahan, Kuhn, & Shaver, 1974; Lockheed, 1976).

Tresemer first concluded that the literature showed there were no significant sex differences in FOS (1976), but then determined that the social context of the success was crucial, and that "incompatability between gender role and success" was determined by this factor (1977, p. 47). Overall, the research raises serious questions but resolves very few. The result is a body of literature fraught with contradictions.

[4] See n. 3.

Horner's study itself provides two corroborations of the interpretation that competition is the critical variable. One is her instrument: the TAT cue presents a highly competitive situation. After first term finals, which is only the first round, Anne is at the top of her medical school class. This also means that many people are at the bottom. Medical school, one of the most competitive educational experiences, prepares students for a high-status, high-pressure profession—if they make it. So the subjects are being asked to make sense of one person (no colleagues or friends are mentioned; they are all down there somewhere beneath Anne) doing well as she starts down a highly competitive path. A sociological observer would point out that these subjects are being asked to make sense of one person in the process of joining an elite minority that many of her peers would like to join but from which they will be excluded. Some will win, some will lose out. Second, Horner has succeeded in validating the existence of success anxiety only in a competitive context: she has told us that performance decrements validated her findings when anagram tasks were assigned in a competitive situation and that the results were inconclusive when the situation was not competitive (1968).

Horner conceives of success as competitive and isolated, achieved without the cooperation of others. In her revised scoring system (Horner, Tresemer, Berens, & Watson, Note 2), the subject who attempts to insert any colleagues or friends into the cue character's life is seen as exhibiting success anxiety. Subjects who adhere to the idea of the protagonist making it alone are considered less anxious about success. Tresemer (1977) cites four studies which showed small but consistent sex differences using this measure.

If, as I have suggested, Horner's studies and Zuckerman and Alison's questionnaire indicate a connection between sex differences and a definition of success as isolated and competitive, what does this tell us from the viewpoint of developmental research on women's self-concepts? Why should this definition of success produce anxiety in women? And why doesn't it produce anxiety in most men? How we define anxiety becomes a central question here.

Defining Anxiety: The Impact of Constructivist Theory

So much depends on definitions. Horner defines anxiety as a response "aroused . . . when one expects that the consequences of the action will be negative" (Horner, 1968, p. 15). Another definition of anxiety emerges from the recent work of Robert Kegan (1977), whose theory is grounded in the work of Piaget, Kohlberg, Fingarette, and Erikson. Kegan used the concept of a developing "structure of knowing" as an alternative to a pathological model in his work with thirty-nine voluntarily hospitalized psychiatric patients. He studied the process of ego equilibrium, which he sees as a "dynamic, sense-making, constructing activity." He writes, "Our world design or theory or structure-of-knowing" is what allows us to "construct a meaning" for our experiences and thus to "have" those experiences (1977, p. 99).

Kegan is careful to point out that "meaning" is not as cognitive and affect-free as it may sound, for cognition and affect cannot be separated. In fact, meaning-making involves one's whole being. As Fingarette (1963) showed, making meaning is in part an "existential process of generating a new vision which shall serve as the context for a new commitment" (p. 64). That is, this "cognitive" activity exists at the level at which existential decisions are made, and at which it is often necessary to "leap into nothingness" (p. 101), risking all the concepts that previously made the world make sense. It is at this level of emotion and personal risk that Kegan places the experience of anxiety. He describes it as the sense of disintegration which occurs when a meaning-making organism finds itself unable to make meaning.

From this perspective, anxiety takes on new dimensions. Because it arises from the inability to make meaning, and meaning-making is so connected with personal and existential commitment, there is much more to the anxiety experience than fear of what comes next. If we use Kegan's definition of anxiety, the women in Horner's and Zuckerman's samples are not simply afraid. They are unable to take competitive success and construct around it a vision, a new way of making sense, to which they can feel personally committed.

Why should it be hard for women to commit themselves to competitive success, and easy for men? Developmentalists from Piaget (1972) to Kohlberg (1969) and Gilligan (1977) have noted sex differences in the structures which people bring to the activity of making meaning. We are treading on dangerous ground here, for feminists have taken great pains to show that many experiments which claim to uncover sex differences have proven inadequate when examined, or to depend on the projections of the experimenter far more than on the facts. Yet Piaget's study of children's games, *The Moral Judgment of the Child*, has been replicated (Lever, 1976) showing that boys and girls regard rules in different ways. Kohlberg's work, based on an all-male sample, led to the development of an instrument for measuring moral development which appeared to have a built-in sex bias. Women were consistently scored at an "immature" stage. But Gilligan's studies of women's moral judgment corroborate the existence of sex differences in moral reasoning without implying that women's reasoning is less advanced than men's. Chodorow (1974) points out even more fundamental sex differences in the formation of self-concept and gender-identity. Each of these theorists illuminates the antagonism between women's structures of knowing and equating success with succeeding in competition.

Piaget found that girls, when faced with an argument over the rules of a game, tended to end the game and start over (or do something else) while boys would legislate their way through the issue. This illustrates one aspect of the structure with which the girls are operating and which the boys' structure lacks: the girls preserve the relationships of the players of the game, while the boys preserve the rules.

Gilligan showed that women's constructions of moral dilemmas tended to be more contextual than men's, based on a morality of interpersonal responsibilities rather than a morality of rights. The women she interviewed referred repeatedly to relationships in explaining their moral reasoning: the "reciprocity of care" (p. 503) of which she writes cannot exist unless more than one person is taken into account. This construction of reality conflicts directly with Horner's scoring system, which considers the inclusion of these necessary others to indicate fear of success. Similarly, it conflicts with Zuckerman and Alison's assumption that a preference for cooperation indicates fear of success.

Chodorow (1974, 1978) points out that women form their gender-identity and thus much of their self-concept in a relationship, the one with their mothers, in a way men do not, since a boy's role-model for this process is usually absent (in this culture) most of his waking hours. The mother-daughter relationship, she points out, continues into adulthood. Rather than replacing the mother with the father as her love object, she argues, the girl adds the father to the relationship and thus lives with a "constellation" of relationships and affections for the rest of her life. This constellation is, to be sure, fraught with problems as the girl becomes a woman. Taking a constructivist view, however, we could argue that in grappling with such problems, a woman learns to make meaning in a particularly female way and develops a contextual rather than an individualistic structure of knowing.

This line of reasoning sketches out a perspective which female subjects are likely to bring to the TAT cue or fear-of-success questionnaire. Their structure of knowing is more oriented toward preserving and fostering relationships than toward winning. What happens when this structure confronts Anne's individual competitive success, or any test item which implies that competitive success is more valuable than cooperative achievement?

Kegan helps us here with his discussion of anxiety as a phenomenon which involves active ability as well as an inability. The individual is able to see that assimilating the environmental event, that is, accepting it as it appears into the meaning one is currently able to construct, would distort the event. Yet the individual is unable to change the structure of knowing to accommodate that event. Women bring a relational, contextual structure of knowing to the cue they are asked to make sense of, and thus find they cannot accommodate it to this kind of competitive success. Changing one's way of knowing in response to a four-minute apperceptive test or an agree-disagree item seems unlikely—hence the anxiety.

Further Evidence from Horner's Original Data

The projective stories that Horner quotes from her subjects contain evidence that this kind of inability to make meaning is exactly what is going on in at least some of the subjects. Specifically, certain data that Horner scored as indicative of fear of success did not include anxiety related to sex roles, but included guilt, conflict, or "concern," as Horner put it, over the outcome of Anne's competitive success. Examples of this appear in Horner's 1970 paper.

> Anne has planned for a long time to be a doctor. She has worked hard in her schoolwork to enable her to learn better how to fulfill her dream. Now her hard work has paid off. Unfortunately, Anne suddenly no longer feels so certain that she really wants to be a doctor. She wonders if perhaps this isn't normal. . . . Anne decides not to continue with her medical work but to continue with courses that she never allowed herself to take before but that have a deeper personal meaning for her. (p. 61)

In this story, Anne is seen by the respondent as suddenly reevaluating what it is that she wants. She decides to quit medical school and take courses that "have a deeper personal meaning for her." The respondent experiences some kind of crisis of meaning-making as she sees Anne dissatisfied with the implications of her competitive success, and changing direction to seek deeper meaning. Is this a learned *fear* of the outcome, a motive to avoid competitive success, or is it insight?

In another story written by one of Horner's subjects, ambivalence over Anne's success is again evident.

> Anne is completely ecstatic but at the same time feels guilty. She wishes that she could stop studying so hard, but parental and personal pressures drive her. She will finally have a nervous breakdown and quit medical school and marry a successful young doctor. (1970, p. 61)

Here Anne is seen as happy yet guilty. Horner scores this as a motive to avoid the situation, and implies an inability on the part of the respondent to accept what she merits, the pleasure of success. Yet constructivist theorists view a constant reassessment of external events as a positive force in psychological growth. Fingarette (1963) uses the example of a cloud which resembled a poorly formed rabbit but which, on a second look resembles a ship. Clouds in the sky, like the stellar constellations, are the original natural-and-organic projective test, and it seems reasonable to ask if the subject who saw both happiness and guilt in Anne's experience was seeing both a rabbit and a ship. Given this interpretation of her projection, she could be seen as anxious because she is reformulating—"re-cognizing," as Kegan likes to say—her experience. Again, the anxiety results from seeing another side.

Horner does refer to "an awareness of some of the *reality*-based sources of the motive to avoid success and the actual price one must pay for overcoming societal pressures and pursuing one's interest despite them" (Horner, 1972). This is her first reference to the real costs of success, and I would suggest that it does not go far enough. Horner is referring to the costs for women in particular because competitive success is not viewed as appropriate to the traditional female sex role. But men also experience some negative consequences of competitive success (Slater, 1970; Kanter, 1975; Maccoby, 1976). In the previous story, the student may have been projecting her own experience of the costs of academic success which can exist for either sex. Such projections could indicate reality-based fears, especially for a bright student for whom "parental pressure" has been very real. Horner's view of this story as an example of a learned, sex-typed fear is supported, however, by the last sentence in which Anne marries what she could not be, a doctor.

In another story, the subject initially exhibits ambivalence, but her values and meaning-making structures finally determine the resolution she creates.

> Anne cannot help but be pleased; yet she is unhappy. She had not wanted to be a doctor . . . she had half hoped her grades would be too poor to continue, but she had been too proud to allow that to happen. She had worked extraordinarily hard and her grades showed it. "It is not enough," Anne thinks. "I am not happy." She is not sure what she wants—only feels the pressure to achieve something, even if it's something she doesn't want. Anne says, "To hell with the whole business" and goes into social work—not as glamorous, prestigious, or lucrative; but she is happy. (p. 61)

The consequences to Anne in this story are not negative unless glamour, prestige, and money are the values by which we measure success. She ends up, in this story, *happy*. And it is here that we see meaning-making in action, and action being projected on the basis of that meaning: medicine is not what Anne wants, social work is. Horner could conclude that the subject is scaling down her aspirations or reverting to a sex-role stereotype. Yet the respondent could be making sense of her own ambivalence, sorting out her values, and rejecting competition, a grueling schedule, and three particular values that are associated in this country with medicine but not with social work. She has chosen a field in which relationships are more highly valued, in which training gives more attention to context, and in which competition is supposedly less of a daily experience. Thus, this example does not include consequences defined as negative by a universal value scheme. Instead, the story shows us anxiety rooted in the mismatch between event and structure of knowing, a questioning of competitive success, and, finally, a happy ending.

These stories illustrate that as the subjects attempt to make meaning of Anne's situation, they become anxious. Their structure of knowing, with its relational values, does not fit with the event of the Anne cue, and their inability to make meaning results in anxiety.

However, if this reaction is a function of the structure brought to bear on an event, why aren't men anxious? They too, presumably, construct reality and experience anxiety when their meaning-making activity fails. The work of Piaget, Gilligan, and Chodorow points to an incompatibility between competitive, lone success and meaning structures that are particular to females. The male equivalents of these structures are more rule-focused, individualistic, and rights-oriented. They are also more dependent on a sense of self apart and in a positional stance, as opposed to the female sense of self as a part of the context. With these structures, John (changed from Anne for male subjects) has played by the rules and won; has the right to feel good about succeeding because he worked for it; and has a solid sense of his positional identity as apart from others who are less competent. Horner offers this story as a typical male response to the cue:

> John is a conscientious young man who worked hard. He is pleased with himself. John has always wanted to go into medicine and is very dedicated. His hard work has paid off. He is thinking that he must not let up now, but must work even harder than he did before. His good marks have encouraged him. (He may even consider going into research now.) While others with good first term marks sluff off, John continues working hard and eventually graduates at the top of his class (specializing in neurology). (1970, p. 64)

Most of the men Horner tested were able to fit the John cue and the competitive definition of success comfortably into their structures. The female respondents, however, failed to make sense of the cue as a happy event because their meaning-making orientations were contextual, relational, and oriented toward the personal. The difficulty of assimilating the event to these structures created anxiety.

The Inadequacy of Old Solutions

What are the implications of this new view of Horner's experiment for social change and for women? Horner concluded that women's success anxiety creates a barrier between them and success, and that this barrier should be removed. Here Horner is in the bind of many feminist advocates of social change. She correctly points out (1972) that something is wrong with a society that ties women to a stereotype of nonachievement and incompetence. However, by saying that women have internalized this stereotype and that this is the source of their barrier against success, she also finds herself saying that there is something wrong with women. Other feminists would say that there is something wrong with this definition of success and that there is something right with women's inability to accommodate this definition.

Support for the latter proposition can be found in recent literature on the lives of those who have been successful in the narrow competitive sense. Michael Maccoby's notion of the Gamesman (1976) highlights the costs of success. This new success-personality on the corporate scene is "more detached and emotionally inaccessible" (p. 100) than his forerunners, the entrepreneur and the organization man. The result, according to Maccoby, is a loss of meaning, anomic paralysis, and despair. Maccoby documents the great loss entailed in successful corporate maneuvering at the expense of emotion and close personal relationships. Thus, it is not only for women that these emotional costs exist. They exist for both sexes. But women, having grown up with a set of relationship-oriented structures, are quicker to sense the problems of this way of living.

Unfortunately, this understanding has not informed the creation of corporate social structures which more and more women are now entering. No one has documented their experience from a constructivist standpoint. Rosabeth Kanter, however, has looked at their position in the organization from a structuralist sociological perspective, and points out the links between a "masculinist ethic" (p. 43) and a "spirit of managerialism" (p. 42) which assume hierarchy and denigrate relationships. Building on the work of Davis (1967), Kanter argues that relationships were the single differentiating factor between the behavior of men and women in the corporation, and cites the importance of maintaining relationships to women who choose not to be promoted if this means losing close relationships. Horner has documented the anxiety of able women who choose to "stay behind" (1972).

Thus, when women enter the domain of corporate power, they are faced with a choice between competitive success as defined by the corporate, capitalist culture, and the emotional roots and sense of meaning that successful gamesmen have left behind. If they choose the meaning their structures of knowing find in relationships, they cannot work up to their capacity, and therefore experience frustration and anxiety. Their dilemma is further complicated by the built-in anxiety Kegan has defined as the misfit between structure and environment, which would exist for them whichever path they chose within the corporate environment.

The popular wisdom based on Horner's work recommended changing women so that they could "succeed" in this environment and function with less anxiety. But Kegan and Gilligan would argue that anxiety is part of development and, while it need not reach proportions requiring clinical intervention, a certain amount of anxiety is necessary. The problem is that corporations, and for that matter most institutions, are not designed to promote this kind of development. The dilemma of relational thinking versus competition does not even exist for them, since they have already chosen competition. It appears to be the corporate environment, then, that needs to be changed. The survival of men (Maccoby, 1976; Slater, 1970) as well as women depends on this.

This gives us an entirely different agenda for women in complex organizations. It no longer seems appropriate to rout out success anxiety and replace it with acceptance of the masculine rules of the game. Rather, women now need to focus on affirming the structures and values they bring to the question of competition versus relationships and start reconstructing institutions according to what women know.

Reference Notes

1. Major, B. N., & Sherman, R. C. The competitive woman: Fear of success, attractiveness, and competitor sex. Paper presented at the 83rd Annual Meeting of the American Psychological Association, Chicago, August 30–September 2, 1975.
2. Horner, M., Tresemer, D., Berens, A. E., & Watson, R. I. Scoring manual for an empirically derived scoring system for motive to avoid success. Paper presented at the 81st Annual Meeting of the American Psychological Association, Montreal, August 27–31, 1973.
3. Pappo, M. *Fear of success: A theoretical analysis and the construction and validation of a measuring instrument.* Doctoral dissertation, Columbia University, 1972. Available in the Sophia Smith Collection, Neilsen Library, Smith College.
4. Horner, M., & Fleming, J. Sex and race differences in fear of success imagery. Unpublished manuscript, Harvard University, 1973.

References

Alper, T. G. The relationship between role orientation and achievement motivation in college women. *Journal of Personality*, 1973, 41, 9–31.

Alper, T. G. Achievement motivation in college women: A now-you-see-it-now-you-don't phenomenon. *American Psychologist*, 1974, 29, 194–203.

Bright, M. V. Factors related to the traditionality or innovativeness of career choices in black college women. Unpublished master's thesis, Howard University, 1970

Brown, M., Jennings, J., & Vanik, V. The motive to avoid success: A further examination. *Journal of Research in Personality*, 1974, 8, 172–176.

Chodorow, N. Family structure and feminine personality. In M. Rosaldo & L. Lamphere (Eds.), *Women, culture and society.* Stanford: Stanford University Press, 1974.

Chodorow, N. *The reproduction of mothering: Psychoanalysis and the sociology of gender.* Berkeley: University of California Press, 1978.

Davis, K. *Human relations at work.* New York: McGraw-Hill, 1967.

Esposito, R. P. The relationship between the motive to avoid success and vocational choice. *Journal of Vocational Behavior*, 1977, 10, 347–357.

Fingarette, H. *The self in transformation.* New York: Harper & Row, 1963.

Gilligan, C. F. In a different voice: Women's conceptions of the self and of morality. *Harvard Educational Review*, 1977, 47, 481–517. [Also in this anthology on pp. 187–223.]

Griffore, R. F. Fear of success and task difficulty effects on graduate students' final exam performance. *Journal of Educational Psychology*, 1977, 69, 556–563.

Horner, M. S. *Sex differences in achievement motivation and performance in competitive and noncompetitive situations* (Doctoral dissertation, University of Michigan, 1968). University Microfilms No. 6912135.

Horner, M. S. Femininity and successful achievement: A basic inconsistency. In J. Bardwick (Ed.), *Feminine personality and conflict.* Belmont, Calif.: Brooks/Cole, 1970.

Horner, M. S. Toward an understanding of achievement-related conflicts in women. *Journal of Social Issues*, 1972, 28, 157–176.

Horner, M. S. Why bright women fear success. In *The female experience.* Del Mar, Calif.: Communications Research Machines, 1973.

Kanter, R. Women and the structure of organizations. In M. Millman (Ed.), *Another voice.* New York: Doubleday/Anchor, 1975.

Karabenick, S. A. Effects of fear of success, fear of failure, type of opponent and feedback on female achievement performance. *Journal of Research in Personality*, 1976, 10, 369–385.

Karabenick, S. A. Fear of success, achievement and affiliation dispositions and the performance of men and women under individual and competitive conditions. *Journal of Personality*, 1977, 45, 117–149.

Kegan, R. *Ego and truth: Personality and the Piaget paradigm.* Unpublished doctoral dissertation, Harvard University, 1977.

Kohlberg, L. Stage and sequence: The cognitive-developmental approach to socialization. In

D. A. Goslin (Ed.), *Handbook of socialization theory and research*. Chicago: Rand McNally, 1969.

Kohlberg, L. A cognitive-developmental analysis of children's sex-role concepts and attitudes. In E. Maccoby (Ed.), *The development of sex differences*. Stanford, Calif.: Stanford University Press, 1974.

Kohlberg, L., & Kramer, R. Continuities and discontinuities in childhood and adult moral development. *Human Development*, 1969, 12, 93-120.

Lockheed, M. E. Female motive to avoid success: A psychological barrier or a response to deviancy? *Sex Roles*, 1975, 1, 41-50.

Lever, J. Games children play. *Social Problems*, 1976, 23, 478-487.

Maccoby, M. *The gamesman*. New York: Simon & Schuster, 1976.

Makosky, V. P. Sex role compatibility of task and competitor, and fear of success as variables affecting women's performance. *Sex Roles*, 1976, 2, 237-248.

Mednick, M., & Puryear, G. R. Race and fear of success in college women, 1968 and 1971. *Journal of Consulting and Clinical Psychology*, 1976, 44, 787-789.

Midgeley, N., & Abrams, S. Fear of success and locus of control in young women. *Journal of Consulting and Clinical Psychology*, 1974, 42, 737-741.

Monahan, L., Kohn, D., & Shaver, P. Intrapsychic versus cultural explanations of the "fear of success" motive. *Journal of Personality and Social Psychology*, 1974, 29, 60-64.

Olsen, T., & Willemsen, V. Fear of success: Fact or artifact? *Journal of Psychology*, 1978, 98, 65-70.

Piaget, J. *The moral judgment of the child*. New York: Free Press, 1965. (Originally published, 1932)

Shaver, P. Questions concerning fear of success and its conceptual relatives. *Sex Roles*, 1976, 2, 305-320.

Slater, P. *The pursuit of loneliness*. Boston: Beacon Press, 1970.

Sorrentino, R. M., & Short, J. A. Performance in women as a function of fear of success and sex role orientation, 1973. (ERIC Document Reproduction Service No. ED 080929 CG 008220)

Tresemer, D. W. The cumulative record of research on fear of success. *Sex Roles*, 1976, 2, 217-236.

Tresemer, D. W. *Fear of success*. New York: Plenum Publishers, 1977.

Weinreich-Haste, H. Sex differences in fear of success among British students. *British Journal of Social and Clinical Psychology*, 1978, 17, 37-42.

Weston, P. J., & Mednick, M. T. Race, social class and the motive to avoid success in women. *Journal of Cross Cultural Psychology*, 1970, 1, 284-291.

Zuckerman, M., & Alison, S. N. An objective measure of fear of success: Construction and validation. *Journal of Personality Assessment*, 1976, 40, 424-427.

Zuckerman, M., & Wheeler, L. To dispel fantasies about the fantasy-based measure of fear of success. *Psychological Bulletin*, 1975, 82, 932-946.

In a Different Voice: Women's Conceptions of Self and of Morality

CAROL GILLIGAN

As theories of developmental psychology continue to define educational goals and practice, it has become imperative for educators and researchers to scrutinize not only the underlying assumptions of such theories but also the model of adulthood toward which they point. Carol Gilligan examines the limitations of several theories, most notably Kohlberg's stage theory of moral development, and concludes that developmental theory has not given adequate expression to the concerns and experience of women. Through a review of psychological and literary sources, she illustrates the feminine construction of reality. From her own research data, interviews with women contemplating abortion, she then derives an alternative sequence for the development of women's moral judgments. Finally, she argues for an expanded conception of adulthood that would result from the integration of the "feminine voice" into developmental theory.

The arc of developmental theory leads from infantile dependence to adult autonomy, tracing a path characterized by an increasing differentiation of self from other and a progressive freeing of thought from contextual constraints. The vision of Luther, journeying from the rejection of a self defined by others to the assertive boldness of "Here I stand" and the image of Plato's allegorical man in the cave, separating at last the shadows from the sun, have taken powerful hold on the psychological understanding of what constitutes development. Thus, the individual, meeting fully the developmental challenges of adolescence as set for him by Piaget, Erikson, and Kohlberg, thinks formally, proceeding from theory to fact, and defines both the self and the moral autonomously, that is, apart from the identification and conventions that had comprised the particulars of his childhood world. So

The research reported here was partially supported by a grant from the Spencer Foundation. I wish to thank Mary Belenky for her collaboration and colleagueship in the abortion decision study and Michael Murphy for his comments and help in preparing this manuscript.

Harvard Educational Review   Vol. 47   No. 4   November 1977, 481–517

equipped, he is presumed ready to live as an adult, to love and work in a way that is both intimate and generative, to develop an ethical sense of caring and a genital mode of relating in which giving and taking fuse in the ultimate reconciliation of the tension between self and other.

Yet the men whose theories have largely informed this understanding of development have all been plagued by the same problem, the problem of women, whose sexuality remains more diffuse, whose perception of self is so much more tenaciously embedded in relationships with others and whose moral dilemmas hold them in a mode of judgment that is insistently contextual. The solution has been to consider women as either deviant or deficient in their development.

That there is a discrepancy between concepts of womanhood and adulthood is nowhere more clearly evident than in the series of studies on sex-role stereotypes reported by Broverman, Vogel, Broverman, Clarkson, and Rosenkrantz (1972). The repeated finding of these studies is that the qualities deemed necessary for adulthood—the capacity for autonomous thinking, clear decision making, and responsible action—are those associated with masculinity but considered undesirable as attributes of the feminine self. The stereotypes suggest a splitting of love and work that relegates the expressive capacities requisite for the former to women while the instrumental abilities necessary for the latter reside in the masculine domain. Yet, looked at from a different perspective, these stereotypes reflect a conception of adulthood that is itself out of balance, favoring the separateness of the individual self over its connection to others and leaning more toward an autonomous life of work than toward the interdependence of love and care.

This difference in point of view is the subject of this essay, which seeks to identify in the feminine experience and construction of social reality a distinctive voice, recognizable in the different perspective it brings to bear on the construction and resolution of moral problems. The first section begins with the repeated observation of difference in women's concepts of self and of morality. This difference is identified in previous psychological descriptions of women's moral judgments and described as it again appears in current research data. Examples drawn from interviews with women in and around a university community are used to illustrate the characteristics of the feminine voice. The relational bias in women's thinking that has, in the past, been seen to compromise their moral judgment and impede their development now begins to emerge in a new developmental light. Instead of being seen as a developmental deficiency, this bias appears to reflect a different social and moral understanding.

This alternative conception is enlarged in the second section through consideration of research interviews with women facing the moral dilemma of whether to continue or abort a pregnancy. Since the research design allowed women to define as well as resolve the moral problem, developmental distinctions could be derived directly from the categories of women's thought. The responses of women to structured interview questions regarding the pregnancy decision formed the basis for describing a developmental sequence that traces progressive differentiations in their understanding and judgment of conflicts between self and other. While the sequence of women's moral development follows the three-level progression of all social developmental theory, from an egocentric through a societal to a universal perspective, this progression takes place within a distinct moral conception. This conception differs from that derived by Kohlberg from his all-male longitudinal research data.

This difference then becomes the basis in the third section for challenging the current assessment of women's moral judgment at the same time that it brings to bear a new perspective on developmental assessment in general. The inclusion in the overall conception of development of those categories derived from the study of women's moral judgment enlarges developmental understanding, enabling it to encompass better the thinking of both sexes. This is particularly true with respect to the construction and resolution of the dilemmas of adult life. Since the conception of adulthood retrospectively shapes the theoretical understanding of the development that precedes it, the changes in that conception that follow from the more central inclusion of women's judgments recast developmental understanding and lead to a reconsideration of the substance of social and moral development.

Characteristics of the Feminine Voice

The revolutionary contribution of Piaget's work is the experimental confirmation and refinement of Kant's assertion that knowledge is actively constructed rather than passively received. Time, space, self, and other, as well as the categories of developmental theory, all arise out of the active interchange between the individual and the physical and social world in which he lives and of which he strives to make sense. The development of cognition is the process of reappropriating reality at progressively more complex levels of apprehension, as the structures of thinking expand to encompass the increasing richness and intricacy of experience.

Moral development, in the work of Piaget and Kohlberg, refers specifically to the expanding conception of the social world as it is reflected in the understanding and resolution of the inevitable conflicts that arise in the relations between self and others. The moral judgment is a statement of priority, an attempt at rational resolution in a situation where, from a different point of view, the choice itself seems to do violence to justice.

Kohlberg (1969), in his extension of the early work of Piaget, discovered six stages of moral judgment, which he claimed formed an invariant sequence, each successive stage representing a more adequate construction of the moral problem, which in turn provides the basis for its more just resolution. The stages divide into three levels, each of which denotes a significant expansion of the moral point of view from an egocentric through a societal to a universal ethical conception. With this expansion in perspective comes the capacity to free moral judgment from the individual needs and social conventions with which it had earlier been confused and anchor it instead in principles of justice that are universal in application. These principles provide criteria upon which both individual and societal claims can be impartially assessed. In Kohlberg's view, at the highest stages of development morality is freed from both psychological and historical constraints, and the individual can judge independently of his own particular needs and of the values of those around him.

That the moral sensibility of women differs from that of men was noted by Freud (1925/1961) in the following by now well-quoted statement:

> I cannot evade the notion (though I hesitate to give it expression) that for women the level of what is ethically normal is different from what it is in man. Their superego is never so inexorable, so impersonal, so independent of its emotional origins as we require it to be in men. Character-traits which critics of every epoch have brought up against women—that they show less sense of justice than men, that they are less ready to submit to the great exigencies of life, that they are more often influenced in their judgments by feelings of affection or hostility—all these would be amply accounted for by the modification in the formation of their super-ego which we have inferred above. (pp. 257–258)

While Freud's explanation lies in the deviation of female from male development around the construction and resolution of the Oedipal problem, the same observations about the nature of morality in women emerge from the work of Piaget and Kohlberg. Piaget (1932/1965), in his study of the rules of children's games, observed that, in the games they played, girls were "less explicit about agreement [than boys] and less concerned with legal elaboration" (p. 93). In contrast to the boys' interest in the codification of rules, the girls adopted a more pragmatic attitude, regarding "a rule as good so long as the game repays it" (p. 83). As a result, in comparison to boys, girls were found to be "more tolerant and more easily reconciled to innovations" (p. 52).

Kohlberg (1971) also identifies a strong interpersonal bias in the moral judgments of women, which leads them to be considered as typically at the third of his six-stage developmental sequence. At that stage, the good is identified with "what pleases or helps others and is approved of by them" (p. 164). This mode of judgment is conventional in its conformity to generally held notions of the good but also psychological in its concern with intention and consequence as the basis for judging the morality of action.

That women fall largely into this level of moral judgment is hardly surprising when we read from the Broverman et al. (1972) list that prominent among the twelve attributes considered to be desirable for women are tact, gentleness, awareness of the feelings of others, strong need for security, and easy expression of tender feelings. And yet, herein lies the paradox, for the very traits that have traditionally defined the "goodness" of women, their care for and sensitivity to the needs of others, are those that mark them as deficient in moral development. The infusion of feeling into their judgments keeps them from developing a more independent and abstract ethical conception in which concern for others derives from principles of justice rather than from compassion and care. Kohlberg, however, is less pessimistic than Freud in his assessment, for he sees the development of women as extending beyond the interpersonal level, following the same path toward independent, principled judgment that he discovered in the research on men from which his stages were derived. In Kohlberg's view, women's development will proceed beyond Stage Three when they are challenged to solve moral problems that require them to see beyond the relationships that have in the past generally bound their moral experience.

What then do women say when asked to construct the moral domain; how do we identify the characteristically "feminine" voice? A Radcliffe undergraduate, responding to the question, "If you had to say what morality meant to you, how would you sum it up?," replies:

> When I think of the word morality, I think of obligations. I usually think of it as conflicts between personal desires and social things, social considerations, or personal desires of yourself versus personal desires of another person or people or whatever. Morality is that whole realm of how you decide these conflicts. A moral person is one who would decide, like by placing themselves more often than not as equals, a truly moral person would always consider another person as their equal . . . in a situation of social interaction, something is morally wrong where the individual ends up screwing a lot of people. And it is morally right when everyone comes out better of.[1]

Yet when asked if she can think of someone whom she would consider a genuinely moral person, she replies, "Well, immediately I think of Albert Schweitzer because he has obviously given his life to help others." Obligation and sacrifice override the ideal of equality, setting up a basic contradiction in her thinking.

Another undergraduate responds to the question, "What does it mean to say something is morally right or wrong?," by also speaking first of responsibilities and obligations:

> Just that it has to do with responsibilties and obligations and values, mainly values. . . . In my life situation I relate morality with interpersonal relationships that have to do with respect for the other person and myself. [Why respect other people?] Because they have a consciousness or feelings that can be hurt, an awareness that can be hurt.

The concern about hurting others persists as a major theme in the responses of two other Radcliffe students:

> [Why be moral?] Millions of people have to live together peacefully. I personally don't want to hurt other people. That's a real criterion, a main criterion for me. It underlies my sense of justice. It isn't nice to inflict pain. I empathize with anyone in pain. Not hurting others is important in my own private morals. Years ago, I would have jumped out of a window not to hurt my boyfriend. That was pathological. Even today though, I want approval and love and I don't want enemies. Maybe that's why there is morality—so people can win approval, love and friendship.

> My main moral principle is not hurting other people as long as you aren't going against your own conscience and as long as you remain true to yourself. . . . There are many moral issues such as abortion, the draft, killing, stealing, monogamy, etc. If something is a controversial issue like these, then I always say it is up to the individual. The individual has to decide and then follow his own con-

---

[1] The Radcliffe women whose responses are cited were interviewed as part of a pilot study on undergraduate moral development conducted by the author in 1970.

science. There are no moral absolutes. . . . Laws are pragmatic instruments, but they are not absolutes. A viable society can't make exceptions all the time, but I would personally. . . . I'm afraid I'm heading for some big crisis with my boy-friend someday, and someone will get hurt, and he'll get more hurt than I will. I feel an obligation to not hurt him, but also an obligation to not lie. I don't know if it is possible to not lie and not hurt.

The common thread that runs through these statements, the wish not to hurt others and the hope that in morality lies a way of solving conflicts so that no one will get hurt, is striking in that it is independently introduced by each of the four women as the most specific item in their response to a most general question. The moral person is one who helps others; goodness is service, meeting one's obligations and responsibilities to others, if possible, without sacrificing oneself. While the first of the four women ends by denying the conflict she initially introduced, the last woman anticipates a conflict between remaining true to herself and adhering to her principle of not hurting others. The dilemma that would test the limits of this judgment would be one where helping others is seen to be at the price of hurting the self.

The reticence about taking stands on "controversial issues," the willingness to "make exceptions all the time" expressed in the final example above, is echoed repeatedly by other Radcliffe students, as in the following two examples:

I never feel that I can condemn anyone else. I have a very relativistic position. The basic idea that I cling to is the sanctity of human life. I am inhibited about impressing my beliefs on others.

I could never argue that my belief on a moral question is anything that another person should accept. I don't believe in absolutes. . . . If there is an absolute for moral decisions, it is human life.

Or as a thirty-one-year-old Wellesley graduate says, in explaining why she would find it difficult to steal a drug to save her own life despite her belief that it would be right to steal for another: "It's just very hard to defend yourself against the rules. I mean, we live by consensus, and you take an action simply for yourself, by yourself, there's no consensus there, and that is relatively indefensible in this society now."

What begins to emerge is a sense of vulnerability that impedes these women from taking a stand, what George Eliot (1860/1965) regards as the girl's "susceptibility" to adverse judgments of others, which stems from her lack of power and consequent inability to do something in the world. While relativism in men, the unwillingness to make moral judgments that Kohlberg and Kramer (1969) and Kohlberg and Gilligan (1971) have associated with the adolescent crisis of identity and belief, takes the form of calling into question the concept of morality itself, the women's reluctance to judge stems rather from their uncertainty about their right to make moral statements or, perhaps, the price for them that such judgment seems to entail. This contrast echoes that made by Matina Horner (1972), who differentiated the ideological fear of success expressed by men from the personal conflicts about succeeding that riddled the women's responses to stories of competitive achievement.

> Most of the men who responded with the expectation of negative consequences because of success were not concerned about their masculinity but were instead likely to have expressed existential concerns about finding a "non-materialistic happiness and satisfaction in life." These concerns, which reflect changing attitudes toward traditional kinds of success or achievement in our society, played little, if any, part in the female stories. Most of the women who were high in fear of success imagery continued to be concerned about the discrepancy between success in the situation described and feminine identity. (pp. 163–164)

When women feel excluded from direct participation in society, they see themselves as subject to a consensus or judgment made and enforced by the men on whose protection and support they depend and by whose names they are known. A divorced middle-aged woman, mother of adolescent daughters, resident of a sophisticated university community, tells the story as follows:

> As a woman, I feel I never understood that I was a person, that I can make decisions and I have a right to make decisions. I always felt that that belonged to my father or my husband in some way or church which was always represented by a male clergyman. They were the three men in my life: father, husband, and clergyman, and they had much more to say about what I should or shouldn't do. They were really authority figures which I accepted. I didn't rebel against that. It only has lately occurred to me that I never even rebelled against it, and my girls are much more conscious of this, not in the militant sense, but just in the recognizing sense. . . . I still let things happen to me rather than make them happen, than to make choices, although I know all about choices. I know the procedures and the steps and all. [Do you have any clues about why this might be true?] Well, I think in one sense, there is less responsibility involved. Because if you make a dumb decision, you have to take the rap. If it happens to you, well, you can complain about it. I think that if you don't grow up feeling that you ever had any choices, you don't either have the sense that you have emotional responsibility. With this sense of choice comes this sense of responsibility.

The essence of the moral decision is the exercise of choice and the willingness to accept responsibility for that choice. To the extent that women perceive themselves as having no choice, they correspondingly excuse themselves from the responsibility that decision entails. Childlike in the vulnerability of their dependence and consequent fear of abandonment, they claim to wish only to please but in return for their goodness they expect to be loved and cared for. This, then, is an "altruism" always at risk, for it presupposes an innocence constantly in danger of being compromised by an awareness of the trade-off that has been made. Asked to describe herself, a Radcliffe senior responds:

> I have heard of the onion skin theory. I see myself as an onion, as a block of different layers, the external layers for people that I don't know that well, the agreeable, the social, and as you go inward there are more sides for people I know that I show. I am not sure about the innermost, whether there is a core, or whether I have just picked up everything as I was growing up, these different influences. I think I have a neutral attitude towards myself, but I do think in terms of good and bad. . . . Good—I try to be considerate and thoughtful of other people and I try to be fair in situations and be tolerant. I use the words but I try and work

> them out practically. . . . Bad things—I am not sure if they are bad, if they are altruistic or I am doing them basically for approval of other people. [Which things are these?] The values I have when I try to act them out. They deal mostly with interpersonal type relations. . . . If I were doing it for approval, it would be a very tenuous thing. If I didn't get the right feedback, there might go all my values.

Ibsen's play, *A Doll House* (1879/1965), depicts the explosion of just such a world through the eruption of a moral dilemma that calls into question the notion of goodness that lies at its center. Nora, the "squirrel wife," living with her husband as she had lived with her father, puts into action this conception of goodness as sacrifice and, with the best of intentions, takes the law into her own hands. The crisis that ensues, most painfully for her in the repudiation of that goodness by the very person who was its recipient and beneficiary, causes her to reject the suicide that she had initially seen as its ultimate expression and chose instead to seek new and firmer answers to the adolescent questions of identity and belief.

The availability of choice and with it the onus of responsibility has now invaded the most private sector of the woman's domain and threatens a similar explosion. For centuries, women's sexuality anchored them in passivity, in a receptive rather than active stance, where the events of conception and childbirth could be controlled only by a withholding in which their own sexual needs were either denied or sacrificed. That such a sacrifice entailed a cost to their intelligence as well was seen by Freud (1908/1959) when he tied the "undoubted intellectual inferiority of so many women" to "the inhibition of thought necessitated by sexual suppression" (p. 199). The strategies of withholding and denial that women have employed in the politics of sexual relations appear similar to their evasion or withholding of judgment in the moral realm. The hesitance expressed in the previous examples to impose even a belief in the value of human life on others, like the reluctance to claim one's sexuality, bespeaks a self uncertain of its strength, unwilling to deal with consequence, and thus avoiding confrontation.

Thus women have traditionally deferred to the judgment of men, although often while intimating a sensibility of their own which is at variance with that judgment. Maggie Tulliver, in *The Mill on the Floss* (Eliot, 1860/1965) responds to the accusations that ensue from the discovery of her secretly continued relationship with Phillip Wakeham by acceding to her brother's moral judgment while at the same time asserting a different set of standards by which she attests her own superiority:

> I don't want to defend myself. . . . I know I've been wrong—often continually. But yet, sometimes when I have done wrong, it has been because I have feelings that you would be the better for if you had them. If *you* were in fault ever, if you had done anything very wrong, I should be sorry for the pain it brought you; I should not want punishment to be heaped on you. (p. 188)

An eloquent defense, Kohlberg would argue, of a Stage Three moral position, an assertion of the age-old split between thinking and feeling, justice and mercy, that underlies many of the clichés and stereotypes concerning the difference between the sexes. But considered from another point of view, it is a moment of confrontation, replacing a former evasion, between two modes of judging, two differing constructions of the moral domain—one traditionally associated with masculinity and the public world of social power, the other with femininity and the privacy of domestic interchange. While the developmental ordering of these two points of view has been to consider the masculine as the more adequate and thus as replacing the feminine as the individual moves toward higher stages, their reconciliation remains unclear.

The Development of Women's Moral Judgment

Recent evidence for a divergence in moral development between men and women comes from the research of Haan (Note 1) and Holstein (1976) whose findings lead them to question the possibility of a "sex-related bias" in Kolhberg's scoring system. This system is based on Kohlberg's six-stage description of moral development. Kohlberg's stages divide into three levels, which he designates as preconventional, conventional, and postconventional, thus denoting the major shifts in moral perspective around a center of moral understanding that equates justice with the maintenance of existing social systems. While the preconventional conception of justice is based on the needs of the self, the conventional judgment derives from an understanding of society. This understanding is in turn superseded by a postconventional or principled conception of justice where the good is formulated in universal terms. The quarrel with Kohlberg's stage scoring does not pertain to the structural differentiation of his levels but rather to questions of stage and sequence. Kohlberg's stages begin with an obedience and punishment orientation (Stage One), and go from there in invariant order to instrumental hedonism (Stage Two), interpersonal concordance (Stage Three), law and order (Stage Four), social contract (Stage Five), and universal ethical principles (Stage Six).

The bias that Haan and Holstein question in this scoring system has to do with the subordination of the interpersonal to the societal definition of the good in the transition from Stage Three to Stage Four. This is the transition that has repeatedly been found to be problematic for women. In 1969, Kohlberg and Kramer identified Stage Three as the characteristic mode of women's moral judgments, claiming that, since women's lives were interpersonally based, this stage was not only "functional" for them but also adequate for resolving the moral conflicts that they faced. Turiel (1973) reported that while girls reached Stage Three sooner than did boys, their judgments tended to remain at that stage while the boys' development continued further along Kohlberg's scale. Gilligan, Kohlberg, Lerner, and Belenky (1971) found a similar association between sex and moral-judgment stage in a study of high-school students, with the girls' responses being scored predominantly at Stage Three while the boys' responses were more often scored at Stage Four.

This repeated finding of developmental inferiority in women may, however, have more to do with the standard by which development has been measured than with the quality of women's thinking per se. Haan's data (Note 1) on the Berkeley Free Speech Movement and Holstein's (1976) three-year longitudinal study of adolescents and their parents indicate that the moral judgments of women differ from those of men in the greater extent to which women's judgments are tied to feelings of empathy and compassion and are concerned more with the resolution of "real-life" as opposed to hypothetical dilemmas (Note 1, p. 34). However, as long as the categories by which development is assessed are derived within a male perspective from male research data, divergence from the masculine standard can be seen only as a failure of development. As a result, the thinking of women is often classified with that of children. The systematic exclusion from consideration of alternative criteria that might better encompass the development of women indicates not only the limitations of a theory framed by men and validated by research samples disproportionately male and adolescent but also the effects of the diffidence prevalent among women, their reluctance to speak publicly in their own voice, given the constraints imposed on them by the politics of differential power between the sexes.

In order to go beyond the question, "How much like men do women think, how capable are they of engaging in the abstract and hypothetical construction of reality?" it is necessary to identify and define in formal terms developmental criteria that encompass the categories of women's thinking. Such criteria would include the progressive differentiations, comprehensiveness, and adequacy that characterize higher-stage resolution of the "more frequently occurring, real-life moral dilemmas of interpersonal, empathic, fellow-feeling concerns" (Haan, Note 1, p. 34), which have long been the center of women's moral judgments and experience. To ascertain whether the feminine construction of the moral domain relies on a language different from that of men, but one which deserves equal credence in the definition of what constitutes development, it is necessary first to find the places where women have the power to choose and thus are willing to speak in their own voice.

When birth control and abortion provide women with effective means for controlling their fertility, the dilemma of choice enters the center of women's lives. Then the relationships that have traditionally defined women's identities and framed their moral judgments no longer flow inevitably from their reproductive capacity but become matters of decision over which they have control. Released from the passivity and reticence of a sexuality that binds them in dependence, it becomes possible for women to question with Freud what it is that they want and to assert their own answers to that question. However, while society may affirm publicly the woman's right to choose for herself, the exercise of such choice brings her privately into conflict with the conventions of femininity, particularly the moral equation of goodness with self-sacrifice. While independent assertion in judgment and action is considered the hallmark of adulthood and constitutes as well the standard of masculine development, it is rather in their care and concern for others that women have both judged themselves and been judged.

The conflict between self and other thus constitutes the central moral problem for women, posing a dilemma whose resolution requires a reconciliation between femininity and adulthood. In the absence of such a reconciliation, the moral problem cannot be resolved. The "good woman" masks assertion in evasion, denying responsibility by claiming only to meet the needs of others, while the "bad woman" forgoes or renounces the commitments that bind her in self-deception and betrayal. It is precisely this dilemma—the conflict between compassion and autonomy, between virtue and power—which the feminine voice struggles to resolve in its effort to reclaim the self and to solve the moral problem in such a way that no one is hurt.

When a woman considers whether to continue or abort a pregnancy, she contemplates a decision that affects both self and others and engages directly the critical moral issue of hurting. Since the choice is ultimately hers and therefore one for which she is responsible, it raises precisely those questions of judgment that have been most problematic for women. Now she is asked whether she wishes to interrupt that stream of life which has for centuries immersed her in the passivity of dependence while at the same time imposing on her the responsibility for care. Thus the abortion decision brings to the core of feminine apprehension, to what Joan Didion (1972) calls "the irreconcilable difference of it—that sense of living one's deepest life underwater, that dark involvement with blood and birth and death" (p. 14), the adult questions of responsibility and choice.

How women deal with such choices has been the subject of my research, designed to clarify, through considering the ways in which women construct and resolve the abortion decision, the nature and development of women's moral judgment. Twenty-nine women, diverse in age, race, and social class, were referred by abortion and pregnancy counseling services and participated in the study for a variety of reasons. Some came to gain further clarification with respect to a decision about which they were in conflict, some in response to a counselor's concern about repeated abortions, and others out of an interest in and/or willingness to contribute to ongoing research. Although the pregnancies occurred under a variety of circumstances in the lives of these women, certain commonalities could be discerned. The adolescents often failed to use birth control because they denied or discredited their capacity to bear children. Some of the older women attributed the pregnancy to the omission of contraceptive measures in circumstances where intercourse had not been anticipated. Since the pregnancies often coincided with efforts on the part of the women to end a relationship, they may be seen as a manifestation of ambivalence or as a way of putting the relationship to the ultimate test of commitment. For these women, the pregnancy appeared to be a way of testing truth, making the baby an ally in the search for male support and protection or, that failing, a companion victim of his rejection. There were, finally, some women who became pregnant either as a result of a failure of birth control or intentionally as part of a joint decision that later was reconsidered. Of the twenty-nine women, four decided to have the baby, one miscarried, twenty-one chose abortion, and three remained in doubt about the decision.

In the initial part of the interview, the women were asked to discuss the decision that confronted them, how they were dealing with it, the alternatives they were considering, their reasons for and against each option, the people involved, the conflicts entailed, and the ways in which making this decision affected their self-concepts and their relationships with others. Then, in the second part of the interview, moral judgment was assessed in the hypothetical mode by presenting for resolution three of Kohlberg's standard research dilemmas.

While the structural progression from a preconventional through a conventional to a postconventional moral perspective can readily be discerned in the women's responses to both actual and hypothetical dilemmas, the conventions that shape women's moral judgments differ from those that apply to men. The construction of the abortion dilemma, in particular, reveals the existence of a distinct moral language whose evolution informs the sequence of women's development. This is the language of selfishness and responsibility, which defines the moral problem as one of obligation to exercise care and avoid hurt. The infliction of hurt is considered selfish and immoral in its reflection of unconcern, while the expression of care is seen as the fulfillment of moral responsibility. The reiterative use of the language of selfishness and responsibility and the underlying moral orientation it reflects sets the women apart from the men whom Kohlberg studied and may be seen as the critical reason for their failure to develop within the constraints of his system.

In the developmental sequence that follows, women's moral judgments proceed from an initial focus on the self at the *first level* to the discovery, in the transition to the *second level,* of the concept of responsibility as the basis for a new equilibrium between self and others. The elaboration of this concept of responsibility and its fusion with a maternal concept of morality, which seeks to ensure protection for the dependent and unequal, characterizes the *second level* of judgment. At this level the good is equated with caring for others. However, when the conventions of feminine goodness legitimize only others as the recipients of moral care, the logical inequality between self and other and the psychological violence that it engenders create the disequilibrium that initiates the *second* transition. The relationship between self and others is then reconsidered in an effort to sort out the confusion between conformity and care inherent in the conventional definition of feminine goodness and to establish a new equilibrium, which dissipates the tension between selfishness and responsibility. At the *third level,* the self becomes the arbiter of an independent judgment that now subsumes both conventions and individual needs under the moral principle of nonviolence. Judgment remains psychological in its concern with the intention and consequences of action, but it now becomes universal in its condemnation of exploitation and hurt.

Level I: Orientation to Individual Survival

In its initial and simplest construction, the abortion decision centers on the self. The concern is pragmatic, and the issue is individual survival. At this level, "should" is undifferentiated from "would," and others influence the decision only through their power to affect its consequences. An eighteen-year-old, asked what she thought when she found herself pregnant, replies: "I really didn't think anything except that I didn't want it. [Why was that?] I didn't want it, I wasn't ready for it, and next year will be my last year and I want to go to school."

Asked if there was a right decision, she says, "There is no right decision. [Why?]

I didn't want it." For her the question of right decision would emerge only if her own needs were in conflict; then she would have to decide which needs should take precedence. This was the dilemma of another eighteen-year-old, who saw having a baby as a way of increasing her freedom by providing "the perfect chance to get married and move away from home," but also as restricting her freedom "to do a lot of things."

At this first level, the self, which is the sole object of concern, is constrained by lack of power; the wish "to do a lot of things" is constantly belied by the limitations of what, in fact, is being done. Relationships are, for the most part, disappointing: "The only thing you are ever going to get out of going with a guy is to get hurt." As a result, women may in some instances deliberately choose isolation to protect themselves against hurt. When asked how she would describe herself to herself, a nineteen-year-old, who held herself responsible for the accidental death of a younger brother, answers as follows:

> I really don't know. I never thought about it. I don't know. I know basically the outline of a character. I am very independent. I don't really want to have to ask anybody for anything and I am a loner in life. I prefer to be by myself than around anybody else. I manage to keep my friends at a limited number with the point that I have very few friends. I don't know what else there is. I am a loner and I enjoy it. Here today and gone tomorrow.

The primacy of the concern with survival is explicitly acknowledged by a sixteen-year-old delinquent in response to Kohlberg's Heinz dilemma, which asks if it is right for a desperate husband to steal an outrageously overpriced drug to save the life of his dying wife:

> I think survival is one of the first things in life and that people fight for. I think it is the most important thing, more important than stealing. Stealing might be wrong, but if you have to steal to survive yourself or even kill, that is what you should do. . . . Preservation of oneself, I think, is the most important thing; it comes before anything in life.

The First Transition: From Selfishness to Responsibility

In the transition which follows and criticizes this level of judgment, the words selfishness and responsibility first appear. Their reference initially is to the self in a redefinition of the self-interest which has thus far served as the basis for judgment. The transitional issue is one of attachment or connection to others. The pregnancy catches up the issue not only by representing an immediate, literal connection, but also by affirming, in the most concrete and physical way, the capacity to assume adult feminine roles. However, while having a baby seems at first to offer respite from the loneliness of adolescence and to solve conflicts over dependence and independence, in reality the continuation of an adolescent pregnancy generally compounds these problems, increasing social isolation and precluding further steps toward independence.

To be a mother in the societal as well as the physical sense requires the assumption of parental responsibility for the care and protection of a child. However, in order to be able to care for another, one must first be able to care responsibly for oneself. The growth from childhood to adulthood, conceived as a move from selfishness to responsibility, is articulated explicitly in these terms by a seventeen-year-old who describes her response to her pregnancy as follows:

> I started feeling really good about being pregnant instead of feeling really bad, because I wasn't looking at the situation realistically. I was looking at it from my own sort of selfish needs because I was lonely and felt lonely and stuff. . . . Things weren't really going good for me, so I was looking at it that I could have a baby that I could take care of or something that was part of me, and that made me feel good . . . but I wasn't looking at the realistic side . . . about the responsibility I would have to take on . . . I came to this decision that I was going to have an abortion [because] I realized how much responsibility goes with having a child. Like you have to be there, you can't be out of the house all the time which is one thing I like to do . . . and I decided that I have to take on responsibility for myself and I have to work out a lot of things.

Stating her former mode of judgment, the wish to have a baby as a way of combating loneliness and feeling connected, she now criticizes that judgment as both "selfish" and "unrealistic." The contradiction between wishes for a baby and for the freedom to be "out of the house all the time"—that is, for connection and also for independence—is resolved in terms of a new priority, as the criterion for judgment changes. The dilemma now assumes moral definition as the emergent conflict between wish and necessity is seen as a disparity between "would" and "should." In this construction the "selfishness" of willful decision is counterposed to the "responsibility" of moral choice:

> What I want to do is to have the baby, but what I feel I should do which is what I need to do, is have an abortion right now, because sometimes what you want isn't right. Sometimes what is necessary comes before what you want, because it might not always lead to the right thing.

While the pregnancy itself confirms femininity—"I started feeling really good; it sort of made me feel, like being pregnant, I started feeling like a woman"—the abortion decision becomes an opportunity for the adult exercise of responsible choice.

> [How would you describe yourself to yourself?] I am looking at myself differently in the way that I have had a really heavy decision put upon me, and I have never really had too many hard decisions in my life, and I have made it. It has taken some responsibility to do this. I have changed in that way, that I have made a hard decision. And that has been good. Because before, I would not have looked at it realistically, in my opinion. I would have gone by what I wanted to do, and I wanted it, and even if it wasn't right. So I see myself as I'm becoming more mature in ways of making decisions and taking care of myself, doing something for myself. I think it is going to help me in other ways, if I have other decisions to make put upon me, which would take some responsibility. And I would know that I could make them.

In the epiphany of this cognitive reconstruction, the old becomes transformed in terms of the new. The wish to "do something for myself" remains, but the terms of its fulfillment change as the decision affirms both femininity and adulthood in its integration of responsibility and care. Morality, says another adolescent, "is the way you think about yourself . . . sooner or later you have to make up your mind to start taking care of yourself. Abortion, if you do it for the right reasons, is helping yourself to start over and do different things."

Since this transition signals an enhancement in self-worth, it requires a conception of self which includes the possibility for doing "the right thing," the ability to see in oneself the potential for social acceptance. When such confidence is seriously in doubt, the transitional questions may be raised but development is impeded. The failure to make this first transition, despite an understanding of the issues involved, is illustrated by a woman in her late twenties Her struggle with the conflict between selfishness and responsibility pervades but fails to resolve her dilemma of whether or not to have a third abortion.

> I think you have to think about the people who are involved, including yourself. You have responsibilities to yourself . . . and to make a right, whatever that is, decision in this depends on your knowledge and awareness of the responsibilities that you have and whether you can survive with a child and what it will do to your relationship with the father or how it will affect him emotionally.

Rejecting the idea of selling the baby and making "a lot of money in a black market kind of thing . . . because mostly I operate on principles and it would just rub me the wrong way to think I would be selling my own child," she struggles with a concept of responsibility which repeatedly turns back on the question of her own survival. Transition seems blocked by a self-image which is insistently contradictory:

> [How would you describe yourself to yourself?] I see myself as impulsive, practical—that is a contradiction—and moral and amoral, a contradiction. Actually the only thing that is consistent and not contradictory is the fact that I am very lazy which everyone has always told me is really a symptom of something else which I have never been able to put my finger on exactly. It has taken me a long time to like myself. In fact there are times when I don't, which I think is healthy to a point and sometimes I think I like myself too much and I probably evade myself too much, which avoids responsibility to myself and to other people who like me. I am pretty unfaithful to myself. . . I have a hard time even thinking that I am a human being, simply because so much rotten stuff goes on and people are so crummy and insensitive.

Seeing herself as avoiding responsibility, she can find no basis upon which to resolve the pregnancy dilemma. Instead, her inability to arrive at any clear sense of decision only contributes further to her overall sense of failure. Criticizing her parents for having betrayed her during adolescence by coercing her to have an abortion she did not want, she now betrays herself and criticizes that as well. In this light, it is less surprising that she considered selling her child, since she felt herself to have, in effect, been sold by her parents for the sake of maintaining their social status.

The Second Level: Goodness as Self-Sacrifice

The transition from selfishness to responsibility is a move toward social participation. Whereas at the first level, morality is seen as a matter of sanctions imposed by a society of which one is more subject than citizen, at the second level, moral judgment comes to rely on shared norms and expectations. The woman at this level validates her claim to social membership through the adoption of societal values. Consensual judgment becomes paramount and goodness the overriding concern as survival is now seen to depend on acceptance by others.

Here the conventional feminine voice emerges with great clarity, defining the self and proclaiming its worth on the basis of the ability to care for and protect others. The woman now constructs the world perfused with the assumptions about feminine goodness reflected in the stereotypes of the Broverman et al. (1972) studies. There the attributes considered desirable for women all presume an other, a recipient of the "tact, gentleness and easy expression of feeling" which allow the woman to respond sensitively while evoking in return the care which meets her own "very strong need for security" (p. 63). The strength of this position lies in its capacity for caring; its limitation is the restriction it imposes on direct expression. Both qualities are elucidated by a nineteen-year-old who contrasts her reluctance to criticize with her boyfriend's straightforwardness:

> I never want to hurt anyone, and I tell them in a very nice way, and I have respect for their own opinions, and they can do the things the way that they want, and he usually tells people right off the bat. . . . He does a lot of things out in public which I do in private. . . . it is better, the other [his way], but I just could never do it.

While her judgment clearly exists, it is not expressed, at least not in public. Concern for the feelings of others imposes a deference which she nevertheless criticizes in an awareness that, under the name of consideration, a vulnerability and a duplicity are concealed.

At the second level of judgment, it is specifically over the issue of hurting that conflict arises with respect to the abortion decision. When no option exists that can be construed as being in the best interest of everyone, when responsibilities conflict and decision entails the sacrifice of somebody's needs, then the woman confronts the seemingly impossible task of choosing the victim. A nineteen-year-old, fearing the consequences for herself of a second abortion but facing the opposition of both her family and her lover to the continuation of the pregnancy, describes the dilemma as follows:

> I don't know what choices are open to me; it is either to have it or the abortion; these are the choices open to me. It is just that either way I don't . . . I think what confuses me is it is a choice of either hurting myself or hurting other people around me. What is more important? If there could be a happy medium, it would be fine, but there isn't. It is either hurting someone on this side or hurting myself.

While the feminine identification of goodness with self-sacrifice seems clearly to dictate the "right" resolution of this dilemma, the stakes may be high for the woman herself, and the sacrifice of the fetus, in any event, compromises the altruism of an abortion motivated by a concern for others. Since femininity itself is in conflict in an abortion intended as an expression of love and care, this is a resolution which readily explodes in its own contradiction.

"I don't think anyone should have to choose between two things that they love," says a twenty-five-year-old woman who assumed responsibility not only for her lover but also for his wife and children in having an abortion she did not want:

> I just wanted the child and I really don't believe in abortions. Who can say when life begins. I think that life begins at conception and . . . I felt like there were changes happening in my body and I felt very protective . . . [but] I felt a responsibility, my responsibility if anything ever happened to her [his wife]. He made me feel that I had to make a choice and there was only one choice to make and that was to have an abortion and I could always have children another time and he made me feel if I didn't have it that it would drive us apart.

The abortion decision was, in her mind, a choice not to choose with respect to the pregnancy—"That was my choice, I had to do it." Instead, it was a decision to subordinate the pregnancy to the continuation of a relationship that she saw as encompassing her life—"Since I met him, he has been my life. I do everything for him; my life sort of revolves around him." Since she wanted to have the baby and also to continue the relationship, either choice could be construed as selfish. Furthermore, since both alternatives entailed hurting someone, neither could be considered moral. Faced with a decision which, in her own terms, was untenable, she sought to avoid responsibility for the choice she made, construing the decision as a sacrifice of her own needs to those of her lover. However, this public sacrifice in the name of responsibility engendered a private resentment that erupted in anger, compromising the very relationship that it had been intended to sustain.

> Afterwards we went through a bad time because I hate to say it and I was wrong, but I blamed him. I gave in to him. But when it came down to it, I made the decision. I could have said, 'I am going to have this child whether you want me to or not,' and I just didn't do it.

Pregnant again by the same man, she recognizes in retrospect that the choice in fact had been hers, as she returns once again to what now appears to have been missed opportunity for growth. Seeking, this time, to make rather than abdicate the decision, she sees the issue as one of "strength" as she struggles to free herself from the powerlessness of her own dependence:

> I think that right now I think of myself as someone who can become a lot stronger. Because of the circumstances, I just go along like with the tide. I never really had anything of my own before . . . [this time] I hope to come on strong and make a big decision, whether it is right or wrong.

Because the morality of self-sacrifice had justified the previous abortion, she now must suspend that judgment if she is to claim her own voice and accept responsibility for choice.

She thereby calls into question the underlying assumption of Level Two, which leads the woman to consider herself responsible for the actions of others, while holding others responsible for the choices she makes. This notion of reciprocity, backwards in its assumptions about control, disguises assertion as response. By reversing responsibility, it generates a series of indirect actions, which leave everyone feeling manipulated and betrayed. The logic of this position is confused in that the morality of mutual care is embedded in the psychology of dependence. Assertion becomes personally dangerous in its risk of criticism and abandonment, as well as potentially immoral in its power to hurt. This confusion is captured by Kohlberg's (1969) definition of Stage Three moral judgment, which joins the need for approval with the wish to care for and help others.

When thus caught between the passivity of dependence and the activity of care, the woman becomes suspended in an immobility of both judgment and action. "If I were drowning, I couldn't reach out a hand to save myself, so unwilling am I to set myself up against fate" (p. 7), begins the central character of Margaret Drabble's novel, *The Waterfall* (1971), in an effort to absolve herself of responsibility as she at the same time relinquishes control. Facing the same moral conflict which George Eliot depicted in *The Mill on the Floss*, Drabble's heroine proceeds to relive Maggie Tulliver's dilemma but turns inward in her search for the way in which to retell that story. What is initially suspended and then called into question is the judgment which "had in the past made it seem better to renounce myself than them" (Drabble, p. 50).

The Second Transition: From Goodness to Truth

The second transition begins with the reconsideration of the relationship between self and other, as the woman starts to scrutinize the logic of self-sacrifice in the service of a morality of care. In the interview data, this transition is announced by the reappearance of the word selfish. Retrieving the judgmental initiative, the woman begins to ask whether it is selfish or responsible, moral or immoral, to include her own needs within the compass of her care and concern. This question leads her to reexamine the concept of responsibility, juxtaposing the outward concern with what other people think with a new inner judgment.

In separating the voice of the self from those of others, the woman asks if it is possible to be responsible to herself as well as to others and thus to reconcile the disparity between hurt and care. The exercise of such responsibility, however, requires a new kind of judgment whose first demand is for honesty. To be responsible, it is necessary first to acknowledge what it is that one is doing. The criterion for judgment thus shifts from "goodness" to "truth" as the morality of action comes to be assessed not on the basis of its appearance in the eyes of others, but in terms of the realities of its intention and consequence.

A twenty-four-year-old married Catholic woman, pregnant again two months following the birth of her first child, identifies her dilemma as one of choice: "You have to now decide; because it is now available, you have to make a decision. And if it wasn't available, there was no choice open; you just do what you have to do." In the absence of legal abortion, a morality of self-sacrifice was necessary in order to insure protection and care for the dependent child. However, when such sacrifice becomes optional, the entire problem is recast.

The abortion decision is framed by this woman first in terms of her responsibilities to others: having a second child at this time would be contrary to medical advice and would strain both the emotional and financial resources of the family. However, there is, she says, a third reason for having an abortion, "sort of an emotional reason. I don't know if it is selfish or not, but it would really be tying myself down and right now I am not ready to be tied down with two."

Against this combination of selfish and responsible reasons for abortion is her Catholic belief that

> . . . it is taking a life, and it is. Even though it is not formed, it is the potential, and to me it is still taking a life. But I have to think of mine, my son's and my husband's, to think about, and at first I think that I thought it was for selfish reasons, but it is not. I believe that too, some of it is selfish. I don't want another one right now; I am not ready for it.

The dilemma arises over the issue of justification for taking a life: "I can't cover it over, because I believe this and if I do try to cover it over, I know that I am going to be in a mess. It will be denying what I am really doing." Asking "Am I doing the right thing; is it moral?," she counterposes to her belief against abortion her concern with the consequences of continuing the pregnancy. While concluding that "I can't be so morally strict as to hurt three other people with a decision just because of my moral beliefs," the issue of goodness still remains critical to her resolution of the dilemma:

> The moral factor is there. To me it is taking a life, and I am going to take that upon myself, that decision upon myself and I have feelings about it, and talked to a priest . . . but he said it is there and it will be from now on, and it is up to the person if they can live with the idea and still believe they are good.

The criteria for goodness, however, move inward as the ability to have an abortion and still consider herself good comes to hinge on the issue of selfishness with which she struggles to come to terms. Asked if acting morally is acting according to what is best for the self or whether it is a matter of self-sacrifice, she replies:

> I don't know if I really understand the question. . . . Like in my situation where I want to have the abortion and if I didn't it would be self-sacrificing, I am really in the middle of both those ways . . . but I think that my morality is strong and if these reasons—financial, physical reality and also for the whole family involved— were not here, that I wouldn't have to do it, and then it would be a self-sacrifice.

The importance of clarifying her own participation in the decision is evident in her attempt to ascertain her feelings in order to determine whether or not she was "putting them under" in deciding to end the pregnancy. Whereas in the first transition, from selfishness to responsibility, women made lists in order to bring to their consideration needs other than their own, now, in the second transition, it is the needs of the self which have to be deliberately uncovered. Confronting the reality of her own wish for an abortion, she now must deal with the problem of selfishness and the qualification that she feels it imposes on the "goodness" of her decision. The primacy of this concern is apparent in her description of herself:

> I think in a way I am selfish for one thing, and very emotional, very . . . and I think that I am a very real person and an understanding person and I can handle life situations fairly well, so I am basing a lot of it on my ability to do the things that I feel are right and best for me and whoever I am involved with. I think I was very fair to myself about the decision, and I really think that I have been truthful, not hiding anything, bringing out all the feelings involved. I feel it is a good decision and an honest one, a real decision.

Thus she strives to encompass the needs of both self and others, to be responsible to others and thus to be "good" but also to be responsible to herself and thus to be "honest" and "real."

While from one point of view, attention to one's own needs is considered selfish, when looked at from a different perspective, it is a matter of honesty and fairness. This is the essence of the transitional shift toward a new conception of goodness which turns inward in an acknowledgement of the self and an acceptance of responsibility for decision. While outward justification, the concern with "good reasons," remains critical for this particular woman: "I still think abortion is wrong, and it will be unless the situation can justify what you are doing." But the search for justification has produced a change in her thinking, "not drastically, but a little bit." She realizes that in continuing the pregnancy she would punish not only herself but also her husband, toward whom she had begun to feel "turned off and irritated." This leads her to consider the consequences self-sacrifice can have both for the self and for others. "God," she says, "can punish, but He can also forgive." What remains in question is whether her claim to forgiveness is compromised by a decision that not only meets the needs of others but that also is "right and best for me."

The concern with selfishness and its equation with immorality recur in an interview with another Catholic woman whose arrival for an abortion was punctuated by the statement, "I have always thought abortion was a fancy word for murder." Initially explaining this murder as one of lesser degree—"I am doing it because I have to do it. I am not doing it the least bit because I want to," she judges it "not quite as bad. You can rationalize that it is not quite the same." Since "keeping the child for lots and lots of reasons was just sort of impractical and out," she considers her options to be either abortion or adoption. However, having previously given up one child for adoption, she says: "I knew that psychologically there was no way that I could hack another adoption. It took me about four-and-a-half years to get my head on straight; there was just no way I was going to go through it again." The decision thus reduces in her eyes to a choice between murdering the fetus or damaging herself. The choice is further complicated by the fact that by continuing the pregnancy she would hurt not only herself but also her parents, with whom she lived. In the face of these manifold moral contradictions, the psychological demand for honesty that arises in counseling finally allows decision:

On my own, I was doing it not so much for myself; I was doing it for my parents. I was doing it because the doctor told me to do it, but I had never resolved in my mind that I was doing it for me. Because it goes right back to the fact that I never believed in abortions. . . . Actually, I had to sit down and admit, no, I really don't want to go the mother route now. I honestly don't feel that I want to be a mother, and that is not really such a bad thing to say after all. But that is not how I felt up until talking to Maureen [her counselor]. It was just a horrible way to feel, so I just wasn't going to feel it, and I just blocked it right out.

As long as her consideration remains "moral," abortion can be justified only as an act of sacrifice, a submission to necessity where the absence of choice precludes responsibility. In this way, she can avoid self-condemnation, since, "When you get into moral stuff then you are getting into self-respect and that stuff, and at least if I do something that I feel is morally wrong, then I tend to lose some of my self-respect as a person." Her evasion of responsibility, critical to maintaining the innocence necessary for self-respect, contradicts the reality of her own participation in the abortion decision. The dishonesty in her plea of victimization creates the conflict that generates the need for a more inclusive understanding. She must now resolve the emerging contradiction in her thinking between two uses of the term right: "I am saying that abortion is morally wrong, but the situation is right, and I am going to do it. But the thing is that eventually they are going to have to go together, and I am going to have to put them together somehow." Asked how this could be done, she replies:

I would have to change morally wrong to morally right. [How?] I have no idea. I don't think you can take something that you feel is morally wrong because the situation makes it right and put the two together. They are not together, they are opposite. They don't go together. Something is wrong, but all of a sudden because you are doing it, it is right.

This discrepancy recalls a similar conflict she faced over the question of euthanasia, also considered by her to be morally wrong until she "took care of a couple of patients who had flat EEGs and saw the job that it was doing on their families." Recalling that experience, she says:

You really don't know your black and whites until you really get into them and are being confronted with it. If you stop and think about my feelings on euthanasia until I got into it, and then my feelings about abortion until I got into it, I thought both of them were murder. Right and wrong and no middle but there is a gray.

In discovering the gray and questioning the moral judgments which formerly she considered to be absolute, she confronts the moral crisis of the second transition. Now the conventions which in the past had guided her moral judgment become subject to a new criticism, as she questions not only the justification for hurting others in the name of morality but also the "rightness" of hurting herself. However, to sustain such criticism in the face of conventions that equate goodness with self-sacrifice, the woman must verify her capacity for independent judgment and the legitimacy of her own point of view.

Once again transition hinges on self-concept. When uncertainty about her own worth prevents a woman from claiming equality, self-assertion falls prey to the old criticism of selfishness. Then the morality that condones self-destruction in the name of responsible care is not repudiated as inadequate but rather is abandoned in the face of its threat to survival. Moral obligation, rather than expanding to include the self, is rejected completely as the failure of conventional reciprocity leaves the woman unwilling any longer to protect others at what is now seen to be her own expense. In the absence of morality, survival, however "selfish" or "immoral," returns as the paramount concern.

A musician in her late twenties illustrates this transitional impasse. Having led an independent life which centered on her work, she considered herself "fairly strong-willed, fairly in control, fairly rational and objective" until she became involved in an intense love affair and discovered in her capacity to love "an entirely new dimension" in herself. Admitting in retrospect to "tremendous naiveté and idealism," she had entertained "some vague ideas that some day I would like a child to concretize our relationship . . . having always associated having a child with all the creative aspects of my life." Abjuring, with her lover, the use of contraceptives because, "as the relationship was sort of an ideal relationship in our minds, we liked the idea of not using foreign objects or anything artificial," she saw herself as having relinquished control, becoming instead "just simply vague and allowing events to just carry me along." Just as she began in her own thinking to confront "the realities of that situation"—the possibility of pregnancy and the fact that her lover was married—she found herself pregnant. "Caught" between her wish to end a relationship that "seemed more and more defeating" and her wish for a baby, which "would be a connection that would last a long time," she is paralyzed by her inability to resolve the dilemma which her ambivalence creates.

The pregnancy poses a conflict between her "moral" belief that "once a certain life has begun, it shouldn't be stopped artificially" and her "amazing" discovery that to have the baby she would "need much more [support] than I thought." Despite her moral conviction that she "should" have the child, she doubts that she could psychologically deal with "having the child alone and taking the responsibility for it." Thus a conflict erupts between what she considers to be her moral obligation to protect life and her inability to do so under the circumstances of this pregnancy. Seeing it as "my decision and my responsibility for making the decision whether to have or have not the child," she struggles to find a viable basis on which to resolve the dilemma.

Capable of arguing either for or against abortion "with a philosophical logic," she says, on the one hand, that in an overpopulated world one should have children only under ideal conditions for care but, on the other, that one should end a life only when it is impossible to sustain it. She describes her impasse in response to the question of whether there is a difference between what she wants to do and what she thinks she should do:

> Yes, and there always has. I have always been confronted with that precise situation in a lot of my choices, and I have been trying to figure out what are the things that make me believe that these are things I should do as opposed to what I feel I want to do. [In this situation?] It is not that clear cut. I both want the child and feel I should have it, and I also think I should have the abortion and want it, but I would say it is my stronger feeling, and that I don't have enough confidence in my work yet and that is really where it is all hinged, I think . . . [the abortion] would solve the problem and I know I can't handle the pregnancy.

Characterizing this solution as "emotional and pragmatic" and attributing it to her lack of confidence in her work, she contrasts it with the "better thought out and more logical and more correct" resolution of her lover who thinks that she should have the child and raise it without either his presence or financial support. Confronted with this reflected image of herself as ultimately giving and good, as self-sustaining in her own creativity and thus able to meet the needs of others while imposing no demands of her own in return, she questions not the image itself but her own adequacy in filling it. Concluding that she is not yet capable of doing so, she is reduced in her own eyes to what she sees as a selfish and highly compromised fight

> for my survival. But in one way or another, I am going to suffer. Maybe I am going to suffer mentally and emotionally having the abortion, or I would suffer what I think is possibly something worse. So I suppose it is the lesser of two evils. I think it is a matter of choosing which one I know that I can survive through. It is really. I think it is selfish, I suppose, because it does have to do with that. I just realized that. I guess it does have to do with whether I would survive or not. [Why is this selfish?] Well, you know, it is. Because I am concerned with my survival first, as opposed to the survival of the relationship or the survival of the child, another human being . . . I guess I am setting priorities, and I guess I am setting my needs to survive first. . . . I guess I see it in negative terms a lot . . . but I do think of other positive things; that I am still going to have some life left, maybe. I don't know.

In the face of this failure of reciprocity of care, in the disappointment of abandonment where connection was sought, survival is seen to hinge on her work which is "where I derive the meaning of what I am. That's the known factor." While uncertainty about her work makes this survival precarious, the choice for abortion is also distressing in that she considers it to be "highly introverted—that in this one respect, having an abortion would be going a step backward; going outside to love someone else and having a child would be a step forward." The sense of retrenchment that the severing of connection signifies is apparent in her anticipation of the cost which abortion would entail:

> Probably what I will do is I will cut off my feelings, and when they will return or what would happen to them after that, I don't know. So that I don't feel anything at all, and I would probably just be very cold and go through it very coldly. . . . The more you do that to yourself, the more difficult it becomes to love again or to trust again or to feel again. . . . Each time I move away from that, it

becomes easier, not more difficult, but easier to avoid committing myself to a relationship. And I am really concerned about cutting off that whole feeling aspect.

Caught between selfishness and responsibility, unable to find in the circumstances of this choice a way of caring which does not at the same time destroy, she confronts a dilemma which reduces to a conflict between morality and survival. Adulthood and femininity fly apart in the failure of this attempt at integration as the choice to work becomes a decision not only to renounce this particular relationship and child but also to obliterate the vulnerability that love and care engender.

The Third Level: The Morality of Nonviolence

In contrast, a twenty-five-year-old woman, facing a similar disappointment, finds a way to reconcile the initially disparate concepts of selfishness and responsibility through a transformed understanding of self and a corresponding redefinition of morality. Examining the assumptions underlying the conventions of feminine self-abnegation and moral self-sacrifice, she comes to reject these conventions as immoral in their power to hurt. By elevating nonviolence—the injunction against hurting—to a principle governing all moral judgment and action, she is able to assert a moral equality between self and other. Care then becomes a universal obligation, the self-chosen ethic of a postconventional judgment that reconstructs the dilemma in a way that allows the assumption of responsibility for choice.

In this woman's life, the current pregnancy brings to the surface the unfinished business of an earlier pregnancy and of the relationship in which both pregnancies occurred. The first pregnancy was discovered after her lover had left and was terminated by an abortion experienced as a purging expression of her anger at having been rejected. Remembering the abortion only as a relief, she nevertheless describes that time in her life as one in which she "hit rock bottom." Having hoped then to "take control of my life," she instead resumed the relationship when the man reappeared. Now, two years later, having once again "left my diaphragm in the drawer," she again becomes pregnant. Although initially "ecstatic" at the news, her elation dissipates when her lover tells her that he will leave if she chooses to have the child. Under these circumstances, she considers a second abortion but is unable to keep the repeated appointments she makes because of her reluctance to accept the responsibility for that choice. While the first abortion seemed an "honest mistake," she says that a second would make her feel "like a walking slaughter-house." Since she would need financial support to raise the child, her initial strategy was to take the matter to "the welfare people" in the hope that they would refuse to provide the necessary funds and thus resolve her dilemma:

> In that way, you know, the responsibility would be off my shoulders, and I could say, it's not my fault, you know, the state denied me the money that I would need to do it. But it turned out that it was possible to do it, and so I was, you know, right back where I started. And I had an appointment for an abortion, and I kept calling and cancelling it and then remaking the appointment and cancelling it, and I just couldn't make up my mind.

Confronting the need to choose between the two evils of hurting herself or ending the incipient life of the child, she finds, in a reconstruction of the dilemma itself, a basis for a new priority that allows decision. In doing so, she comes to see the conflict as arising from a faulty construction of reality. Her thinking recapitulates the developmental sequence, as she considers but rejects as inadequate the components of earlier-stage resolutions. An expanded conception of responsibility now reshapes moral judgment and guides resolution of the dilemma, whose pros and cons she considers as follows:

> Well, the pros for having the baby are all the admiration that you would get from, you know, being a single woman, alone, martyr, struggling, having the adoring love of this beautiful Gerber baby . . . just more of a home life than I have had in a long time, and that basically was it, which is pretty fantasyland; it is not very realistic. . . . Cons against having the baby: it was going to hasten what is looking to be the inevitable end of the relationship with the man I am presently with. . . . I was going to have to go on welfare, my parents were going to hate me for the rest of my life, I was going to lose a really good job that I have, I would lose a lot of independence . . . solitude . . . and I would have to be put in a position of asking help from a lot of people a lot of the time. Cons against having the abortion is having to face up to the guilt . . . and pros for having the abortion are I would be able to handle my deteriorating relation with S. with a lot more capability and a lot more responsibility for him and for myself . . . and I would not have to go through the realization that for the next twenty-five years of my life I would be punishing myself for being foolish enough to get pregnant again and forcing myself to bring up a kid just because I did this. Having to face the guilt of a second abortion seemed like, not exactly, well, exactly the lesser of the two evils but also the one that would pay off for me personally in the long run because by looking at why I am pregnant again and subsequently have decided to have a second abortion, I have to face up to some things about myself.

Although she doesn't "feel good about having a second abortion," she nevertheless concludes,

> I would not be doing myself or the child or the world any kind of favor having this child. . . . I don't need to pay off my imaginary debts to the world through this child, and I don't think that it is right to bring a child into the world and use it for that purpose.

Asked to describe herself, she indicates how closely her transformed moral understanding is tied to a changing self-concept:

> I have been thinking about that a lot lately, and it comes up different than what my usual subconscious perception of myself is. Usually paying off some sort of debt, going around serving people who are not really worthy of my attentions because somewhere in my life I think I got the impression that my needs are really secondary to other people's, and that if I feel, if I make any demands on other people to fulfill my needs, I'd feel guilty for it and submerge my own in favor of other people's, which later backfires on me, and I feel a great deal of resentment for other people that I am doing things for, which causes friction and the eventual

deterioration of the relationship. And then I start all over again. How would I describe myself to myself? Pretty frustrated and a lot angrier than I admit, a lot more aggressive than I admit.

Reflecting on the virtues which comprise the conventional definition of the feminine self, a definition which she hears articulated in her mother's voice, she says, "I am beginning to think that all these virtues are really not getting me anywhere. I have begun to notice." Tied to this recognition is an acknowledgement of her power and worth, both previously excluded from the image she projected:

> I am suddenly beginning to realize that the things that I like to do, the things I am interested in, and the things that I believe and the kind of person I am is not so bad that I have to constantly be sitting on the shelf and letting it gather dust. I am a lot more worthwhile than what my past actions have led other people to believe.

Her notion of a "good person," which previously was limited to her mother's example of hard work, patience and self-sacrifice, now changes to include the value that she herself places on directness and honesty. Although she believes that this new self-assertion will lead her "to feel a lot better about myself" she recognizes that it will also expose her to criticism:

> Other people may say, 'Boy, she's aggressive, and I don't like that,' but at least, you know, they will know that they don't like that. They are not going to say, 'I like the way she manipulates herself to fit right around me.' . . . What I want to do is just be a more self-determined person and a more singular person.

While within her old framework abortion had seemed a way of "copping out" instead of being a "responsible person [who] pays for his mistakes and pays and pays and is always there when she says she will be there and even when she doesn't say she will be there is there," now, her "conception of what I think is right for myself and my conception of self-worth is changing." She can consider this emergent self "also a good person," as her concept of goodness expands to encompass "the feeling of self-worth; you are not going to sell yourself short and you are not going to make yourself do things that, you know, are really stupid and that you don't want to do." This reorientation centers on the awareness that

> I have a responsibility to myself, and you know, for once I am beginning to realize that that really matters to me . . . instead of doing what I want for myself and feeling guilty over how selfish I am, you realize that that is a very usual way for people to live . . . doing what you want to do because you feel that your wants and your needs are important, if to no one else, then to you, and that's reason enough to do something that you want to do.

Once obligation extends to include the self as well as others, the disparity between selfishness and responsibility is reconciled. Although the conflict between self and other remains, the moral problem is restructured in an awareness that the occurrence of the dilemma itself precludes non-violent resolution. The abortion decision is now seen to be a "serious" choice affecting both self and others: "This is a life that I have taken, a conscious decision to terminate, and that is just very heavy, a very heavy thing." While accepting the necessity of abortion as a highly compromised resolution, she turns her attention to the pregnancy itself, which she now considers to denote a failure of responsibility, a failure to care for and protect both self and other.

As in the first transition, although now in different terms, the conflict precipitated by the pregnancy catches up the issues critical to development. These issues now concern the worth of the self in relation to others, the claiming of the power to choose, and the acceptance of responsibility for choice. By provoking a confrontation with these issues, the crisis can become "a very auspicious time; you can use the pregnancy as sort of a learning, teeing-off point, which makes it useful in a way." This possibility for growth inherent in a crisis which allows confrontation with a construction of reality whose acceptance previously had impeded development was first identified by Coles (1964) in his study of the children of Little Rock. This same sense of possibility is expressed by the women who see, in their resolution of the abortion dilemma, a reconstructed understanding which creates the opportunity for "a new beginning," a chance "to take control of my life."

For this woman, the first step in taking control was to end the relationship in which she had considered herself "reduced to a nonentity," but to do so in a responsible way. Recognizing hurt as the inevitable concomitant of rejection, she strives to minimize that hurt "by dealing with [his] needs as best I can without compromising my own . . . that's a big point for me, because the thing in my life to this point has been always compromising, and I am not willing to do that any more." Instead, she seeks to act in a "decent, human kind of way . . . one that leaves maybe a slightly shook but not totally destroyed person." Thus the "nonentity" confronts her power to destroy which formerly had impeded any assertion, as she consider the possibility for a new kind of action that leaves both self and other intact.

The moral concern remains a concern with hurting as she considers Kohlberg's Heinz dilemma in terms of the question, "who is going to be hurt more, the druggist who loses some money or the person who loses their life?" The right to property and right to life are weighed not in the abstract, in terms of their logical priority, but rather in the particular, in terms of the actual consequences that the violation of these rights would have in the lives of the people involved. Thinking remains contextual and admixed with feelings of care, as the moral imperative to avoid hurt begins to be informed by a psychological understanding of the meaning of nonviolence.

Thus, release from the intimidation of inequality finally allows the expression of a judgment that previously had been withheld. What women then enunciate is not a new morality, but a moral conception disentangled from the constraints that formerly had confused its perception and impeded its articulation. The willingness to express and take responsibility for judgment stems from the recognition of the psychological and moral necessity for an equation of worth between self and other. Responsibility for care then includes both self and other, and the obligation not to hurt, freed from conventional constraints, is reconstructed as a universal guide to moral choice.

The reality of hurt centers the judgment of a twenty-nine-year-old woman, married and the mother of a preschool child, as she struggles with the dilemma posed by a second pregnancy whose timing conflicts with her completion of an advanced degree. Saying that "I cannot deliberately do something that is bad or would hurt another person because I can't live with having done that," she nevertheless confronts a situation in which hurt has become inevitable. Seeking that solution which would best protect both herself and others, she indicates, in her definition of morality, the ineluctable sense of connection which infuses and colors all of her thinking:

> [Morality is] doing what is appropriate and what is just within your circumstances, but ideally it is not going to affect—I was going to say, ideally it wouldn't negatively affect another person, but that is ridiculous, because decisions are always going to affect another person. But you see, what I am trying to say is that it is the person that is the center of the decision making, of that decision making about what's right and what's wrong.

The person who is the center of this decision making begins by denying, but then goes on to acknowledge, the conflicting nature both of her own needs and of her various responsibilities. Seeing the pregnancy as a manifestation of the inner conflict between her wish, on the one hand, "to be a college president" and, on the other, "to be making pottery and flowers and having kids and staying at home," she struggles with contradiction between femininity and adulthood. Considering abortion as the "better" choice—because "in the end, meaning this time next year or this time two weeks from now, it will be less of a personal strain on us individually and on us as a family for me not to be pregnant at this time," she concludes that the decision has

> got to be, first of all, something that the woman can live with—a decision that the woman can live with, one way or another, or at least try to live with, and that it be based on where she is at and other people, significant people in her life, are at.

At the beginning of the interview she had presented the dilemma in its conventional feminine construction, as a conflict between her own wish to have a baby and the wish of others for her to complete her education. On the basis of this construction she deemed it "selfish" to continue the pregnancy because it was something "I want to do." However, as she begins to examine her thinking, she comes to abandon as false this conceptualization of the problem, acknowledging the truth of her own internal conflict and elaborating the tension which she feels between her femininity and the adulthood of her work life. She describes herself as "going in two directions" and values that part of herself which is "incredibly passionate and sensitive"—her capacity to recognize and meet, often with anticipation, the needs of others. Seeing her "compassion" as "something I don't want to lose" she regards it as endangered by her pursuit of professional advancement. Thus the self-deception of her initial presentation, its attempt to sustain the fiction of her own innocence, stems from her fear that to say that *she* does not want to have another baby at this time would be an acknowledgement to me that I am an ambitious person and that I want to have power and responsibility for others and that I want to live a life that extends from 9 to 5 every day and into the evenings and on weekends, because that is what the power and responsibility means. It means that my family would necessarily come second . . . there would be such an incredible conflict about which is tops, and I don't want that for myself.

Asked about her concept of "an ambitious person" she says that to be ambitious means to be

power hungry [and] insensitive. [Why insensitive?] Because people are stomped on in the process. A person on the way up stomps on people, whether it is family or other colleagues or clientele, on the way up. [Inevitably?] Not always, but I have seen it so often in my limited years of working that it is scary to me. It is scary because I don't want to change like that.

Because the acquisition of adult power is seen to entail the loss of feminine sensitivity and compassion, the conflict between femininity and adulthood becomes construed as a moral problem. The discovery of the principle of nonviolence begins to direct attention to the moral dilemma itself and initiates the search for a resolution that can encompass both femininity and adulthood.

Developmental Theory Reconsidered

The developmental conception delineated at the outset, which has so consistently found the development of women to be either aberrant or incomplete, has been limited insofar as it has been predominantly a male conception, giving lip-service, a place on the chart, to the interdependence of intimacy and care but constantly stressing, at their expense, the importance and value of autonomous judgment and action. To admit to this conception the truth of the feminine perspective is to recognize for both sexes the central importance in adult life of the connection between self and other, the universality of the need for compassion and care. The concept of the separate self and of the moral principle uncompromised by the constraints of reality is an adolescent ideal, the elaborately wrought philosophy of a Stephen Daedalus, whose flight we know to be in jeopardy. Erikson (1964), in contrasting the ideological morality of the adolescent with the ethics of adult care, attempts to grapple with this problem of integration, but is impeded by the limitations of his own previous developmental conception. When his developmental stages chart a path where the sole precursor to the intimacy of adult relationships is the trust established in infancy and all intervening experience is marked only as steps toward greater independence, then separation itself becomes the model and the measure of growth. The observation that for women, identity has as much to do with connection as with separation led Erikson into trouble largely because of his failure to integrate this insight into the mainstream of his developmental theory (Erikson, 1968).

The morality of responsibility which women describe stands apart from the morality of rights which underlies Kohlberg's conception of the highest stages of moral judgment. Kohlberg (Note 3) sees the progression toward these stages as resulting from the generalization of the self-centered adolescent rejection of societal morality into a principled conception of individual natural rights. To illustrate this progression, he cites as an example of integrated Stage Five judgment, "possibly moving to Stage Six," the following response of a twenty-five-year-old subject from his male longitudinal sample:

> [What does the word morality mean to you?] Nobody in the world knows the answer. I think it is recognizing the right of the individual, the rights of other individuals, not interfering with those rights. Act as fairly as you would have them treat you. I think it is basically to preserve the human being's right to existence. I think that is the most important. Secondly, the human being's right to do as he pleases, again without interfering with somebody else's rights. (p. 29)

Another version of the same conception is evident in the following interview response of a male college senior whose moral judgment also was scored by Kohlberg (Note 4) as at Stage Five or Six:

> [Morality] is a prescription, it is a thing to follow, and the idea of having a concept of morality is to try to figure out what it is that people can do in order to make life with each other livable, make for a kind of balance, a kind of equilibrium, a harmony in which everybody feels he has a place and an equal share in things, and it's doing that—doing that is kind of contributing to a state of affairs that go beyond the individual in the absence of which, the individual has no chance for self-fulfillment of any kind. Fairness; morality is kind of essential, it seems to me, for creating the kind of environment, interaction between people, that is prerequisite to this fulfillment of most individual goals and so on. If you want other people to not interfere with your pursuit of whatever you are into, you have to play the game.

In contrast, a woman in her late twenties responds to a similar question by defining a morality not of rights but of responsibility:

> [What makes something a moral issue?] Some sense of trying to uncover a right path in which to live, and always in my mind is that the world is full of real and recognizable trouble, and is it heading for some sort of doom and is it right to bring children into this world when we currently have an overpopulation problem, and is it right to spend money on a pair of shoes when I have a pair of shoes and other people are shoeless. . . . It is part of a self-critical view, part of saying, how am I spending my time and in what sense am I working? I think I have a real drive to, I have a real maternal drive to take care of someone. To take care of my mother, to take care of children, to take care of other people's children, to take care of my own children, to take care of the world. I think that goes back to your other question, and when I am dealing with moral issues, I am sort of saying to myself constantly, are you taking care of all the things that you think are important and in what ways are you wasting yourself and wasting those issues?

While the postconventional nature of this woman's perspective seems clear, her judgments of Kohlberg's hypothetical moral dilemmas do not meet his criteria for scoring at the principled level. Kohlberg regards this as a disparity between normative and metaethical judgments which he sees as indicative of the transition between conventional and principled thinking. From another perspective, however, this judgment represents a different moral conception, disentangled from societal conventions and raised to the principled level. In this conception, moral judgment is oriented toward issues of responsibility. The way in which the responsibility orientation guides moral decision at the postconventional level is described by the following woman in her thirties:

> [Is there a right way to make moral decisions?] The only way I know is to try to be as awake as possible, to try to know the range of what you feel, to try to consider all that's involved, to be as aware as you can be to what's going on, as conscious as you can of where you're walking. [Are there principles that guide you?] The principle would have something to do with responsibility, responsibility and caring about yourself and others. . . . But it's not that on the one hand you choose to be responsible and on the other hand you choose to be irresponsible—both ways you can be responsible. That's why there's not just a principle that once you take hold of you settle—the principle put into practice here is still going to leave you with conflict.

The moral imperative that emerges repeatedly in the women's interviews is an injunction to care, a responsibility to discern and alleviate the "real and recognizable trouble" of this world. For the men Kohlberg studied, the moral imperative appeared rather as an injunction to respect the rights of others and thus to protect from interference the right to life and self-fulfillment. Women's insistence on care is at first self-critical rather than self-protective, while men initially conceive obligation to others negatively in terms of noninterference. Development for both sexes then would seem to entail an integration of rights and responsibilities through the discovery of the complementarity of these disparate views. For the women I have studied, this integration between rights and responsibilities appears to take place through a principled understanding of equity and reciprocity. This understanding tempers the self-destructive potential of a self-critical morality by asserting the equal right of all persons to care. For the men in Kohlberg's sample as well as for those in a longitudinal study of Harvard undergraduates (Gilligan & Murphy, Note 5) it appears to be the recognition through experience of the need for a more active responsibility in taking care that corrects the potential indifference of a morality of noninterference and turns attention from the logic to the consequences of choice. In the development of a postconventional ethic understanding, women come to see the violence generated by inequitable relationships, while men come to realize the limitations of a conception of justice blinded to the real inequities of human life.

Kohlberg's dilemmas, in the hypothetical abstraction of their presentation, divest the moral actors from the history and psychology of their individual lives and separate the moral problem from the social contingencies of its possible occurrence. In doing so, the dilemmas are useful for the distillation and refinement of the "objective principles of justice" toward which Kohlberg's stages strive. However, the reconstruction of the dilemma in its contextual particularity allows the understanding of cause and consequence which engages the compassion and tolerance considered by previous theorists to qualify the feminine sense of justice. Only when substance is given to the skeletal lives of hypothetical people is it possible to consider the social injustices which their moral problems may reflect and to imagine the individual suffering their occurrence may signify or their resolution engender.

The proclivity of women to reconstruct hypothetical dilemmas in terms of the real, to request or supply the information missing about the nature of the people and the places where they live, shifts their judgment away from the hierarchical ordering of principles and the formal procedures of decision making that are critical for scoring at Kohlberg's highest stages. This insistence on the particular signifies an orientation to the dilemma and to moral problems in general that differs from any of Kohlberg's stage descriptions. Given the constraints of Kohlberg's system and the biases in his research sample, this different orientation can only be construed as a failure in development. While several of the women in the research sample clearly articulated what Kohlberg regarded as a postconventional metaethical position, none of them were considered by Kohlberg to be principled in their normative moral judgments of his hypothetical moral dilemmas (Note 4). Instead, the women's judgments pointed toward an identification of the violence inherent in the dilemma itself which was seen to compromise the justice of any of its possible resolutions. This construction of the dilemma led the women to recast the moral judgment from a consideration of the good to a choice between evils.

The woman whose judgment of the abortion dilemma concluded the developmental sequence presented in the preceding section saw Kohlberg's Heinz dilemma in these terms and judged Heinz's action in terms of a choice between selfishness and sacrifice. For Heinz to steal the drug, given the circumstances of his life (which she inferred from his inability to pay two thousand dollars), he would have "to do something which is not in his best interest, in that he is going to get sent away, and that is a supreme sacrifice, a sacrifice which I would say a person truly in love might be willing to make." However, not to steal the drug "would be selfish on his part . . . he would just have to feel guilty about not allowing her a chance to live longer." Heinz's decision to steal is considered not in terms of the logical priority of life over property which justifies its rightness, but rather in terms of the actual consequences that stealing would have for a man of limited means and little social power.

Considered in the light of its probable outcomes—his wife dead, or Heinz in jail, brutalized by the violence of that experience and his life compromised by a record of felony—the dilemma itself changes. Its resolution has less to do with the relative weights of life and property in an abstract moral conception than with the collision it has produced between two lives, formerly conjoined but now in opposition, where the continuation of one life can now occur only at the expense of the other. Given this construction, it becomes clear why consideration revolves around the issue of sacrifice and why guilt becomes the inevitable concomitant of either resolution.

Demonstrating the reticence noted in the first section about making moral judgments, this woman explains her reluctance to judge in terms of her belief that everybody's existence is so different that I kind of say to myself, that might be something that I wouldn't do, but I can't say that it is right or wrong for that person. I can only deal with what is appropriate for me to do when I am faced with specific problems.

Asked if she would apply to others her own injunction against hurting, she says:

See, I can't say that it is wrong. I can't say that it is right or that it's wrong because I don't know what the person did that the other person did something to hurt him . . . so it is not right that the person got hurt, but it is right that the person who just lost the job has got to get that anger up and out. It doesn't put any bread on his table, but it is released. I don't mean to be copping out. I really am trying to see how to answer these questions for you.

Her difficulty in answering Kohlberg's questions, her sense of strain with the construction which they impose on the dilemma, stems from their divergence from her own frame of reference:

I don't even think I use the words right and wrong anymore, and I know I don't use the word moral, because I am not sure I know what it means. . . . We are talking about an unjust society, we are talking about a whole lot of things that are not right, that are truly wrong, to use the word that I don't use very often, and I have no control to change that. If I could change it, I certainly would, but I can only make my small contribution from day to day, and if I don't intentionally hurt somebody, that is my contribution to a better society. And so a chunk of that contribution is also not to pass judgment on other people, particularly when I don't know the circumstances of why they are doing certain things.

The reluctance to judge remains a reluctance to hurt, but one that stems now not from a sense of personal vulnerability but rather from a recognition of the limitations of judgment itself. The deference of the conventional feminine perspective can thus be seen to continue at the postconventional level, not as moral relativism but rather as part of a reconstructed moral understanding. Moral judgment is renounced in an awareness of the psychological and social determinism of all human behavior at the same time as moral concern is reaffirmed in recognition of the reality of human pain and suffering.

I have a real thing about hurting people and always have, and that gets a little complicated at times, because, for example, you don't want to hurt your child. I don't want to hurt my child but if I don't hurt her sometimes, then that's hurting her more, you see, and so that was a terrible dilemma for me.

Moral dilemmas are terrible in that they entail hurt; she sees Heinz's decision as "the result of anguish, who am I hurting, why do I have to hurt them." While the morality of Heinz's theft is not in question, given the circumstances which necessitated it, what is at issue is his willingness to substitute himself for his wife and become, in her stead, the victim of exploitation by a society which breeds and legitimizes the druggist's irresponsibility and whose injustice is thus manifest in the very occurrence of the dilemma.

The same sense that the wrong questions are being asked is evident in the response of another woman who justified Heinz's action on a similar basis, saying "I don't think that exploitation should really be a right." When women begin to make direct moral statements, the issues they repeatedly address are those of exploitation and hurt. In doing so, they raise the issue of nonviolence in precisely the same psychological context that brought Erikson (1969) to pause in his consideration of the truth of Gandhi's life.

In the pivotal letter, around which the judgment of his book turns, Erikson confronts the contradiction between the philosophy of nonviolence that informed Gandhi's dealing with the British and the psychology of violence that marred his relationships with his family and with the children of the ashram. It was this contradiction, Erikson confesses,

> which almost brought *me* to the point where I felt unable to continue writing *this* book because I seemed to sense the presence of a kind of untruth in the very protestation of truth; of something unclean when all the words spelled out an unreal purity; and, above all, of displaced violence where nonviolence was the professed issue. (p. 231)

In an effort to untangle the relationship between the spiritual truth of Satyagraha and the truth of his own psychoanalytic understanding, Erikson reminds Gandhi that "Truth, you once said, 'excludes the use of violence because man is not capable of knowing the absolute truth and therefore is not competent to punish'" (p. 241). The affinity between Satyagraha and psychoanalysis lies in their shared commitment to seeing life as an "experiment in truth," in their being

> somehow joined in a universal "therapeutics," committed to the Hippocratic principle that one can test truth (or the healing power inherent in a sick situation) only by action which avoids harm—or better, by action which maximizes mutuality and minimizes the violence caused by unilateral coercion or threat. (p. 247)

Erikson takes Gandhi to task for his failure to acknowledge the relativity of truth. This failure is manifest in the coercion of Gandhi's claim to exclusive possession of the truth, his "unwillingness to learn from *anybody anything* except what was approved by the 'inner voice'" (p. 236). This claim led Gandhi, in the guise of love, to impose his truth on others without awareness or regard for the extent to which he thereby did violence to their integrity.

The moral dilemma, arising inevitably out of a conflict of truths, is by definition a "sick situation" in that its either/or formulation leaves no room for an outcome that does not do violence. The resolution of such dilemmas, however, lies not in the self-deception of rationalized violence—"I was" said Gandhi, "a cruelly kind husband. I regarded myself as her teacher and so harassed her out of my blind love for her" (p. 233)—but rather in the replacement of the underlying antagonism with a mutuality of respect and care.

Gandhi, whom Kohlberg has mentioned as exemplifying Stage Six moral judgment and whom Erikson sought as a model of an adult ethical sensibility, instead is criticized by a judgment that refuses to look away from or condone the infliction of harm. In denying the validity of his wife's reluctance to open her home to strangers and in his blindness to the different reality of adolescent sexuality and temptation, Gandhi compromised in his everyday life the ethic of nonviolence to which in principle and in public he was so steadfastly committed.

The blind willingness to sacrifice people to truth, however, has always been the danger of an ethics abstracted from life. This willingness links Gandhi to the biblical Abraham, who prepared to sacrifice the life of his son in order to demonstrate the integrity and supremacy of his faith. Both men, in the limitations of their fatherhood, stand in implicit contrast to the woman who comes before Solomon and verifies her motherhood by relinquishing truth in order to save the life of her child. It is the ethics of an adulthood that has become principled at the expense of care that Erikson comes to criticize in his assessment of Gandhi's life.

This same criticism is dramatized explicitly as a contrast between the sexes in *The Merchant of Venice* (1598/1912), where Shakespeare goes through an extraordinary complication of sexual identity (dressing a male actor as a female character who in turn poses as a male judge) in order to bring into the masculine citadel of justice the feminine plea for mercy. The limitation of the contractual conception of justice is illustrated through the absurdity of its literal execution, while the "need to make exceptions all the time" is demonstrated contrapuntally in the matter of the rings. Portia, in calling for mercy, argues for that resolution in which no one is hurt, and as the men are forgiven for their failure to keep both their rings and their word, Antonio in turn foregoes his "right" to ruin Shylock.

The research findings that have been reported in this essay suggest that women impose a distinctive construction on moral problems, seeing moral dilemmas in terms of conflicting responsibilities. This construction was found to develop through a sequence of three levels and two transitions, each level representing a more complex understanding of the relationship between self and other and each transition involving a critical reinterpretation of the moral conflict between selfishness and responsibility. The development of women's moral judgment appears to proceed from an initial concern with survival, to a focus on goodness, and finally to a principled understanding of nonviolence as the most adequate guide to the just resolution of moral conflicts.

In counterposing to Kohlberg's longitudinal research on the development of hypothetical moral judgment in men a cross-sectional study of women's responses to actual dilemmas of moral conflict and choice, this essay precludes the possibility of generalization in either direction and leaves to further research the task of sorting out the different variables of occasion and sex. Longitudinal studies of women's moral judgments are necessary in order to validate the claims of stage and sequence presented here. Similarly, the contrast drawn between the moral judgments of men and women awaits for its confirmation a more systematic comparison of the responses of both sexes. Kohlberg's research on moral development has confounded the variables of age, sex, type of decision, and type of dilemma by presenting a single configuration (the responses of adolescent males to hypothetical dilemmas of conflicting rights) as the basis for a universal stage sequence. This paper underscores the need for systematic treatment of these variables and points toward their study as a critical task for future moral development research.

For the present, my aim has been to demonstrate the centrality of the concepts of responsibility and care in women's constructions of the moral domain, to indicate the close tie in women's thinking between conceptions of the self and conceptions of morality, and, finally, to argue the need for an expanded developmental theory that would include, rather than rule out from developmental consideration, the difference in the feminine voice. Such an inclusion seems essential, not only for explaining the development of women but also for understanding in both sexes the characteristics and precursors of an adult moral conception.

Reference Notes

1. Haan, N. *Activism as moral protest: Moral judgments of hypothetical dilemmas and an actual situation of civil disobedience.* Unpublished manuscript, University of California at Berkeley, 1971.
2. Turiel, E. *A comparative analysis of moral knowledge and moral judgment in males and females.* Unpublished manuscript, Harvard University, 1973.
3. Kohlberg, L. *Continuities and discontinuities in childhood and adult moral development revisited.* Unpublished paper, Harvard University, 1973.
4. Kohlberg, L. Personal communication, August, 1976.
5. Gilligan, C., & Murphy, M. *The philosopher and the "dilemma of the fact": Moral development in late adolescence and adulthood.* Unpublished manuscript, Harvard University, 1977.

References

Broverman, I., Vogel, S., Broverman, D., Clarkson, F., & Rosenkrantz, P. Sex-role stereotypes: A current appraisal. *Journal of Social Issues,* 1972, **28,** 59–78.

Coles, R. *Children of crisis.* Boston: Little, Brown, 1964.

Didion, J. The women's movement. *New York Times Book Review,* July 30, 1972, pp. 1–2; 14.

Drabble, M. *The waterfall.* Hammondsworth, Eng.: Penguin Books, 1969.

Eliot, G. *The mill on the floss.* New York: New American Library, 1965. (Originally published, 1860.)

Erikson, E. H. *Insight and responsibility.* New York: W. W. Norton, 1964.

Erikson, E. H. *Identity: Youth and crisis.* New York: W. W. Norton, 1968.

Erikson, E. H. *Gandhi's truth.* New York: W. W. Norton, 1969.

Freud, S. "Civilized" sexual morality and modern nervous illness. In J. Strachey (Ed.), *The standard edition of the complete psychological works of Sigmund Freud* (Vol. 9). London: Hogarth Press, 1959. (Originally published, 1908.)

Freud, S. Some psychical consequences of the anatomical distinction between the sexes. In J. Strachey (Ed.), *The standard edition of the complete psychological works of Sigmund Freud* (Vol. 19). London: Hogarth Press, 1961. (Originally published, 1925.)

Gilligan, C., Kohlberg, L., Lerner, J., & Belenky, M. Moral reasoning about sexual dilemmas: The development of an interview and scoring system. *Technical Report of the President's Commission on Obscenity and Pornography* (Vol. 1) [415 060–137]. Washington, D.C.: U.S. Government Printing Office, 1971.

Haan, N. Hypothetical and actual moral reasoning in a situation of civil disobedience. *Journal of Personality and Social Psychology,* 1975, **32,** 255–270.

Holstein, C. Development of moral judgment: A longitudinal study of males and females. *Child Development,* 1976, **47,** 51–61.

Horner, M. Toward an understanding of achievement-related conflicts in women. *Journal of Social Issues,* 1972, **29,** 157–174.

Ibsen, H. *A doll's house.* In *Ibsen plays.* Hammondsworth, Eng.: Penguin Books, 1965. (Originally published, 1879.)

Kohlberg, L. From is to ought: How to commit the naturalistic fallacy and get away with it in the study of moral development. In T. Mischel (Ed.), *Cognitive development and epistemology.* New York: Academic Press, 1971.

Kohlberg, L., & Gilligan, C. The adolescent as a philosopher: The discovery of the self in a postconventional world. *Daedalus,* 1971, **100,** 1051–1056.

Kohlberg, L., & Kramer, R. Continuities and discontinuities in childhood and adult moral development. *Human Development,* 1969, **12,** 93–120.

Piaget, J. *The moral judgment of the child.* New York: The Free Press, 1965. (Originally published, 1932.)

Shakespeare, W. *The merchant of Venice.* In *The comedies of Shakespeare.* London: Oxford University Press, 1912. (Originally published, 1598.)

Woman's Place in Man's Life Cycle

CAROL GILLIGAN

Drawing on literary and psychological sources, Carol Gilligan documents the way in which theories of the life cycle, by taking for their model the lives of men, have failed to account for the experience of women. Arguing that this bias has promoted a social science concern with autonomy and achievement at the expense of attachment and intimacy, she suggests that systematic attention to women's lives, in both theory and research, will allow an integration of these concerns into a more balanced conception of human development.

In the second act of *The Cherry Orchard*, Lopakhin, the young merchant, describes his life of hard work and success. Failing to convince Madame Ranevskaya to cut down the cherry orchard to save her estate, he will go on, in the next act, to buy it himself. He is the self-made man, who, in purchasing "the estate where grandfather and father were slaves," seeks to eradicate the "awkward, unhappy life" of the past, replacing the cherry orchard with summer cottages where coming generations "will see a new life" (Act III). Elaborating this developmental vision, he describes the image of man that underlies and supports this activity: "At times when I can't go to sleep, I think: Lord, thou gavest us immense forests, unbounded fields and the widest horizons, and living in the midst of them we should indeed be giants." At which point, Madame Ranevskaya interrupts him, saying, "You feel the need for giants—They are good only in fairy tales, anywhere else they only frighten us" (Act II).

Conceptions of the life cycle represent attempts to order and make coherent the unfolding experiences and perceptions, the changing wishes and realities of everyday life. But the truth of such conceptions depends in part on the position of the observer. The brief excerpt from Chekhov's play (1904/1956) suggests that when the observer is a woman, the truth may be of a different sort. This discrepancy in judgment between men and women is the center of my consideration.

This essay traces the extent to which psychological theories of human development, theories that have informed both educational philosophy and classroom practice, have enshrined a view of human life similar to Lopahkin's while dismissing the ironic commentary in which Chekhov embeds this view. The specific issue I address is that of sex differences, and my focus is on the observation and assessment of sex differences by life-cycle theorists. In talking about sex differences, however, I risk the criticism which such generalization invariably invites. As Virginia Woolf said, when embarking on a similar endeavor: "When a subject is highly controversial—and any question about sex

Harvard Educational Review   Vol. 49   No. 4   November 1979, 431–446

is that—one cannot hope to tell the truth. One can only show how one came to hold whatever opinion one does hold" (1929, p. 4).

At a time when efforts are being made to eradicate discrimination between the sexes in the search for equality and justice, the differences between the sexes are being rediscovered in the social sciences. This discovery occurs when theories formerly considered to be sexually neutral in their scientific objectivity are found instead to reflect a consistent observational and evaluative bias. Then the presumed neutrality of science, like that of language itself, gives way to the recognition that the categories of knowledge are human constructions. The fascination with point of view and the corresponding recognition of the relativity of truth that has informed the fiction of the twentieth century begin to infuse our scientific understanding as well when we begin to notice how accustomed we have become to seeing life through men's eyes.

A recent discovery of this sort pertains to the apparently innocent classic by Strunk and White (1959), *The Elements of Style*. The Supreme Court ruling on the subject of discrimination in classroom texts led one teacher of English to notice that the elementary rules of English usage were being taught through examples which counterposed the birth of Napoleon, the writings of Coleridge, and statements such as, "He was an interesting talker, a man who had traveled all over the world and lived in half a dozen countries" (p. 7) with "Well, Susan, this is a fine mess you are in" (p. 3) or, less drastically, "He saw a woman, accompanied by two children, walking slowly down the road" (p. 8).

Psychological theorists have fallen as innocently as Strunk and White into the same observational bias. Implicitly adopting the male life as the norm, they have tried to fashion women out of a masculine cloth. It all goes back, of course, to Adam and Eve, a story which shows, among other things, that, if you make a woman out of a man you are bound to get into trouble. In the life cycle, as in the Garden of Eden, it is the woman who has been the deviant.

The penchant of developmental theorists to project a masculine image, and one that appears frightening to women, goes back at least to Freud (1905/1961), who built his theory of psychosexual development around the experiences of the male child that culminate in the Oedipus complex. In the 1920s, Freud struggled to resolve the contradictions posed for his theory by the different configuration of female sexuality and the different dynamics of the young girl's early family relationships. After trying to fit women into his masculine conception, seeing them as envying that which they missed, he came instead to acknowledge, in the strength and persistence of women's pre-Oedipal attachments to their mothers, a developmental difference. However, he considered this difference in women's development to be responsible for what he saw as women's developmental failure.

Deprived by nature of the impetus for a clear-cut Oedipal resolution, women's superego, the heir to the Oedipus complex, consequently was compromised. It was never, Freud observed, "so inexorable, so impersonal, so independent of its emotional origins as we require it to be in men" (1925/1961, p. 257). From this observation of difference, "that for women the level of what is ethically normal is different from what it is in men" (p. 257), Freud concluded that "women have less sense of justice than men, that they are less ready to submit to the great exigencies of life, that they are more often influenced in their judgments by feelings of affection and hostility" (pp. 257–258).

Chodorow (1974, 1978) addresses this evaluative bias in the assessment of sex differences in her attempt to account for "the reproduction within each generation of certain general and nearly universal differences that characterize masculine and feminine personality and roles" (1974, p. 43). Writing from a psychoanalytic perspective, she attributes these continuing differences between the sexes not to anatomy but rather to "the fact that women, universally, are largely responsible for early child care and for (at least) later female socialization" (1974, p. 43). Because this early social environment differs for and is experienced differently by male and female children, basic sex differences recur in personality development. As a result, "in any given society, feminine personality comes to define itself in relation and connection to other people more than masculine personality does. (In psychoanalytic terms, women are less individuated than men; they have more flexible ego boundaries.)" (1974, p. 44).

In her analysis, Chodorow relies primarily on Stoller's research on the development of gender identity and gender-identity disturbances. Stoller's work indicates that male and female identity, the unchanging core of personality formation, is "with rare exception firmly and irreversibly established for both sexes by the time a child is around three" (Chodorow, 1978, p. 150). Given that for both sexes the primary caretaker in the first three years of life is typically female, the interpersonal dynamics of gender identity formation are different for boys and girls. Female identity formation takes place in a context of ongoing relationship as "mothers tend to experience their daughters as more like, and continuous with, themselves. Correspondingly, girls tend to remain part of the dyadic primary mother-child relationship itself. This means that a girl continues to experience herself as involved in issues of merging and separation, and in an attachment characterized by primary identification and the fusion of identification and object choice" (1978, p. 166).

In contrast, "mothers experience their sons as a male opposite" and, as a result, "boys are more likely to have been pushed out of the preoedipal relationship and to have had to curtail their primary love and sense of empathic tie with their mother" (1978, p. 166). Consequently, boys' development entails a "more emphatic individuation and a more defensive firming of ego boundaries." For boys, but not for girls, "issues of differentiation have become intertwined with sexual issues" (1978, p. 167).

Thus Chodorow refutes the masculine bias of psychoanalytic theory, claiming that the existence of sex differences in the early experiences of individuation and relationship "does not mean that women have 'weaker ego boundaries' than men or are more prone to psychosis" (1978, p. 167). What it means instead is that "the earliest mode of individuation, the primary construction of the ego and its inner object-world, the earliest conflicts and the earliest unconscious definitions of self, the earliest threats to individuation, and the earliest anxieties which call up defenses, all differ for boys and girls because of differences in the character of the early mother-child relationship for each" (1978, p. 167). Because of these differences, "girls emerge from this period with a basis for 'empathy' built into their primary definition of self in a way that boys do not" (1978, p. 167). Chodorow thus replaces Freud's negative and derivative description of female psychology with a more positive and direct account of her own:

Girls emerge with a stronger basis for experiencing another's needs and feelings as one's own (or of thinking that one is so experiencing another's needs and feelings). Furthermore, girls do not define themselves in terms of the denial of preoedipal relational modes to the same extent as do boys. Therefore, regression to these modes tends not to feel as much a basic threat to their ego. From very early, then, because they are parented by a person of the same gender . . . girls come to experience themselves as less differentiated than boys, as more continuous with and related to the external object-world, and as differently oriented to their inner object-world as well. (1978, p. 167)

Consequently, "issues of dependency, in particular, are handled and experienced differently by men and women" (Chodorow, 1974, p. 44). For boys and men, separation and individuation are critically tied to gender identity since separation from the mother is essential for the development of masculinity. "For girls and women, by contrast, issues of femininity or feminine identity are not problematic in the same way" (1974, p. 44); they do not depend on the achievement of separation from the mother or on the progress of individuation. Since, in Chodorow's analysis, masculinity is defined through separation while femininity is defined through attachment, male gender identity will be threatened by intimacy while female gender identity will be threatened by individuation. Thus males will tend to have difficulty with relationships while females will tend to have problems with separation. The quality of embeddedness in social interaction and personal relationships that characterizes women's lives in contrast to men's, however, becomes not only a descriptive difference but also a developmental liability when the milestones of childhood and adolescent development are described by markers of increasing separation. Then women's failure to separate becomes by definition a failure to develop.

The sex differences in personality formation that Chodorow delineates in her analysis of early childhood relationships as well as the bias she points out in the evaluation of these differences, reappear in the middle childhood years in the studies of children's games. Children's games have been considered by Mead (1934) and Piaget (1932/1965) as the crucible of social development during the school years. In games children learn to take the role of the other and come to see themselves through another's eyes. In games they learn respect for rules and come to understand the ways rules can be made and changed.

Lever (1976), considering the peer group to be the agent of socialization during the elementary school years and play to be a major activity of socialization at that time, set out to discover whether there were sex differences in the games that children play. Studying 181 fifth-grade, white, middle-class, Connecticut children, ages 10 and 11, she observed the organization and structure of their playtime activities. She watched the children as they played during the school recess, lunch, and in physical education class, and, in addition, kept diaries of their accounts as to how they spent their out-of-school time.

From this study, Lever reports the following sex differences: boys play more out of doors than girls do; boys more often play in large and age-heterogeneous groups; they play competitive games more often than girls do, and their games last longer than girls' games (Lever, 1976). The last is in some ways the most interesting finding. Boys' games appeared to last longer not only because they required a higher level of skill and were thus less likely to become boring, but also because when disputes arose in the course of a game, the boys were able to resolve the disputes more effectively than the girls: "During the course of this study, boys were seen quarrelling all the time, but not once was a game terminated because of a quarrel and no game was interrupted for more than seven minutes. In the gravest debates, the final word was always to 'repeat the play,' generally followed by a chorus of 'cheater's proof' " (1976, p. 482). In fact, it seemed that the boys enjoyed the legal debates as much as they did the game itself, and even marginal players of lesser size or skill participated equally in these recurrent squabbles. In contrast, the eruption of disputes among girls tended to end the game.

Thus Lever extends and corroborates the observations reported by Piaget (1932/1965) in his naturalistic study of the rules of the game, where he found boys becoming increasingly fascinated with the legal elaboration of rules and the development of fair procedures for adjudicating conflicts, a fascination that, he noted, did not hold for girls. Girls, Piaget observed, had a more "pragmatic" attitude toward rules, "regarding a rule as good as long as the game repaid it" (1932/1965, p. 83). As a result, he considered girls to be more tolerant in their attitudes toward rules, more willing to make exceptions, and more easily reconciled to innovations. However, and presumably as a result, he concluded that the legal sense which he considered essential to moral development "is far less developed in little girls than in boys" (1932/1965, p. 77).

This same bias that led Piaget to equate male development with child development also colors Lever's work. The assumption that shapes her discussion of results is that the male model is the better one. It seems, in any case, more adaptive since as Lever points out it fits the requirements Riesman (1961) describes for success in modern corporate life. In contrast, the sensitivity and care for the feelings of others that girls develop through their primarily dyadic play relationships have little market value and can even impede professional success. Lever clearly implies that, given the realities of adult life, if a girl does not want to be dependent on men, she will have to learn to play like a boy.

Since Piaget argues that children learn the respect for rules necessary for moral development by playing rule-bound games, and Kohlberg (1971) adds that these lessons are most effectively learned through the opportunities for role-taking that arise in the course of resolving disputes, the moral lessons inherent in girls' play appear to be fewer than for boys. Traditional girls' games like jump rope and hopscotch are turn-taking games where competition is indirect in that one person's success does not necessarily signify another's failure. Consequently, disputes requiring adjudication are less likely to occur. In fact, most of the girls whom Lever interviewed claimed that when a quarrel broke out, they ended the game. Rather than elaborating a system of rules for resolving disputes, girls directed their efforts instead toward sustaining affective ties.

Lever concludes that from the games they play boys learn both independence and the organizational skills necessary for coordinating the activities of large and diverse groups of people. By participating in controlled and socially approved competitive situations, they learn to deal with competition in a relatively forthright manner—to play with their enemies and compete with their friends, all in accordance with the rules of the game. In contrast, girls' play tends to occur in smaller, more intimate groups, often the best-friend dyad, and in private places. This play replicates the

social pattern of primary human relationships in that its organization is more cooperative and points less toward learning to take the role of the generalized other than it
does toward the development of the empathy and sensitivity necessary for taking the
role of the particular other.

Chodorow's analysis of sex differences in personality formation in early childhood is
thus extended by Lever's observations of sex differences in the play activities of middle
childhood. Together these accounts suggest that boys and girls arrive at puberty with a
different interpersonal orientation and a different range of social experiences. While
Sullivan (1953), tracing the sequence of male development, posits the experience of a
close same-sex friendship in preadolescence as necessary for the subsequent integration
of sexuality and intimacy, no corresponding account is available to describe girls' development at this critical juncture. Instead, since adolescence is considered a crucial
time for separation and individuation, the period of "the second individuation
process" (Blos, 1967), it has been in adolescence that female development has appeared most divergent and thus most problematic.

"Puberty," Freud said, "which brings about so great an accession of libido in boys, is
marked in girls by a fresh wave of repression" (1905/1961, p. 220) necessary for the
transformation of the young girls' "masculine sexuality" into the "specifically
feminine" sexuality of her adulthood. Freud posits this transformation on the girl's acknowledgement and acceptance of "the fact of her castration." In his account puberty
brings for girls a new awareness of "the wound to her narcissism" and leads her to develop, "like a scar, a sense of inferiority" (Freud, 1925/1961, p. 253). Since
adolescence is, in Erikson's expansion of Freud's psychoanalytic account, the time
when the ego takes on an identity which confirms the individual in relation to society,
the girl arrives at this juncture in development either psychologically at risk or with a
different agenda.

The problem that female adolescence presents for psychologists of human development is apparent in Erikson's account. Erikson (1950) charts eight stages of psychosocial development in which adolescence is the fifth. The task of this stage is to forge a
coherent sense of self, to verify an identity that can span the discontinuity of puberty
and make possible the adult capacity to love and to work. The preparation for the successful resolution of the adolescent identity crisis is delineated in Erikson's description
of the preceding four stages. If in infancy the initial crisis of trust vs. mistrust generates
enough hope to sustain the child through the arduous life cycle that lies ahead, the
task at hand clearly becomes one of individuation. Erikson's second stage centers on
the crisis of autonomy versus shame and doubt, the walking child's emerging sense of
separateness and agency. From there, development goes on to the crisis of initiative
versus guilt, successful resolution of which represents a further move in the direction of
autonomy. Next, following the inevitable disappointment of the magical wishes of the
oedipal period, the child realizes with respect to his parents that to beat them he must
first join them and learn to do what they do so well. Thus in the middle childhood
years, development comes to hinge on the crisis of industry versus inferiority, as the
demonstration of competence becomes critical to the child's developing self-esteem.
This is the time when children strive to learn and master the technology of their culture in order to recognize themselves and be recognized as capable of becoming adults.

Next comes adolescence, the celebration of the autonomous, initiating, industrious self through the forging of an identity based on an ideology that can support and justify adult commitments. But about whom is Erikson talking?

Once again it turns out to be the male child—the coming generation of men like George Bernard Shaw, William James, Martin Luther, and Mahatma Gandhi—who provide Erikson with his most vivid illustrations. For the woman, Erikson (1968) says, the sequence is a bit different. She holds her identity in abeyance as she prepares to attract the man by whose name she will be known, by whose status she will be defined, the man who will rescue her from emptiness and loneliness by filling "the inner space" (Erikson, 1968). While for men, identity precedes intimacy and generativity in the optimal cycle of human separation and attachment, for women these tasks seem instead to be fused. Intimacy precedes, or rather goes along with, identity as the female comes to know herself as she is known, through her relationships with others.

Two things are essential to note at this point. The first is that, despite Erikson's observation of sex differences, his chart of life-cycle stages remains unchanged: identity continues to precede intimacy as the male diagonal continues to define his life-cycle conception. The second is that in the male life cycle there is little preparation for the intimacy of the first adult stage. Only the initial stage of trust versus mistrust suggests the type of mutuality that Erikson means by intimacy and generativity and Freud by genitality. The rest is separateness, with the result that development itself comes to be identified with separation, and attachments appear as developmental impediments, as we have repeatedly found to be the case in the assessment of women.

Erikson's description of male identity as forged in relation to the world and of female identity as awakened in a relationship of intimacy with another person, however controversial, is hardly new. In Bettelheim's discussion of fairy tales in *The Uses of Enchantment* (1976) an identical portrayal appears. While Bettelheim argues, in refutation of those critics who see in fairy tales a sexist literature, that opposite models exist and could readily be found, nevertheless the ones upon which he focuses his discussion of adolescence conform to the pattern we have begun to observe.

The dynamics of male adolescence are illustrated archetypically by the conflict between father and son in "The Three Languages" (Bettelheim, 1976). Here a son, considered hopelessly stupid by his father, is given one last chance at education and sent for a year to study with a famous master. But when he returns, all he has learned is "what the dogs bark" (1976, p. 97). After two further attempts of this sort, the father gives up in disgust and orders his servants to take the child into the forest and kill him. The servants, however, those perpetual rescuers of disowned and abandoned children, take pity on the child and decide simply to leave him in the forest. From there, his wanderings take him to a land beset by furious dogs whose barking permits nobody to rest and who periodically devour one of the inhabitants. Now it turns out that our hero has learned just the right thing: he can talk with the dogs and is able to quiet them, thus restoring peace to the land. The other knowledge he acquires serves him equally well, and he emerges triumphant from his adolescent confrontation with his father, a giant of the life-cycle conception.

In contrast, the dynamics of female adolescence are depicted through the telling of a very different story. In the world of the fairy tale, the girl's first bleeding is followed by a period of intense passivity in which nothing seems to be happening. Yet in the deep sleep of Snow White and Sleeping Beauty, Bettelheim sees that inner concentration which he considers to be the necessary counterpart to the activity of adventure. The adolescent heroines awaken from their sleep not to conquer the world but to marry the prince. Their feminine identity is inwardly and interpersonally defined. As in Erikson's observation, for women, identity and intimacy are more intricately conjoined. The sex differences depicted in the world of the fairy tales, like the fantasy of the woman warrior in Maxine Hong Kingston's (1977) recent autobiographical novel (which in turn echoes the old stories of Troilus and Cressida and Tancred and Chlorinda) indicate repeatedly that active adventure is a male activity, and if women are to embark on such endeavors, they must at least dress like men.

These observations about sex difference support the conclusion reached by McClelland that "sex role turns out to be one of the most important determinants of human behavior. Psychologists have found sex differences in their studies from the moment they started doing empirical research" (1975, p. 81). But since it is difficult to say "different" without saying "better" or "worse," and since there is a tendency to construct a single scale of measurement, and since that scale has been derived and standardized on the basis of men's observations and interpretations of research data predominantly or exclusively drawn from studies of males, psychologists have tended, in McClelland's words, "to regard male behavior as the 'norm' and female behavior as some kind of deviation from that norm" (1975, p. 81). Thus when women do not conform to the standards of psychological expectation, the conclusion has generally been that something is wrong with the women.

What Horner (1972) found to be wrong with women was the anxiety they showed about competitive achievement. From the beginning, research on human motivation using the Thematic Apperception Test (TAT) was plagued by evidence of sex differences which appeared to confuse and complicate data analysis. The TAT presents for interpretation an ambiguous cue — a picture about which a story is to be written or a brief story stem to be completed. Such stories in reflecting projective imagination are considered to reveal the ways in which people construe what they perceive — that is, the concepts and interpretations they bring to their experience and thus presumably the kind of sense that they make of their lives. Prior to Horner's work, it was clear that women made a different kind of sense than men of situations of competitive achievement, that in some way they saw the situation differently or the situation aroused in them some different response.

On the basis of his studies of men, McClelland (1961) had divided the concept of achievement motivation into what appeared to be its two logical components, a motive to approach success ("hope success") and a motive to avoid failure ("fear failure"). When Horner (1972) began to analyze the problematic projective data on female achievement motivation, she identified as a third category the unlikely motivation to avoid success ("fear success"). Women appeared to have a problem with competitive achievement, and that problem seemed, in Horner's interpretation, to emanate from a perceived conflict between femininity and success, the dilemma of the female adolescent who struggles to integrate her feminine aspirations and the identifications of her early childhood with the more masculine competence she has acquired at school. Thus Horner reports, "When success is likely or possible, threatened by the negative consequences they expect to follow success, young women become anxious and their positive achievement strivings become thwarted" (1972, p. 171). She concludes that this fear "exists because for most women, the anticipation of success in competitive achievement activity, especially against men, produced anticipation of certain negative consequences, for example, threat of social rejection and loss of femininity."

It is, however, possible to view such conflicts about success in a different light. Sassen (1980) on the basis of her reanalysis of the data presented in Horner's thesis, suggests that the conflicts expressed by the women might instead indicate "a heightened perception of the 'other side' of competitive success, that is, the great emotional costs at which success achieved through competition is often gained—an understanding which, while confused, indicates some underlying sense that something is rotten in the state in which success is defined as having better grades than everyone else" (p. 15). Sassen points out that Horner found success anxiety to be present in women only when achievement was directly competitive, that is, where one person's success was at the expense of another's failure.

From Horner's examples of fear of success, it is impossible to differentiate between neurotic or realistic anxiety about the consequences of achievement, the questioning of conventional definitions of success, and the discovery of personal goals other than conventional success. The construction of the problem posed by success as a problem of identity and ideology that appears in Horner's illustrations, if taken at face value rather than assumed to be derivative, suggests Erikson's distinction between a conventional and neohumanist identity, or, in cognitive terms, the distinction between conventional and postconventional thought (Loevinger, 1970; Inhelder & Piaget, 1958; Kohlberg, 1971; Perry, 1968).

In his elaboration of the identity crisis, Erikson discusses the life of George Bernard Shaw to illustrate the young person's sense of being co-opted prematurely by success in a career he cannot wholeheartedly endorse. Shaw at seventy, reflecting upon his life, describes his crisis at the age of twenty as one caused not by lack of success or the absence of recognition, but by too much of both:

> I made good in spite of myself, and found, to my dismay, that Business, instead of expelling me as the worthless imposter I was, was fastening upon me with no intention of letting me go. Behold me, therefore, in my twentieth year, with a business training, in an occupation which I detested as cordially as any sane person lets himself detest anything he cannot escape from. In March, 1876, I broke loose. (Erikson, 1968, p. 143)

At this point Shaw settled down to study and to write as he pleased. Hardly interpreted as evidence of developmental difficulty, of neurotic anxiety about achievement and competition, Shaw's refusal suggested to Erikson, "the extraordinary workings of an extraordinary personality coming to the fore" (1968, p. 144).

We might on these grounds begin to ask not why women have conflicts about succeeding but why men show such readiness to adopt and celebrate a rather narrow vision of success. Remembering Piaget's observation, corroborated by Lever, that boys in their games are concerned more with rules while girls are more concerned with relationships, often at the expense of the game itself; remembering also that, in Chodorow's analysis, men's social orientation is positional and women's orientation is personal, we begin to understand why, when Anne becomes John in Horner's tale of competitive success and the stories are written by men, fear of success tends to disappear.

John is considered by other men to have played by the rules and won. He has the *right* to feel good about his success. Confirmed in his sense of his own identity as separate from those who, compared to him, are less competent, his positional sense of self is affirmed. For Anne, it is possible that the position she could obtain by being at the top of her medical school class may not, in fact, be what she wants.

"It is obvious," Virginia Woolf said, "that the values of women differ very often from the values which have been made by the other sex" (1929, p. 76). Yet, she adds, it is the masculine values that prevail. As a result, women come to question the "normality" of their feelings and to alter their judgments in deference to the opinion of others. In the nineteenth-century novels written by women, Woolf sees at work "a mind slightly pulled from the straight, altering its clear vision in the anger and confusion of deference to external authority" (1929, p. 77). The same deference that Woolf identifies in nineteenth-century fiction can be seen as well in the judgments of twentieth-century women. Women's reluctance to make moral judgments, the difficulty they experience in finding or speaking publicly in their own voice, emerge repeatedly in the form of qualification and self-doubt, in intimations of a divided judgment, a public and private assessment which are fundamentally at odds (Gilligan, 1977).

Yet the deference and confusion that Woolf criticizes in women derive from the values she sees as their strength. Women's deference is rooted not only in their social circumstances but also in the substance of their moral concern. Sensitivity to the needs of others and the assumption of responsibility for taking care lead women to attend to voices other than their own and to include in their judgment other points of view. Women's moral weakness, manifest in an apparent diffusion and confusion of judgment, is thus inseparable from women's moral strength, an overriding concern with relationships and responsibilities. The reluctance to judge can itself be indicative of the same care and concern for others that infuses the psychology of women's development and is responsible for what is characteristically seen as problematic in its nature.

Thus women not only define themselves in a context of human relationship but also judge themselves in terms of their ability to care. Woman's place in man's life cycle has been that of nurturer, caretaker, and helpmate, the weaver of those networks of relationships on which she in turn relies. While women have thus taken care of men, however, men have in their theories of psychological development tended either to assume or devalue that care. The focus on individuation and individual achievement that has dominated the description of child and adolescent development has recently been extended to the depiction of adult development as well. Levinson, in his study, *The Seasons of a Man's Life* (1978), elaborates a view of adult development in which relationships are portrayed as a means to an end of individual achievement and success. In the critical relationships of early adulthood, the "Mentor" and the "Special Woman" are defined by the role they play in facilitating the man's realization of his "Dream." Along similar lines Vaillant (1977), in his study of men, considers altruism a defense, characteristic of mature ego functioning and associated with successful "adaptation to life," but conceived as derivative rather than primary in contrast to Chodorow's analysis, in which empathy is considered "built-in" to the woman's primary definition of self.

The discovery now being celebrated by men in mid-life of the importance of intimacy, relationships, and care is something that women have known from the beginning. However, because that knowledge has been considered "intuitive" or "instinctive," a function of anatomy coupled with destiny, psychologists have neglected to describe its development. In my research, I have found that women's moral development centers on the elaboration of that knowledge. Women's moral development thus delineates a critical line of psychological development whose importance for both sexes becomes apparent in the intergenerational framework of a life-cycle perspective. While the subject of moral development provides the final illustration of the reiterative pattern in the observation and assessment of sex differences in the literature on human development, it also indicates more particularly why the nature and significance of women's development has for so long been obscured and considered shrouded in mystery.

The criticism that Freud (1961) makes of women's sense of justice, seeing it as compromised in its refusal of blind impartiality, reappears not only in the work of Piaget (1934) but also in that of Kohlberg (1958). While girls are an aside in Piaget's account of *The Moral Judgment of the Child* (1934), an odd curiosity to whom he devotes four brief entries in an index that omits "boys" altogether because "the child" is assumed to be male, in Kohlberg's research on moral development, females simply do not exist. Kohlberg's six stages that describe the development of moral judgment from childhood to adulthood were derived empirically from a longitudinal study of eighty-four boys from the United States. While Kohlberg (1973) claims universality for his stage sequence and considers his conception of justice as fairness to have been naturalistically derived, those groups not included in his original sample rarely reach his higher stages (Edwards, 1975; Gilligan, 1977). Prominent among those found to be deficient in moral development when measured by Kohlberg's scale are women whose judgments on his scale seemed to exemplify the third stage in his six-stage sequence. At this stage morality is conceived in terms of relationships, and goodness is equated with helping and pleasing others. This concept of goodness was considered by Kohlberg and Kramer (1969) to be functional in the lives of mature women insofar as those lives took place in the home and thus were relationally bound. Only if women were to go out of the house to enter the arena of male activity would they realize the inadequacy of their Stage Three perspective and progress like men toward higher stages where morality is societally or universally defined in accordance with a conception of justice as fairness.

In this version of human development, however, a particular conception of maturity is assumed, based on the study of men's lives and reflecting the importance of individuation in their development. When one begins instead with women and derives developmental constructs from their lives, then a different conception of development emerges the expansion and elaboration of which can also be traced through stages that comprise a developmental sequence. In Loevinger's (1966) test for measuring ego development that was drawn from studies of females, fifteen of the thirty-six sentence stems to complete begin with the subject of human relationships (for example, "Raising a family. . . .; If my mother. . . .; Being with other people. . . .; When I am with a man. . . .; When a child won't join in group activities. . . .") (Loevinger & Wessler, 1970, p. 141). Thus ego development is described and measured by Loevinger through conception of relationships as well as by the concept of identity that measures the progress of individuation.

Research on moral judgment has shown that when the categories of women's thinking are examined in detail (Gilligan, 1977) the outline of a moral conception different from that described by Freud, Piaget, or Kohlberg begins to emerge and to inform a different description of moral development. In this conception, the moral problem is seen to arise from conflicting responsibilities rather than from competing rights and to require for its resolution a mode of thinking that is contextual and inductive rather than formal and abstract.

This conception of morality as fundamentally concerned with the capacity for understanding and care also develops through a structural progression of increasing differentiation and integration. This progression witnesses the shift from an egocentric through a societal to the universal moral perspective that Kohlberg described in his research on men, but it does so in different terms. The shift in women's judgment from an egocentric to a conventional to a principled ethical understanding is articulated through their use of a distinct moral language, in which the terms "selfishness" and "responsibility" define the moral problem as one of care. Moral development then consists of the progressive reconstruction of this understanding toward a more adequate conception of care.

The concern with caring centers moral development around the progressive differentiation and integration that characterize the evolution of the understanding of relationships just as the conception of fairness delineates the progressive differentiation and balancing of individual rights. Within the responsibility orientation, the infliction of hurt is the center of moral concern and is considered immoral whether or not it can otherwise be construed as fair or unfair. The reiterative use of the language of selfishness and responsibility to define the moral problem as a problem of care sets women apart from the men whom Kohlberg studied and from whose thinking he derived his six stages. This different construction of the moral problem by women may be seen as the critical reason for their failure to develop within the constraints of Kohlberg's system.

Regarding all constructions of responsibility as evidence of a conventional moral understanding, Kohlberg defines the highest stages of moral development as deriving from a reflective understanding of human rights. That the morality of rights differs from the morality of responsibility in its emphasis on separation rather than attachment, in its consideration of the individual rather than the relationship as primary, is illustrated by two quotations that exemplify these different orientations. The first comes from a twenty-five-year-old man who participated in Kohlberg's longitudinal study. The quotation itself is cited by Kohlberg to illustrate the principled conception of morality that he scores as "integrated [Stage] Five judgment, possibly moving to Stage Six."

[What does the word morality mean to you?] Nobody in the world knows the answer. I think it is recognizing the right of the individual, the rights of other individuals, not interfering with those rights. Act as fairly as you would have them treat you. I think it is basically to preserve the human being's right to existence. I think that is the most important. Secondly, the human being's right to do as he pleases, again without interfering with somebody else's rights.

[How have your views on morality changed since the last interview?] I think I am more aware of an individual's rights now. I used to be looking at it strictly from my point of view, just for me. Now I think I am more aware of what the individual has a right to. (Note 1, p. 29)

"Clearly," Kohlberg states,

these responses represent attainment of the third level of moral theory. Moving to a perspective outside of that of his society, he identifies morality with justice (fairness, rights, the Golden Rule), with recognition of the rights of others as these are defined naturally or intrinsically. The human's right to do as he pleases without interfering with somebody else's rights is a formula defining rights prior to social legislation and opinion which defines what society may expect rather than being defined by it. (Note 1, pp. 29–30)

The second quotation comes from my interview with a woman, also twenty-five years old and at the time of the interview a third-year student at Harvard Law School. She described her conception of morality as follows:

[Is there really some correct solution to moral problems or is everybody's opinion equally right?] No, I don't think everybody's opinion is equally right. I think that in some situations . . . there may be opinions that are equally valid and one could conscientiously adopt one of several courses of action. But there are other situations which I think there are right and wrong answers, that sort of inhere in the nature of existence, of all individuals here who need to live with each other to live. We need to depend on each other and hopefully it is not only a physical need but a need of fulfillment in ourselves, that a person's life is enriched by cooperating with other people and striving to live in harmony with everybody else, and to that end, there are right and wrong, there are things which promote that end and that move away from it, and in that way, it is possible to choose in certain cases among different courses of action, that obviously promote or harm that goal.

[Is there a time in the past when you would have thought about these things differently?] Oh, yah. I think that I went through a time when I thought that things were pretty relative, that I can't tell you what to do and you can't tell me what to do, because you've got your conscience and I've got mine . . . .

[When was that?] When I was in high school, I guess that it just sort of dawned on me that my own ideas changed and because my own judgments changed, I felt I couldn't judge another person's judgment . . . but now I think even when it is only the person himself who is going to be affected, I say it is wrong to the extent it doesn't cohere with what I know about human nature and what I know about you, and just from what I think is true about the operation of the universe, I could say I think you are making a mistake.

[What led you to change, do you think?] Just seeing more of life, just recognizing that there are an awful lot of things that are common among people . . . there are certain things that you come to learn promote a better life and better relationships and more personal fulfillment than other things that in general tend to do the opposite and the things that promote these things, you would call morally right.

These responses also represent a reflective reconstruction of morality following a period of relativistic questioning and doubt, but the reconstruction of moral understanding is based not on the primacy and universality of individual rights, but rather on what she herself describes as a "very strong sense of being responsible to the world." Within this construction, the moral dilemma changes from how to exercise one's rights without interfering with the rights of others to how "to lead a moral life which includes obligations to myself and my family and people in general." The problem then becomes one of limiting responsibilities without abandoning moral concern. When asked to describe herself, this woman says that she values

> having other people that I am tied to and also having people that I am responsible to. I have a very strong sense of being responsible to the world, that I can't just live for my enjoyment, but just the fact of being in the world gives me an obligation to do what I can to make the world a better place to live in, no matter how small a scale that may be on.

Thus while Kohlberg's subject worries about people interfering with one another's rights, this woman worries about "the possibility of omission, of your not helping others when you could help them."

The issue this law student raises is addressed by Loevinger's fifth "autonomous" stage of ego development. The terms of its resolution lie in achieving partial autonomy from an excessive sense of responsibility by recognizing that other people have responsibility for their own destiny (Loevinger, 1968). The autonomous stage in Loevinger's account witnesses a relinquishing of moral dichotomies and their replacement with "a feeling for the complexity and multifaceted character of real people and real situations" (1970, p. 6).

Whereas the rights conception of morality that informs Kohlberg's principled level [Stages Five and Six] is geared to arriving at an objectively fair or just resolution to the moral dilemmas to which "all rational men can agree" (Kohlberg, 1976), the responsibility conception focuses instead on the limitations of any particular resolution and describes the conflicts that remain. This limitation of moral judgment and choice is described by a woman in her thirties when she says that her guiding principle in making moral decisions has to do with "responsibility and caring about yourself and others, not just a principle that once you take hold of, you settle [the moral problem]. The principle put into practice is still going to leave you with conflict."

Given the substance and orientation of these women's judgments, it becomes clear why a morality of rights and noninterference may appear to women as frightening in its potential justification of indifference and unconcern. At the same time, however, it also becomes clear why, from a male perspective, women's judgments appear inconclusive and diffuse, given their insistent contextual relativism. Women's moral judgments thus elucidate the pattern that we have observed in the differences between the sexes, but provide an alternative conception of maturity by which these differences can be developmentally considered. The psychology of women that has consistently been described as distinctive in its greater orientation toward relationships of interdependence implies a more contextual mode of judgment and a different moral understanding. Given the differences in women's conceptions of self and morality, it is not surprising that women bring to the life cycle a different point of view and that they order human experience in terms of different priorities.

The myth of Demeter and Persephone, which McClelland cites as exemplifying the feminine attitude toward power, was associated with the Eleusinian Mysteries celebrated in ancient Greece for over two thousand years (1975, p. 96). As told in the Homeric *Hymn to Demeter* (1971), the story of Persephone indicates the strengths of "interdependence, building up resources and giving" (McClelland, 1975, p. 96) that McClelland found in his research on power motivation to characterize the mature feminine style. Although, McClelland says, "it is fashionable to conclude that no one knows what went on in the Mysteries, it is known that they were probably the most important religious ceremonies, even partly on the historical record, which were organized by and for women, especially at the onset before men by means of the cult of Dionysus began to take them over" (1975, p. 96). Thus McClelland regards the myth as "a special presentation of feminine psychology" (1975). It is, as well, a life-cycle story par excellence.

Persephone, the daughter of Demeter, while out playing in the meadows with her girl friends, sees a beautiful narcissus which she runs to pick. As she does so, the earth opens and she is snatched away by Pluto, who takes her to his underworld kingdom. Demeter, goddess of the earth, so mourns the loss of her daughter that she refuses to allow anything to grow. The crops that sustain life on earth shrivel and dry up, killing men and animals alike, until Zeus takes pity on man's suffering and persuades his brother to return Persephone to her mother. But before she leaves, Persephone eats some pomegranate seeds which insures that she will spend six months of every year in the underworld.

The elusive mystery of women's development lies in its recognition of the continuing importance of attachment in the human life cycle. Woman's place in man's life cycle has been to protect this recognition while the developmental litany intones the celebration of separation, autonomy, individuation, and natural rights. The myth of Persephone speaks directly to the distortion in this view by reminding us that narcissism leads to death, that the fertility of the earth is in some mysterious way tied to the continuation of the mother-daughter relationship, and that the life cycle itself arises from an alternation between the world of women and that of men. My intention in this essay has been to suggest that only when life-cycle theorists equally divide their attention and begin to live with women as they have lived with men will their vision encompass the experience of both sexes and their theories become correspondingly more fertile.

Reference Note

1. Kohlberg, L. *Continuities and discontinuities in childhood and adult moral development revisited.* Unpublished manuscript, Harvard University, 1973.

References

Bettelheim, B. *The uses of enchantment.* New York: Knopf, 1976.

Blos, P. The second individuation process of adolescence. In A. Freud (Ed.), *The psychoanalytic study of the child* (Vol. 22). New York: International Universities Press, 1967.

Chekhov, A. *The cherry orchard.* (Stark Young, trans.). New York: Modern Library, 1956. (Originally published, 1904.)

Chodorow, N. Family structure and feminine personality. In M. Rosaldo & L. Lamphere (Eds.), *Women, culture and society*. Stanford, Calif.: Stanford University Press, 1974.

Chodorow, N. *The reproduction of mothering*. Berkeley: University of California Press, 1978.

Edwards, C. P. Societal complexity and moral development: A Kenyan study. *Ethos*, 1975, **3**, 505-527.

Erikson, E. *Identity: Youth and crisis*. New York: Norton, 1968.

Freud, S. Female sexuality. In J. Strachey (Ed.), *The standard edition of the complete psychological works of Sigmund Freud* (Vol. 21). London: Hogarth Press, 1961. (Originally published, 1931.)

Freud, S. Some psychical consequences of the anatomical distinction between the sexes. In J. Strachey (Ed.), *The standard edition of the complete psychological works of Sigmund Freud* (Vol. 19). London: Hogarth Press, 1961. (Originally published, 1925.)

Freud, S. Three essays on sexuality. In J. Strachey (Ed.), *The standard edition of the complete psychological works of Sigmund Freud* (Vol. 7). London: Hogarth Press, 1961. (Originally published, 1905.)

Gilligan, C. In a different voice: Women's conceptions of the self and of morality. *Harvard Educational Review*, 1977, **47**, 481-517. [Also in this anthology on pp. 187-223.]

The Homeric Hymn (C. Boer, trans.). Chicago: Swallow Press, 1971.

Horner, M. Toward an understanding of achievement-related conflicts in women. *Journal of Social Issues*, 1972, **28** (2), 157-174.

Inhelder, B., & Piaget, J. *The growth of logical thinking from childhood to adolescence*. New York: Basic Books, 1958.

Kingston, M. H. *The woman warrior*. New York: Vintage Books, 1977.

Kohlberg, L., & Kramer, R. Continuities and discontinuities in childhood and adult moral development. *Human Development*, 1969, **12**, 93-120.

Kohlberg, L. From is to ought: How to commit the naturalistic fallacy and get away with it in the study of moral development. In T. Mischel (Ed.), *Cognitive development and epistemology*. New York: Academic Press, 1971.

Lever, J. Sex differences in the games children play. *Social Problems*, 1976, **23**, 478-487.

Levinson, D. *The seasons of a man's life*. New York: Knopf, 1978.

Loevinger, J., & Wessler, R. *The meaning and measurement of ego development*. San Francisco: Jossey-Bass, 1970.

McClelland, D. *The achieving society*. New York: Van Nostrand, 1961.

McClelland, D. *Power: The inner experience*. New York: Irvington Publishers, 1975.

Mead, G. H. *Mind, self and society*. Chicago: University of Chicago Press, 1934.

Perry, W. *Forms of intellectual and ethical development in the college years*. New York: Holt, Rinehart & Winston, 1968.

Piaget, J. *The moral judgment of the child*. New York: Free Press, 1965. (Originally published, 1932.)

Riesman, D. *The lonely crowd*. New Haven: Yale University Press, 1961.

Sassen, G. Success-anxiety in women: A constructivist theory of its sources and its significance. *Harvard Educational Review*, 1980, **50**, 13-24. [Also in this anthology on pp. 175-186.]

Strunk, W., & White, E. B. *The elements of style*. New York: Macmillan, 1959.

Sullivan, H. S. *The interpersonal theory of psychiatry*. New York: Norton, 1953.

Vaillant, G. *Adaptation to life*. Boston: Little, Brown, 1977.

Woolf, V. *A room of one's own*. New York: Harcourt, Brace & World, 1929.

In Response to Gilligan

SUSAN SQUIER
SARA RUDDICK

IN A DIFFERENT VOICE:
PSYCHOLOGICAL THEORY AND WOMEN'S DEVELOPMENT
by Carol Gilligan.
Cambridge, Mass.: Harvard University Press, 1982. 184 pp.

Feminists have argued, for some time, that "psychology constructs the female."[1] Now it seems that psychology also omits the female from its account of moral development, or worse, distorts and insults the female experience it includes. This is the crucial point of Carol Gilligan's important study, *In a Different Voice: Psychological Theory and Women's Development*. Offered as a meditation on the pitfalls in theory-building and as an exploration of the "different voice" whose themes have been ignored by psychological theory, Gilligan's book will change your thinking not only about moral development but also about the nature and meaning of relationships for women and men. Further, if you are a teacher, it may change the way you think about your subject — and the way you teach.

In an introductory chapter, which ranges from Freud and Kohlberg to Erikson, Piaget, Chodorow, and even to fairy tales, Gilligan demonstrates that women's divergence from the standard model of moral development has been seen not as a problem in the theory but rather as a problem in *women*.* The result, she argues, has been a vicious cycle, damaging not only to women but to society as a whole. Bereft of an accurate language in which to describe women's moral actions, both women and men are blind to the content of women's experience and the structure of their development. Gilligan's book represents an excitingly successful first attempt to remove the distortions and clarify the nature of female moral development.

---

* Earlier versions of chapters one and three appeared in the *Harvard Educational Review* as "Woman's Place in Man's Life Cycle," **49** (1979), 431–446; and "In a Different Voice: Women's Conceptions of the Self and of Morality," **47** (1977) 481–517. Both of these articles are included in this anthology on pp. 187–223, 244–239.—ED.

[1] Naomi Weisstein, "Psychology Constructs the Female, On the Fantasy Life of the Male Psychologist," in *Women's Liberation and Literature*, ed. Elaine Showalter (New York: Harcourt Brace Jovanovich, 1971), pp. 271–286.

Harvard Educational Review   Vol. 53   No. 3   August 1983, 338–342

The different voice Gilligan identifies is defined by theme, not gender; its association with women is neither absolute nor invariable but is an empirical finding admitting of exception and degree. Gilligan's research in itself supports the claim that most women tend to have a conception of morality different from that of most men. After having discovered that there is a distinctive female moral voice, Gilligan turned to the work of other psychologists, especially Nancy Chodorow, to explain how this gender difference could arise from early parent-child relations. Citing Chodorow, she notes that in societies where children are raised primarily by women, girls tend to define themselves in relation to others, whereas boys tend to define themselves in opposition to others.[2] Gilligan suggests that two conceptions of morality arise from these early differences. The "activity of care" is more central to many women's moral vision, which focuses on an understanding of responsibilities that are integral to relationships. By contrast, in many men's moral vision, fairness is the central virtue, and moral dilemmas turn upon adjudicating the rights of autonomous selves according to systems of rules designed to reflect fairness.

Gilligan recognizes that for too long we have used the wrong lens — one based on typical male development — to examine women's development. *In A Different Voice* abandons the use of this lens and lets women speak for themselves, telling their own stories of moral conflict, crisis, and decision. From the structure, language, and content of these vivid female narratives, Gilligan derives a theory of moral development dramatically different from that which male-derived theories would predict. In brief, she claims that, from earliest identity throughout moral development, a female self is a self-in-relationship. For women, moral failure and success turn upon avoiding hurt and providing care; moral problems involve a conflict of responsibilities more often than rights. Furthermore, moral problems so conceived require a way of thinking that is not formal and abstract but contextual and narrative. In short, the women to whom Gilligan listens tend to see moral dilemmas as existing *between people* in a particular social context and as requiring, for their solution, virtues of responsibility and care.

Because for them identity is so tied to intimacy, women tend to conceptualize the self differently from men. Central to this alternative conception of the self is a distinctive way of apprehending relationships — as networks or webs rather than as hierarchies. One of the most dramatically convincing sections of *In A Different Voice* demonstrates this by describing the research of Gilligan and Susan Pollak in which they compared the stories that women and men invented in response to a number of pictures from the Thematic Apperception Test. Presented with the picture of "two trapeze artists grasping each other's wrists, the man hanging by his knees from the trapeze and the woman in mid-air" (p. 41), women and men generated strikingly different stories. For a statistically significant number of the men, the picture of two acrobats performing high in the air with no visible safety net elicited tales of betrayal, injury, even death. In contrast, a significant number of the women invented a safety net as they told their stories, creating a safe intimacy between the two acrobats. For Gilligan, this divergence suggests that "men and women may perceive danger in different social situations and construe danger in

_____

[2] Chodorow, *The Reproduction of Mothering* (Berkeley: Univ. of California Press, 1978).

different ways" (p. 42). She suggests two reasons why men see danger in being connected to others: identity for many men is likely to depend on autonomy and on
disconnection from others; relationships for them tend to imply a hierarchy in
which, if there is no recourse to rules of fairness, people will get hurt. In contrast,
many women are likely to find danger in lack of connection because for them the
self is constructed in intimacy and depends upon a web of relationships characterized by responsibility and caring.

In her treatment of a study in which she interviewed women before and after
they made a decision about having an abortion, Gilligan moves beyond the form
and content of the female moral voice to describe a distinct path of moral *development* for women. Indeed, the delineation of this path is one more of this study's
many accomplishments. Although the catalyst for moral change in both men's and
women's lives is usually a crisis that initiates growth, the nature of the crisis is often
different. For men, typically, an intimate encounter with another triggers growth.
Such intimacy is no shock for women who have constructed identity in terms of
relationships since childhood. Crises for women, however, are often triggered by
situations in which they are forced to acknowledge their own needs. In deciding
about abortion, for example, they may be unable to find "a way of caring that does
not at the same time destroy," a way of being non-violent to themselves as well as
others (p. 90). Often they feel both hurt and abandoned by those whom they have
trusted and hurtful to others such as parents or lovers. The "safety net" of relationships fails them (chs. 3–4). Such a crisis can lead a woman to a new preoccupation
with personal survival or a painful nihilism. However, it can also move her to a
more developed moral vision.

In the latter, happier case, Gilligan finds in women's responses to their abortion
decisions a sequential development of the "ethic of care" (p. 74). In this sequence,
a woman's initial preoccupation with survival is followed by an appreciation of
"goodness." At first being "good" consists primarily of pleasing others in order to
gain approval. This conventional goodness is followed in turn by authentic goodness. A woman now aims to help rather than to please, "seeing and responding to
need, taking care of the world by sustaining the web of connection so that no one
is left alone" (p. 62). Finally, development may move a woman to a responsible caring attitude, toward both self and other, which acknowledges the truth of feelings
and the realities of moral life. The moral questions remain the same: How much
suffering are you going to cause? Why do you have the right to cause human suffering? Can exploitation ever be a right? Eventually, however, the questions apply not
only to others but to the woman herself. By this level of development, women comprehend "successively, the self-blinding nature of the opposition between selfishness
and responsibility, the challenge of the concept of rights to the virtue of selflessness,
and the way in which an understanding of rights transforms the understanding of
care and relationships" (p. 138). Gilligan calls this final level of women's moral development an awareness of "truth and interdependence" (pp. 108–109). Women at
this level recognize the reality of human pain and suffering; they seek mutually
caring and responsible relationships between self and other.

It is heartening to think that Gilligan's work may help to transform developmental psychology, correcting the blindness and distortion she persuasively documents.

Scholars from other disciplines will find their own ways of using her work. For example, in her provocative brief comparison of George Eliot's *The Mill on the Floss* and Margaret Drabble's *The Waterfall*, Gilligan herself suggests some implications for feminist writers and critics (ch. 5). Following her example, critics may be moved to return to those novels where intimacy, aggression, and the necessity for moral choices intertwine in complex ways. For example, in reading works by male writers, we can watch for instances in which violence and death are responses to "dangerous" intimacy, or in which disaster follows when a character chooses personal relations over public rules. Conversely, we can ask if women characters who are credible to women readers are portrayed as endangered or crazed by the remoteness of intimates or the care-less-ness of men. Gilligan's description of the muting of an authentic voice in women who are over-invested in being conventionally "good" suggests that critics may do well to reconsider the development of voice in women writers. For example, one might ask how rights and responsibilities, or laws and relationships, interact for women writers split between concerns for the rules of their genre and literary tradition, and a different concern for the fictional and actual relationships about which they write.

In addition to invigorating scholarly work, Gilligan boldly challenges the conceptual categories through which we understand political and social life. In this time of a lethally escalating arms race and of arms reduction negotiations shackled by the very system of complex regulations designed to free them, *In a Different Voice* offers a crucial corrective to the prevailing impersonal and legalistic view of moral decisionmaking. In a world where we routinely create the enemy as "other," where we matter-of-factly hurt and exploit not only individuals but whole races and classes of people, Gilligan prompts us to look past our preconceptions, to acknowledge our responsibilities to each other, and to care.

In a Different Voice excites dialogue; Gilligan explicitly invites investigators from other disciplines and from different social classes and racial groups to extend and test her results. We, the writers, are neither prepared for, nor especially interested in, assessing her methodology. Instead, we take her work as a lively hypothesis that transforms our own work. In conversations together, we have several times imagined debating with Gilligan some of her specific interpretations or concepts. Yet we have seriously questioned the book only when she seemed to downplay what we see as its political implications.

By her own account, Gilligan means solely to identify differences in moral voice and not to make value judgments. She asks that women's experience and moral vision be joined with men's so that we may have an adequate *human* psychology and morality. Certainly, in their ideal forms, the moral visions of care and fairness and of connection and autonomy supplement each other. Yet in our eyes, Gilligan is too sanguine about both women's and men's moralities as they are lived out in our society.

For example, she does not mention that the "safety nets" in which women put their faith are too often fictions which cannot really protect them or their loved ones. More seriously, she does not emphasize the ways that women's focus on their own families and communities limits their ability—or even willingness—to contest exploitation. Although Gilligan herself hopes for a world in which "no one is left out" and quotes many women who share her view, it seems to us that a kind of "family selfishness" is at least as prevalent among women as is a wide social vision.

Finally, we believe that Gilligan underestimates the real powerlessness and consequent suffering of women. We would strongly emphasize what she clearly implies: the conflicts in women's moral development — between being "good" and seeing truthfully, between seeking to please and respecting the self — arise in a social context where men deny, distort, and insult female experience. We would also focus more sharply on a frequent moral of her own stories: women in the United States now, no matter how developed their morality, need great good luck to realize their vision in either intimate relations or public endeavors; for most women, the effort to be responsibly caring is painful and personally costly.

Our main concern, however, is that Gilligan does not make sufficiently explicit the critique of traditionally male visions and institutions which her book embodies. Not only does she withhold judgment on some shockingly arrogant and disconnected male voices — of both psychologists and their subjects — but at times she uses language that seems to belie her book's implications. For example, in speaking of women's need for *self*-respect, Gilligan chooses the legalistic and impersonal notion of rights. When speaking of intimate relations, Gilligan could more accurately have spoken simply of *caring* for the self and being responsive to its needs. Clearly, a healthy language of rights is indispensable for abused persons or peoples; in public discourse, women, like any members of an oppressed group, must assert their "rights" in the language that the public understands. Yet, the need to appeal to rights indicates a failure of care. Thus, acknowledging rights is only a minimal — though necessary — step in rectifying that failure. Adopting the concept of rights will do little to institute a caring community. After all, despite the goodness and vision of many individual men, we have managed to institutionalize injustice under the guise of fairness.

Gilligan's prospect of a two-sided, complementary *human* morality sometimes seems to pass over the *content* of the rules by which we play and the deadly nature of our games. Throughout the world and across the ages, men have written a story of needless misery, exploitation, and violence from which all people suffer. Women's care has developed within that story and in contrast to it. Our greed and fearfulness have contributed to the plot; our tears and love allow the conflict to continue. To fail to see this cruel and wasteful story for what it is would be one more exercise in complicity.

Gilligan's idea that women and men complement each other reminds us of an image that comforted Virginia Woolf in *A Room of One's Own*.[3] A man and a woman get into a taxi together and are driven off. "The sight of two people coming down the street and meeting at the corner seems to ease the mind of some strain, I thought, watching the taxi turn and make off. Perhaps to think, as I had been thinking these two days, of one sex as distinct from the other is an effort" (p. 100). It *is* a strain to identify differences between men and women, still more threatening to judge the differences one finds. It *is* an effort for women to identify with each

---

[3] *A Room of One's Own* (New York: Harcourt, Brace and World, 1929).

other as a class, to maintain the stance of critical outsiders, challenging from a *female* perspective the "realities" and values we have been trained to accept. We take comfort in Woolf's image and Gilligan's humanism. We do not want to hurt men or to idealize ourselves and exacerbate divisions among political comrades. But it is no favor to anyone if we minimize the damage wrought by the ideal of disconnected autonomy expected of men. It would be a *failure* in caring for both women and men to trust conceptions of rights and fairness which are killing us. Gilligan has written a profound and challenging book; its seriousness requires us to explore and extend its radical, political implications.

The Danger of Fairy Tales

DONNA HULSIZER

THE CINDERELLA COMPLEX
by Colette Dowling.
New York: Summit Books, 1981. 266 pp.; New York: Pocket Books, 1982. 289 pp.

The Cinderella Complex is a fascinating and dangerous book. It is fascinating because it touches a nerve. Many women will recognize the feeling Colette Dowling describes and be relieved that she has given it a name — fear of independence — and has suggested a cure. The book is dangerous, I believe, because her argument is unsound, and in the present climate of conservatism, it may be put to unsavory uses. Once again, women are found deficient; once again these deficiencies are only vaguely defined; once again it is up to women themselves to correct their flaws.

Dowling is a journalist, and her book reflects both the virtues and the limits of the craft. Lively, personal, and easy to read, *The Cinderella Complex* is an amalgam of confession, interviews, and psychological literature. Liberally laced with citations from *Vogue*, *Psychology Today*, and the *New York Times*, the book also draws upon the literature on sex differences and the psychology of women. Dowling invokes Matina Horner and Simone de Beauvoir and offers vivid stories of women crippled by this hidden fear. Beginning each of her seven chapters with anecdotes from her own life, she then marshals support for her view from the experiences of other women and from research. Among other topics, she considers psychoanalytic theory and sex differences in development, socialization, achievement, and earnings; she also cites observations of clinicians who work with women. She ends with a flimsy prescription for escaping the fear of independence.

Her interviews with women of diverse ages, educational backgrounds, and circumstances illustrate her theme well. Indeed, many serve as cautionary tales. However, she never tells us how many women she interviewed, how she found them, or what questions she asked them. Her reading of the research and theoretical literature is both selective and superficial, careful enough to lend the gloss of authority to her work but too shallow to support her claims. Since Dowling apparently does not aspire to scholarly rigor, that would be an unfair standard to apply in judging her book. I wish, however, that she had been more humble in her conclusions and prescriptions.

Harvard Educational Review   Vol. 52   No. 3   August 1982, 352–356

The book also suffers that disease peculiar to journalists—chronic capitalization. Here we find such entities as Gender Panic, Energy Leak, the Competent One, the Good Woman, and the overarching concept, the Cinderella Complex. This may seem a trivial point, but I believe it is not. This simple visual alteration in words promotes the reification of such terms and ideas. They take on a life of their own, enter the vernacular, and become labels that people apply to their experiences, comforting themselves by being able to reduce complex and often painful phenomena to a popular phrase. Such simplification does a disservice to the intricacy of human experience and encourages false consciousness.

The main problem with Dowling's thesis is that the phenomenon she claims to have unearthed—fear of independence—is ill-defined. The closest she comes to a definition is her statement "that personal, psychological dependency—the deep wish to be taken care of by others—is the chief force holding women down today" (p. 31). "This network of distorted attitudes and fears that keeps women in a kind of half-light, retreating from the full use of their minds and creativity" is the Cinderella Complex (p. 31). The source of this complex is "the psychological need to avoid independence" (p. 30).

Are we to assume that avoiding independence and wanting to be cared for are the same thing? This is a questionable equation, since the latter seems to be an undeniably basic human impulse. It is perhaps more acceptable for women to express such a wish. Few researchers, journalistic or otherwise, question men about issues of care and dependence, despite the fact that giving and receiving care are crucial to sustaining connections with others, an activity routinely undertaken by both sexes. Dowling forgets that men, too, want to be taken care of—and usually are, by wives.

Dowling also neglects the fact that women traditionally have cared *for* others. Adopting uncritically the view that women's activities in the nurturance of families are uncreative, stultifying, and dull, she characterizes this role as one of parasitic dependency. Jean Baker Miller aptly summarizes the attitude to which Dowling falls prey: "Most so-called women's work is not recognized as real activity. One reason for this attitude may be that such work is usually associated with helping others' development, rather than with self-enhancement or self-development. This is seen as *not doing anything*."[1]

Dowling's definitional confusion is compounded when she tackles the dependence/independence dichotomy. If fear of independence is what is holding women back, then presumably the author envisions a utopia of independence to which they must aspire. The outline of this utopia emerges from a closer look at her use of the terms "dependence" and "independence." Dowling identifies many influences that contribute to women's training in dependence: learned helplessness, restrictive mothers, fathers who discourage intellectual achievement, and husbands and lovers who disparage their partners, to name a few. But the real problem seems to be "excessive affiliative needs," that "need to experience *relationship* above all else" (p. 111, Dowling's italics). This need for attachment inhibits women's capacity for productive work, and they are warned to fight the impulse.

[1] *Toward a New Psychology of Women* (Boston: Beacon Press, 1976), p. 52, Miller's italics.

Women are relational creatures, she says, and "though it cripples us, we have let it go unquestioned" (p. 133). She thus equates dependence with attachment, finds this to be an affliction of not just some but "virtually all women," and rails against its pernicious effects on women's lives. Where was she, I wonder, during the sixties and seventies when women were questioning their traditional relationships, examining their costs, and seeking alternatives? Many women rushed to abandon old ways and are now rethinking the dilemma of how to both love and work.

For Dowling, being truly independent means accepting "the adult reality that we, alone, are responsible for ourselves" (p. 14). It means being active rather than reactive, taking risks, being "clear and unconflicted" (p. 220), and assuming responsibility for our own problems. She speaks of a kind of self-reliance and self-sufficiency that are impossible if one is involved, as most people are, in a web of social relationships. Her notion of autonomy sounds more like isolation, and her idea of independence teeters on the brink of narcissism. Dowling's misty utopia seems not only completely unrealistic but also frankly unappetizing.

It is a remarkably asocial and ahistorical utopia. She ignores the fact that most societies have neither valued nor accommodated themselves to the experiences and aspirations of women. This remains true in our society despite laudable achievements in the struggle for equal rights for women. Most women still earn less than men; there is still a dearth of good daycare facilities; women are still denied positions of power in fields (such as education) in which they are numerically dominant — the litany is familiar. Yet Dowling would have us believe that this is women's fault, paralyzed as they are by hidden fears of independence. She has turned a problem with deep historical and social roots into a problem of the individual female psyche.

She also implies that men do not suffer this defect, that they learn to become their own caretakers and so have less need for the ties that bind. But most men do not stand alone. They have mentors and wives to sustain them in their quest for success. They are not necessarily "free and unconflicted," or active rather then reactive[2]; in fact, many will admit ruefully that their greater autonomy is often attained at the cost of the attachments that Dowling finds so constraining.

"Springing free" is Dowling's shorthand phrase for the process of achieving independence. This requires that women relinquish their "sense of cultural disadvantage" (p. 133). She believes that their preoccupation with issues of fairness keeps them from confronting the truth that "women prevent themselves from advancing" (p. 103). Having thus pointed an accusing finger at women, Dowling offers help. In her final, breathlessly optimistic chapter, she suggests a method by which women can free themselves from these neurotic conflicts. This involves emancipation from within, "paying scrupulous attention to yourself," watching personality quirks "coolly and objectively," and then coming to accept the parts of the self revealed by this scrutiny (pp. 211–212).

Dowling warns that the process is painful; it takes courage. But the rewards are great. Women who have "sprung free" can expect powerful emotional experiences,

---

[2] Daniel J. Levinson, with Charlotte N. Darrow, Edward B. Klein, Maria H. Levinson, and Braxton McKee, *The Seasons of a Man's Life* (New York: Knopf, 1978).

renewed energy, and "freedom to succeed." This self-cure is based on the work of Karen Horney and is but one example of Dowling's faulty use of psychological theory. In a long footnote, she observes that one of Horney's important, and at the time unorthodox, contributions to psychoanalytic thought about women was her insistence on the interplay of the individual and the social, the internal and the external, in the shaping of human personality (pp. 253–254). It is difficult to see, then, how Dowling draws from this a method of self-help that is exclusively intra-psychic.

Given the book's emphasis on productivity, work, and achievement, it comes as something of a shock to find that the ultimate goal of this cure is "emotional spontaneity" (p. 227.) Readers find themselves in a time warp. From the tough individualism Dowling first advocates, so apt for the grim mood of the eighties, she suddenly flings us back into the emotive sixties, in which self-expression and soul-searching were extolled as a panacea for everything from war to psychosis. But it is this spontaneity, Dowling asserts, that permits women to enter into the utopia of independence.

The Cinderella Complex is a fundamentally misanthropic book. I was tempted at first to call it "misogynist," since it is women's lack of courage and flawed psyches that the author begins and ends by deploring. However, I soon noticed that men fare no better. Husbands "bellow," are passive-aggressive and self-preoccupied, and drink a lot. Fathers are intrusive, controlling, and authoritarian. She continuously makes invidious comparisons between men and women: "men are stretchers . . . women are shrinkers" (p. 176). Here is Dowling on the subject of parents: "Father is active; Mother is passive. Father is able to rely on himself; Mother is helpless and dependent" (p. 118).

Mothers are especially culpable. They are shadowy and fearful, overly solicitous of their baby daughters and wary of risk and conflict: "The peacemaker, a kind of half-person who chooses to tag along safely behind her husband, Mother is protected from the more abrasive aspects of life in the world" (p. 118). Here Dowling fails to confront the historical fact that for centuries most women were constrained to the role of wifely adjunct. Again we find her denigrating "women's work," as though caring for a family entailed no risks or abrasive aspects. Jean Baker Miller points out that raising children requires "learning for change," a complex process that, in their traditional role, women have engaged in daily: "What one learned yesterday is not good enough and does not apply today. One cannot hope to use it exactly, or even by analogy, because the situation has already changed."[3] An intricate skill, this, surely beyond the capabilities of a "half-person." We are a society that places great emphasis on the ability to raise successful children; indeed, we have even begun to teach people how "to parent." Yet we persist in failing to support women — and it still is women who have the major responsibility for child care in most families — in this complicated task and to reward them for a job well done.

But it is her female contemporaries who most arouse Dowling's indignation. They are characterized as cowardly, irrational, and depressed. They act as under-paid drones in the work force or as compulsive child-rearers to avoid "working."

[3] *Toward a New Psychology of Women*, p. 55.

They choose low-paying careers and look to others for their sense of self. Worst of all, they do not really want to succeed and so "sabotage [their] own originality" (p. 103). Although surely the author believes that she writes on behalf of women, to jolt them from their illusions and help them to "spring free," her tone is unsympathetic and disgusted. Although she argues that women are trained in dependency from infancy, she also believes they should nonetheless be horrified by this deficiency and strive to undo years of socialization through a naïve, nebulous process of intrapsychic unraveling.

Dowling embraces the literature on fear of success with special relish, and I will examine this issue at some length because it exemplifies her careless use of social science research and her failure to consider alternative explanations. According to Dowling, Matina Horner found that women fear success because they believed "that doing well professionally would jeopardize their relationships with men. It was as simple as that" (p. 172). Dowling sees this as further evidence that women are held back by their excessive need for affiliation, a problem "unique to the female psyche" (p. 170).

The work of Georgia Sassen suggests that it is not so simple.[4] Sassen reanalyzed some of Horner's original data on fear of success and found that it was a particular kind of success that women were avoiding — competitive success in which one person's gain would be another's loss. From her review of the literature on fear of success, Sassen concluded that the question of sex differences is far from settled. Some studies show more men than women exhibiting fear of success, while others show no sex differences. It is a field, Sassen says, "fraught with contradictions." She found, further, that no sex differences appeared in those studies that analyzed immobilizing or self-sabotaging behavior — exactly the behavior Dowling chastises women for displaying. However, sex differences did surface when experiments tested for fear of competitive success.

Although Dowling observes that the idea of success "meant something quite different for women than it did for men" (p. 170), she does not follow through on the implications of this observation. Fortunately, other women — among them Georgia Sassen, Nancy Chodorow, and Carol Gilligan — have illuminated women's different way of constructing meaning.[5] Sassen argues that women are critical of, and thus avoid, competitive success as it is narrowly defined in our culture, not simply because they fear the loss of relationships with men, but because this definition of success is at odds with their more personal, contextual, relational way of making sense of the world. Chodorow suggests that this sense of relatedness is not a warp in the female personality but rather the result of a social structure that makes women responsible for the early care and socialization of children. Gilligan goes further, insisting that this sense of connection to others is a vital human strength, too long ignored or disparaged by psychological theorists and researchers.

Dowling fails to consider that independence also may mean something different to women and that her notion of independence in particular is one that women,

[4] "Success Anxiety in Women: A Constructivist Interpretation of Its Source and Its Significance," *Harvard Educational Review*, **50** (1980), 13–24; also on pp. 175–186 of this anthology.

[5] Sassen, "Success Anxiety"; Chodorow, *The Reproduction of Mothering* (Berkeley: Univ. of California Press, 1978); Gilligan, *In a Different Voice* (Cambridge, Mass.: Harvard Univ. Press, 1982).

with good reason, may wish to avoid. She overlooks the possibilities of such concepts as interdependence, or what W. R. D. Fairbairn has called "mature dependency."[6] These ideas imply a balancing of autonomy and attachment — not a capitulation to one or the other extreme — and honor the needs of men and women for both independence and intimacy, for achievement and care. We live as social beings in an intricate social environment, and our social relations exact costs as well as provide benefits. It simply is not possible, even if one would choose it, to live in unfettered autonomy, in which one never needs to balance the wishes of others against those of the self; in which one possesses ultimate freedom and control; in which one's life is molded more by actions than reactions. A utopia of interdependence seems far more appealing, far more adaptive for the species as a whole — as well as for each of the sexes — and far more realistic in a world that relentlessly reminds us of our inevitable connections and our need to rely on and cooperate with each other across sexes, classes, and nations.

[6] *Psychoanalytic Studies of the Personality* (London: Routledge & Kegan Paul, 1972).

Sex Differences and Math Achievement

LORELEI R. BRUSH

WOMEN AND THE MATHEMATICAL MYSTIQUE
edited by Lynn H. Fox, Linda Brody, and Dianne Tobin.
Baltimore: Johns Hopkins University Press, 1980. 211 pp.

Women and the Mathematical Mystique, one of several recent books on the issue of women's participation and achievement in mathematics, contributes substantially to our knowledge of this topic.[1] It is an updated compilation of papers first presented at the 1976 Hyman Blumberg Symposium on Research in Early Childhood Education, a conference on sex differences in mathematical talent and achievement. The papers are intended for educational researchers, but the inclusion of practical suggestions makes them useful for teachers and administrators as well. Although emphasis is on the intellectually talented who complete calculus in high school and study college-level mathematics, many of the suggested "causes" of sex differences in participation and the intervention strategies recommended to increase women's participation are equally applicable to less talented students.

The book begins with a statement of the fact that many women do not enroll in optional mathematics courses. In search of an explanation, the authors of two chapters describe studies exploring the differences in personality and experience between women who continue to study mathematics and those who do not. Four chapters are devoted to the discussion of sex differences in achievement and attitudes toward mathematics, and five chapters describe courses, or other intervention strategies, that may encourage women to continue their study of mathematics.

Several contributors demonstrate that sex differences exist in enrollment in optional high school mathematics courses. Elizabeth Fennema, for example, provides evidence of sex differences in math enrollment of Wisconsin high school students. She found that in 1975-1976 substantially fewer females than males took elective mathematics courses in high school. Similarly, Lucy Sells reports data from her study of applicants to the University of California at Berkeley in 1972. Of the male applicants in the sample, 57 percent had completed trigonometry or a higher-level

---

[1] Sheila Tobias, *Overcoming Math Anxiety* (Boston: Houghton-Mifflin, 1980); Lorelei Brush, *Encouraging Girls in Mathematics* (Cambridge: Abt Press, 1980); Stanley Kogelman and Joseph Warren, *Mind Over Math* (New York: McGraw-Hill, 1979); Michele A. Wittig and Anne C. Petersen, eds., *Sex-Related Differences in Cognitive Functioning* (New York: Academic Press, 1979).

Harvard Educational Review   Vol. 52   No. 1   February 1982, 105–108

high school mathematics course, while only 8 percent of the female applicants had done so. This remarkable difference meant that 92 percent of the women applicants would be barred from majors with advanced mathematics prerequisites.

Research on salary differences suggests a further ramification of this lack of preparation: lower earning potential. In their nationwide sample of job offers to people with new bachelor's degrees, the College Placement Council found that salaries offered to people with training in mathematics were much higher than those offered people without college-level mathematics.[2] Engineering majors, for example, had an average annual salary offer of $18,372 whereas majors in the humanities and social sciences averaged only $11,810. Majors in economics, business, and the sciences fell between these extremes.

A recent report in *Science* achieved nationwide publicity by suggesting that the reason for the enrollment differences is the differing abilities of the sexes, that women are simply less able in mathematics than men. This report by Camilla Benbow and Julian Stanley presented data suggesting lower achievement for girls in comparison to boys in the Johns Hopkins Study of Mathematically Precocious Youth.[3] Since several chapters in this book refer to the same data, we can carefully examine their findings.

For example, Lynn Fox and Sanford J. Cohn report on the Scholastic Aptitude Test scores of the junior high school students from the Johns Hopkins study. In 1972, although 44 percent of the participants were girls, among seventh graders 8 percent of the boys received higher scores than the highest-scoring girl, and among eighth graders 27 percent of the boys scored higher than the highest-scoring girl. This seems serious indeed. However, over time that degree of difference has diminished. Since 1973 the percentages of seventh-grade boys outscoring the highest-scoring girl has consistently dropped, and by 1979 there was no percentage difference. Moreover, although mean scores continue to favor males, that gap is also closing, suggesting that girls' lower scores may be due to factors other than native ability.

In support of this possibility, contributors to *Women and the Mathematical Mystique* catalogue other reasons that may explain sex differences in achievement and enrollment in math courses. Fennema describes some studies that report a sex difference in self-confidence in mathematical ability. The import of this difference is that achievement and talent do not necessarily predict who will enroll in mathematics: a girl who is equally as able as a boy may not choose to take mathematics simply because she is insecure about her ability. Other contributors suggest that differences in values and life patterns also relate to differences in interest in mathematics. Linda Brody and Lynn Fox report on a study in which mathematically precocious students completed the Allport-Vernon-Lindzey Study of Values. In both the control and experimental groups, boys scored significantly higher on the theoretical scale while girls scored significantly higher on the social scale. Tobin and Fox describe studies which indicate that girls seemed less oriented toward careers

---

[2] College Placement Council, *National Average Monthly Salaries* (Bethlehem, Pa.: College Placement Council, 1979).

[3] Benbow and Stanley, "Sex Differences in Mathematical Ability: Fact or Artifact?," *Science*, **210** (1980), 1262–1264.

than boys, and that even those gifted girls who were oriented toward careers seemed less likely than boys to report an interest in careers in mathematics or the sciences.

It is useful to note the attitudes that seem to characterize girls who do go on to study higher levels of mathematics. According to Ravenna Helson, they are able and interested in mathematics, perceptive and open to new experiences, reflective and reserved, value cognitive skills and autonomy, and enjoy puzzles. More important than these individual differences, at least for those wanting to encourage girls in the fields of mathematics or science, are the external factors affecting their study of mathematics. Patricia Lund Casserly reports that girls who take advanced placement mathematics are homogeneously tracked fairly early in school, some as early as fourth grade, but typically by seventh grade. This early tracking might encourage them to stay in mathematics. Casserly found that such students are often recruited by teachers to take the next course in the sequence and are encouraged by parents to continue. Also, being among other girls who are accelerated helps to supply the needed social interactions. In addition, the young women in Casserly's report seem to have been given information about careers in mathematics and the importance of such training for future work. Often they have participated in quantitative work or experiences outside of school that have helped to provide a perspective on the world of work and the usefulness of mathematics to it.

The range of explanations for sex differences in mathematics presented in this volume is impressive, but not exhaustive. The authors concentrate on psychological and sociological explanations, not biological ones. For example, they do not discuss theories of genetic, hormonal, or cortical differences between males and females that are sometimes associated with differences in spatial or mathematical ability. Although the authors focus on the effects of parents, teachers, and peers on girls' decisions to continue in math, they have not gone into detail on the stereotype of mathematics as a male domain, exemplified by many problem sets presented in math books and on standardized math tests which focus on males' engaging in traditionally male activities. Fortunately, Michele A. Wittig and Anne C. Petersen's recent work amply covers these areas.[4]

A particular strength of *Women and the Mathematical Mystique* is that Fox translates the reported results into several intervention strategies in the final chapter. First, she recommends that schools recognize the importance of early identification of talented girls and the fact that their early placement in accelerated mathematics classes will encourage them to continue. An acceleration program that keeps girls with their peers and in their own school is likely to be most successful; it will meet the social values of the students while providing them with mathematical training at an appropriate level. Second, girls need more information on the practical uses of mathematics for careers. They need to be encouraged to keep their options open by taking as much mathematics as possible. Because of the findings that girls may lose interest in math when its "social relevance" is not stressed, Fox suggests that courses include more applied mathematics. It may also be useful for schools to provide girls with the opportunity to meet women who have careers requiring mathe-

---

[4] Wittig and Petersen, *Sex-Related Differences*.

matical skills. Finally, explicit encouragement by teachers is more important for girls than for boys. Teachers can convince talented girls to take advanced courses and can help them to overcome a lack of self-confidence.

Women and the Mathematical Mystique provides a useful summary of research, oriented toward the person seeking directions for future work on cognitive abilities, the mathematically gifted, or reasons for the avoidance of mathematics. The book supplies valuable reviews of intervention strategies for teachers and administrators, outlining ways in which our schools might change in order to ensure that girls and boys alike are prepared for a fuller range of options in the job market they will ultimately enter.

PART V
Ethnic Minority Voices

Employment and Education of Mexican-American Women: The Interplay of Modernity and Ethnicity in Eight Families

MAXINE BACA ZINN

Acculturation has been the major framework used to explain changes in Mexican-American families. It assumes that changing conjugal roles are associated with a corresponding decline in ethnicity. Instead of viewing traditional Mexican values as determinants of conjugal roles and changes in those roles as the consequence of acculturation, the study examined the effect on conjugal interation of wives' employment outside the home and level of education. It was found that as women acquired extradomestic resources, they achieved greater equality in conjugal decisionmaking without sacrificing ethnicity in other realms of family life.

Past research on changes in ethnic families has emphasized cultural values and given less attention to social and economic conditions. This study examines the effect of outside employment and level of education on the relative power of wives in Mexican-American families and questions the assumption that changes in conjugal roles are associated with acculturation. The data are derived from interviews with and participant observation of eight Chicano families over a ten-month period. Middle-class families, working-class families, and families with employed wives and nonemployed wives were equally represented. All families were in roughly the same stage of the family life cycle. I found support for the proposition that power rests on economic and other resources external to the marriage. Employed wives used their economic independence and extra-domestic knowledge and skills to increase their power in family decision making. While the four families with employed wives exhibited different patterns of marital power from those with nonemployed wives, especially in decision making, they also identified themselves as ethnics, valuing ethnic customs in rituals, kin gatherings, and daily family activities.

Findings refute the depiction of family change as a simple substitution of modern patterns for traditional ones. Recent discussions in ethnic family research represent improvements over the stereotyped interpretations that have characterized such re-

Harvard Educational Review   Vol. 50   No. 1   February 1980, 47–62

search in the past. However, this type of research continues to be limited by an overreliance on the acculturation framework which restricts analysis to cultural values surrounding familial roles. Few writers have explored the possibility that changes in family patterns are fostered by specific familial conditions such as socioeconomic status, level of education, occupation, and residence. I investigated the effect of wives' employment and education on conjugal power in Mexican-American families to indicate some shortcomings of exclusively cultural interpretations and to offer evidence for alternative explanations.

Family structure in industrial and urban societies has undergone a transition from a patriarchal pattern to one considered more egalitarian. Social scientists have viewed social and economic organization as the primary determinants of family organization: "power relationships within the family are considered to be dependent upon economic roles within the larger society" (McLaughlin, 1973, p. 111). Although this interpretation of changes in traditional family relationships is widely accepted, changes in ethnic or minority family structure are viewed somewhat differently; cultural values rather than social and economic organization are thought to be the primary factors. The authoritarian Mexican-American family, dominated by a macho male, is thought to be a product of traditional Mexican culture. The idea of male superiority is heavily emphasized in the literature. The father is seen as having full authority over his wife and children, and all major decisions are his responsibility (Alvirez & Bean, 1976). Wives are described as passive, submissive, and dependent upon their husbands.

Studies conducted in the past few years, however, dispute the rigidity of patriarchy in Mexican-American families (Grebler, Moore, & Guzman, 1970; Hawkes & Taylor, 1975; Cromwell & Cromwell, 1978). Changes in this traditional family structure have been attributed to acculturation — to the acquisition of the predominant values in the United States about familial roles. Tharp, Meadow, Lenhoff, and Satterfield (1968), for example, say that "social science has long assumed that the processes of acculturation operate with widespread and profound effects on the minority ethnic group family" (p. 404). While this portrayal has typified ethnic families in general, it has assigned "too great a role to the influence of cultural factors in shaping family patterns of Mexican-Americans" (Alvirez & Bean, 1976, p. 289). This creates conceptual problems because it "invites the idea that certain patterns are derivative of beliefs and values passed on from generation to generation," rather than to social and economic conditions (Alvirez & Bean, 1976, p. 289). It also implies that egalitarian marital roles and ethnic family patterns are mutually exclusive.

Mexican-American families are usually divided into two types. One is the patriarchal-traditional family whose structure is determined by Mexican cultural values. The second is a more modern-egalitarian type whose structure is created when the larger society's values supersede Mexican cultural values and the traditional authority of husband/father gives way to greater sharing in family decision making. This latter view has two shortcomings. Modernization is confused with acculturation and mechanistically applied to family roles. Haraven's (1976) critique of modernization as a single explanatory and predictive framework for studying family change notes these limitations. She proposes that "the search for an overall modernization process is less fruitful than the acceptance of a complex and diversified model of behavior in which individuals adopt modern patterns in one area of their lives and hold on to traditional patterns in other areas" (p. 205). She further maintains that cultural distinctions have remained despite modernization: "Traditional patterns have persisted among families of different cultural and ethnic groups, contradicting established notions that individuals uniformly shed their traditional customs as the larger society becomes modernized" (Haraven, 1977, p. 58).

The second limitation of this approach is that conjugal power constitutes only one dimension of family organization. It is possible that power relationships between husbands and wives move away from strict male dominance as a result of social and economic changes, while ethnic cultural patterns remain in other dimensions of family life. Few studies have been conducted on the effects of educational attainment or of employment on the lifestyle of Mexican-Americans (Alvirez & Bean, 1976, p. 286). And yet, it is precisely these two factors—education and occupation—that family sociologists have found to be associated with differences in conjugal roles and conjugal power. Some research findings indicate that married women who work outside the home have greater power in their families than those who work at home (Blood & Wolfe, 1960; Blood, 1963; Heer, 1963; Buric & Zelevic, 1967; Safilios-Rothschild, 1969, 1970; Scanzoni, 1970; Bahr, 1974). This is most often explained in terms of the resources which wives acquire outside the home. They develop new financial, intellectual, and skill resources and, consequently, become less dependent upon their husbands (Wolfe, 1959).

Mexican-American families whose structure departs from the traditional patriarchy are often those in which women are employed (Taylor, 1933; Humphrey, 1944; Clark, 1969; Gouldner, 1959; Hawkes, 1975), but this phenomenon has so far inspired no systematic study. With increasing numbers of Mexican-American women entering the labor force, the relationship between wives' employment and family roles can no longer be overlooked (Arroyo, 1973; Cooney, 1975).

This paper examines both conjugal power and ethnicity within the larger context of wives' extra-domestic activity. Conjugal roles, conjugal power, and ethnicity were compared in families with employed wives and nonemployed wives to assess the impact of their extra-domestic activities on family roles. I sought to identify ethnicity in all families rather than assuming that nonpatriarchal families are acculturated. Ethnicity was defined as a distinct group identification based on perceived similarities within a group, self-labeling in group terms, and patterned distinctions in values, customs, and rituals of family life. My questions concerned the effect extra-domestic activity of wives has on conjugal roles and conjugal power, and the degree to which ethnicity is discernible in families where conjugal roles are not rigidly sex-segregated.

Data were gathered by focused interview and participant observation. The interview was designed for flexibility in gathering information about a wide range of behaviors in varying family situations and made it possible to lead the informants in the directions dictated by the research project while still varying the approaches used to gather the information (Runcie, 1976). Interviews were conducted conversationally, over long time periods, and the sequence of questions was varied according to the immediate situations of each family. Observation was used to gather information on behavior as it occurred, data which could not be obtained through the use of interviews alone (Selltiz, Wrightsman, & Cook, 1976). This made it possible to check the validity of the interviews.

Previous research on the relationship between wives' employment and conjugal roles helped define the issues and formulate interview questions (Blood & Wolfe, 1960; Blood, 1963; Hoffman, 1963). These questions were then used as guides and refashioned as the research progressed. By selecting an open-ended research strategy, we could confront reality from the perspective of those Mexican–Americans who were informants by raising issues and then letting both women and men speak for themselves. The findings suggested further areas to be probed as the research progressed.

Families were selected through a local community-education program that provided contact with families in which wives were employed as staff members and families in which wives were unemployed. I began by taking an active part in all program activities: accompanying staff members on home and classroom visits, attending and participating in workshops, and just hanging around the program center helping with numerous tasks. These shared activities provided the basis for a relationship that allowed me to establish the necessary credibility for conducting research on their private lives. I was invited to their parties, ritual celebrations, and other family gatherings, and allowed simply to spend time with each family.

A sample of eight families, four with employed wives and four with nonemployed housewives, was selected. The study was conducted in an urban New Mexico setting during a ten-month period in 1975. Middle-class families, defined in terms of the husband's white-collar occupational category, and working-class families, defined in terms of the husband's blue-collar occupational category, were equally represented. Families were in roughly the same stage of the family life cycle. All had teenage children and some had grade school children and/or adult children. In addition, all employed wives had or were in the process of completing a four-year college degree. Brief descriptions of the sample families follow.

Employed Wives: Working Class

Mrs. Lopez, a paraprofessional working with parents in the community-education program, had held this position for three years, and had worked outside of the home part-time for the past seven years. She was completing her bachelor of arts degree at the local college. Her husband was a surveyor's assistant in the highway department. They had five children, aged ten through twenty-three.

Mrs. Santiago was also a paraprofessional working with parents in the community-education program, and had worked in this position for four years, and outside the home part-time for nine years. She was completing her bachelor of arts degree at the local college. Mr. Santiago was an equipment mechanic in the highway department. The Santiagos had six children, aged nine through nineteen.

Employed Wives: Middle Class

Mrs. Delgado had been the parent coordinator of the community-education program for the past three years. She had a bachelor's degree and had previously been a teacher in the local school system. Her husband was a real-estate broker. They had four children, aged seventeen through thirty.

Mrs. Tenorio had been the registered nurse for the community-education program for two years. For the previous six years she worked for a doctor in private practice.

She was completing work for her bachelor of arts degree at the local college. Mr. Tenorio was a supervisor in the post office. The Tenorios had four children, aged fourteen through twenty-four.

Nonemployed Wives: Working Class

MRS. MENDOZA had not worked outside the home since her marriage. Her husband worked in a lumber yard. The Mendozas had seven children, aged nine through twenty-four.

MRS. VASQUEZ had never worked outside the home. Mr. Vasquez was a truck driver. They had four children, aged eight through nineteen.

Nonemployed Wives: Middle Class

MRS. SEDILLO had never worked outside the home. Mr. Sedillo was a lawyer in private practice. The Sedillos had four children, aged ten through eighteen.

MRS. RENDON had never worked outside the home. Mr. Rendon was an engineer in the highway department. The Rendons had four children, aged twelve through twenty-six.

The findings cannot be considered representative of Mexican-American families in general, particularly because of the sample size and selection procedure. The value of the present research lies in the relationships that the data suggest and not in the proof that these relationships are characteristic of all Mexican-American families. The extent to which the findings may be generalized to other Chicano families is a matter for further research.

Differences in family power were found between families with employed and nonemployed wives. In all families where women were not employed, tasks and decision making were typically sex-segregated. However, in all families with employed wives, tasks and decision making were shared. This is consistent with other research associating wives' employment with an increase in marital power and supports the central proposition of the resource theory that power in marriage rests on economic and other resources derived outside the family (Blood & Wolfe, 1960).

Even though employed wives had greater power than nonemployed wives, the ideology of patriarchy was strongly asserted in all eight families. Both husbands and wives reiterated that the husband should be the head of the family. Although all families said this, in only those in which the wife stayed at home was there evidence of the patriarchal behavior thought to be characteristic of Mexican-American families—that is, the husband demanding and receiving obedience from wife and children, making all family and financial decisions, and representing the household in dealings with the outside world (Hawkes & Taylor, 1975).

In families where wives were employed, patriarchal ideology was not accompanied by male dominance or by sex segregation in decision making and in the execution of family tasks. The finding that families could be patriarchal in ideology but not in practice points to the need to distinguish between traditional values and actual behavior. In families with nonemployed wives, husbands and wives were responsible for work and decisions in their respective spheres of activity—wives in the domestic sphere and husbands outside it. Families with employed wives operated as systems in which both husbands and wives were linked to extra-domestic institutions, and women's linkages gave them rights which they brought to bear on marital interaction. Husbands of these wives, unlike husbands of homemakers, were involved in domestic activities and shared decision making with their wives. Thus, extra-domestic activities of employed wives resulted in a transformation of family roles. Yet the families also identified with a group which they perceived to be distinct and separate from Anglos. Three of the four families in which wives shared power revealed similarities in the rituals and customs of family living.

Decision Making and Household Labor

In families with employed wives, the division of household labor was not equal, but wives did make and enforce decisions about sharing housework. Wives, husbands, and children participated in household tasks, but there was disorganization, and often conflict in the family about who should do the work. The fact that women were not continuously available or always willing to perform requisite daily tasks forced the involvement of husbands and children. Employed wives spoke often of how grateful they were for the help of their husbands, but at times felt as if they did not do enough. Mrs. Delgado expressed her feelings in the following way.

> Nowadays women are not expected to do everything for their families as they were at one time. Now that more women have jobs, men have to get more involved in the family. Years ago it was the women, and only the women, who took care of the children, who did the shopping and the cooking, who did the dishes and the laundry, and cleaned the house. Today husbands do all of these things. Well, not as much as they should. At least they do some of them if they are told to.

Mrs. Delgado often complained that her husband did not help as much as she thought he should, but I saw him washing dishes a number of times and noted that he cooked dinner on several occasions when she attended late meetings. Sometimes when I dropped by, both husband and wife would be engaged in domestic tasks. Mr. Delgado seemed almost apologetic, and told me several times that he was just helping out because his wife was tired that day.

Mr. Tenorio, too, expressed little enthusiasm for his participation in domestic maintenance. But he "had no choice," as he expressed it: "Hoy en día la mujer tiene que trabajar [In this day and age the woman has to go to work]. Since she helps the family, I have to help her. It's only fair."

Like Mrs. Delgado, Mrs. Tenorio had trouble getting her husband to do as much housework as she thought he should. She attributed this to his fear of what friends might say if they saw him doing housework. She said: "Let's face it, if the wife is working, and the family is going to make it, they [husbands] have to help. Like mine, if the kids can't do it, or I can't do it, he has to do housework. But he wouldn't want his friends to see him."

When the two working-class women were specifically questioned about how their working had affected their family lives, they also spoke of the changing distribution of household tasks. They had been employed on a full-time basis outside the home only since the nonprofessional positions were made available to them in the community-education program. Mrs. Lopez commented: "When I stayed home, I was in charge of everything. I did everything and if I didn't do it, Nabor [husband] would complain. Well, when I started working I told him that he had to give me a hand or I would go crazy. Now he does and he even gets on the kids to do their share." Mrs. Santiago also reported greater family participation in household chores:

> Since I've gone to work, the kids have more responsibilities. Sometimes I have to tell them what to do, but you know, they're more independent now. They don't rely on me so much. Believe it, even Juan [husband] helps, but this has been a long time in coming. At first, he reacted by going against me; he wouldn't get after the kids, but things are different now. And it's good for the whole family. Just this morning when I was getting ready for work, there was Christopher sewing his pants.

Mr. Santiago sometimes seemed to resent the division of his wife's time and attention. Yet he conceded that it was necessary for him to give her a hand: "porque siempre hay trabajo en la casa [because there is always housework to be done]." Since his wife was working and going to college, he felt that she deserved help.

Clearly, it was the wives in these four families who made and enforced the decision that their husbands should help with housework. Their husbands' participation reflects an important alteration in family roles. It is significant in the context of traditional Mexican–American patriarchy where "any demand by the wife . . . may be perceived as a demand for submission by her. Similarly, any request for assistance with the children or in housework is regarded as an affront to his dignity" (Penalosa, 1968, p. 685). The fact that husbands did housework, despite their objections, is seen as an indication of their wives' power in the marital relationship.

This is consistent with other research which shows that when the wife is employed, her household labor decreases, while that of the husband increases. Bahr (1974) provides a fairly clear picture of the relationship between the division of labor and wives' employment:

> When a wife becomes employed she has less time for housework and consequently is likely to get at least some help from her husband. Nevertheless, working or not, it appears that housework is still primarily her responsibility. Husbands of employed wives get particularly involved in child care, although they also do considerably more housework than husbands of nonemployed wives. (p. 184)

This raises questions about the effect that husbands' sharing of household responsibilities has on the distribution of power. Goode (1963) proposes that even when husbands perform household chores, they gain power since the household becomes a further domain for the exercise of their prerogatives in decision making. Bahr (1974) also suggests that employment decreases a wife's power within the household but increases it in the area of finances. A different interpretation is offered in *Woman, Culture and Society* (Rosaldo & Lamphere, 1973). In her theoretical overview, Rosaldo contends that men and women are most equal in societies where they share some of the child-rearing and household responsibilities. Hoffman (1963) agrees that the employment of mothers outside the home decreases their decision making in household tasks and increases that of their husbands, but points out that the decisions involved are of relatively little concern to other family members. Power, on the other hand, involves decisions which may have important effects on others.

This distinction between power and control helps to eliminate some of the ambiguity surrounding the relationship between wives' employment and marital power. Hoffman (1963) argues that the employment of wives outside the home increases their power vis-à-vis that of their husbands:

> The theory is that by her employment the mother obtains control of a certain amount of money, thus gaining greater control over financial decisions. This financial control may also enable her to gain more extensive familial power. Furthermore, because she is working and earning money, she gains a new concept of her own worth and thus becomes more assertive. In short, both the husband and the wife are more likely to accept the legitimacy of the working women's claim to power. (p. 217)

My data support Hoffman's view. Wives who were employed gained power by participating in extra-domestic institutions, while their husbands gained only additional domestic responsibility by participating in household activities. The domestic sphere is not equal to the public sphere in terms of the resources upon which power is based.

The relationship between wives' employment and the power they exerted in the families may be clarified by classifying decisions as internal or external (Blood, 1963). Internal decisions may be defined as domestic in nature, while external decisions are extra-domestic in nature. While housewives did control household activities, it cannot be said that they participated equally in making the decisions which were most important to the family. As Safilios Rothschild (1969) points out, all areas of decision making do not have equal weight. One housewife summed up the separate spheres of decision-making responsibility which could be seen in all four housewife families: "Women run the home and men work and take care of business. That's the way we do it anyway, and that's the way it should be."

Control of routine domestic activities should not be confused with women's dominance (Schneider & Smith, 1973) as it does not pose a threat to men's authority in the family. The fact that husbands can leave the household responsibilities to their wives yet impose their will in virtually every other area of decision making is discussed by Polatnick (1975): "Men's authority as family provider/family 'head' carried right over into child-rearing matters. Men may have surrendered the regular responsibilities and routine decision making, but they retain power where important decisions are concerned [including what the routine will be]" (p. 223).

My findings support this interpretation. While husbands of housewives left routine household matters to their wives, their control of external resources allowed them to retain power and authority in their families. On the other hand, all four employed wives had their own spending money, three of the four had their own checking accounts, and all of them had cars which they had purchased. Decision making in these families was different from that in families of housewives in that these wives were involved in external as well as internal decisions.

Multiple Resources and Conjugal Power

The relationship between wives' extra-domestic roles and their power is most clearly revealed in the multiple resources which they used to influence family decision making. Employed wives had several links with organizations outside of their families. Three of them were also attending college (Lopez, Santiago, Tenorio). The other activist, Mrs. Delgado, took graduate courses periodically. This gave all of them additional sources of power.

The way in which multiple extra-domestic resources constituted a basis for the exercise of wives' power may be considered in the context of Hallenbeck's (1966) five types of familial power:

> (1) reward power, based on the ability of a person possessing power to provide rewards for the one influenced; (2) coercive power, based on the powerful one's ability to mediate punishments for the one influenced; (3) legitimate power, based on the influenced one's belief that the powerful one has the right to control his behavior or opinions; (4) referent power, based on the influenced one's identification with the powerful one's perceptions of superior knowledge and skill in the powerful one; and (5) expert power, based on the influenced one's perception of superior knowledge and skill in the powerful one. (p. 200)

Reward power, legitimate power, referent power, and expert power were all exercised by the employed wives. They were able to offer their husbands certain rewards as inducement for compliance in a variety of matters. For example, Mr. Santiago frequently told his wife that she should get another job and drop out of school because it was wrong for her to be absent from home so often, and it was unsafe for her to attend night classes alone. But Mrs. Santiago held fast to her goal of completing her education by reminding him of the better life her degree would bring: "I tell him all the time, if I didn't work we wouldn't have all these extras, and I never let him forget that my degree will mean more money." Mrs. Delgado also used her economic contribution to obtain her husband's agreement to apply for a job. She told me that she had wanted to apply for a position for over a month, but her husband was firmly convinced that it would take up too much of her time. She raised the issue and argued with him frequently until he was persuaded by the benefits a higher salary would bring.

Other types of power did not stem from economic resources. The women commanded power by virtue of their role as workers. The fact that they were employed outside the home gave them certain rights and thus legitimized their power. French and Raven (1960) claim that legitimate power derives primarily from cultural values of masculinity and femininity, but they indicate that position in a social structure may also legitimize power. They explain that rights inherent in some roles can constitute a basis for legitimate power: "The acceptance of an office as *right* is a basis for legitimate power—a judge has a right to levy fines, a foreman should assign work, a priest is justified in prescribing religious beliefs, and it is the management's prerogative to make certain decisions" (p. 265). Husbands of employed wives accepted the rightful influence of their wives, and this legitimized their power. Speaking of his dislike for housework, Mr. Tenorio said: "I sure don't like to be doing this, but she has a right to ask me now that she works all day." Mrs. Lopez also felt that now that she had outside obligations, she was entitled to more rights. "I have a right to certain considerations now. Oh boy, he sure likes to brag about me working and going to school. Well, it's not easy. And he knows the only way I can make it is if he pitches in. Sure it's hard, but I like calling the shots now and then." Mrs. Delgado told me that she had a right to say no if her husband asked for money and she needed it for something else. She stressed that she worked hard for her money, and she had a right to say how it was to be spent.

To the extent that employed wives had legitimate power, they had authority in their families. According to Weber (1947), "When power rests on legitimacy [that is, the notion that an individual has the 'right' to impose his will], and when it is exercised within a hierarchy of roles, it is defined as authority" (p. 152). In these four families, wives' authority was based on the rights associated with their extra-familial roles.

Wives' employment and their participation in extra-domestic organizations also gave them referent power—the ability to influence their husbands based on husband's identification with their accomplishments. French and Raven (1960) speak of "a feeling of oneness" and "conformity based on identification" (p. 266). Such identification of husbands with their wives is illustrated in the following situation: Mrs. Lopez, who was graduating from college, was given the opportunity to enter a master's degree program, but to do so she would have to move to a distant city to go to school for a year. After many deliberations with her husband and children, the decision was made that she would move with four of her school-aged children for a year, while the other children would remain behind with their father. Mr. Lopez expressed his feelings on the decision in the following manner:

> We have been close in our marriage, and now our lives are changing. Now that Linda has the chance to get her master's, things are going to be different for all of us. Who would have thought that she would go and leave me here? But if you want the good things in life you have to take some hardships like this separation. It will be hard for a year, but you can't stop progress, no matter who it is.

Mr. Lopez's identification with his wife and the good things which this opportunity presented enabled him to view the situation in terms of the family's oneness even though a temporary separation would be involved. Mr. Delgado, too, seemed to identify with his wife's position and responsibilities in the community-education program. Speaking to me at the yearly dance, he commented: "I don't care for doing things like this, but here I am at this dance. I'd rather not come, but since she's running the show tonight, I thought I better show her some support by coming." Mr. Tenorio's joining of a community organization may also be viewed as an identification with his wife's community activism by following her example.

Expert power was also used by these women. Their jobs in the community-education program and their education gave them the basis for their expert power. They made numerous references to their "expertise" as a basis for decision making in their families. Speaking about her power in the family, Mrs. Lopez stated:

> A few years ago, I would have told you that I had power because I could get my way with Raul, but I don't think I did compared to the way I have it now. If you're talking about real power, I have it now. You know why? Because since I've been in college, I know more and I don't hesitate to express my opinion. He knows that, and he asks me about things he never would have.

Mrs. Santiago also pointed to her education as a source of power:

> Going to school has given me more power because now I know more. I know how things should be in families, and I try to apply them to my family. Now we do things together more. Well, we try to anyway. Before, he decided everything, but now it's a different story.

Mrs. Tenorio's observation that husbands cannot "put anything over" on employed wives throws additional light on the importance of expert power:

> Sure I make decisions in my family, but that seems natural. A husband knows that he can't put anything over on his wife when she is out in the world facing the same problems that he is. She knows more, and her husband knows she knows more.

These findings should not lead us to overestimate the effect that resources had on the lives of the four external activists. They were busy, overworked women, coping with daily strains that were not present in housewife families. Each of them told me again and again how difficult it was to meet the demands of job, college, and family. Their attempts to balance these conflicting roles was an indication of their willingness to adapt to new and diverse situations and to behave in ways that transcended the traditional definitions of their gender roles.

Scholars have used acculturation and modernization to explain changes in conjugal power relationships in ethnic families. The dynamics or causal relationships of the egalitarian process are ambiguous, but the general point of view is that acculturation precedes shifts in the balance of power. My research questions the assumption that a move away from traditional conjugal roles in Mexican–American families is necessarily associated with acculturation and a corresponding decline in ethnicity. Data gathered on ethnicity were divided into two separate components: family activities and group ethnic identification.

Three of the four families where wives exercised power revealed similarities in rituals and customs of family living. All of the families were Catholic, and their activities with kin often revolved around religious celebrations. Baptisms, weddings, funerals, and Sunday Mass seemed to provide a strong sense of solidarity. Of course, people can behave ethnically at gatherings with kin, and yet be much like non-Chicano families in day-to-day activities. But all families, including those with working wives, revealed similarities in their use of the Spanish language, their preference for Mexican and Spanish food, and their choice of Spanish or Mexican music.

Language is an important indicator of ethnicity since it plays a central role in the efforts of cultural groups to maintain and develop their heritage (Frances, 1947; Schermerhorn, 1970). Sources reveal that Chicanos have retained their Spanish language for well over a century in the midst of United States culture (Gonzales, 1967; Skrabanek, 1970). Similarly, seven of the eight families studied spoke Spanish. In every household with shared decision making, Spanish was spoken by both parents and children, although some expressed dismay that they did not speak it as often as they thought they should. The one family in which Spanish was not spoken was a traditional family in which the wife remained at home.

Visiting with the Tenorios, I commented on how well their children spoke Spanish. Mr. Tenorio told me that they were taught to speak English first because he did not want them to suffer by not knowing English when they got to school. But he also thought that might have been a mistake:

> Sure, they suffer if they don't speak English too well when they go to the first grade, but they also suffer by not knowing our beautiful language as well as they should. Which is worse? I didn't speak English when I went to first grade but I learned it, and I've done all right.

Many of the primary informants spoke both Spanish and English, mixing the two languages even in the same sentence. In the cases of both Mrs. Tenorio and Mrs. Lopez, jokes or funny remarks were made in Spanish. Mrs. Lopez made the following comment:

> We should raise our kids as whole people instead of creating kids with split personalities. That's what happened to me when I was growing up. I was Anglo at school and Chicano at home. That's not even healthy, and that's why we should teach our kids both at home and in school. I'm all for bilingual education.

Mrs. Delgado told me that she often made her children speak Spanish just to keep in practice: "Sometimes I say, okay now, we're all going to speak Spanish until noon, and then we do that until someone forgets and then we go back and forth like we always do using both Spanish and English."

The importance of food in maintaining ethnicity has been noted elsewhere (Mindel & Habenstein, 1976). Ethnic foods were commonly prepared in all of the families—frijoles, chile, tortillas, and special festive foods such as tamales, posole, and biscochitos. The practice of cooking a pot of frijoles and reheating them through the week was commonly observed. This proves to be especially handy for the employed wives since their jobs left less time for elaborate meal preparation during the week. Comments made by all four external activists pointed to the importance of ethnic food in their daily lives:

> *Tenorio:* You would think we would get tired of frijoles, but we can't go too long without them. Once we went to Denver for a few days and the first thing the kids asked for when we got back was my tortillas and frijoles.

> *Lopez:* My husband has to have his tortillas every day. Before I got so busy, it was no problem. But now how can I make tortillas every day when I have to go to class or a meeting, or if I'm tired and just don't feel like it? So now what I do is make the dough for him, and keep it in a sack in the refrigerator, and when I can't make the tortillas, he makes them himself.

Listening to Spanish or Mexican music was also common in these households. For instance, the music and news programs of a Spanish-language radio station were heard daily. As Mrs. Santiago said, "When we all get together, it's like a fiesta. Our food, la música. We go crazy with Spanish. That's the way it should be. You can let loose and enjoy yourself with your own kind."

Mrs. Santiago's comment also represents the ethnic identification found in all eight families. In each family, members perceived themselves to be distinct from the Anglo population, although the labels they used to identify themselves varied. They called themselves Spanish, Mexican, and Chicano, and sometimes all three. The following comments from families with working wives confirm their ethnic identification.

> *Lopez:* We're more open than Anglos in our religion. We're more emotional. Spanish people make religion a part of our daily lives.

> *Santiago:* We don't keep up our customs just to keep them up. We do things because they're good for us. I teach my kids to stand up for their rights as Chicanos.

> *Delgado:* Yesterday we went to the grand opening of the Southwest National Bank. People call it the taco bank because it is the Spanish people who run the show there. I think it's about time our people had something like that in this town.

Tenorio: I am fiercely proud of being Chicano. We have a heritage to be proud of. I would do anything to defend it.

The tendency of ethnic group members to associate primarily with members of their own group has been noted by Paredes (1968) and others (Gordon, 1964; Greeley, 1974; Yancey, 1976). According to Paredes:

Mexican-Americans who speak good English and have received advanced education in American colleges . . . would seem completely acculturated, having adapted to American culture and functioning in a very successful way. At the same time, when they are away from the courtroom, school, or office, they think of themselves as Mexicanos. Not only will they speak Spanish among themselves, but it is quite obvious that they place a high value on many aspects of Mexican culture and are proud of their background. They do, in a sense, live double lives, functioning as Americans in the affairs of the community at large, and as Mexicans within their own closed circle. (p. 111)

This pattern was clearly revealed in all but one of the research families. The four wives with extra-domestic associations did, as Paredes describes, function successfully and competently in the public sphere. Still, they preferred to spend time away from work with their own people. Mrs. Tenorio essentially echoes Mrs. Santiago in remarking that extended family activities are important: "You can just relax with your people."

Conclusions and Implications for Further Research

The findings of this study argue against the depiction of family change as a simple substitution of modern patterns for traditional patterns. Husbands and wives took on new behaviors that were more congruent with the wives' economic and educational roles, but held on to ethnic customs in other areas of family life. The four families with shared power were more egalitarian than the others, but this did not mean that they renounced their ethnic affiliation. They were modern and ethnic at the same time.

Future research on Mexican-American families must examine the ways in which family roles are affected by both cultural expectations and specific external linkages of family members with societal institutions. Both cultural values and extra-domestic roles of husbands and wives require further study before we can say to what extent differences in conjugal relationships result from cultural values surrounding roles and to what extent they result from specific socioeconomic conditions, including educational and occupational statuses of husbands and wives.

Wives' employment was found to have a greater impact on conjugal roles than the social class of families. Both middle-class and working-class external activists had greater power in their families than did the housewives, and no difference between the power of middle-class wives and working-class wives could be observed. This contrasts with studies of conjugal power which conclude that working-class wives gain greater power through employment than do middle-class wives (Heer, 1963; Scanzoni, 1970). However, a sample this size does not provide a sufficient basis for comparing the effects of class on conjugal decision making.

Moreover, in this study social class was assessed in the conventional manner—that is, in terms of the husband's occupational status. Two of the employed wives were defined as belonging to the working-class based on their husband's blue-collar work, but all four employed wives did white-collar work themselves. Even though the two working-class employed wives received lower salaries, they were equal to the middle-class employed wives in their educational status. This may have cancelled out class differences, reflecting the conceptual and empirical problems of defining class position of families in terms of the male head. Acker (1973) remarks, "the assumption that a woman's status is determined by that of the man to whom she is attached implies that women have no status resources of their own. In a society where women as well as men have resources of education, occupation and income, it is obviously not true that women have no basis for determining their own status. If women do have such resources, why do we assume that they are inoperative if they are married?" (p. 176). In this study, social class was assessed in the conventional manner to compare employed wives and housewives. Though it seemed at the outset that meaningful relationships could only be made if social class were defined in the same way, in fact, we found that the resources of the working-class external activists were not much different from those of their middle-class counterparts.

Some kinds of employment carry with them more types of resources and hence provide greater potential power than others. The four employed wives of this study were engaged in careers which were interesting to them and which were perceived as important by the community. Their work in community education enhanced their alternatives and decreased their dependence on husbands. Furthermore, these wives' college education gave them special status and prestige. It was their education which constituted the most prestigious resource brought to bear on conjugal interaction. It is possible that had these women regarded themselves as working in jobs rather than as having careers, their power would have been considerably less. This points to the need for research which compares the relative and separate impact of wives' and husbands' resources to further our understanding of conjugal roles and conjugal power.

References

Acker, J. Women and social stratification: A case of intellectual sexism. In J. Huber (Ed.), *Changing women in a changing society*. Chicago: University of Chicago Press, 1973.

Alvirez, D., & Bean, F. D. The Mexican-American family. In C. H. Mindel & R. W. Habenstein (Eds.), *Ethnic families in America*. New York: Elsevier, 1976.

Arroyo, L. E. Industrial and occupational distribution of Chicano workers. *Aztlan*, 1973, **4**, 343–360.

Bahr, S. J. Effects of power and division of labor in the family. In L. W. Hoffman & F. L. Nye (Eds.), *Working mothers*. San Francisco: Jossey Bass, 1974.

Blood, R. O., & Wolfe, D. M. *Husbands and wives*. New York: Free Press, 1960.

Blood, R. O. The husband-wife relationship. In L. W. Hoffman & F. L. Nye (Eds.), *The employed mother in America*. Chicago: Rand McNally, 1963.

Buric, O., & Zelevic, A. Family authority, marital satisfaction and the social network in Yugoslavia. *Journal of Marriage and the Family*, 1967, **29**, 325–366.

Clark, M. *Health in the Mexican–American culture*. Berkeley: University of California Press, 1969.

Cooney, R. S. Changing labor force participation of Mexican-American wives: A comparison with Anglos and Blacks. *Social Science Quarterly*, 1975, **56**, 202–226.

Cromwell, V. L., & Cromwell, R. E. Perceived dominance in decision making and conflict resolution among Anglo, Black, and Chicano couples. *Journal of Marriage and the Family*, 1978, **40**, 749–759.

Frances, E. K. The nature of the ethnic group. *American Journal of Sociology*, 1947, **52** 393-400.

French, J. R. P., & Raven, B. The bases of social power. In D. Cartwright & A. Zander (Eds.), *Group dynamics: Research and theory* (2nd ed.). Elmsford, N. Y.: Row Peterson, 1960.

Gonzales, N. L. *The Spanish-Americans of New Mexico*. Albuquerque: University of New Mexico Press, 1967.

Goode, W. J. *World revolution and family patterns*. New York: Free Press, 1963.

Gordon, M. M. *Assimilation in American life*. New York: Oxford University Press, 1964.

Gouldner, N. *The Mexican in the Northern urban area: A comparison of two generations*. Unpublished master's thesis, University of Minnesota, 1959.

Grebler, L., Moore, J. W., & Guzman, R. C. *The Mexican-American people: The nation's second largest minority*. New York: Free Press, 1970.

Greeley, A. M. *Ethnicity in the United States: A preliminary reconnaissance*. New York: Wiley, 1974.

Hallenbeck, P. N. An analysis of power dynamics in marriage. *Journal of Marriage and the Family*, 1966, **28**, 200-203.

Haraven, T. K. Modernization and family history: Perspectives on social change. *Signs*, 1976, **2**, 190-206.

Haraven, T. K. Family time and historical time. *Daedalus*, 1977, **106**, 57-70.

Hawkes, G. R., & Taylor, M. Power structure in Mexican and Mexican-American farm labor families. *Journal of Marriage and the Family*, 1975, **37**, 807-811.

Heer, D. M. Dominance and the working wife. In F. I. Nye & L. W. Hoffman (Eds.), *The employed mother in America*. Chicago: Rand McNally, 1963.

Hoffman, L. W. Parental power relations and the division of household tasks. In L. W. Hoffman & F. L. Nye (Eds.), *The employed mother in America*. Chicago: Rand McNally, 1963.

Humphrey, N. D. The changing structure of the Detroit Mexican family. *American Sociological Review*, 1944, **9**, 622-626.

McLaughlin, V. Y. Patterns of work and family organization. In T. K. Rabb & R. I. Rotberg (Eds.), *The family in history*. New York: Harper & Row, 1973.

Mindel, C. H., & Habenstein, R. W. *Ethnic families in America*. New York: Elsevier, 1976.

Paredes, A. Folk medicine and the intercultural jest. In J. Helm (Ed.), *Spanish-speaking people in the United States*. Seattle: University of Washington Press, 1968.

Penalosa, F. Mexican family roles. *Journal of Marriage and the Family*, 1968, **30**, 682-685.

Polatnick, M. Why men don't rear children: A power analysis. In J. W. Petras (Ed.), *Sex: Male gender: Masculine*. New York: Alfred, 1975.

Rosaldo, M., & Lamphere, L. *Women, culture and society*. Stanford: Stanford University Press, 1973.

Runcie, J. F. *Experiencing social research*. Homewood, Ill.: Dorsey Press, 1976.

Safilios-Rothschild, C. Family sociology or wives' family sociology? A cross-cultural examination of decision making. *Journal of Marriage and the Family*, 1969, **31**, 290-301.

Safilios-Rothschild, C. The study of family power structure: A review, 1960-1969. *Journal of Marriage and the Family*, 1970, **32**, 539-552.

Scanzoni, J. *Opportunity and the family*. New York: Free Press, 1970.

Schermerhorn, R. A. *Comparative ethnic relations*. New York: Random House, 1970.

Schneider, D. M., & Smith, R. T. *Class differences and sex roles in American family and kinship structure*. Englewood Cliffs, N. J.: Prentice Hall, 1973.

Selltiz, C., Wrightsman, L. S., & Cook, S. W. *Research methods in social relations* (3rd ed.). New York: Holt, Rinehart & Winston, 1976.

Skrabanek, R. L. Language maintenance among Mexican-Americans. *International Journal of Comparative Sociology*, 1970, **8**, 272-282.

Taylor, P. S. Mexican labor in the United States. *Migration Statistics IV*. University of California Publications in Economics, 1933.

Tharp, R. G., Meadow, A., Lennhoff, S., & Satterfield, D. Changes in marriages roles accompanying the acculturation of the Mexican-American wife. *Journal of Marriage and the Family*, 1968, **30**, 404-412.

Weber, M. [The theory of social and economic organization] (A. M. Henderson & T. Parsons, Eds.). Glencoe, Ill.: Free Press, 1947. (Originally published, 1924).

Wolfe, D. M. Power and authority in the family. In D. Cartwright (Ed.), *Studies in social power*. Ann Arbor: University of Michigan Press, 1959.

Yancey, W. L., Erickson, E. P., & Juliani, R. Emergent ethnicity: A review and reformulation. *American Sociological Review*, 1976, 41, 391–403.

A Historical View of
Chicanas in Literature

CONCEPCIÓN M. VALADEZ

La Chicana, The Mexican-American Woman
by Alfredo Mirandé and Evangelina Enríquez.
Chicago: The University of Chicago Press, 1979. 283 pp.

Scholarly writing about Chicanas has not been a major focus of academic research, though Mexican and Mexican-American women have made important contributions which have been barely acknowledged or neglected altogether. *La Chicana* is an important addition to the literature on the women of one of this country's major ethnic groups.

Alfredo Mirandé, a sociologist, and Evangelina Enríquez, a student of comparative literature, have written a comprehensive account of the place of Chicanas in the history and culture of Mexico and the United States. In their introduction, the authors assert that Chicanas have been victims of internal colonialism, and as a result suffer a triple oppression: "They are victims of attempted cultural genocide as the dominant group has sought insidiously to destroy Chicano culture and render its institutions subordinate and dependent. . . . As women, Chicanas experience the universal oppression that comes from being female. . . . Finally, Chicanas carry an additional burden of internal oppression by the cultural heritage that tends to be dominated by males and exaggerates male domination over women" (pp. 12–13). Although the angry and accusatory tone of the introduction does not permeate the book, the same points are made by forceful voices in Spanish, accompanied by excellent English translations, telling of injustices described in the Aztec codices, the early colonial period, as well as accounts by more recent historical figures.

La Chicana is a comprehensive resource useful for general readers, as well as for academics in the area of women's studies, Chicano studies, sociology, and cultural anthropology. The book presents Chicana history, woman's role in the family, the interaction of work, education, and the Chicana, as well as Chicanas in literature and Chicana feminism.

The word *Chicana*, as used by Mirandé and Enríquez, refers to all women of Mexican descent, whether or not they prefer to be known as Latinas, Hispanas,

Harvard Educational Review   Vol. 51   No. 1   February 1981, 223–225

Mexicans, or even Americans. The authors note that Chicanas may be bilingual in Spanish and English, or monolingual in either English or Spanish. Diversity also spans the degrees of assimilation into mainstream United States culture, ranging from women totally unidentified with this country to those totally assimilated. Additionally, women vary in their acceptance of the traditional female role (p. 11). "Some cultural expectations of Chicanas date back to Aztec models — such as being the heart of the home, bearing and rearing children, being clean and tidy, dedicating oneself to a husband, and preserving one's respectability in the eyes of the community" (p. 15). The authors cite evidence from the *Florentine Codex*, a pre-Colombian Aztec pictographic manuscript with text written by fifteenth-century Spanish friars as first-hand accounts of roles and behaviors, modes of dress, hair ornaments, and adornments common to men and women of various stations in Aztec society. In a subsequent discussion of the family, the Aztec codices cite the most important virtues parents prescribed for their daughters:

> tenacidad de aguantar las dificultades de la vida [tenacity in enduring the difficulties of life]
> decencia y honestidad [decency and honesty]
> devoción y piedad [devotion and piety]
> conocimientos y habilidad en los oficios mujeriles [knowledge and mastery of feminine duties]
> diligencia [diligence]
> castidad [chastity]
> obedencia [obedience]
> modestia [modesty] (p. 99)

The contemporary concept of honor in Chicano families is also rooted in Aztec society. The authors claim that "the Aztec family was not an extended system like the traditional Chinese family, yet there was a great emphasis on familism. One was expected to obey and respect the family and, most importantly, not to dishonor it" (p. 99). A woman could dishonor her family, however, by committing adultery or by being immodest in conduct or dress. Mirandé and Enríquez also discuss the strict monitoring of maternal behavior. The centuries-old legend of "La Llorona," a ghost who is recognized by her mournful wail as she searches for the children she rejected or neglected, reinforces women's matriarchal role.

The authors effectively use census data concerning Mexican-American women in the labor force in their discussion of changing dynamics in society as traditional homebound roles are altered. Research by sociologists Leonarda Ybarra and Maxine Baca Zinn indicates that shifts in decision making occur after women enter the labor force (p. 117). In such households, many women for the first time begin to share the decision-making process with their spouses.

Among the sections most skillfully written by Mirandé and Enríquez is the chapter that traces the sociohistorical and cultural views of Chicanas through literature, beginning with accounts of Anglo travelers in the mid-nineteenth century to present self-portrayals by Chicanas. These early travelers were both attracted and repulsed, comparing the clothing and demeanor of Mexican women to those of the women in their own families. By the end of the nineteenth century, a romanticized stereotype of women had developed, evident in such novels as *Ramona* by the American novelist, Helen Hunt Jackson, published in 1844. Describing her title character, the author wrote:

> Ramona is distinguished by her ancestry, her flawless brown beauty, and her enduring sunny nature. . . . Ramona is a half-breed whose unhappy conception remains a mystery to her and all those who surround her. The pastoral freshness she is endowed with is amplified by her personal virtues and lovely spirit. (pp. 147–148)

A third type of Anglo writing about Chicanas is labelled "social Darwinist," which includes John Steinbeck's *Tortilla Flat* and Frank Norris's *Mac Teague*. In the social chains constructed by these writers, according to Mirandé and Enríquez, Mexican women are relegated to the lowest link, viewed as motivated primarily by bestial lust. The authors substantiate their claim that the treatment of Chicanas in Anglo literature proceeds from an encounter between "two very different cultures which produce a series (of writings) of initial attraction that quickly gives way to rejection, seduction, and finally, relegation to inferior status of one by the other" (p. 158).

Mirandé and Enríquez are not much more lenient in their evaluation of the way Chicanos write about women, contending that Chicanos' literary work remains dominated by a masculine universe (p. 160). Women are considered either good or bad, and there is a preponderance of prostitutes and easily intimidated women. Mothers are the only group of women Chicano authors consistently present in a positive light. Mothers in Chicano literature are warm, enduring, uncomplaining, and strong. An example in José Montoya's bilingual poem, "La Jefita," which begins,

> When I remember the campos
>   y las noches and the sounds
> of those nights en carpas o
> Bagones I remember my jefita's
> Palote
> Clik-clok; clik-clak-clok
> Y su tocesita.
>
> (I swear, she never slept!) (p. 165)
> . . . .

The poem portrays a man's vivid memory of his mother in a migrant camp, as she begins the daily ritual of lighting the fire, rolling out the tortillas, and starting breakfast in the darkness, while her family sleeps a bit longer. The young boy's awe of his mother's stamina is captured very effectively.

Images of Chicanas in their own works reveal a common concern about assimilation into mainstream Anglo culture. They write little about the insidious, profound influence of Anglo culture on the language, education, and life-style of Chicanas. Georgia M. Cobos's poem, "Suffer Little Children," on the other hand, serves as a commentary on the destructive power schools have on Chicano children's ethnic pride:

> Pride and love are lost within the yellow cumulative folder—
> That one which limits and relegates my boys to hoods and slaves,
> And my girls to early ugliness and pain. (p. 180)

Some write of the seductive powers of Anglo pop culture, while others write about relationships between males and females. Some literature questions traditional sex roles. A succinct poem by Bernice Zamora, "Pueblo, 1950," protests the cultural double standard in relations between the sexes:

> I remember you, Fred Montoya.
> You were the first *vato* ever to kiss me.
> I was twelve years old.
> My mother said shame on you.
> My teacher said shame on you, and
> I said shame on me, and nobody said a word to you. (p. 186)

Another characteristic aspect of literature written by Chicanos focuses on relationships across familial generations. Mirandé and Enríquez note that, in Chicana literature, women relate to one another in nonstereotyped ways and are themselves nonstereotyped. They relate to one another as equals, regardless of age. The authors value assertiveness and individuality as a significant advance in Chicano literature, a feature not found in the literature produced by Anglo writers or by Chicanos.

La Chicana affirms that Chicanas have been relegated to a low status by the dominant society for being members of an ethnic group, and that they have been considered inferior in a world that values males more than females.[1] Chicanas also have inherited the cultural expectations of an ethnic group in which men are accorded preferential treatment. A major portion of the work, however, testifies to Chicanas' resourcefulness and talents. Chicana women have been leading contributors to the history, politics, and economic development of both Mexico and the United States. As mothers, they have been charged with keeping and transmitting ethnic traditions and values,[2] the continuity or modification of which lies in their hands.[3]

La Chicana celebrates the Chicana as a gracious woman who continues to emerge as strong, decisive, and idealistic. Mirandé and Enríquez provide valuable insights into the complex character of this woman who bridges two distinct worlds, each with its own dynamism and set of traditions.

---

[1] See Michelle Z. Rosaldo and Louise Lamphere, eds., *Woman, Culture and Society* (Stanford: Stanford Univ. Press, 1974).

[2] George Spindler, *Education and Cultural Process: Towards an Anthropology of Education* (New York: Holt, Rinehart & Winston, 1974).

[3] Concepción M. Valadez, "Chicanas and Education," paper presented at the Spanish Department Colloquium, Univ. of California, Irvine, 1980.

A Canadian Perspective on Black American Authors

MARGARET ATWOOD

MIDNIGHT BIRDS: STORIES OF CONTEMPORARY BLACK WOMEN WRITERS
edited by Mary Helen Washington.
New York: Anchor Books, 1980. 274 pp.

Midnight Birds is a collection of fifteen recent short stories written by women who are black and American. There is an excellent preface by Mary Helen Washington, and each writer introduces herself in a brief preliminary piece that makes the book handy for teaching. Although the book's subtitle mentions "women," "contemporary," and "black," it does not bother with "American." (Black women do exist elsewhere.)

It is also of note that this book is being reviewed in an issue devoted to the Third World. It is noteworthy as well that I am female, but neither black nor American. I am in fact Canadian, a citizen of a country which was dominated until recently by one imperial power and now by another. Could I then have something in common with the writers in this collection? I remember the bemused expression on the faces of a group of American feminists when I tried to explain to them why their Canadian sisters had locked themselves in the washroom during a joint conference. "Ask Alice Walker," I said. "She'll tell you."

The writers themselves have no doubt about their identity as Americans, nor should they. Their prose is American, their settings are American; even their shared assumption that things can be improved almost by sheer faith is at its core profoundly American. These women are not writing about genital mutilation, polygamy, or purdah, which luckily are not problems they have to deal with directly. These women are writing—these women *can* write, which distinguishes them from most women in Third World countries, who have not been taught to write at all—in the most basic sense of the word. These authors are as American as jazz and lynching. By what strange squint—the same one, presumably, that sees white male American writers as the norm and everyone else as the exception—might they be designated by the editors of this journal as in the "Third World" category?*

* This review originally appeared in a special issue of *HER* (February 1981), "Education As Transformation: Identity, Change, and Development."—ED.

Harvard Educational Review   Vol. 51   No. 1   February 1981, 221–223

It certainly cannot be a reflection of the quality of the writing. This is American writing at its finest, by turns earthy, sinuous, thoughtful, and full of power. *Midnight Birds* includes such well-known names as Alice Walker, Toni Morrison, Toni Cade Bambara, and Ntozake Shange, as well as those not quite so well-known but which deserve to be: Alexis Deveaux, Paulette Childress White, Frenchy Hodges, Gayle Jones, and Sherley Anne Williams. Prose techniques range from the window-pane clarity of Alice Walker to the verbal improvizations of Alexis Deveaux and Ntozake Shange. The writers are concerned with the need to forge or rediscover a language of their own, since the mainstream white male language they were taught they ought to think in has served them badly. Perhaps white Americans would rather not see the visions of these women as visions of their own society, but as visions of a Third World, somewhere foreign? Isn't Harlem in New York? There are many more worlds than three, even in America, and some of them overlap.

I once met an academic who specialized in Commonwealth literature. When I asked him why he had chosen to do that, he said that being at the periphery rather than at the center it was much easier to trace the patterns of relationship between writer and audience, to investigate the social function of literature. A member of an imperial culture—a Roman rather than a Gaul—can take things for granted to the point of ignorance or amnesia in a way that a Gaul cannot. Black American women are, paradoxically, both Romans and Gauls, but these writers identify most of the time with the Gauls.

This makes a difference in their own attitudes toward what they are doing. For instance, if you were to ask a white American male writer whom he is writing for, you would probably get some abstract answer, unless he is a member of an ethnic minority. But the writers in *Midnight Birds* know exactly whom they are writing for. They are writing for other black American women, and they believe in the power of their words. They see themselves as giving a voice to the voiceless. They perceive writing as the forging of saving myths, the naming of forgotten pasts, the telling of truths. They do not want their books to be admired merely for aesthetic qualities. They want them to be taken back into the society from which they have sprung and to change that society.

These writers think it is important that a people be able to see its own reflection in the mirror of art. These writers see art very much as a mirror, when they are not seeing it as some even more practical tool such as a shovel. Almost every author writes about the extent to which she has created art from her own experience and derived the power to do so from her own community. Alexis Deveaux stands for many:

> Writing helps me unravel the images and forces at work in my own life, and therefore, by extension, in the lives of Black women and Black people around me. I hope to communicate something not just about my life, but about *our* life. It's all one life—isn't it? And I'm very concerned about the images of Black women in literature because whatever is written down becomes the word, and stays. . . . I want to say something about the Black woman as a three-dimensional human being. So often we've seen her depicted as . . . ugly and useless. I want to change that. In the most radical and revolutionary ways possible. (p. 15)

Both the writers' attitudes and the readers' anticipated responses depend on factors which we are used to thinking of as extra-literary, which should probably lead us to reexamine what we mean by this term. Can art and the world really be separated? Perhaps art for art's sake is a luxury, one you can afford only when you are well-fed. Despite their private successes, these women are still very close to hunger.

As in early feminist theory, there is still some tension between the desire to create heroic figures and the pull towards truth-telling. Gayle Jones, for instance, has been criticized for not making her characters more admirable. The editor comments:

> Diane Johnson said in *The New York Review of Books* that a white reader, like herself, could not relate to such dehumanized pictures of black life and lamented that all of Jones's women characters were brutalized and dull. . . . One wishes for the heroic voice, for the healing of the past; but it is presumptuous to demand that these things appear before their time. (p. 127)

There will always be a conflict between readers who want writers to create good role models and those writers who feel that a picture of life that omits the rock bottom would be profoundly untrue. For the most part, these writers resolve this conflict in that most American of ways: by seeing the ordinary as heroic.

White American feminists might have some trouble, too, with the way men are dealt with here, though nobody from a colony would. In a colony, both men and women are oppressed, the women doubly so, though the men feel emasculated by having their decision-making powers taken from them. The writers in *Midnight Birds* display a tenderness, a pity, towards their black male characters that would be hard to match among contemporary white American feminists. The men are often dying of dope, bullet wounds, and other forms of violence slow and swift, and the women characters, although often badly treated by them, cannot turn their backs on them. One of the most harrowing scenes in the book is from Toni Morrison's *Sula*, in which a woman burns her own son to death because he has become a hopeless addict; yet even this act is rendered as profoundly maternal.

In a recent discussion about writing, someone described to me a cartoon in *The New Yorker*: a small girl is hunched over a book, in tears, and her mother is warning the returning father, "Shh! Beth is dying!" The girl's capacity to be moved is seen as comic. But isn't that moment what the act of writing is supposed to aim for? Not sentimentality, to be sure — and these writers are rarely sentimental — but empathy on the part of the reader. These writers have no doubts about that. They want to involve the reader, they want to move her, and, at their best, they succeed. Universal literature is not literature that ignores the local, the particular. On the contrary, it is literature that renders the particular so concretely that even readers from outside the constituency can be moved. It is not the Third World — some place foreign — that these women are writing about, but it is a world very different from the one most people who read books in America inhabit. Or rather it is the same world, though it is seen, with honesty, passion, and painful clarity, through different windows.

Notes on Contributors

MARGARET ATWOOD, Canadian poet, author, and critic, has been the recipient of numerous awards for her poetry and fiction. Among her recent writings are *Life Before Man* (1980), *Bodily Harm* (1981), and *Murder in the Dark* (1983).

HELEN PHELPS BAILEY, who is now retired, was formerly Professor of French and Dean of Studies at Barnard College. She is the author of *Hamlet in France* (1964).

JEANNE BOYDSTON is Assistant Professor of History at Rutgers University, where her professional interests are United States women's history. She is coeditor of an anthology of the writings of Catharine Beecher, Harriet Beecher Stowe, and Isabella Beecher Hooker, tentatively titled *The Limits of Sisterhood* (forthcoming).

BARBARA M. BRENZEL, Associate Professor and Chair of the Department of Education at Wellesley College, is author of *Daughters of the State: A Social Portrait of the First Reform School for Girls, 1856–1905* (1983) and *Female Adolescents in the Two Wars: A Journal of Early Adolescence* (1984).

LORELEI R. BRUSH is Executive Associate at Aurora Associates, Washington, DC. Her present work is in program evaluation, working with child and family programs. She designed and is presently helping to implement a cost management program for Head Start. She is the author of *Encouraging Girls in Mathematics: The Problem and the Solution* (1980) and of *Women and Mathematics: Balancing the Equation* (forthcoming).

BARBARA GATES, when her review was written in 1975, was a teacher of English at The Group School, Cambridge, Massachusetts, and coordinator of its language arts program. She was coauthor with Adria Reich of a curriculum for teachers and counselors working with women in lower income and ethnic groups, a project funded by the Rockefeller Family Fund.

CAROL GILLIGAN, Associate Professor of Education at Harvard University, is currently doing research in adolescent development, focusing on the high school years. She is also continuing her study of how people think about moral conflict and choice. She is the author of *In a Different Voice* (1982).

RUTH HUBBARD, Professor of Biology at Harvard University, is concerned with women's studies and the sociology of science. She is coeditor, with Marian Lowe, of *Woman's Nature: Rationalizations of Inequality* (1983) and the author of numerous articles in journals and anthologies.

DONNA HULSIZER is Director of Corporate Development, The Youth Employment Company, Washington, DC. She has worked as a writing and editorial consultant for numerous organizations and is interested in women's and adult development.

CAROL NAGY JACKLIN is Professor of Psychology and Director of the Program for the Study of Women and Men in Society at the University of Southern California. A prolific writer in the fields of child development and infant behavior, with special emphasis upon sex differences, her present work in progress is a longitudinal study of hormonal and parental contributions to sex differences from birth to third grade, with particular attention to the development of aggression and the prediction of school behavior.

JACQUELINE JONES, whose professional interest is nineteenth-century social history, is Associate Professor of History at Wellesley College. She is author of *Soldiers of Light and Love: Northern Teachers and Georgian Blacks, 1865–1973* (1980) and *Labor of Love, Labor of Sorrow: Black Women, Work, and the Family from Slavery to the Present* (forthcoming).

JANE ROLAND MARTIN is Professor of Philosophy at the University of Massachusetts, Boston. Her major professional interest is the philosophy of education, especially gender and education. She was a Fellow of the Bunting Institute of Radcliffe College (1980–1981) and a Visiting Distinguished Women's Studies Scholar, University of New Hampshire (1983–1984).

MARGARET MEAD, who died in 1978, was Curator of Natural History and Adjunct Professor of Anthropology at Columbia University. Her publications on temperamental differences between the sexes in various societies brought her early recognition. Among her best-known work in the field of anthropology are *Coming of Age in Samoa* (1928) and *Sex and Temperament in Three Primitive Societies* (1935). Her autobiography, *Blackberry Winter: My Earlier Years*, was widely praised on publication in 1972.

ARUN P. MUKHERJEE is Assistant Professor of English at the University of Regina, Saskatchewan, Canada. Among her current professional interests are Canadian immigrant literature, children's literature, and women's education.

KATHLEEN MURPHEY is currently a foreign expert in English at the Public College of Beijing, People's Republic of China, in the Foreign Languages Institute. She was formerly Assistant Professor of Education at Bowling Green University, Department of Educational Foundations and was a tutor at The Group School, Cambridge, Massachusetts.

PATRICIA ANN PALMIERI is Assistant Professor of Education at Dartmouth College. Her interests include the history of women's higher education and of women in the professions. She is the author of "Here Was Fellowship: A Social Portrait of the Academic Women at Wellesley College, 1895–1920," *History of Education Quarterly* (1983). In 1985, she will serve on the editorial board of the *History of Education Annual*.

ADRIA REICH, when this review was written in 1975, was a teacher of history and women's studies at The Group School, Cambridge, Massachusetts. She was coauthor of a curriculum for teaching and counseling low income and ethnic women, a project funded by the Rockefeller Family Fund, the author of several articles on women's issues, and a teacher-training consultant for Antioch College.

SARA RUDDICK is a member of the faculty, Seminar College, The New School for Social Research, New York. A contributing editor to current feminist literature, her professional interests include feminist and pacifist theory and philosophical psychology.

TERRY SAARIO is Vice President, Community Relations, the Pillsbury Company, Minneapolis, with a special interest in corporate philanthropy. She was formerly Director of Contributions and Community Affairs for The Standard Oil Company and a consultant to the Ford Foundation and the Carnegie Foundation.

GEORGIA SASSEN is Clinical Associate in the Division of Psychiatry at the University of Massachusetts Medical Center. Among her immediate professional concerns are families at mid-life, including problems of women at mid-life, and adjustment to the dependency of aging family members.

ALIX KATES SHULMAN, who teaches in the Graduate Writing Program in the Department of English, New York University, is the author of *Memoirs of an Ex-Prom Queen* (1972), *Burning Questions* (1978), and *On the Stroll* (1981).

PATRICIA MEYER SPACKS, whose chief professional interests are eighteenth-century fiction and women's writing, is Professor of English at Yale University. Her works include *The Female Imagination* (1975), *Imagining a Self* (1976), and *The Adolescent Idea* (1981).

SUSAN MERRILL SQUIER is Assistant Professor of English, State University of New York, Stony Brook. Her professional interests are modern British literature and feminist theory and criticism. She is editor of *Women Writers and the City: Essays in Feminist Literary Criticism* (1984) and author of *Virginia Woolf and the Politics of City Space* (forthcoming).

ORDWAY TEAD, who died in 1973, was the author of several books, including *Equalizing Educational Opportunities Beyond the Secondary Schools* (1947) and *Administration: Its Purpose and Performance* (1959). He was Chairman of the Board of Higher Education of New York State (1938–1953) and was both Professor of Industrial Relations and Lecturer of Personnel Administration at Columbia University. He was also editor of social and economic books for Harper & Row (1938–1953).

CAROL KEHR TITTLE is Professor in the School of Education, University of North Carolina at Greensboro, and coauthor (with E. R. Denker) of *Returning Women in Higher Education* (1980) and author of *Career and Family: Sex Roles and Adolescent Life Plans* (1981).

ROBERT ULICH, who died in 1977, was Professor Emeritus of Education, Harvard University. Among his many books are *History of Educational Thought* (1945), *Three Thousand Years of Educational Thought* (1947), and *Philosophy of Education* (1961). He was also editor of *Education and the Idea of Mankind* and served as an associate editor for the *Harvard Educational Review* from 1945–1950.

CONCEPCION M. VALADEZ is Assistant Professor in the Graduate School of Education at the University of California, Los Angeles. Deeply concerned with the education of linguistic and cultural minorities, she has written prolifically, in both English and Spanish, in the field of bilingual education. She is the author of *Basic Skills in Urban Schools: A View from the Bilingual Classroom* (1979).

ESTHER MANNING WESTERVELT, who died in 1975, was an expert in the field of women's education and development. She was Alumnae Professor and Holder of the Alumnae Endowed Chair at Simmons College and served as Executive Codirector of the National Coalition for Research on Women's Education and Development, as well as Project Consultant to the U.S. Office of Education.

MARCIA WESTKOTT is Associate Professor of Sociology at the University of Colorado, Colorado Springs. Her forthcoming book, now in progress, will be titled *A Feminist Theory of Feminine Psychology: Revisioning Karen Horney's Social Psychology.*

ANN WITHORN, Associate Professor of Social Policy at the College of Public and Community Service, University of Massachusetts, Boston, is primarily concerned with social welfare policy, women and welfare, and alternative educational models. She is the author of *The Circle Game: Services for the Poor in Massachusetts* (1982) and *Serving the People: Social Services and Social Change* (1984).

MAXINE BACA ZINN is Associate Professor of Sociology, the University of Michigan, Flint. Her major professional interests are sociology of the family, sex and gender differentiation, and race and ethnic relations. She is an associate editor of *The Social Science Journal* and a contributor to journals in the field of sociology in the area of Hispanic culture.

Index

Abortion, 10; and moral judgment, 188, 196–215, 218, 242. *See also* Birth control; Moral development

Abrahams, H. J., 66

Abrams, S., 176

Academic achievement, *see* Intellectual performance

Academic administrators, woman as, *see* Education

Achievement tests, *see* Tests and testing

Acker, J., 272

Adler, Polly, 35

Adolescence: social relationships during, 8; of girls in Lancaster school, 26–27; developmental challenge of, 187; identity crisis in, 192, 229, 230, 232; studies of, 196; pregnancy during, 199–201, 202; ideological morality in, 215, 216, 221; female development in, 229–231; fairy-tale view of, 230–231. *See also* Age; Children

Adulthood: as portrayed in children's primers, 106, 108, 109; independence of, 187, 196; concept of, 188, 189, (Erikson and) 215, 221, 229; moral judgment and, 196, 197, 210, 222; -femininity conflict, 196, 210, 214, 215; pregnancy and, 199–201; and responsibility, 200–201; critical relationships of, 233. *See also* Age; Motherhood; Parenthood; Relationships; Responsibility

Advertising: exploitation by, 10. *See also* Exploitation

Affirmative action, 70, 72, 76, 77, 79

Age: of "wayward girls," 22, 23, 26–29, 30; of marriage, and employment, 31; as issue for women, 39; and admission to graduate study, 76; and academic achievement/intellectual performance, 78–79; and gender identity, 226. *See also* Adolescence; Adulthood; Children

Algerian Women's Union Congress, 80

Alison, S. N., 178, 179, 180

Allmendinger, David, Jr., 86

Allport-Vernon-Lindzey Study of Values, 253

Alper, T. G., 175

Altruism, 12, 15, 193, 203, 233. *See also* Self-sacrifice

Alvirez, D., 260, 261

American Association of University Women, 67, 84n5; study of members of, 9

American Council on Education, 72, 74; Commission on the Education of Women, 69

American Legion, 41

American Men of Science, 92, 94

American Missionary Association, 146

American Women (Commission on the Status of Women), 69

Ames, Marcus, 27, 31

Amherst College, 50

Androgyny, *see* Behavior

Antioch College, 50

Anxiety: defined, 179–180, 181. *See also* Success (fear of)

Apgar, Virginia, 39

Arden, Elizabeth, 35, 41

Arms race, 243. *See also* Politics

Arroyo, L. E., 261

Association of American Colleges, 76

Association of Collegiate Alumnae, 67, 84

Astaire, Fred, 42

Astin, H. S., 77

Athletics, 118–119

Atlantic Monthly, 51, 142

Atwood, Margaret, 138, 282

Autonomy, *see* Independence

Aztec codices, 275, 276

Bahr, S. J., 261, 265

Bailey, Helen Phelps, 282

Balch, Emily Greene, 86n11

Bambara, Toni Cade, 280

Bank Street textbook series, 104, 109. *See also* Textbooks

Barnard College, 61

Barney, Nora Blatch (Mrs. Lee de Forest), 38

Barron, N. M., 111

Basic Opportunity Grants, 74

Bauchens, Anne, 40

Bayer, A. E., 77

Bean, F. D., 260, 261

Beard, Mary, 90

Beauty, 38–39. *See also* Self-image

Beauvoir, Simone de, 246

Beecher, Catherine, 145, 167; founds female seminaries, 3, 66; glorification of maternal role by, 68, 69, 144; philosophy of education of, 161, 173

Behavior: "proper"/traditional or "normal," 3, 11, 70, 84, 129, 231; sex differences in, (and child's development) 100, (as portrayed by basal reading textbooks) 102–110, (and fear of success), 250; of teacher, and sex role development,

tivation for, 7, 73; choice of (vs. not working outside the home), 8, 51, 52, 68; and professional collaboration with men, 9, 11, 37–38, 92–93, 94; economic conditions and, 9, 53, 73, 87, 261; in volunteer work, 15, 72; exploitation in, 15, 44, 46; domesticity vs. (19th century), 18, 43; in domestic service (training for) 23, 29–31, (importance of) 31, 43–46, (female relationships in) 31, 43, 44–46; of immigrant women, 31, 44, 46, 87; of black women, 31, 45, 72; diversity of, 53; in clerical work, 53, 116, 118, 120; probability of, 62; post-motherhood, 69; domesticity-related, 84, 89, 92, 93; by women's colleges, 93, 94; 1970s statistics on, 110, 118; "women's work," 118, 126–127, (teaching) 66, 72, 75, 103, 115, 144, 146, 159, (nursing, health professions, social work) 72, 75, 92, 103, (home economics) 84, 92, 93, (psychology) 92, 93, (clerical work) 118, (denigration of) 146, 247, 249. *See also* Career(s); Domestic help; Domesticity; Education; Occupations and professions; Teaching

Enríquez, Evangelina (coauthor): *La Chicana, The Mexican-American Woman* reviewed, 275–278

Environmental categories: sex differences in (as portrayed by textbooks), 108. *See also* Occupations and professions

Environmental theories: of reform, 20, 23, 28–29; of child development, 100–101; of personality formation, 151, 226. *See also* Family, the; Urbanization Epstein, Cynthia Fuchs: *Woman's Place: Options and Limits in Professional Careers* reviewed, 11–12, 16

Equal Pay Act, 120. *See also* Law and legislation; Salaries

Erikson, Erik H., 179, 187, 215, 220, 221, 229–232 *passim*, 240

Esposito, R. P., 176

Ethics and Education (Peters), 164

Ethnicity, 259–272, 275–278; defined, 261

Etter, Lyz, 130n1

Europe: reform institutions in, 19–20; women in professions in, 73

Euthanasia, 207

Executive Order #11246, 120. *See also* Law and legislation

Expectations, *see* Values and expectations

Exploitation, 244; by advertising, 10; sexual, 15; in employment, 15, 44, 46; of "wayward girls," 27; academic social science, 154, 155; self-, 156; as moral issue, 220; limitations on struggle against, 243. *See also* Values and expectations

Fairbairn, W. R. D., 251

Fairy tales: sexism in, 230–231, 240; and "Cinderella Complex," 246–251

Family, the: nuclear, 10, 15, 16, 44; extended, 12, 16; single women and, 15, 38; mid-19th-century view of women's influence on, 17–18, 21, 66; and family-style institutional life, 18, 20, 22,

23, 26, 28, 29, 30, 31; of "wayward girls," 25, 32; and "hired help," 44; role of, in industrialization process, 45; limit on size of, 68; socialization/transmission of values by, 99, 100–101, 165; and devaluation/alienation of women, 151; Mexican-American (Chicano), 259–272, 275–278; power relationships within, 260–272; transformation (by wife's employment) of roles in, 264–265. *See also* Children; Hereditarianism; Marriage; Motherhood; Parenthood; Society

Fay, Francis, and Fay Commission (1854), 19n5

Female Eunuch, The (Germaine Greer): review of, 12–14, 15–16

Female seminaries, *see* Women's colleges

Female worship, 127

Feminine "attributes," 190, 202, 212, 276. *See also* Altruism; Behavior; "Goodness"; Stereotyping; Values and expectations

Feminine Mystique, The (Friedan), 69, 87

"Feminine voice," 187–222

Femininity: and careerism as "deviance," 87–88; in males, school reinforcement of, 121; vs. success, 175, 177, 231–232; -adulthood conflict, 196, 210, 214, 215; pregnancy as confirmation of, 200, 201; -abortion conflict, 203; and feminine identity, 227. *See also* Gender identity

Feminism: and opposition to marriage, 12; male support of, 13, 92; "radical," 14–15, 88, 139; positive approach to, 16; and higher education for women, 50, 67–70, 93; and "antipathy" toward science, 91; and feminist literature, 135, 136, 141–142, 161; and feminist criticism of social sciences/psychology, 149–157, 240; and feminist research, 161. *See also* Writing

Fennema, Elizabeth, 252, 253

Ferreira, Janet, 130n1

Fingarette, H., 179, 182

Firestone, Shulamith, 11n1; *The Dialectic of Sex: The Case for Feminist Revolution* reviewed, 14–16

Fleming, J., 178n3

Florentine Codex, 276

Fonwit, Kathy, 131

Food: ethnicity and, 270

Ford Foundation, 103n1, 111n3

Fox, Lynn, 253

Frances, E. K., 269

Frankfort, Roberta: *Collegiate Women: Domesticity and Career in Turn-of-the-Century America* reviewed, 82–90

Fraser, D. B., 68

Frasher, R., 112

Freedom, 156, 248–249; "insecurity as," 13; sexual, 13–14, 15; of choice, 71; denial of, 155. *See also* Choice(s); Independence

Freeman, Alice (Mrs. George Herbert Palmer), 83, 84–85

French, J. R. P., 267, 268

Frenkel-Brunswik, Else, 38

Freud, Sigmund, 194, 196, 230, 234, 235, 240; Oedipal conflict theory of, 15, 16, 190, 225, 226, 229; and Freudian dicta, 87

ucation; Women's colleges; *individual institutions*
"Hired help," 44. *See also* Domestic help
Hirst, Paul, 166–167, 172, 173
Hodges, Frenchy, 280
Hoffman, L. W., 262, 265, 266
Hoffman, Nancy: *Woman's "True" Profession: Voices from the History of Teaching* reviewed, 143–146
Hofstadter, Richard, 65, 83
Holiday, Judy, 41
Holmen, M. G., 111
Holstein, C., 195
Home economics, *see* Education
Home making: education/employment combined with, 8–9, 11, 31, 36, 38, 41, 51; "creative," 15; as career, decline of interest in, 72. *See also* Domesticity
Homeric Hymn, The (Boer, trans.), 238
Hopper, Hedda, 41
Hormones: and sex role development, 121; and differences in spatial or mathematical ability, 254
Horner, Matina S., 175–184 *passim*, 192, 231–232, 246, 250
Horney, Karen, 249
Howe, Samuel Gridley, 30
Howe Sanborn Report (1865), 26
Hubbard, Ruth, 282
Hughes, Bishop John Joseph, 24
Hull House, 89
Hulsizer, Donna, 283
Human relations: feminine instinct for, 52, 92. *See also* Relationships
Human rights, *see* Rights
Humphrey, N. D., 261
Hurst, Fannie, 37–38
Hutchinson, Anne, 3
Huxley, Thomas Henry, 160
Hyde, Ida, 93n2
Hyman Blumberg Symposium on Research in Early Childhood Education (1976), 252

Ibsen, Henrik: *A Doll's House*, 194
Identity: adolescent crisis of, 192, 229, 230, 232. *See also* Gender identity
Illiteracy, 136; and social history, 19
Immigration and immigrants, 17, 18, 20, 24, 25, 145; and employment, 31, 44, 46, 87; and teaching of immigrant pupils, 143, 146. *See also* Mexican-American families
In a Different Voice: Psychological Theory and Women's Development (Gilligan): review of, 240–245
Income, *see* Salaries
Independence: marriage vs., 15, 260; pseudo, men's toleration of, 16; "cult of domesticity"/femininity/compassion vs., 86, 196, 197; adult, 187, 196; pregnancy and, 199, 200; mutual care vs., 204; game-playing and, 228; child's progress toward, 229; fear of, 246, 247–249; vs. "mature dependency" or interdependence, 250–251; eco-

nomic, and power, 259, 261. *See also* Freedom; Relationships
India: independence of (1947), 126; Education Commission of, 126
Indian education, 126–128. *See also* Education
Industrialization, 18, 31, 43, 45, 87. *See also* Modernization; Urbanization
"Inferiority" of women, *see* Status
Inhelder, B., 232
Institute for Social Research (Frankfurt), 152
Institutional life: and deinstitutionalization (in Massachusetts), 33–34. *See also* Reform school(s)
Intellectual performance: age/motherhood and, 78–79; "inferior" (Freud), 194. *See also* Tests and testing
Intelligence tests, 111. *See also* Tests and testing
Iowa Tests: of Basic Skills and of Educational Development, 112n4. *See also* Tests and testing
Irish potato famine (1845) and Irish immigrants, 24, 25. *See also* Immigration and immigrants
Irony of Early School Reform, The (Katz), 21
Isolation: of mothers, 51, 199; vs. relationships, 199, 248. *See also* Independence
Italy: women in medieval universities of, 65; "women's table" at Zoological Station, Naples, 93
Jacklin, Carol, 121; et al., 103, 112, 113, 115n10, 283
Jackson, Helen Hunt: *Ramona*, 277
Jackson, Mahalia, 42
James, Roslyn, 130
James, William, 58, 230
Jauhar, 128
Jefferson, Thomas, 65
Jennings, J., 178n3
Jews, 92n1
Johns Hopkins University, 85, 93; School of Medicine, 37; Study of Mathematically Precocious Youth, 253
Johnson, Adelaide, 39
Johnson, Diane, 281
Johnson, Dr. Samuel, 138
Jones, Gayle, 280, 281
Jones, Jacqueline, 283
Joplin, Janis, 42
Jubilee (Walker), 138
Juvenile reform, 17–34

Kaestle, Carl F., 24
Kagan, J., 100
Kalia, Narendra Nath: *Sexism in Indian Education: The Lies We Tell Our Children* reviewed, 126–128
Kameros, Debbie, 130
Kant, Immanuel, 189
Kanter, Rosabeth, 182, 184
Karabenick, S. A., 176
Katz, Michael: *The Irony of Early School Reform*, 21
Katzman, David: *Seven Days a Week: Women and Domestic Service in Industrializing America*, 43
Kegan, Robert, 179, 180, 181, 182, 184
Keller, Helen, 40

171–172, 180, 189, 196, 216, 217, 221, 225, 231, 234, 235, 241; women defined in relationship to, 150, 215, 249; and success anxiety, 175, 182, 183, 192–193; and rules of the game, 180, 184, 190, 227–228; and gender identity, 180, 226, 227; and "masculinist ethic," 184; and adulthood/parenthood stereotypes, 188, 232, 249; women's thinking compared with that of, 196; morality as viewed by, 216, 217, 221, 235–236; life cycle of, woman's place in, 224–238; and masculine bias of psychoanalytic theory and psychology, 226, 231, 244; "independence" of, 248; mathematics as domain of, 254; domestic activities and responsibilities of, 264–266; black women writers' attitude toward, 281. *See also* Gender roles; Sex bias; Sex differences

Mann, Horace, 21, 30
Mansfield, Katherine, 137
Margolis, Diane, 158n
Marine Biological Laboratory (Woods Hole, Massachusetts), 93
Marlin, M. J., 111
Marriage: combined with or vs. career, 7, 41, 51, 78, 83, 84–85, 88; women's choice of, 8, 15, 38, 69; social pressures for, 8, 62, 196; feminist opposition to, 12; alternative to, 13; modified idea of, 15; age at, and employment, 31; information about, in biographies, 37; and professional collaboration, 37–38; and divorce, 38, 41; of college graduates, 50, 62; and mobility, 78; domesticity equated with, 86–87; power relationships within, 260–272. *See also* Domesticity; Family, the
Martin, Jane Roland, 283
Martin, Michael, 158n
Marxist tradition, 152, 153
Mary Ingraham Bunting Institute (Radcliffe College), 158n
Mary Sharp College, 66
"Masculine" careers, "Masculinist ethic," *see* Males
Massachusetts: state records of, 19; deinstitutionalization in, 33–34
Massachusetts Board of State Charities, 19, 24, 26, 28, 29
Massachusetts legislature and Commissioners, 17, 19, 20, 22, 25, 27, 28n28
Massachusetts State Schools, *see* State Industrial School for Girls (Lancaster, Massachusetts); State Primary School (Monson, Massachusetts)
Mathematics, 75, 252–255
"Matriolatry," 68. *See also* Motherhood
Mead, G. H., 227
Mead, Margaret, 100, 283
Meadow, A., 260
Mednick, M., 178n3
Menstrual period, 68, 230
Merchant of Venice, The (Shakespeare), 221
Metropolitan Achievement Tests, 112n4. *See also* Tests and testing
Metzger, W. P., 65
Mexican-American families, 259–272, 275–278

Mexico, 278
Midgeley, N., 176
Midnight Birds: Stories of Contemporary Black Women Writers (Washington, ed.): review of, 279–281
Miller, Jean Baker, 247, 249
Millet, Kate: *Sexual Politics*, 10
Millikan, Robert, 93
Mill on the Floss, The (Eliot), 194, 204, 243
Mindel, C. H., 270
Minorities: in higher education, 71. *See also* Blacks; Ethnicity; Mexican-American families
Mirandé, Alfredo (coauthor): *La Chicana, The Mexican-American Woman* reviewed, 275–278
Mischel, W., 100
Mitchell, Margaret, 10
Mobility: marriage and, 78
Modernization: and consequences of, 18, 19, 20, 43, 269; confused with acculturation, 260–261. *See also* Industrialization; Technology; Values and expectations
Monahan, L., 178n3
Money, John, 121
Monroe, Marilyn, 40, 41
Monson, Massachusetts, State Primary School, 28
Montessori, Maria, 160–161, 170
Montoya, José, 277
Moore, J. W., 260
Moore, Marianne, 41
Moral development: education and, 21, 22, 31, 32; and female views on morality, 176, 188, 191–196, 201, 202–219 *passim*, 236–237; Kohlberg's theory of stages of, 180, 189–199 *passim*, 204, 213–221 *passim*, 234–237 *passim*; sex bias in measurement of, 180, 195–196, 215, 218, 221, 225–226, 228, 234, 240; sex difference in, 180, 190, 194–195, 198, 233, 234, 237, 241–242; and moral dilemma, 180, 184, 194–198 *passim*, 216–217, 241, 244, 248, (abortion as) 188, 196–215, 218, 242, ("Heinz" dilemma) 199, 213, 218–220; "inferior," 195, 215; Erikson's theory of, 215, 221; and adolescent view of morality, 215, 216, 221; and male view of morality, 216, 217, 221, 235–236; psychological theory of, 240. *See also* Values and expectations
Moral Judgment of the Child, The (Piaget), 180, 234
Moravian Seminary (Bethlehem, Pennsylvania), 66
Morrison, Toni, 280; *Sula*, 281
Motherhood: and employment, 7, 9, 31, 37, 38, 83, 269; and child care, 7, 136, 226, 249, (courses in) 56, (as "utterly unintellectual") 68, (facilities for) 76, 77, 248, (by husbands) 265; women's choice/postponement of, 8; technology and child-bearing, 15; "destruction" of, 16; and influence on/education of children, 17, 32, 52, 66, 160, 166, 167–174, 278; isolation of, 51, 199; glorification of, 68, 69, 144; end of, and employment, 69; and academic achievement, 78; and maternity leave, 79; and writing, 136; as social institution, examination of, 157, 173;

Pearson product moment correlation coefficients, 105
Peirce, Bradford K., 17, 27
Penalosa, F., 265
Perry, W., 232
Persephone myth, 238
Personality: influences on, 100, 249; feminist challenge to society's view of, 151; sex differences in development of, 226, 227, 229. *See also* Behavior
Pestalozzi, Johann Heinrich, 158, 162, 165, 170, 171; *Leonard and Gertrude*, 160
Peters, R. S., 166–173 *passim; Ethics and Education*, 164; *The Logic of Education*, 164
Petersen, Anne C., 254
Phelps, Almira, 67
Piaget, Jean, 179, 187, 240; sex differences noted by, 180, 183, 190, 227, 228, 232; *The Moral Judgment of the Child*, 180, 234; and moral development, 189, 234, 235
Piche, Marie, 133
Pierce, Christine, 159
Plath, Sylvia, 41
Plato, 158–163 *passim*, 170, 173, 187; *Republic*, 159, 161
"Pleasure principle," 13
Polatnick, M., 266
Politics: participation in, 3, 4, 40, 57–58, 69, 88, 92, 93, 127, 243, 278; exclusion from, 162; of differential power between sexes, 196. *See also* Power
Pollak, Susan, 241
Population, *see* Census, U.S. Bureau of the
Population explosion, 9
Porter, Katherine Anne, 137, 138
Positivism, 152, 153
Potter, B. A., 103
Potter, E. H., 101, 102, 103
Poverty: women and, 17, 18; and reform, 18, 19, 24–25, 32, 33; social history of, 19; academic social-science exploitation of, 154. *See also* Economic conditions
Power: corporate, 184; differential, between sexes, 196; within family, 260–272, (control vs.) 265–266, (five types of) 267. *See also* Relationships
Pregnancy: as testing of relationship, 197; adolescent, 202, (and adulthood) 199–201. *See also* Abortion; Birth control; Motherhood
Primers, *see* Textbooks
Princeton University, 50
Priorities for Action (Carnegie Commission), 71
Professions, *see* Occupations and professions
Progressive era, 89, 90
Psychoanalytic theory, 246, 249; Satyagraha compared to, 220; masculine bias of, 226
Psychology, 52, 157, 237, 243, 246, 249; "of women's oppression," 10; and special curriculum for women, 68; as "woman's field," 92, 93; developmental, and role models, 100–101; from men's viewpoint, 231, 244; "constructs the

female," 240. *See also* Social sciences; Values and expectations
Psychology Today magazine, 246
Public education, *see* Education
Public Health Service Act (1971), 70, 76
Public High Schools, New York City (NYC Board of Education), 117
Puryear, G. R., 178n3

Quinn, R. P., 118

Radcliffe College, 61, 88, 94–95, 158n; students interviewed, 191, 192, 193
Ramona (Jackson), 277
Rand, Gertrude, 37
Rationality theory (of teaching), *see* Teaching
Rauhe Haus, Das (Hamburg, Germany), 20
Raven, B., 267, 268
Reading: basal textbooks for, 101–110. *See also* Education; Illiteracy
Reform: social (by women), 4, 89, 90, (domesticity seen as) 17–34; educational, 5, 8, 20, 22, 51, 120; tax, 8; juvenile, 17–34, (environmental theories of) 20, 23, 28–29; poverty and, 18, 19, 24–25, 32, 33
Reform school(s): for girls (Lancaster, Massachusetts), 17–34; for boys (Westborough, Massachusetts), 21, 27, 33–34
Reich, Adria, 283–284
Relationships: late adolescent social, 8; "reciprocity" or "activity" of care in, 14, 180, 197, 198, 202, 204, 208, 209, 217, 233, 241–242, 244, 247; of single women, 15, 38, 85; lesbian, 16; between domestic worker and employer, 31, 43, 44–46; feminine effectiveness in, 52, 92; sex differences in, 91, 103, 180–181, 226, 227, 233, 241; children's friendships, (as portrayed in basal reading texts) 103, (preadolescent) 229; between literary stereotypes and sex role development, 110; male-female, (as source of female stereotype) 150, (cultural double standard in) 278; mother-daughter/parent-child, 180–181, 226, 238, 241; "constellation" of, 181; as factor in corporate power, 184; and self-perception or self-definition, 188, 233; pregnancy as testing of, 197; isolation vs., 199, 248; trust (established in infancy) in, 215, 229, 230; "safety net" of, 241, 242, 243; dependence equated with, 247–248; power, within family, 260–272. *See also* Family, the; Independence
Relativism, 192; moral, 219, 237
Religion: women as upholders of, 17; and religious training, 20, 21, 23, 29; and Catholics in Protestant institution, 24, 25; and educational institutions, 61; and female worship in Indian creation myths, 127. *See also* Roman Catholic Church
Republic (Plato), 159, 161
Research: new design for, in study of educated